P9-CDU-635

# DESPERATE
## NETWORKS

# DESPERATE
# NETWORKS

## Bill Carter

**BROADWAY BOOKS**

NEW YORK

PUBLISHED BY BROADWAY BOOKS

Copyright © 2006 by Bill Carter

All Rights Reserved

A hardcover edition of this book was originally published
in 2006 by Doubleday.

Published in the United States by Broadway Books, an imprint of
The Doubleday Broadway Publishing Group,
a division of Random House, Inc., New York.

www.broadway.com

BROADWAY BOOKS and its logo, a letter B bisected on the diagonal,
are trademarks of Random House, Inc.

Book design by Fearn Cutler de Vicq

Library of Congress Control Number: 2006296658

ISBN 978-0-7679-1974-6

PRINTED IN THE UNITED STATES OF AMERICA

1  3  5  7  9  10  8  6  4  2

First Paperback Edition

To Caela and Dan;
I love you, Miss P. and Bub

# CONTENTS

ACKNOWLEDGMENTS                                       *ix*

PROLOGUE: A CALL TO A HIT MAN                          *1*

ONE: "BEAUTIFUL GIRLS"                                  9

TWO: *FRIENDS* AND ENEMIES                             27

THREE: MUST-SEE-SOMETHING-ELSE TV                      49

FOUR: THE TRIBE HAS SPOKEN                             67

FIVE: REALITY . . . WHAT A CONCEPT                     *91*

SIX: MY FICKLE FRIEND, THE SUMMER WIND                *111*

SEVEN: SUPERSIZE ME                                   *135*

EIGHT: "I'VE BEEN THERE"                              *161*

NINE: *IDOL* MINDS                                    *175*

TEN: AN UNOPENED PACKAGE                              *197*

ELEVEN: *FRIENDS* TO THE END                          *211*

TWELVE: GIRLS' SHOWS                                      225

THIRTEEN: "YOU'RE FIRED!"                                 253

FOURTEEN: *LOST* CAUSES                                   277

FIFTEEN: I SAW THE NEWS TODAY, OH BOY                     309

SIXTEEN: THE RESIDUE OF DESIGN                            333

EPILOGUE: A BRAND-NEW DAY                                 373

AFTERWORD                                                 391

INDEX                                                     395

# ACKNOWLEDGMENTS

This is the third book I have written about the network television industry, and like the others it is almost completely the product of my own firsthand reporting. Over a period of about eighteen months I conducted interviews with many of the most important executives, producers, writers, stars, and talent agents in the business—a number of them on several occasions. I received almost unfailing cooperation from this long list of people. They all have my thanks.

In addition to my own reporting, I drew some information and occasional quotes from published articles in a number of newspapers and magazines, including the *Washington Post,* the *Los Angeles Times, Time, Newsweek, The New Yorker, Newsday, New York* magazine, the *San Jose Mercury News, Advertising Age, Broadcasting and Cable, Variety,* and the *Hollywood Reporter.* I also found some helpful material in several books, including *Disney War,* by James B. Stewart, and *Jump In,* by Mark Burnett. And an ABC interview with Teri Hatcher and the other stars of *Desperate Housewives* provided some useful information.

I also was able to mine a bit of my own previous work in the *New York Times.* I have been privileged to cover television since 1989 for the *Times* and I am always mindful of how valuable my association with the *Times* has been in my career. That has been especially true with this book, because my editors and supervisors at the paper kindly consented to allow me time to work on this project, and they have been consistently supportive throughout its completion. I want to thank several editors and executives, beginning with Bill Keller, Jill Abramson, and Bill Schmidt, and including Sam Sifton, Jim Schacter, and Steve Reddicliffe, for their patience and assistance.

At Doubleday, I want to thank Phyllis Grann for her unflagging interest in this book and her assistant, Karyn Marcus, for her agile help. My agent, Kathy Robbins, has always been my staunch advocate and never more so than in this effort.

A number of personal friends, professional colleagues, and family members made helpful contributions, from useful suggestions to words of support. I want to thank Phil and Denise Andrews, Frank and Diane Guercio, Gerry Uehlinger, Eric Mink, John Schwartz, Jack Steinberg, Fred Conrad, Maureen Dowd, Alessandra Stanley, Dinitia Smith, Lorne Manly, Lawrie Mifflin, Karin Davison, Peter Lassally, Richard Carter, Jr., Nikki Carter, Richard Carter III, John Carter, Alexandra Carter, Greg Lembrich, Catherine Carter O'Neill and Dan O'Neill, Bridget and Danny O'Neill, and, as always, my parents, Richard and Teresa Carter.

A number of public relations professionals provided me with enormous help. I want to thank especially Carole Robinson of MTV Networks; Michael Mand of the Creative Artists Agency; Chris Ender and Gil Schwartz of CBS; Kevin Brockman and Jeffrey Schneider of ABC; Joe Earley and Scott Grogin of the Fox Broadcasting Company; Rebecca Marks, Kathy Kelly-Brown, Anna Perez, Allison Gollust, Barbara Levin, and Jeff DeRome of NBC; Steven Melnick of Twentieth Century Fox Television; Sharan Magnuson of Warner Brothers Television; Paula Askanas of Sony Pictures Television; and Jim Dowd of the Dowd Agency.

Many people offered recollections and comments and asked not to be named, but I want all of them to know how much I appreciate their contributions.

I wish I could thank everyone who generously consented to formal interviews, but that would fill pages. I do need to acknowledge several people who provided crucial stories, details, and information.

On the agency side, I want to thank especially Rick Rosen at

Endeavor and Alan Berger and Lee Gabler at CAA for their invaluable insights.

From the studios, Peter Roth of Warner Brothers was, as always, wonderfully generous to me.

From the production side, Marc Cherry tells his own tale almost as well as he does those of Susan, Bree, Lynette, and Gabrielle. It was a privilege to share it. Mark Burnett has been available, open, and helpful to me since the day I met him five years ago, and it was no different during this project. I appreciate it greatly. Thanks also to Conrad Riggs.

Thom Sherman started out at ABC but wound up on the production side with *Lost*. I appreciate how willingly he shared with me the details of his personal adventure. Thanks as well to Julie McNamara and Heather Kadin.

Ben Silverman was good enough to clue me in to the emerging trend of reality television five years ago, and he has remained, now as executive producer of *The Office,* a reliable and enthusiastic resource.

In the area known in television as "talent," I want especially to mention Donald Trump, who loves talking television and real estate, and Simon Cowell, who loves talking television and music. Thanks to both for talking so much with me.

I also want to express special appreciation to Conan O'Brien.

From news, I want to acknowledge the generous contribution of Dan Rather.

From Fox, I first want to thank Mike Darnell, one of the most fascinating and fun people to talk to about television that I have met in the business. Peter Liguori, Gail Berman, and Sandy Grushow all supplied great material. Preston Beckman has been at the television game for many years at two networks and has a store of tales, insights, and theories to prove it. I want to thank him for sharing so many of them.

From ABC, Steve McPherson totally lived up to his reputation for being a straight-shooting, insightful, and smart executive, and I am grateful to him. David Westin had one of the toughest years any executive could have but was open and generous to me in recounting it.

Susan Lyne has moved on from ABC to Martha Stewart Living

Omnimedia, but she remains sharp, perceptive, and insightful about television and kindly shared all those qualities with me.

At NBC, Bob Wright has for two decades been accessible and generous to me, and he was once again with this project. I am deeply grateful to him. Randy Falco also kindly shared his time and thoughts with me. Marc Graboff had roles in so many of the events in this tale that he was invaluable me. Ghen Maynard has since left the network, but he was exceptionally helpful and I thank him. Kevin Reilly came to NBC at a testing time and had enormous demands on him, but he was extraordinarily open and helpful throughout. Dick Ebersol has been in my Rolodex for almost thirty years, and no one has ever been easier or more fun for me to talk to.

Jeff Zucker has been among the best stories for me to cover in the past fifteen years. I first met him when he was an up-and-coming young producer at the *Today* show. I have followed—and chronicled—his meteoric career steps ever since. But as he moved up he never changed at all in his willingness to talk with me enthusiastically about the state of television as he saw it. He was just as open and engaging throughout the process of this book, and I deeply appreciate it.

At CBS, Kelly Kahl is one the sharpest young executives in television, and I benefited greatly from his recollections. Andrew Heyward gave me a thoughtful interview from the perspective of CBS News. I want to thank Nina Tassler for being such a terrific storyteller and David Poltrack for being so insightful from the research side.

Leslie Moonves first came on my radar screen when he moved up to run the Warner Brothers television studio. From my first time talking with him it was apparent that this was a dynamic executive and also one who enjoyed the give-and-take of the interview process as much as anyone I had ever dealt with. That was never more true than over the past eighteen months, and he has my great thanks.

This effort surely could not have been accomplished without the support of the people I love most. So I am most grateful to my children, Caela Ellen Carter and Daniel Houston Carter, who could not be more of an inspiration to me, and my wife, Beth Keating Carter, who, besides being the sharpest-eyed reader and editor I have ever had, is, pure and simple, the best thing that ever happened to me.

# A CALL TO A HIT MAN

As the 2004–2005 television season hit its first benchmark, the close of the November sweep rating period, Bob Wright, the NBC chairman, sitting at his desk in his big office on the fifty-second floor of 30 Rockefeller Plaza in Manhattan, found himself troubled. He was troubled enough to do something highly irregular.

He asked his assistant to place a call for him, a direct call to a television writer/producer not in his network's employ, someone Wright did not even know.

Bob Wright had established himself as the dean of CEOs in the TV business. He had run NBC—with enormous success—for almost two decades. He understood the contemporary television business as well as anybody—and he saw with clear-eyed realism the coming threats to the network industry, with its outdated business model: a single revenue stream based entirely on advertising.

Wright's most recent and biggest coup, one he had worked on doggedly for long months after long months, was the hugely complicated 2003 purchase of the entertainment assets held by Vivendi Universal. Wright, in presenting his case for the acquisition to the General Electric owners of NBC, had described the necessity of adding Universal in survival terms. NBC simply had to get bigger, had to add a movie studio, a big television production arm, and a well-stocked library of intellectual content, or it simply would not be able to compete with its Big Media rivals, like Viacom, Time Warner, Disney, and News Corp. The old network structure of prime-time lineups designed to amass enormous numbers of viewers all at the same time was everywhere under attack. TiVo machines that let viewers watch shows without commercials, the digitalization of video signals that would multiply the number of channels available, and Internet programs that would make television as vulnerable to illegal downloading as music all made network television's position vulnerable. As much as anyone in the industry, Wright realized that a revolution was barreling down on the media business, and the broadcast networks were going to be on the bloody front lines of the coming action.

And yet the chairman of the vast NBC Universal media conglomerate felt driven on a late-fall afternoon to make this telephone call, not because he had to discover how NBC had failed to pick up on some crucial new wrinkle on the technology side or on a critical new business opportunity, but because he simply had to find out how in the world NBC had managed to miss out on one little hour-long television show.

It was killing Bob Wright that ABC had *Desperate Housewives* and NBC didn't.

ABC's new Sunday-night comedy/drama had exploded as a national phenomenon—the kind only network television still could create—from its first week on the air. The man Wright wanted to speak to that afternoon was Marc Cherry, the show's creator and chief producer, who had emerged from the outermost ring of show business obscurity as a sudden television hit maker.

Cherry could not help but be well aware who Bob Wright was, but he did not know Bob Wright personally. In the preceding seven years, he would have been as likely to be speaking to Orville Wright as to Bob Wright. But that fall, Cherry's life had changed in oh so many ways.

Cherry greeted Wright's unexpected call with surprise, and Bob, always a gracious man, began by congratulating Cherry on the spectacular early success of *Desperate Housewives*. He told Cherry, "It's good for the whole network industry when somebody has a hit like that."

Cherry thanked him, and Wright went on with a few pleasantries about the show and the attention it was getting.

But, of course, none of that was the real point of the call. Suddenly, Wright changed the tenor of the conversation: "Can I ask you a question?" Wright said. "This is a yes-or-no question: Did you bring this to NBC?"

Cherry got the drift quickly. "Yes, I brought it to NBC first," he said.

Wright, his suspicions confirmed, asked Cherry what had happened. Cherry filled him in, to the best of his recollection, about how the script he had written had been delivered to NBC's comedy development department.

Wright wanted to know if Cherry had the names of the people who might have seen the script. Cherry, figuring a heaping helping of blame was about to be dished out, offered a few names; then he said, "Well, they told me it was great and everything, and then they told me that they weren't so sure it was a comedy. So they were sending it over to drama. The next thing I got back was word that they were going to take a pass on it."

When he hung up with Cherry, Wright concluded that he would have many more calls to make, calls to NBC development executives and the top managers at NBC Entertainment. He was determined to learn exactly what had happened, how NBC had missed this opportunity. As much as he was convinced that the future of television would be ruled by unpredictable, sweeping change, Wright knew one thing had not changed and would not change. No matter how they viewed television—on their computer monitors, on their cell phones, or on TV screens as big as medieval tapestries—people would still want to see hit shows. If you had hits, it would not matter where and how the revenue came in; you would always be in business.

•  •  •

Until the fall of 2004, ABC had spent most of a decade consistently *disproving* one of the hoariest axioms of network television: that prime-time programming was a cyclical business, where the losers would surely become winners eventually.

Maybe no more, the analysts and critics and competitors said; maybe ABC was the proof that television had changed irrevocably, that a network really on the skids could no longer launch a smash hit show that could turn around its fortunes, that a network could simply fail again and again until it ceased to matter as a competitive entity.

In the space of eleven days, between September 22 and October 3, 2004, ABC shut the analysts and critics up. Even that early in the season, much of the nation was talking about not one but two new shows on ABC. *Desperate Housewives* was, with more than 21 million viewers, the most-watched new show on ABC since 1996. Another new show, *Lost,* had also taken off immediately, drawing more than 18 million viewers and becoming a phenomenon from its first week on the air. Besides their explosive starts, both shows shared unusually turbulent backstories in how they reached the air, the kind that seemed to attach to every big hit the networks managed to find.

The timing of the twin hits had profound consequences for ABC and its network competitors. With *Desperate Housewives* and *Lost,* a network had two instant breakout hits in the same season for the first time since NBC introduced *ER* and *Friends* in 1994.

Those two shows had ushered in a decade of dominance for NBC. Now, ten years later, that network saw the returns from its onetime bonanza finally falling to dust, and its own failure to replenish its roster of hits over that decade left NBC vulnerable to playing a painful game of role reversal with ABC. Suddenly, ABC had the hits; NBC didn't.

And, as Bob Wright knew, it was no time for a network to be so bereft. The smash hit show was, more than ever, the lifeline for network television, the mother lode from which the Big Four networks, ABC, CBS, NBC, and Fox, along with the two part-time networks, WB and UPN, extracted more than $20 billion in advertising each year. Those billions were still the oxygen of the network business, and designer-suited men (as ever, it was mostly men) in well-appointed offices in Manhattan and Burbank, California, now squirmed mightily with the effort to keep that air supply flowing.

Already diminished by inroads from cable, the networks faced ever more serious threats from all kinds of digital and broadband competitors, endless temptations for viewers, especially the young ones they lusted after, to drift to other forms of entertainment and diversion. Having the smoking-hot hit, the "appointment show," the "must-see TV" that cable channels could not yet afford to produce, that a computer screen or BlackBerry or iPod could not hope to duplicate, was more than ever a life-or-death proposition for the business.

In 2005, the networks themselves, noticing the tide of ad dollars drifting away, to Internet sites and other locations, set out with the fervor of the newly converted to find ways to build new revenue streams by feeding their programming into all those new micro- and magna-sized outlets. Disney lined up a deal to play episodes of *Desperate Housewives* and *Lost* on Apple's latest invention, the video iPod (a palm-sized picture of strikingly good quality)—charging $1.99 for each episode ordered. NBC countered with a similar Apple iPod deal for a range of programs, including its still-potent late-night franchises, *The Tonight Show* and *Late Night*. CBS partnered with the Comcast cable empire to offer many of its shows on the increasingly popular technology of video-on-demand, which allowed viewers to catch up on episodes of their favorite shows for just 99 cents each.

Behind every one of the deals was a critical assumption: that each network would have hit shows that viewers would be willing to pay to see.

Finding those hits was no easier than it had ever been, of course. It took a combination of boldness, vision, and extreme patience to be able to identify one standout show among the hundreds of ideas floated every year. And that's why network executives almost never found any. Instead, they mostly hoped that a breakthrough show would fall into their laps, the way most of the smash hits on television did.

The plain truth was that no matter how much they spent on script development, which stars they signed to multimillion-dollar deals, how many notes they gave on story beats and character arcs, hits most often arrived on a network executive's doorstep by chance, by whim, by blind, stupid luck.

Network executives, highly paid and widely catered to, simply had to be ready to embrace it, fondle it, shower it with loving attention when a hit stumbled down the street and rang their doorbell. Most often, they weren't.

•   •   •

The 2004–2005 season was a watershed for network television, marked by sudden upheavals that rocked the business. Outside the entertainment divisions, a combination of retirement, scandal, and untimely death produced a sea change in network news, with all four of the Old Lions of broadcast journalism, Tom Brokaw, Dan Rather, Peter Jennings, and Ted Koppel, gone from their anchor chairs in the span of one year. In their wake, network news, already a fading shadow of its former greatness, was inevitably a further diminished thing.

In entertainment, with the big hit show more than ever the coin of the ratings realm, the effects of finding and owning the most and best of them became increasingly magnified. To understand the fate of each network in the 2004–2005 season, you had to track back where and how the hits had come from, three or even five years previously. The net impact of hits accumulated (or squandered) over that period generated a seismic shift in the 2004–2005 season, one that had been boiling under the surface of the four-network competition since the late 1990s.

Fox, the upstart fourth (and still not full-time) network, rode a wave of reality and sports programming and actually surpassed its far more established rivals for the entire season in the competition for viewers between the ages of 18 and 49, the standard that every network but CBS used as the only benchmark of success.

At the same time, after years of disavowing the overarching significance of that 18-to-49 audience, CBS found itself in position to win by that younger standard—and every other. No longer could the network be dismissed as appealing only to old people. In 2004, it was storming NBC's last stronghold, its Thursday-night lineup. Behind a pair of totally unexpected and now long-running hits, CBS had conquered Thursday night, which by dint of the amount of ad dollars committed was unquestionably the most important night of television.

NBC, a network that literally compared itself to the New York Yankees for the consistent excellence of its record, stood by helplessly as its own store of once-great hits slowly melted away, leading to a precipitous and hugely costly plunge.

And ABC, a network written off for dead in the press and most Hollywood conversations, effected the most startling change of all. Awash in so much failure that it terminated the executive team that put its new roster of programs into production, ABC found its redemption in shows those executives had left behind.

Which was only fitting, because, like something out of Dickens, success in network television usually depended on the stirring rise of the orphaned, the rejected, and the abandoned.

# CHAPTER ONE

# "BEAUTIFUL GIRLS"

On a sunny Tuesday afternoon in Manhattan in mid-May 2005, few people in the great city had reason to be as buoyant, as self-satisfied, as downright gleeful as the reserved, handsome, impeccably dressed fifty-four-year-old man sitting in a prominent aisle seat in the orchestra section of Avery Fisher Hall in Lincoln Center.

For Robert A. Iger, this was a day of real triumph, not merely because ABC, the network he had been associated with for virtually his entire career, all the way back to 1977, had emerged from a seemingly endless dark night of failure and financial loss to sudden, spectacular success, but also because he had survived one of the most precarious apprenticeships in media history. He had finally been designated as the successor to Michael Eisner, chairman of the Walt Disney Company.

That appointment had come just two months earlier, and it was due in no small measure to the startling turnaround at ABC during the just-completed 2004–2005 television season. Iger, once the top programmer at ABC himself, had presided, in his capacity as the number-two Disney executive, over nearly ten years of flops. The network seemed to be allergic to hit television shows. A batch of the biggest hits in recent years—*Survivor, CSI, American Idol, The*

*Apprentice*—had all turned up first at ABC, only to have the network recoil in rejection.

Much of the blame for those mind-blowing misreads had been laid at the feet of Iger and Eisner, in constant stories of how their crippling control over the network's decision making had undermined the efforts of the network's creative executives to find the shows ABC needed so badly. Iger dismissed the stories as inaccurate, but certainly they had some effect on his increasingly challenged aspirations to succeed Eisner. If he could not fix ABC in years of trying, why would anyone think he could master the more complex issues facing the Disney Company?

Nor had the 2004 season begun with any great expectations. Just one year earlier, in April, there had been yet another multi-executive pile-up at ABC, as Iger axed both of the managers running the entertainment division and installed a new boss less than a month before the upfront. Nobody ever did something like that in April, because the upfront, an annual sales presentation of the new selections of network prime-time shows, was so important to every network's bottom line.

At the upfront, so called because clients purchased commercial time in network shows *before* the season commenced, the big advertising clients in New York piled into some elegant midtown hall, watched as the network trotted out clips of the new series it had picked up, and then attended a loud, crowded, lavish after-party where many of the young ad buyers lined up at booths to get their photos taken with—and autographed by—the new "stars." For ABC in recent years, that had meant more Ernie Hudson than Tim Allen. Even when ABC did seem to build a successful show with a real star, like the comedy 8 *Simple Rules for Dating My Teenage Daughter,* something awful seemed to happen, like the shocking sudden death of that show's star, John Ritter. ABC had the feel—and maybe the smell—of the chronically snakebitten.

Iger's appointment of Stephen McPherson that April, accompanied by the announcement that he would create a new, improved ABC schedule from the pieces left behind by people who had just been ashcanned, seemed like an engraved invitation to every rattler, cobra, and asp in Hollywood to come and dine again on the carcass of ABC.

This time the snakes went hungry. Now, a year later, no one in Lincoln Center, with the possible exception of McPherson himself, had benefited more from what ABC had wrought in the preceding twelve months than Bob Iger.

As the upfront presentation began, the trim, ruddy-faced McPherson walked out on stage, exuding a stony confidence. Thanks to the turnaround, McPherson had amassed, as a top Hollywood agent, Rick Rosen of Endeavor, put it, "more political capital than anyone else in this business."

McPherson had several people to thank for that success—including Iger, of course, for putting him in the job—but surely no one more than the man waiting behind a decorated screen at the center of the stage.

•   •   •

Behind that screen, the man who had turned television on its head waited, psyching himself up for the performance of his lifetime.

Marc Cherry could not help thinking of the significance of the moment, about how far he had come—all the way from forgotten, ignored, and broke to the toast of network television. Decked out in white tie and tails, Cherry was to be the centerpiece of this day of celebration for ABC.

ABC was so downtrodden a year earlier that its late-night star, Jimmy Kimmel, had brought down the house with a joke about how each of the networks could be identified as a familiar type from high school. ABC was "the fat kid who eats paste"—that same ABC now had what the advertisers craved: the hottest of the hot shows.

Out on stage, McPherson was working quickly through his early material to get to his major announcement: "Ladies and gentlemen, please welcome my friend Marc Cherry!"

The screen parted in the middle and Cherry walked out with a flair that both reveled in and defied his own self-described "Stubby

Kaye" look: round-faced, balding, roly-poly. The white tie and tails got a few laughs. Well, why shouldn't this be a grand moment for this guy, the writer who could not get an interview, never mind a job, and who now had created *Desperate Housewives,* the biggest new scripted television show in years?

Cherry played it up. "Well, I don't know about you guys, but I had the nicest year," he said, soaking in the laughter. He called it an amazing time for his cast, his studio, and "especially my network."

Then he turned to an unseen orchestra leader. "Hit it!" he commanded, turning his shoulder to the back of the stage as music came up and a montage of shots from the first season of *Desperate Housewives* played on video screens above him.

A couple of other guys in tuxes appeared, handing Cherry a top hat and cane. With complete aplomb, he began to belt out "Beautiful Girls," the Sondheim song from *Follies,* in a tenor voice so pure and powerful that many in the audience looked immediately for signs of lip-synching—but saw only a trained musical-theater singer fully in his element.

Cherry sang:

> "Hats off, here they come, those beautiful girls . . .
> That's what you've been waiting for."

Cherry's face loomed huge on the video screens as the camera caught him in close-up.

> "See them in their glory—
> Diamonds and pearls, dazzling jewels by the score. . . ."

Iger, beaming in his tightly controlled way, had to remember how Cherry had called to congratulate him the day the Disney appointment was announced. Bob, surely recognizing what *Desperate Housewives* had meant to the moribund network that had been undermining his career ambitions, told Cherry, "Well, thank you for your part in it."

As Cherry sang, a full chorus line of guys with top hats and canes filed out and joined him.

> *"This is what beauty can be.*
> *Beauty celestial, the best you'll agree . . .*
> *All for you, these beautiful girls!"*

And with another flourish Cherry swept his arm back and said, "Ladies and gentlemen, straight from Wisteria Lane, the Desperate Housewives!"

Now the chorus escorted out a lineup of truly beautiful girls—women really, a group of six actresses, mostly in their forties, who had captured the country's imagination from their first week on the air eight months earlier. Out they walked in floor-length gowns and faux jewels, a couple waving snow-white boas: Marcia Cross, the show's uptight Bree, in a coppery-gold gown with a cleavage-baring cutout; Eva Longoria, the Hispanic sexpot, Gabrielle, in a bejeweled strapless silver number, her long diamond string earrings stretching so far one literally rested in her cleavage.

The fourth in the parade was without boa or jewels, but the flashing smile and elegantly curled brown tresses signaled the central stardom of Teri Hatcher, the emotionally vulnerable Susan of the series, in a striking beaded white V-neck gown. The reception from the audience reinforced the point: Hatcher, the lead in an earlier, now almost forgotten ABC series, *Lois & Clark*, was a megawatt star again after descending so far into has-been land that she found herself, only a few months before her *Housewives* audition, far more desperate in her real life than anything Marc Cherry's scripts had dished up for her.

> *"This is what drives men insane,*
> *Here from our cheery, Wisteria Lane . . ."*

. . .

One day earlier, Monday, at a venue famed for the art of high-kicking, Radio City Music Hall, Jeff Zucker, NBC's increasingly embattled entertainment leader, had been forced to put on a dance of his own. NBC, the network that had dominated ratings and profits over much of the previous two decades, had accomplished a fall of Icarus-like proportions, crashing all the way from first place to fourth (and dead last) in the span of one September-to-May television season. And the only credible message Zucker could deliver that day was along the lines of: Yeah, we blew it.

That afternoon, NBC hoped to package its programs skillfully enough to convince advertisers that the network's aging series and new unknowns were still worth near the same level of investment as the year before. The preceding May, NBC had managed to maintain command of the market with close to $3 billion in upfront sales.

NBC had achieved that feat even though its last truly "must-see" comedy, *Friends*, was gone, replaced by a spin-off, *Joey*, starring one holdover *Friends* cast member, Matt LeBlanc. A year later, *Joey*, completing a season in which it had shed millions of viewers in a yearlong megamolt, was somehow still being offered up as the network's replacement for *Friends* leading off Thursday night.

There were beautiful girls at the NBC upfront show as well, but they weren't singing and dancing. From a set made up to look like the anchor desk from the "Weekend Update" segment on *Saturday Night Live*, Tina Fey and Amy Poehler flayed their network for its woeful performance.

"Buy NBC," Fey urged the advertisers. "Because out of over a hundred TV channels, we're number four—and that's pretty good."

Poehler came back with "We'd like to promise you that this year things will be better—but we can't."

And Fey praised the clarity of NBC's new high-definition technology, saying, "The picture is so clear that last week during *Joey* you could actually see Matt LeBlanc's panic."

NBC was unaccustomed to this kind of humiliation, but in truth it had been a long time coming—six years at least, marked by a succession of executive shakeups and seemingly intractable friction between the network's West Coast entertainment planners and its East Coast corporate leadership. The resulting prime-time schedules, which aimed to sustain the tradition of *Seinfeld* and *Friends,* had flamed out, with nothing but ashes left of entries like *Stark Raving Mad, Cursed, Inside Schwartz, Coupling,* and, most recently, an expensive animated comedy, *Father of the Pride.*

Zucker was back on the stage in Radio City a year after promising greatness for *Joey* and *Father of the Pride.* He was still a package of energy, ambition, and cockiness in a compact frame. He was the utterly New York professional, in a perfectly tailored suit and close-shaved—but not skinned—bald pate. Zucker had lost much in the ratings in the past year but none of his stage presence.

"We totally get it," Zucker told the advertisers. "We did not have the season we told you we'd have."

Still, it was left to Kevin Reilly, Zucker's handpicked choice to take over the entertainment operation in Burbank, California, to absorb the most lashes from the ritual self-flagellation, starring in a video in which he was depicted as slowly going mad over the performance of the previous fall's entries, like *Hawaii, LAX,* and, yes, *Father of the Pride.*

Though all those shows had been put in the pipeline with Reilly running the development staff, Zucker had been in overall charge of NBC Entertainment, a fact not lost on his growing legion of critics. Zucker, just now hitting forty, had been the most conspicuous boy wonder in recent network annals. He had risen like an ICBM in the corporate ranks at NBC, largely on the strength of his brilliant record producing the network's most important (because it makes the most money) program, *Today.*

Now fingers were being pointed at Zucker—some from competitors, but others from at least nominally nonpartisan Hollywood studio and agency executives—for milking old NBC hits like *ER* and *Law & Order* of every drop of ratings juice left in them, and for being too clever by more than half in forestalling the day of reckoning with program stunts and gimmicks.

Ted Harbert, who worked under Zucker as the head of NBC's studio, credited Jeff for his "showman's sense" but said, "Where he wasn't facile was in script development. He could make up for a lot with sheer aggressiveness and scheduling, promoting and market-ing—and that stuff counts. You can get ratings points out of that. But you have to have the source material. And in the end you've got to be able to guide your development people."

Script development became the almost universal knock on Zucker. "Zuck is very smart and a very good news producer," one prominent NBC prime-time series producer said. "But clearly, script development is not his forte."

Zucker had made few real friends during his sojourn in Los Angeles, mostly because he never embraced the Hollywood life or the Hollywood game. He had made his share of enemies, though, mainly with his aggressive personality and his special talent for soaking up all the attention in every room, especially those with reporters in them.

Preston Beckman, the prime-time scheduler for the Fox net-work, who had held the same job at NBC during the glory years of the nineties, before leaving with some bitterness just before Zucker arrived, was blunt in his assessment of Zucker's performance at NBC Entertainment.

"He was taking credit for what other people had done," Beckman said. "You listen to him and it's like: What the fuck have *you* done? There was arrogance; there was haughtiness. He was dismantling what we had built at NBC and making it seem like he invented it all."

Some of the animus, especially from the Fox network, was attrib-utable to competitive jealousy over NBC's long run at the top. Zucker, with his abundant morning-show skills in packaging multi-ple elements to best advantage, had moved NBC's existing prime-time pieces around like a manic choreographer. He was always pushing every angle to build audiences, like the time he commis-sioned an NBC special to capitalize on the sudden fascination with Michael Jackson, telling the press it would be an hour all about "Michael Jackson's face." Zucker said, "Michael Jackson is the ulti-mate traffic accident. People can't take their eyes off him." The only trouble was that the comment ticked off members of the Jackson entourage and made compiling the special much harder.

Still, Zucker put the steps together so well that he had managed to maintain the network's reign at the top for the four years he worked in the West, even without finding a smash hit. But in the season just concluded, all the dancing had stopped, and NBC hit the floor. Now the prospect of witnessing NBC—and Zucker— brought low was unleashing the kind of gleeful schadenfreude that Hollywood specialized in.

For the first time in his career—though surely not his life—Jeff Zucker was facing real pressure, because for the first time his performance was not matching his unrestrained bravado.

Still, it was Reilly, the latest executive in charge of NBC's entertainment division, who was already under the gun, expected to find in one development season the kind of hits that ABC had taken the better part of a decade to unearth.

At the NBC upfront, nobody in attendance thought they saw a hit like that. The center of attention was a quirky new entry called *My Name Is Earl,* a promising comedy, though a fragile-looking candidate for savior of a network. The most expensive new addition, *E-Ring,* the Pentagon thriller NBC had secured from the hit-making producer Jerry Bruckheimer, played utterly flat with the advertisers. In terms of a title, the series certainly fell far short of *Desperate Housewives,* with some in attendance suggesting that *E-Ring* sounded like a birth-control device.

In perhaps the most curious move of the day, NBC's executives seemed to play down the introduction of Martha Stewart, who should have been the network's most talked-about new star. Stewart, after all, was set to make her comeback on television after her highly publicized incarceration. Mark Burnett, the reality-show maestro responsible for the huge hits *The Apprentice* on NBC and *Survivor* on CBS, had lined up Stewart both for a new syndicated show, which NBC owned, and for a second edition of *The Apprentice.*

Despite the potential for making a splash, Stewart was introduced to the advertisers almost as an afterthought. She walked out on stage, looking oddly unprepared and nervously twirling what looked like scripted comments.

Only days earlier, Stewart had wowed advertisers with an upfront presentation for her own company in which she scored by showing a little leg. She elegantly pulled up her pants leg to reveal a new pair of shoes she was extolling, then teasingly told the crowd she was sure they would like to see the *other* ankle—the one with the police security bracelet she was still forced to wear at that point while under house arrest.

At NBC's show, nobody had apparently thought to try to do something equally fun. Instead, Stewart, accustomed to ad-libbing during her television performances, was compelled to read drivel awkwardly off a TelePrompTer. The ungraceful moment left advertisers shaking their heads.

By the end of NBC's upfront, with the crowd milling over drinks and hors d'oeuvres outside in the lovely sunshine in Rockefeller Plaza, Bob Wright, NBC's top executive, professed disappointment that the ratings fall-off at his network was "steeper than anticipated." But he declared it was "nothing to be alarmed about."

•   •   •

Carnegie Hall had been home to CBS's program announcements since 1996, the location consciously chosen to signal CBS's return to its venerable image as the network of high standards—and a high opinion of itself. Leslie Moonves had played Carnegie Hall every May for ten years. He called it "a new record for a Jew without an instrument."

Even without accompaniment, Moonves, a former actor, always treated his Carnegie Hall upfront announcement like a performance, carefully honing a speech full of quips and shots at his competitors, and spending hours to record his scenes in a video that was meant to synopsize the past season, and Les's role—for good and ill—in it.

This, however, was the day Moonves had been waiting for since he first walked into the broken-down retirement home that had been CBS a decade earlier. By 2004, Moonves had become television's highest-profile impresario, one who had fashioned CBS's comeback with the patience and craftsmanship of an old-time TV repairman.

This was to be his year, the year he vanquished the once-proud NBC (and its upstart leader, Zucker), and in so doing won the ratings in prime-time television by every measure there was—total viewers, viewers between the ages of 25 and 54, and even the brass ring, viewers between the ages of 18 and 49.

CBS had not won in that category since antediluvian days, before the Nielsen Company introduced the modern ratings system known as people meters. For most years in the past quarter century, CBS was not even a factor in that competition, with an audience largely made up of post-fifty heavy television viewers in rural counties—in other words, an audience few advertisers cared much about reaching. In 1998, an advertising executive named Bill Croasdale had mocked the CBS audience profile, saying it might be appealing to advertisers if they were selling Depends.

Moonves, a man of deep intensity and thin skin, had bridled under those insults. He was prepared to enjoy the ultimate triumph of the 2004–2005 season. And it was still surely a triumph. CBS owned a long list of the most watched shows on television. The network was going to finish first in category after category, and perhaps best of all, his nemesis, NBC, was in apparent free fall. In Moonves's biggest coup, arguably the crowning achievement of his career, CBS had finally toppled what had been for two solid decades an impregnable fortress, NBC's Thursday-night lineup. Over the preceding two seasons, Moonves had already pulled more overall viewers to CBS on Thursday night; now, finally, he had beaten NBC in the 18-to-49-year-old audience that NBC had made its holy grail.

What Moonves had wrought in his tenure at CBS was truly extraordinary. He had won virtually unanimous acclaim in the industry. "What Les has done is flat-out amazing," said Alan Berger, an agent with Creative Artists Agency. "He turned around an aircraft carrier." Even one of NBC's top executives said, "What he's done in ten years is as worthy of major applause as anything anybody has done in the past quarter century."

But there were nits in the bowl of cherries. ABC had stolen a few cracks of his thunder with the season's biggest sensation, *Desperate Housewives*. And thanks to the ratings bump provided by the Super Bowl and big numbers from postseason baseball, as well as its seemingly endless cavalcade of episodes of the hit talent show *American Idol*, the Fox network, of all entities, was going to nip CBS at the wire in that 18-to-49 category.

Moonves had been tempted to claim victory across the board anyway, adding an asterisk to account for the Super Bowl. In fact, he had made that claim in a full-page ad in the *New York Times* just two days earlier (on NBC's upfront day), which declared CBS the winner in just about everything. (In small print the ad cited the caveat "among regularly scheduled programs," thus excluding sports.) In a fortuitous twist, the ad had run on a page facing a story about NBC, and the accompanying photograph had Zucker apparently looking directly at the blaring CBS announcement of its great achievement.

But here at Carnegie Hall, Moonves, fifty-five, impeccably tailored, square-jawed, his slightly curly hair now showing flecks of gray, a medium-sized man whose powerful presence always made him seem far larger, wasn't going to make a sweeping claim of victory. It sounded too much like the lame spinning coming out of NBC. Instead, Moonves merely said that Fox had edged CBS out on the strength of its Red Sox–Yankees playoff series, blaming Yankee closer Mariano Rivera for blowing it for both the Yanks and CBS.

In reality, the year had been a thrill ride for Moonves—and not always a fun one. His network had never performed better or made so much money; he had married a woman he was clearly crazy about. But CBS News had been caught up in a humiliating scandal in the middle of a presidential election; the face of the news division, Dan Rather, was involved, and his eventual departure from the anchor chair only seemed to underscore the disarray in CBS's onceproud, now perennially third-place news division.

That had played out in public. One potentially bigger challenge had played out more quietly. Moonves found himself pressed into carefully plotting a course for his corporate future, after getting an unwelcome but unmistakable indication of where things were headed at CBS's parent company, Viacom.

But on Wednesday afternoon of upfront week, Les Moonves was in an upbeat and typically aggressive mood. He had a show to put on, and he was nothing if not a showman. The theme this day: We're great and the other guys suck.

That point was driven home right from the opening act. The CBS version of Cherry's ersatz Broadway production number was a real Broadway production number, featuring puppets. CBS had the cast from the musical *Avenue Q* adapt one song from the show especially for the occasion. And so puppets representing Zucker, Iger, and Fox's corporate chief, Rupert Murdoch (though they looked more like Manny, Moe, and Jack), danced around the Carnegie Hall stage singing "It Sucks to Be Me," while the puppet representing Moonves (looking more like a close-shaved Abe Lincoln) sang "It's Great to Be Me."

Why Murdoch or Iger would have been so depressed at the end of their patently successful television seasons was not addressed.

Even after the number, Moonves was far from through with either his celebration of CBS's success or his tweaking of Jeff Zucker. In what had become a tradition of the CBS upfront, Moonves followed up with a starring role in an elaborately produced video. He played a boxing phenom being tutored by the Clint Eastwood character from the film *Million Dollar Baby*. The CBS production team had digitally inserted Moonves into scenes from the actual film so that he seemed to be talking to Eastwood and Morgan Freeman. Moonves was playing the Hilary Swank role, though in the end he did not die (or win an Academy Award).

Instead, he dispatched a series of palookas labeled as rival network shows. But the video's signature moment came when Moonves was hitting the heavy bag far too lightly for Eastwood's taste. That was solved when a photo of Zucker was placed on the bag, whereupon Les blasted it right though the back wall of the gym. "Now I know what a Zucker punch is," Moonves said into the camera.

To add to the insult (if not the literal injury), Moonves introduced a clip from one of NBC's own shows, *Late Night with Conan O'Brien,* which featured the star lambasting his network with jokes about its slide into fourth place—and singing a song about NBC's opportunity to go even lower, "the drive for five."

Still, Moonves was not finished with Zucker. He had decided this upfront was the appropriate time to raise the profile of his favorite programming lieutenant, Nina Tassler, by bringing her on stage to outline the CBS fall schedule. After he introduced her, Tassler opened with the best advice Les had given her: "Jokes about Jeff Zucker are always funny." She began with the line "A priest, a rabbi, and Jeff Zucker go into a bar . . ."

Tassler had certainly earned her elevation in Moonves's eyes, having developed a string of the network's biggest recent hits. There was little question about her greatest achievement. Four years earlier, Tassler had been the executive most responsible for locating and advocating a below-the-radar drama, with spectacular and far-reaching results. That drama, *CSI,* had emerged as the signature franchise for the new CBS.

But Tassler did not deserve all the credit. *CSI,* the show that changed CBS's fortunes more than anything else in Les Moonves's tenure, had made it onto the CBS schedule at the very last minute, thanks, at least in part, to the contributions of a very unconventional program consultant.

At the CBS party, held, as always, at Tavern on the Green (Les liked the location for its class and, coincidentally, because he used to bartend there in his days as an acting student in New York), Moonves held court. He was accompanied by his new wife, the *CBS Early Show* coanchor, Julie Chen. Moonves's mood was buoyant, and he dismissed any suggestions about going too far with the slams on Jeff Zucker. "They always come after me," he said, remembering past skewering at the hands of the other networks.

Besides, he pointed out, there was a lot on the line—hundreds of millions of bucks. He was out to convince these advertisers to divert some of the $3 billion they had spent on NBC the previous season into CBS pockets. Noting that NBC had lost Thursday night for the first time in twenty years, with huge ratings falloffs in *Joey, Will & Grace, The Apprentice,* and even the once-unassailable *ER,* Moonves underscored just how bankrupt NBC's programming efforts had become, telling the advertisers: "And they just renewed the entire night."

The line was to have telling impact, with many of those ad buyers wondering why they were being asked to continue to spend so much money on NBC.

After a couple of beers and servings of shrimp, two of Les's close advisers—two of his "guys," as he always called his close staff members—conceded that the boss had approached this season's upfront presentation with considerable relish. "You should have heard all the Zucker lines we took out," one said.

• • •

The Fox network did include an attempt at a Moonves gag the following afternoon during its presentation in the far less elegant—indeed, downright barnlike—setting of the City Center. Fox, playing to the connection between most of the buyers in the audience and its network sales team, had taken to including a couple of sales personnel in movie parodies to open its presentations.

Always lame, this one, "Sales Wars," which put the Fox sales staff inside scenes from the recently opened *Star Wars* sequel, consisted mainly of jokes about sloppy fat guys eating doughnuts. But the space battle scenes did include an attack on a "Death Star" shaped like the CBS eye logo called, to no real laughter, "Darth Moonves."

Fox didn't really care about Moonves. Fox executives had never really cared much about any other network but NBC. That network they detested, and the enmity between the two had been ratcheted up even before the start of the season over Fox's blatant effort to derail an NBC reality series, *The Contender.* Fox had tried to buy the series itself. When it failed, it decided in familiar Fox fashion to make its own copy (Fox called it a legitimate twist) of the show and rush it onto the air first.

In this case, according to one top Fox network executive, the bit-

terly competitive game with NBC was being played out at the very
highest levels. The decision to copy *The Contender*—in an effort to
undermine NBC—was ordered, according to the Fox executive, by
Rupert Murdoch himself.

The bad blood over *The Contender* inspired some verbal fire-
bombs tossed by Zucker and the then-head of Fox Entertainment,
Gail Berman. Behind the hostility was a deep-rooted system of
rivalry and something akin to class warfare. Fox believed that the
NBC people looked down on them as Johnny-come-lately inferiors.

The fact that Fox could run its network like a guerrilla operation
trying to ambush a rival's shows amazed other network executives.
But Fox had special circumstances. In the 2004–2005 season, Fox's
fall schedule was a patchwork of confusion, thanks to the require-
ment that all its series go off the air for three weeks in October to
make room for baseball coverage. Few scripted shows, no matter
how good, could get any traction in a schedule like that.

That left the field largely open to one of network television's most
idiosyncratic and polarizing figures, Mike Darnell, the head of "alternative series" for Fox. Darnell had been asked to carry the network
through the fall of 2004 almost single-handedly with a schedule
chock-a-block with distinctively Darnell reality entries, like *The Swan*
(a beauty pageant for surgically enhanced women) and *The Rebel Billionaire* with the British mogul Richard Branson (an obvious photo-
copy of *The Apprentice*). That schedule had performed abysmally,
however, and Fox languished in the ratings basement through the end
of the year, leaving Berman's employment standing shaky.

Still, thanks to a remarkable second-half surge, Fox had come
home a winner. Berman moved on to run Paramount Pictures. The
turnaround also carried potential implications for the always-
controversial (mostly by his own design) Darnell. His form of can't-
look-away reality show seemed to be falling out of favor, and for the
first time in years Fox had zero offerings from Darnell on its fall
2005 schedule (though some of that was a calculated bait-and-
switch tactic to attract more ad money in upfront sales). Darnell
was not present in New York that Thursday to ponder those implica-

tions. He was home in L.A.: Mike didn't fly, but he was also superstitious about the upfront; he thought it was bad luck to be there.

The new leader at Fox Entertainment, Peter Liguori, a well-liked former chief at Fox's cable channel FX, had replaced Berman as the face of the network. His message to advertisers emphasized the rise of Fox's classy scripted series, like *House* and *24*. Liguori even put in a good word for the renewal of the much-praised but low-rated comedy *Arrested Development*, which had survived a threat of cancellation—and the intense dislike of Murdoch, who found its appeal elitist and limited—to win a spot leading off Fox's Monday nights, at least for a while. (That show was the main pea in the network's upfront shell game.)

Because this was a season without the boost a Super Bowl provides, overall performance was much on the minds at Fox. Its executives rationalized that all the network had to do was upgrade its fall to be on its way. The second half of the season was no worry at all. That's when Fox would again ride the wave of the hit that had changed the competitive landscape of all of network television, the hit that no one, not even Fox, had really wanted to put on the air: *American Idol*. That the amateur-vocalist talent competition was there at all was yet another example of the priceless advantage in television of simply lucking out.

*Idol* had its customary central presence at the Fox upfront, with an eardrum-piercing performance from the increasingly obscure winner of the previous *Idol* competition, Fantasia Barrino, and a march across the stage by the show's celebrated triumvirate of judges, Randy Jackson, Paula Abdul, and Simon Cowell.

Cowell was much more than an *Idol* judge, of course. He was the biggest star on Fox, the highest paid, and the most crucial to the continuing success of the series (and, by extension, the whole network). Cowell, dressed down as always in form-fitting T-shirt and jeans, drank up the support from the *Idol* fans among the advertisers.

Liguori greeted Cowell warmly. That was better than worrying about just how much money it was going to take to keep him from leaving Fox's bedrock show after one more go-round.

While running smoothly through Fox's lineup of new programs, Liguori had one main message for his audience: "We recognize we have a target on our backs. Everyone is gunning for us."

It wasn't true. *Idol* was still gigantic, but it was moving toward old-news status. Fox had made great strides, but another network had already grabbed the profile of the network on the rise. For the moment anyway, ABC had the shows everyone was talking about, even if CBS had the shows with the most people watching.

# CHAPTER TWO

# FRIENDS AND ENEMIES

Before Leslie Moonves, there was a CBS. Few bothered to pay it much attention, though, because it was a dim place where nobody youthful ever ventured. CBS in the early 1990s was reminiscent of a ramshackle old mansion, once grand but now filled with furniture draped in sheets and covered with dust. The network still seemed to be speaking to children of the Depression, the group that had made CBS the channel of choice since the earliest days of television.

But instead of Gleason and Lucy, CBS was offering *Major Dad* and *Dr. Quinn, Medicine Woman*. CBS still played the mass-audience game long after all of its competitors had made young adults their priority. The network found itself hamstrung by a lineup of stations that were not competitive in most markets, that had the worst broadcast signals in the nation's biggest cities. In the early days of television, CBS had the lowest channel position on the dial: that was channel 2. But as cities grew and signals intersected, channel 2 became the weakest signal to own.

Cable transmission should have rectified that, but by the time cable became a force, CBS's stations had long been neglected. CBS was a network-centric company; it paid less attention to the needs of local television stations than did any of its rivals. As a result, the

CBS station in many of the country's biggest cities was a woebegone loser.

That designation was underscored by two massive blows from Fox, the network that arrogant CBS executives had once dismissed as a snot-nosed, dirty-fingernailed upstart. In December 1993, Fox stole the rights to NFL football games from CBS. Then, the following year, Fox raided eight of CBS's prime affiliated stations.

Thanks to those two blunders, the network was slinking toward oblivion in the 1990s, with a roster of aging shows that mainly appealed to aged viewers—a formula that seemed to guarantee a slow march from irrelevant to irretrievable.

But that was before the arrival of Leslie Moonves. No television studio executive ever carved out a higher profile in as short a time as Moonves did in the early 1990s.

In 1991, Moonves, then forty-three, was already easily identifiable as a rising star. Taking over as head of the Warner Brothers television studio that year, he had quickly established a reputation for both his acumen in putting together popular shows and his hard-driving, aggressive personality.

Early in his tenure at Warner, Moonves got wind of a promising writing/producing team named Kauffman, Crane, and Bright. From one of his young associates, David Janollari, Moonves learned that Marta Kauffman and David Crane had been off-Broadway playwrights in New York. Kevin Bright was their producing partner. They were about to go on the market for an exclusive studio deal.

The main competition in the bidding was Disney's production studio, which was offering the writing team a bit more money. Moonves won out by telling the team's agent, Nancy Josephson of ICM: "Don't go for the extra 10 cents. Go for the extra 10 million."

Moonves landed the deal. His payoff came about a year and a half later. For the 1993 development season, Kauffman, Crane, and Bright had three separate comedy ideas they wanted to pitch around to the networks. They were young, hip, a bit risqué. Moonves figured them as right for ABC, Fox, or NBC.

The first idea was the most ambitious. Kauffman, Crane, and

Bright pitched ABC an idea about a group of wisecracking high school kids who burst into song at regular intervals. The idea was *Grease* for the nineties.

They might have picked their network better. ABC still had bouts of post-traumatic stress disorder from its experience trying a weekly songfest with the infamous crime-show musical *Cop Rock*. The comedy team was politely—but quickly—ushered out of the room.

Moonves had considerably higher hopes for the other two shows at NBC and Fox. His plan was to do a "one and one"—each network could pick one of the two ideas. Moonves brought the young writers first to Fox and had them pitch their two shows. Fox loved one, a traditional three-camera, videotaped comedy. The network said it would start negotiations to buy it.

Next, Moonves brought the group to NBC, which also liked the three-camera show, but with Fox having spoken up for it first, NBC had to be content with negotiating for the second idea, a quirkier, one-camera filmed show about a Ferris Bueller–type high school kid called *Reality Check*.

Moonves had his one and one. The only problem was that Fox was playing hardball in making a deal. For what he considered the more promising three-camera comedy, Moonves was insisting on a $150,000 penalty payment; that is, Fox would pay for the script to be written and pledge to pay an additional $150,000 fee if the show was not ordered to go to pilot. If the pilot was ordered, there was no penalty.

The Fox executive working the deal, Tom Noonan, came back to Moonves and told him the network wanted the script but he could not get the commitment for the penalty money. Moonves turned to NBC, who agreed to pay it.

NBC got *Friends*; Fox kept its 150 grand.

The *Friends* deal done, Moonves also had a drama he wanted NBC to see. The script had floored him, it was so good; but he knew when he read it that it must have been buried in a trunk for an awfully long time. Set in Boston, the script mentioned a Celtics game with Tommy Heinsohn as a player. "I knew he had retired in, like, the seventies," Moonves said.

NBC's development team was also enthusiastic about the show, but because it was a hospital drama, and NBC had already had *St. Elsewhere* set in Boston, they asked for the location to be moved. For no especially good reason, Chicago was the choice. The show was called *ER*.

The production "auspices," as they are called in television, were certainly impressive. The novelist Michael Crichton had written the script—clearly about his days as a resident—and his partner on the series was Steven Spielberg, with whom he had recently worked on *Jurassic Park*.

NBC needed to be assured that the series would have someone in charge day to day—a "showrunner," as it's known in television. And Moonves was fortunate to have in that job John Wells, who had handled *China Beach*.

Given the big names involved, Moonves expected NBC to pony up to land the show. Warren Littlefield, the NBC Entertainment president, promised a two-hour pilot with a commitment for six more episodes. If the network didn't like the pilot and decided not to shoot the episodes, it would have to pay a penalty fee. All sides agreed—or at least Moonves thought so. Unexpectedly, he got a call from Littlefield, who started changing the terms. Littlefield said his budget was stretched and he couldn't agree to the six-episode guarantee. He would order only the pilot—no penalty if it did not go past that point.

That did not sit well with Les Moonves. He believed he had made a deal and NBC was simply reneging. In Moonves's mind, he was free to take the show elsewhere. He picked up the phone and called Jeff Sagansky, then in charge of entertainment at CBS.

Sagansky read the script immediately and called Moonves. He loved the show. But he had a problem. *ER* was an ensemble-acted hospital show set in Chicago. Sagansky was already committed to an ensemble-acted hospital show called *Chicago Hope*. It was being written by David E. Kelley, then the most significant series creator on the CBS payroll, having brought the network the multi-award-winning drama *Picket Fences.* Sagansky told Moonves, "I can't do them both."

Les went back to NBC and made the deal for just a pilot. He was still confident that he had the drama that NBC would select to replace the flagging *L.A. Law* on Thursday nights. (The competition was an existing NBC show, *Homicide,* which Moonves believed stood no chance of ever being a major hit.)

Meanwhile, he was deep into casting for *Friends.* Moonves prided himself on his casting abilities. He loved the process more than almost anything else about his job, and felt a special affinity for the actors being subjected to this often humiliating routine. He had been there himself. The *Friends* roles were being filled with what Moonves saw as spectacular young talent: Matthew Perry, Courteney Cox, David Schwimmer. The only hitch was the part of Rachel. It was the critical role in the pilot, as Moonves saw it—the girl who walked out of her wedding.

He knew whom he wanted: a young actress named Jennifer Aniston. But she was locked up in a show called *Muddling Through,* which CBS was planning to use as a short-run summer entry. Luckily, Moonves had a close friend named Jon Feltheimer, who ran the Columbia-TriStar television studio, which controlled *Muddling Through.* Les asked Feltheimer to allow him to use Aniston in the *Friends* pilot, on the hope that *Muddling Through* would not be picked up for more episodes. It wasn't, and NBC got a star.

(Later, Feltheimer told Moonves he had been stupid. "I should have gotten schmuck insurance," he said. Showbiz executives liked to circumvent accusations of screwing up and missing out on some big score by nailing down some financial protection in case of significant success—schmuck insurance. "I should have gotten, like, 1 percent of the show, which you would have given me," Feltheimer said. Moonves replied, "You're probably right.")

When he moved on to the *ER* casting, Moonves had an even stronger conviction that he had finally found something he had long been looking for: a role to suit an actor he had signed to a talent-holding deal for four years in a row. "I just said: this guy's a star; and I signed him. I thought he was great-looking, unbelievably charming. I thought he had great presence. I said he has what every TV and movie star wants. The guys want to drink beer with him and the women want to sleep with him."

Moonves sent the *ER* script to George Clooney. At the same time, he sent Clooney another pilot script for a legal drama set in San Francisco—a true leading role and so a bigger part than anything in *ER.*

Moonves told Clooney he was sending two scripts without commenting on them. Clooney called back quickly. "I love this *ER* script, I love this guy Dr. Ross." Les reminded Clooney the other part was bigger. "Doesn't matter," Clooney said.

Moonves was delighted—until he remembered he had just given away a part without even consulting the show's production staff. He called John Wells, still excited about his coup. He told him he had secured George Clooney for Dr. Ross. "Who's he?" Wells said. "I don't know who George Clooney is." Moonves told him how great he believed this guy would be; then he sent Clooney over to charm Wells—which he did.

The *Friends* pilot went off fabulously, at least as far as Moonves was concerned. The title changed a couple of times. It started out as *Friends Like Us,* and then became *Six of One,* before being simply called *Friends.* NBC was deeply troubled by one aspect. They sent a note asking about the group's chosen hangout. "Nobody's ever going to believe people in a coffee shop," the note said. "Couldn't you make it a diner?"

Moonves, amazed, asked if they wanted the *Friends* cast to meet in the exact same diner as the cast from *Seinfeld.* The note was dropped.

As soon as the *Friends* pilot was screened, no one had any doubt: It was ticketed for the NBC Thursday-night comedy lineup. Moonves, of course, wanted more; he wanted *ER* to land the open 10 P.M. slot. Moonves was armed to make his case as soon as NBC told him how much they loved the *ER* pilot—except they didn't. Word came back that it had not played well, that Don Ohlmeyer, the head of NBC's West Coast division, did not like the pilot—so much so, Moonves was told, that he had gotten up and walked out of the room.

Moonves was stunned. It didn't seem possible. He went out to lunch at a local hamburger joint and by chance ran into Laurie Opinden, then the top casting executive for NBC. She walked over, shaking her head. "They didn't get it," she said.

It turned out that NBC felt steamrolled. Warner Brothers had submitted its testing on *ER* and the response was off-the-charts great. NBC didn't buy it; it wanted more testing done. When those results came back just as strong, NBC finally jumped aboard.

Moonves got his order for a series; more than that, he got the second jewel in his production crown for the year: two new shows on NBC's Thursday night, including the premier drama position in all of television—Thursday night at 10.

In an exhibition of all-too-common network disregard for viewers, CBS had already decided it would slot *Chicago Hope* in exactly the same time slot: Two new, high-gloss, classy hospital dramas, both set in Chicago, were going head to head at the same hour. Moonves, convinced he had the real thing, regarded CBS's move as a display of utter hubris.

Despite his confidence in *ER,* the competitive pressure had Moonves on edge. In September 1994, *Chicago Hope* premiered with its two-hour pilot on a Sunday; *ER* did the same the following night. Both shows opened well, but *ER* fared better, especially with the younger viewers NBC required. By the time the two shows faced off for the first time the following Thursday at 10, *ER* was pulling away, already the twelfth-most-popular show on television, while *Hope* finished down the track, in forty-sixth place. When Moonves, in New York that Friday morning, got the ratings news, he breathed easier. "We kicked the shit out of them," he said.

At that moment, Leslie Moonves had no idea that he himself, while emerging as one of the central figures in the television industry, would spend most of the next decade on the wrong side of that Thursday night shit kicking.

• • •

$A$s a kid growing up in Valley Stream, Long Island, Leslie Moonves watched little television other than sports and some news. He was, from a young age, a high-culture type. His mother was a Broadway fanatic, and she brought him along to see virtually every show in New York.

His other passion, baseball, he inherited from his father, a serious player first of hardball, then of fast-pitch softball. The elder Moonves owned gas stations, first in Brooklyn adjacent to Ebbets Field, then on Long Island. Les himself played a lot of sports and considered himself a jock of sorts.

For all of that, the Russian-heritage family was "Jewish royalty," as Moonves jokingly put it. His grandfather's sister had married one of the founding fathers of Israel, David Ben-Gurion.

Starting at Bucknell in 1967, Moonves quickly dropped his first plan, to be a doctor. He shifted his major to Spanish. The old Broadway baby also drifted into occasional college theatrical productions. During his senior year, an adviser suggested that if he was truly serious about acting, he should study under Sanford Meisner at the Neighborhood Playhouse in New York. Moonves spent what he always called the greatest two years of his life there, intensely working on acting during the day, tending bar all over town at night.

He got a little off-off-Broadway work, but when a girl he was dating decided to try her luck in California, Moonves followed her out. The relationship ended, but Moonves found a home in Hollywood. He made the rounds looking for acting work, all the time networking, building relationships.

Moonves continued to tend bar, settling at the comedy club The Improv at a time when comedy talent was flocking to L.A. He saw new names all the time: Robin Williams, Freddie Prinze, Andy Kaufman. Moonves's mate behind the bar thought he was a comic, too, though Les cringed every time his friend, a sweet, gentle guy named Kevin Nealon, stepped out on open-mike night and bombed. He stayed at it, though. (And wound up on *Saturday Night Live*.)

The assistant manager at the club was an ambitious guy named

Chris Albrecht, who also became friendly with Moonves. He went on to put *The Sopranos* and *Sex and the City* on television and ultimately to run HBO.

Moonves got an agent. With his swarthy look, square build, and natural talent for affecting menace, he landed a few guest-starring roles, usually as a Latin heavy named something like Pasqual in shows like *Cannon* and *The Six Million Dollar Man*. He kept going on auditions, scrapping, always hustling. But increasingly, he despised the process. "I felt like my hand was always out. Do me a favor. Please hire me."

Moonves looked around at some of his close acting buddies. Gregory Harrison and Mark Harmon were both breaking through. Moonves realized it wasn't happening for him. "I never thought I was that good." He remembered a bit of advice Meisner had given him back in New York: "You should only be an actor if it's the only thing you can do."

There had to be other things he could do. Moonves soaked up information everywhere he went, observing how the business worked, getting himself ready to move on to other things. In 1978, he started producing small-time theater with Harrison and another friend, Frank Levy.

Harrison, then starring in the CBS series *Trapper John, MD*, wanted still to be a Serious Actor. Moonves and he arranged a production of *The Hasty Heart*—a movie hit for Ronald Reagan—for a small theater. Every big career is usually ignited by a break; this was the moment for Moonves.

The third partner, Levy, was friendly with Robert Fryer, who ran the huge Ahmanson Theatre in downtown L.A. Levy invited Fryer down to see Harrison's performance in a Sunday matinee. The night before, the news broke that Natalie Wood had been drowned in a boating accident. Wood was scheduled to appear in Fryer's next show. He needed a replacement—fast.

*The Hasty Heart*, starring Gregory Harrison and Lisa Eilbacher, looked awfully good to him that afternoon. Within a few weeks, Moonves was in charge of a production at a 2,800-seat theater.

Moonves started to make some regular money. More than that, he had an opportunity to use his organizational skills, to display his management ability at things like running a budget, to prove he was a leader. Moonves still got a few calls for auditions, but he turned them all down. He realized immediately that what jazzed him up more than anything else was the action.

A short while later, Moonves interviewed for an entry-level job at NBC. But a young executive just coming into his own there, Warren Littlefield, alerted him to a more promising job with Sol Ilson, an executive then leaving NBC to start up a production company. Les would get a shot at really developing new shows there.

Moonves was already thirty. After only a short time on the job with Ilson's company, he knew that he was born to work in television. But he also was in a hurry. After learning the basics and working under a series of executives, Moonves came to a firm conclusion: "If these are the big guys in this business, I'm going all the way."

After several successful years commissioning TV movies for the Fox studio, Moonves landed at Lorimar Television, where he got his first crack at developing series. Lorimar already had hits like *Knots Landing* on the air. Moonves kicked the unit into overdrive. He developed a close relationship with two comedy producers named Tom Miller and Bob Boyette, and rode with them to enormous success, creating a whole slate of family comedy for ABC on Friday night, which came to be known as "TGIF."

Moonves never forgot some of the highlight moments from those years, including one memorable casting session when a young mother brought in her two nine-month-old babies, named Mary-Kate and Ashley Olsen, to try out for the part of Michelle, the baby on the biggest Miller-Boyette hit, *Full House*.

Moonves was fast-tracked at Lorimar, set to take over as president in 1989, when he learned his studio had been sold out from under him to Warner Brothers.

Just before the July Fourth holiday, Moonves, pondering his options, was set to go on vacation with his wife and three kids to the south of France. His lawyer, Ernie Del, called with some news. Jeffrey Katzenberg, then the number-two executive at Walt Disney, had called Del about Les. He wanted to initiate a job discussion.

The timing was horrible. Moonves was leaving for Europe the next day. But Katzenberg was adamant: Could they meet in the morning before his flight? And could it be discreet?

Moonves agreed. He met Katzenberg at 7 A.M. at a Jack in the Box on a back street in Burbank. Over his habitual Diet Coke, Katzenberg pitched Moonves to come to Disney as president of its network television division. Moonves was seriously interested. He was losing out on control of Lorimar in the Warner deal. Even if the Warner chief, Bob Daly, kept the Lorimar unit separate from his own Warner television studio, Moonves figured he would always be the stepchild in that configuration. The boss of Warner television, Harvey Shepherd, was close to Daly.

But Moonves was under contract and would have to convince Daly to allow him to leave—and Bob Daly had a well-known reputation for never letting anyone out of a contract. Moonves told Katzenberg he was interested and would be back in the country in ten days.

Halfway through his trip, he got a call from Del: The Disney chairman, Michael Eisner, was in Paris for the opening of Euro Disney and wanted to meet Les. Moonves rearranged his plans and stopped off in Paris on his way home. He visited Eisner in his extraordinary apartment overlooking the Eiffel Tower and they discussed the offer Eisner had in mind. It sounded great to Moonves— plenty of stock options that would make him a rich man if the stock paid off. He was ready to jump.

When Moonves returned to L.A., he went straight to Daly, whom he had never even met. It seemed like a win-win. Moonves would solve the dilemma of having two heads of television units for Daly by moving on to Disney. The conversation was brief. In a polite, charming way, Bob Daly said: No way; won't even discuss it. Nobody gets out of contracts, ever.

Moonves contacted everyone he knew: agents, lawyers. All that resulted from his efforts was Daly making a call to Katzenberg to say, in effect: Stay away from my executive.

Moonves closed the Disney chapter with some regret (even years later, he said, he still thought about what might have been). He got along with Harvey Shepherd, but he knew there was a natural rivalry. To the ferociously competitive Moonves, that meant he had to win. He was far more driven than Shepherd, who was on the downside of his career, having already been the top programmer at CBS. In short order, Lorimar had far surpassed Warner's own unit in number of shows on the air.

By 1991, with Lorimar—and Moonves—dominating the television business for Warner Brothers, it made no sense to keep the units separate anymore. They merged, Harvey Shepherd got a deal as a producer, and Leslie Moonves was put in charge.

Only a couple of years later, Moonves was delivering the gift that kept on giving to NBC: *Friends* and *ER,* the highest-rated comedy and drama on television. They were among the record twenty-two Warner shows that Moonves placed on various networks that season.

As he figured it, Les Moonves had two mountains he could aim to climb in 1994. He could set his sights on running the film studio, or he could switch sides and jump to a network as head of entertainment. Both appealed to him, but there was no door ajar for him. At Warner, the company and the film studio were both extremely well run by Daly and his partner, Terry Semel. Opportunities at the networks were foreclosed until his contract with Warner expired in September 1995.

Daly, now among Moonves's biggest fans, opened talks about a new contract in January 1995. Moonves was plainly feeling stymied. "I put *Friends* on," he said. "I put *ER* on. I got twenty-two shows on the air. I can't do this job any better."

The contract discussions included the vague possibility of making Moonves a kind of junior partner to Daly and Semel; but despite his fondness for Daly, the options just did not seem all that appealing to Moonves.

In the spring, Moonves got a call he was not expecting from Bill Haber, one of the principals of the CAA Agency. "Larry Tisch would like to meet you," Haber said. "When will you be in New York?"

Tisch, mainly a stock market investor, had purchased CBS in 1986. The company had been slowly falling apart since, with Tisch selling off pieces, like the record division, and ordering drastic cutbacks in the news division. In prime time, CBS was loaded down with old-fashioned series like *Murder, She Wrote*—shows that attracted lots of viewers, but mainly old ones. Jeff Sagansky had departed a season earlier, in 1994, just before the network's ratings took a back flip down the drainpipe.

Moonves knew CBS was in trouble; he was intrigued. Given the prevailing opinion of Tisch as a stern taskmaster who had eviscerated CBS, Moonves was surprised to find the old man so avuncular, almost grandfatherly.

Tisch asked Moonves what he thought of the people at CBS, why things were going so wrong. Les offered some opinions. He did not campaign for the job, but he easily demonstrated that he knew the competitive landscape; he knew talent; he knew the business inside and out.

Moonves still expected that Warner would make him an offer and he'd stay on. But when Tisch called only a week later, he was ready to deal. A couple of days later, he flew into New York with Ernie Del and met with Tisch at his apartment on Seventy-ninth and Fifth. Tisch was accompanied by his CBS CFO, Peter Keegan. Del began a negotiation, while Moonves repaired to another room and watched television. Del came back a few times to discuss details. Things went smoothly.

It was mid-April 1995. Back in Los Angeles, the new president of CBS's entertainment division, Peter Tortorici, was in the final weeks of putting together his first slate of fall programs.

Tortorici was thinking revolution. He had analyzed the tattered CBS lineup when he succeeded Sagansky, and especially how the network's graybeard audience and dowdy image were leading most advertisers to walk the other way when a CBS salesman appeared.

"We had shows with viewers over seventy," one longtime CBS executive said. "A show like *Lois & Clark* on ABC, which was on at the same time as our *Murder, She Wrote,* had a much smaller audience, but ABC was getting about 50 percent more revenue than we were with Angela Lansbury."

Leslie Moonves had put *Lois & Clark* on ABC. He had a framed magazine cover prominently displayed in his office, showing him surrounded by three stars he had steered onto the air: Jennifer Aniston, George Clooney, and Teri Hatcher of *Lois & Clark.*

At a management retreat the previous December, Tortorici had given his CBS bosses an ultimatum of sorts: If they wanted him to continue the policies of aiming for broad audiences heavily larded with older viewers, he would do that. "We may hold on to a little bit more revenue that way," Tortorici said, "but it's going to get ugly real fast."

The other way to go was risky. CBS could try to aim its new fall shows at a younger audience, make a fundamental shift. It would clearly involve some financial pain, but it might put CBS on the right track. "I'm only going to do it if you have the stomach for it," Tortorici told his bosses. They told him his analysis was right; he should make the necessary changes.

A few months later, before any of the shows Tortorici had commissioned had even been seen, Larry Tisch was in the process of giving his job away to Leslie Moonves.

During the 1995 upfront week that May in New York, Tisch invited Moonves to dinner at an uptown restaurant, Coco Pazzo, often frequented by the media crowd. Moonves worried about how smart it was for them to be seen together with everyone in town for the upfronts. Tisch said nobody would believe they would be stupid enough to be seen together if they were working on an employment deal. Quietly, the paperwork was being finalized.

Moonves got word the deal was closed while attending the ABC post-presentation party Tuesday evening at the Museum of Natural History. The next day, he attended CBS's upfront presentation at the Marriott Marquis on Broadway. It struck Moonves as a sloppy, downmarket affair, with bridge chairs set up in the ballroom for the advertisers, nothing like the classy theaters the other networks used for their presentations.

Watching Tortorici introduce his new program lineup, Moonves was struck by the lackluster presentation. More than that, he was appalled by the content. Tortorici was introducing show after show, with names like *Can't Hurry Love, If Not for You,* and *Dweebs.* The centerpiece was a high-profile new soap opera called *Central Park West,* from Darren Star, who had been assigned credit for the Fox soap hit *Melrose Place. Central Park West* was a show full of young, beautiful people, a show that was radically unlike anything CBS had introduced in years.

"I'm in more trouble than I had any idea of," Moonves said to himself. After the presentation, an excited Joe Abruzzese, the head of sales for CBS, came up to Moonves gushing about the new lineup, asking Moonves if he didn't think it all looked great.

"Yeah, it looks great," Moonves lied. *Obviously, we're starting from the bottom here,* he thought. The task suddenly looked huge and oppressive. "On the flip side," he said to himself, "if I can turn *this* around, it'll be the greatest thing since sliced bread."

Moonves broke the news to Bob Daly when he got back to L.A. The Warner chief was, initially, happy for his lieutenant—he himself had run CBS Entertainment in an earlier day. The next morning, though, he called Moonves. Now he was pissed. "You have a contract; you're too valuable here," he said.

But, of course, the contract was to run out in September. Daly tried a few angles, offered more money. But he could not compete with everything Tisch was offering. This wasn't about the money. Moonves, knowing he was getting a shot to program a whole network, was resolute. The news leaked in June. Daly still held Moonves back, releasing him only in mid-July after extracting a couple of program commitments for Warner from CBS.

•   •   •

Moonves moved into CBS in the summer of 1995 full of trepidation—and a little remorse. The first few months, he told himself the same thing every single day: "I've made the biggest mistake of my life." He missed the team of executives he had assembled at Warner.

The deal had included a clause that would not allow him to steal anyone away for eighteen months.

Alone in CBS's factorylike offices in Television City, Moonves was stuck with what he considered a mess of a schedule, which he hated. Within a couple of weeks, he decided that the work ethic inside the CBS offices was deplorable. He wandered the hallways at 3:30 on a Friday afternoon and found the place three-quarters empty. He sat down and typed up a memo to the staff: "Unless anybody hasn't noticed, we're in third place. My guess is that at ABC and NBC they're still working at 3:30 on Friday. This will no longer be tolerated."

The new schedule collapsed pretty much as Moonves predicted. Not one of the new shows lasted through the season. *Central Park West* was the most notable bust, and for years after Moonves would cite it as a symbol of CBS trying to change its image too fast and too drastically.

Moonves was miserable the entire first year. Losing every week by a huge margin, seeing the headlines—"The Moribund CBS," "The Perennial Last-Place Network"—he was convinced that CBS was so beaten down that its staff felt it had become acceptable to lose. Losing was like death to Moonves. He was having no fun at all. After years of success, this was hell.

Doing something big seemed the only answer, so Moonves went after the biggest star he could think of. He wooed Bill Cosby. It was a pattern Moonves would repeat frequently, signing up stars who had had hits on NBC and ABC when they were younger. As they hit their forties or fifties, Moonves would bring them into CBS: Ted Danson, Rhea Perlman, Tom Selleck, Tim Daly, David Caruso, Amy Brenneman, Ellen DeGeneres, Jason Alexander, Jenna Elfman. The list grew every year—even though almost none of the shows worked.

The deal for Cosby was hugely expensive. Moonves guaranteed $1 million an episode for forty-four episodes—at a time when an average comedy cost only about $600,000 an episode. And the show was hardly the same kid-oriented family comedy Cosby's NBC hit had been in the 1980s—Bill was going to play a sixty-year-old downsized blue-collar worker. But adding a star of that magnitude gave Moonves instant credibility.

It was the start of a strategy that Moonves would employ with the fierce doggedness that defined his personality. He would rebuild CBS piece by piece—"brick by brick," as he liked to put it—never pushing too hard too fast. What he wanted from Cosby was something, anything, positive that he could use to boost morale—the staff's and his own. In was important—essential—to start winning somewhere.

That conviction led to a plan that was the polar opposite of Tortorici's youthquake approach. Les decided he could at least assemble large numbers of people if he was willing to service the core audience CBS had held for seemingly the entire twentieth century: older viewers in rural areas.

He said to the staff, "Let's embrace who we are. We're not selling eighteen to forty-nine; we'll sell twenty-five to fifty-four, or even just total audience. Why are we going to announce we're in this fight that we're never going to win?"

So he announced that CBS was in a different fight, first for households (a totally outmoded means of measuring TV viewing), then for total viewers (which the other networks disdained because they argued that advertisers did not want to pay for hordes of older viewers that they had little or no need of reaching). Advertisers sought young adults mainly because they were scarce. They watched less television; older people watched a lot and so were easily available. There was also an old advertising theory in some quarters that younger people were more likely to switch brands.

CBS went to great lengths, formulating research presentations that proved older viewers did indeed switch brands (though it was impossible to argue that older viewers did not watch a lot more television than younger viewers). CBS argued that its strategy was ideal for a nation whose biggest population segment, the baby boomers, were aging past fifty.

The network had difficulty winning widespread support for the argument. CBS shows routinely were priced far lower, sometimes at only about 30 to 50 percent of what the other networks were getting. Jon Mandel, one of the most influential advertising executives in the country, said, "In order for the CBS argument to work, people would have to age in dog years."

Even some of CBS's own sales executives conceded that the pitch about older viewers was almost entirely spin, noting that the median age of CBS shows was so much older than its competitors'. "That was just killing us," a CBS sales executive said.

In candid moments, Moonves acknowledged throughout his early years at CBS that he had serious regrets about the fact that there was not a single show on the network that his own teenage children watched. Ever.

Moonves knew he would have to change that; but that would come in time. In the short run, CBS picked out shows that had a chance to bring in a few younger people, while making sure they appealed to its big crowd of older folks. A family comedy that Moonves particularly liked in his first development season at CBS had the virtue of including grandparents as key characters. That wasn't the only reason Les liked *Everybody Loves Raymond*. The humor genuinely cracked him up. He became a big early supporter of both the show and its creative team, led by the star, Ray Romano, and a sharp showrunner named Phil Rosenthal.

Rosenthal hit it off with Moonves so well that he became, early on, one of Les's "guys," the coterie of executives and associates that Moonves would eventually build into the most impressively professional programming unit in the business. As soon as he was able, Moonves began to import to CBS executives he knew and trusted from his Warner days. Among the most crucial moves, he installed Kelly Kahl as his chief scheduler, brought in Nina Tassler for drama development, and hired Nancy Tellem as his second in command at CBS Entertainment, though she remained principally his deal maker, the head of business affairs.

But CBS was not led by committee—unless you counted a committee of one. Moonves left no doubt about who ran the place. He had ultimate authority over everything, and he exercised it. He participated in every move of even minute significance, from the smallest casting decisions to the closing of every big deal. He read scripts, supervised promos, hired and fired, was the voice and face of the network in innumerable interviews, and served as cheerleader, coach, and taskmaster of a boss to the executives who worked under him.

Some chafed, but most of them displayed both affection and unwavering loyalty—and Moonves demanded nothing less. To a few, the demands were too much, as was Moonves's occasionally volcanic temper.

"Raise your voice at me? I'm on your side," one former CBS executive said of his volatile encounters with Moonves. "Tell me one guy who ever raised his voice back at Les and still has his job. Nobody."

Kelly Kahl, one of Les's most trusted lieutenants, said, "Is he intimidating? Sure. You get used to it. I feel much worse when he says, 'I'm disappointed.' It's almost like a Dad thing. That's much worse than being screamed at. Screamed at comes and goes. It's not fun, but the frequency is not great." Kahl did give Les credit, however. "I've seen a few times when he goes supernova, and he's really good at it."

Moonves loved the job being done by Chris Ender, the top public relations executive at CBS Entertainment, whom Les had hired away as a fresh-faced kid from Columbia Television's syndication unit. But once, at a press conference when Les was being hounded by unwelcome questions from reporters, he noticed Ender off to one side engaged in a friendly conversation. Les abruptly broke off from the reporters, saying, "That's it," and stormed off in Ender's direction.

"Well, I hope *you're* having a fucking nice conversation," he said in barely contained rage to his PR guy as he brushed by him. Ender later said the incident did not overly disturb him. "If I couldn't get up off the floor every time he yelled at me, I couldn't do this job."

The level Moonves's anger could reach would sometimes shock those not accustomed to it. One new CBS executive was taken aback by what took place at staff meetings. Moonves often displayed a nervous tic when he spoke, using the fingernails on one hand to scratch upward at his cheek. The gesture looked a bit like Marlon Brando's brushstroke in *The Godfather*.

Moonves always seemed totally unaware he was doing it. But as one meeting progressed, the new executive saw that the scratching became more and more agitated when Les was roused to anger. On this occasion, Moonves got so worked up, and the scratching got so fevered, that blood began dripping down his face onto his shirt.

Most of Les's anger focused on the competition. Like any great coach, Moonves fired up his team with us-vs.-them rhetoric. One former CBS executive said, "When I worked at CBS, Les was really good at instilling in his team that the rest of the world, especially NBC, was the devil."

But some staff members thought the notion of having an enemy, *needing* an enemy, was part of Moonves's psychological makeup. One executive who worked closely with Moonves for years said, "To go along with his great talent, you've got an insurmountable ego. One thing about Les, there has to be somebody he hates—internally, externally. It was Jonathan Dolgen at the Paramount film studio. Then it was Kerry McCluggage at Paramount Television. Someone at the competition or inside the network."

Les's good friend Ted Harbert, the former ABC programming chief, often saw the best side of Moonves during annual golf outings with a group of longtime buddies (which also included Ernie Del and Jon Feltheimer) to Pebble Beach and St. Andrews in Scotland. After taking a day or so to decompress, Harbert said, the professional demons evaporated for the whole group, especially Les. "Underneath, Les is the nicest, sweetest guy," Harbert said. "He's a lot of laughs, really kind and generous."

But to challenge him in business was to take on a brawler. Harbert said that Les would sometimes take the slightest rebuttal as an affront. "You poke Les, he'll hit you in the head with a frying pan."

In his early years at CBS, nothing poked at Les as much as the huge success NBC was having, while he looked like a loser week after week. He did not believe NBC was being in any way gracious about their good fortune, for which, thanks to his own role in placing *Friends* and *ER,* he felt at least partially responsible. Instead, NBC seemed insufferably arrogant to Les, and no one more so than his old friend Warren Littlefield.

The two men frequently represented their networks on industry panels, and they would enliven these usually tedious affairs with a series of running jabs—and uppercuts. It got to be performance art of a sort.

"We'd be sitting there on a panel," Moonves said. "And maybe he'd be talking about how great they were doing, which would be turning a knife in my stomach. And then he'd say something dumb, innocently."

And off Les would go. At one panel in New York, Littlefield was asked what mistakes he had made that programming season and he somehow managed to say he couldn't think of even one. Les was right on him. "You can't think of one mistake? Not one? You didn't mis-schedule a movie of the week or miscast one actor? How can you be in this job and not have made one mistake?"

At another television executive panel held in Aspen during HBO's comedy festival there, Warren said the question the moderator asked "presupposes that the guy running the network had nothing to do with its success." Moonves almost came out of his chair to interrupt. "And what better person than you to answer that question?" he said.

Moonves got a huge laugh on that occasion, but he knew he had slashed a little too deeply into Warren, the guy who had given him his first opportunity in television. Don Ohlmeyer, a close, longtime buddy of Moonves, who supervised Littlefield at that point, called Les after the Aspen incident.

"That was going too far, Les," Ohlmeyer said. "You gotta knock this off. You guys are hurting each other."

Moonves agreed. "I love Warren, I really do," he said. "It was my only defense, because my shows weren't working."

Littlefield's were. At that point, in the late 1990s, NBC was riding a wave of success never before seen in the television business. When, in an unrestrained fit of self-promotion, NBC labeled its shows "Must-See TV," nobody could dispute the point—not even Moonves. On Thursday nights, the central pillar of its wonderwall of hits, NBC would outrate its three competitors *combined.* NBC's lineup of shows contained not just smash commercial hits, but a Murderer's Row of television classics that included *Seinfeld, Frasier, Friends, Law & Order,* and *ER.* NBC was taking in hundreds of millions more in revenues each year than its closest competitor, which at that point was ABC. CBS, meanwhile, was still limping along far back up the track, trying to compete with a lineup of pedestrian, stodgy shows like *Diagnosis: Murder; Walker Texas Ranger;* and *Touched by an Angel.* Leslie Moonves's kids still weren't watching his network.

There was only one way for Moonves to fix the situation: Hang in, find better shows, bide his time, and maybe outlast Littlefield and Ohlmeyer at NBC.

The plan had some merit.

# CHAPTER THREE

# MUST-SEE-SOMETHING-ELSE TV

In the late fall of 1998, a few weeks after being dispatched from his job at NBC Entertainment, where he had spent virtually his entire career, Warren Littlefield sat down to a farewell breakfast with the NBC boss, Bob Wright, in New York at the Four Seasons Hotel.

Wright had brought along a couple of sizable bonus checks for Warren, which could not help but put Littlefield in a good, loose mood. The previous month had not been an especially happy time for Littlefield. He had been ushered out the door in October, with less ceremony than he surely deserved for his long stewardship at the network, which encompassed NBC's years of greatness.

And it wasn't as though NBC was in crisis. The network was still winning prime time handily, still raking in buckets of cash. But a few cracks had begun to appear. A string of new comedies had come and gone with none looking like a replacement for *Seinfeld,* which left the air amid enormous fanfare the previous May.

Littlefield had extended himself to the limit to try to convince Jerry Seinfeld, with whom he believed he had a close relationship, to star in and produce another year of the series. Wright and Jack Welch, the GE chairman, made a last-ditch effort themselves, inviting Seinfeld to Wright's Central Park apartment for some desperation wooing. They offered the comic a deal of stupefying magnitude to stay on for one more season: $5 million an episode for twenty-two episodes of television—or $110 million for one year's work. No television star had ever been offered anything close to that level of compensation.

Jerry still said no; he sensed the time was right to move on (and besides, he still could look forward to his stake in the show's billion-dollar-plus syndication revenues). Had Seinfeld said yes, Littlefield might have been granted a reprieve. But with *Seinfeld* gone from Thursday night, the New York management decided that the entertainment team in Burbank needed a transfusion of new blood. Wright believed that NBC was simply failing to "stack up the programs that matched with *Friends* and *ER* and *Seinfeld*."

He decided to make a change before things deteriorated further.

Years later, NBC executives who had worked through several programming regimes pointed to this decision as a turning point for NBC. The network's entertainment division had thrived and dominated under Don Ohlmeyer and Littlefield, a somewhat dysfunctional pairing of personalities, but a well-matched professional team. Ohlmeyer, a big physical presence, ran the entertainment ship in a broad business sense. Littlefield, rust-bearded and almost professorial-looking, did the creative decision making. They often bickered fractiously, but the work they did together made sense—and for a long time the team performed outstandingly well.

But Wright had become impressed with a well-regarded veteran television executive named Scott Sassa, who had been running Ted Turner's cable entertainment networks. After asking around the business, Wright decided that Sassa was "a really hot guy." When he quietly sought out Sassa to recruit him, Scott impressed Wright with his flashy intelligence and fusillade of ideas. That October, Wright named Sassa to replace Littlefield.

Executives who worked for Ohlmeyer and Littlefield, and respected both's abilities, found the choice somewhat bewildering. Sassa had the résumé of a business executive, not a creative executive. And logically, NBC needed someone experienced in handling the myriad creative decisions during a development season. Yet Littlefield, the creative end of the partnership, had been let go in October, right in the teeth of the period where network executives start hearing about future shows.

Most NBC executives suspected that Sassa was eventually ticketed to assume the Ohlmeyer role. But because Don had been the higher-ranked executive, NBC elbowed Littlefield out first, in order to give Ohlmeyer's exit some distance from Warren's. Sassa was indeed elevated to the Ohlmeyer position the next May. The decision to slide Sassa into the Littlefield job first meant that NBC was acquiescing to leaving the oddly matched Ohlmeyer-Sassa pairing in place for eight months, a period that included much of a development season.

Littlefield himself was baffled by NBC's machinations in the entertainment division—and now that he was out of the job and had his bonus checks, he could press Wright about it over breakfast at the Four Seasons.

"You know, just for the hell of it, Bob," Warren said, "explain it to me. I'm gone, but what was the thinking behind Don and Scott as a team? Tell me how you think that's going to play out."

Wright replied that there wasn't all that much to it. He told Warren he expected things would play out normally. Between November and the fixing of the new schedule in May, things would "just be what they would be."

Littlefield always considered Wright to be very bright, and thought his opinions about shows and talent were vastly underrated. Wright had been an early voice of support for the late-night star Conan O'Brien when some at the network wanted to offer the comedian week-by-week contracts. Wright had spotted many good shows in the pilot stage, even some he might otherwise have been expected to abhor, given his well-known conservative leanings. When Littlefield showed him the pilot for the gay-themed *Will & Grace*, for example, Wright had been delighted. He told Littlefield, "I'm thrilled our name is on this show."

But Littlefield had always questioned whether Wright fully

understood what a head of network entertainment really did. Did he or the other NBC corporate chiefs in New York understand that the job went far beyond the actual selection and scheduling of shows? Did they have a clue that the job meant making a hundred decisions, small and large, every day, about which producers to deal with, what ideas were worth pursuing, which were a waste of time, what to do if a promising script fell short, or how to do triage on a good premise poorly executed?

Littlefield did not believe Scott Sassa had the skill set to take care of all that. (Interestingly, neither did Wright, who believed that Ohlmeyer would assume the primary responsibility for the programming during that development season.) At least, Littlefield concluded, Sassa was smart enough to realize his own limitations. Warren had heard the rumors that Sassa was angling to bring in Garth Ancier to run the creative side. Littlefield, who had worked with Ancier in earlier days at NBC and admired Garth's successful career first in the establishment of the Fox network and then during the start-up of the WB network, saw the appointment as appropriate, even shrewd.

Bob Wright was totally on board with the Sassa-Ancier pairing as well. Ancier had pitched himself to Wright for the position and wowed him. Bob believed Ancier had "plenty of credentials to do the job."

The first signs of doubt about how well Ancier would fit with the new NBC corporate culture emerged early in Garth's tenure. Sassa, himself only seven days into the Ohlmeyer position, introduced Ancier at NBC's upfront in May 1999. Scott proudly announced that Garth had prepared all his life for just this career. Sassa pointed out that at an age when most kids had been outdoors playing sports, Garth had been in his room at home creating his own radio interview show.

A short while later, Colin Quinn of *Saturday Night Live*, who was doing a comedy bit for the upfront, recalled Sassa's description of Garth's childhood activities and said, "It must reassure you advertisers to know that the NBC Entertainment president is a loner and a psycho!"

That was all part of the self-deprecating fun of an upfront, of course. At the same event, Conan O'Brien told the advertisers how impressed he was with NBC's new slogan, "Let us entertain you." O'Brien said, "Isn't that a great slogan? I think it's much better than last year's slogan: Let us squander an incredible lead."

The slogan and the comic shot at Ancier would be remembered later as the first sign that NBC's fortunes had taken an ill-starred turn.

•   •   •

No one had any doubt that Garth Ancier was a sweet, decent guy with a great passion for the creative side of television. But he was quiet and reserved, and his diffident, nonconfrontational personality in a place as rough and tumble as NBC was, from the moment he walked in the door, an experiment in disastrously bad chemistry.

"To say it was a macho place is a fair take," said one long-serving female executive. Most of the top NBC executives were aggressive, physically big guys. That certainly described Ohlmeyer, and Dick Ebersol, the sports president, and Randy Falco, the network's chief business executive in New York, and Andy Lack, the news president, and Preston Beckman, the top scheduling executive. Most of those guys had the size—and push—to play power forward in basketball.

Littlefield was not big physically, but he exuded NBC-style aggressiveness. So did John Miller and Vince Manze, the marketing pair who created the network's promotional campaigns. Bob Wright himself was not imposing physically, but he certainly was as a leader. And the whole bruising style of the network could be traced directly to Jack Welch, the GE boss.

"There were a lot of powerful guys there, and they all had opinions," the female executive said.

Kassie Canter, who was the chief corporate communications officer for NBC, and as such the highest-ranking woman, said, "At NBC, you're at a company known for bravado. For better or for worse. They were just these big guys who liked to show it. Big, muscle-flexing guys. And that, in the GE world, is really important."

When the cast of *Friends* first held out for more money, taking a unified stance and demanding equally colossal salary increases for each cast member, NBC executives sent the studio, Warner Brothers, a typically blunt message: We don't care if you dump Matt LeBlanc and go on with just five friends.

That stance gave Warner more leverage in the talks. The cast settled for just over $70,000 an episode apiece, after demanding $100,000 each. But LeBlanc remained on the show. Nobody missed the point that NBC had been perfectly willing to cut him loose, however.

If anything, the NBC executives were even more ruthless with each other. Another long-serving female executive at the network said, "NBC is not a kind and gentle culture. People don't try to help each other. The view at NBC is everybody is trying to kill each other—and they are."

Preston Beckman, the scheduling boss, had a different take. "In the Don and Warren era, we were really aggressive. We were cowboys. Don encouraged it. We would be in his office every day and we'd be fighting with each other. But at the end of the day, we all respected each other."

Ancier's aesthetic, which did seem kinder and gentler, was out of place at NBC. He had been in charge of a network's programming before, but that was at the WB, a fledgling network aimed mainly at teenage girls. Ancier struck no one at NBC as a take-charge type.

"I would sit in his program meetings, and if you didn't know the company, you'd have had no idea who was in charge," said one executive who worked closely with Ancier and liked him enormously as a person. "It would make people crazy, because there was never an agenda. There just weren't any decisions being made. Garth has this tendency to just let everybody speak, and so you would talk for hours about things and never come to any conclusion."

To many who observed him that first year, Ancier had more of an artist's temperament than a manager's. Miller and Manze, Beckman, Shirley Powell, the head PR executive for the West Coast—all of them were under Ancier on the flowchart. But they found him disinterested or distracted when they to went to him with information or questions.

"There were lots of people technically reporting to Garth whom he basically paid no attention to," one of his direct reports said. "So by default we all reported to Scott."

Preston Beckman, who had especially thrived in the big-shoul- dered Ohlmeyer era, was quickly maddened by Ancier's more pas- sive style—it didn't help that Beckman concluded Ancier "didn't know what the fuck he was doing." That was mostly because Garth wanted to be involved with scheduling, and Beckman resented such meddling; under Ohlmeyer, he had mostly had free rein to schedule the network.

They butted heads over a new series from John Wells called *Third Watch*, which premiered in September 1999. Beckman believed Garth had totally messed up the scheduling of the series in the first week of the season.

When the ratings came in the morning after the show's pre- miere, and they were just as disappointing as Beckman had feared, he was livid. He believed Ancier's wrongheaded scheduling was going to cost NBC the ratings win for the week.

On a conference call that morning, Beckman exploded, denouncing what he called the idiotic mistakes in the scheduling.

When the call ended, Sassa called Beckman separately. "Garth's very upset," he said.

"Fuck him," said Beckman. "He's a fucking idiot."

The situation had become untenable. After the first of the year, Beckman got a job offer from Fox. He made plans to leave the net- work he had worked so hard to elevate to go to a place dedicated to bringing it down.

By the time February rolled around, NBC was in deepening trou- ble. Out of the blue, ABC was steamrolling everything in its path with *Who Wants to Be a Millionaire?* The game show had begun in the summer and now was a regular three-night-a-week juggernaut on ABC. NBC was suddenly in second place and falling.

That same February, Wright flew out to California to review the troops. The morning he set for the meeting, NBC was hit with another jolt. The overnight numbers came in and indicated that Fox had staged a ratings blitzkrieg with a two-hour special called *Who Wants to Marry a Multi-Millionaire?* The show, a jaw-dropping spectacle of young women in a beauty-pageant-like contest announcing their willingness to marry, on the spot, an unseen, supposedly rich guy, had set viewers scrambling to TV sets all over the country, drawing an astonishing 25 million viewers in its last half hour.

Wright had already been complaining to NBC's programmers about the fat ratings Fox was accumulating with similar outrageous reality specials. Now ABC had upped the ante with its nonscripted blockbuster game show.

Wright, who told people he was "like crazed" at this success for ABC, simply could not believe a show that was a huge hit in England had flown under NBC's radar. He told Sassa and Ancier, "Okay, now you're going to hire a guy. You're going to have a guy look at the British shows. I don't care if he can't even fly over here. You're going to hire somebody over there who's going to send reports back. Can we at least follow what's going on?"

Wright could smell a trend toward unscripted, reality-based programming, and NBC was completely on the outside of it. First ABC had the game show; now Fox had this monster special.

Wright was so angry about the Fox ratings, he canceled his meeting in Burbank, flying back to New York instead. He did send word, however, that he was furious—"totally mental," as one NBC executive put it—about NBC's failures in the reality genre. "Where are our reality specials?" Wright was asking his program staff. His demands—and his anger—would only grow more intense in the months to come.

·   ·   ·

Garth Ancier had a well-earned reputation for his talent at developing hit television shows. So his first full development season was much anticipated inside NBC. Forget all the issues with his management style; this was where Garth would shine.

But Ancier himself was worried. NBC's finance department had told him he did not have the money to make more than six new drama pilots, by far the fewest of any network. They simply didn't believe he needed more because they now had two *Law & Order* shows up and running, as well as *ER* and *Third Watch* and a new hit that season, *The West Wing*.

Ancier could take no credit for *The West Wing*, because it had been fully executed before he even arrived. Sassa had been an ardent champion of the show, which had been put into motion by Littlefield before he left. To Sassa's credit, he had worked through Bob Wright's concerns about the show (that it was too liberal) and given it powerful promotional backing. It was emerging as exactly the kind of prestige hit NBC was known for.

The same season, NBC had added the *Law & Order* spin-off *Special Victims Unit*, and that was also showing signs of promise. But Ancier believed NBC could truly break out again if it developed the next big prime-time soap-opera franchise, a genre that had gone fallow on the big networks since *Melrose Place*. It was a specialty of Garth's old network, the WB, and he believed he could make his mark at NBC with a breakthrough soap entry, a new creation from one of the old masters, Aaron Spelling, called *Titans*.

Ancier still had to deal with NBC's continuing drought in comedy. The season's great new sitcom hope, *The Mike O'Malley Show*, had lasted exactly two episodes (not nearly long enough for the audience to learn who the hell Mike O'Malley was and why he had a show named after him). But Ancier had a high card up his sleeve. He had in development the first series from one of the former costars of *Seinfeld*, Michael Richards.

That spring, NBC's corporate executives flew to the West Coast to review the new crop of pilots. What they saw left several of them apoplectic. Dick Ebersol, the sports chief, who was also much regarded for his entertainment savvy (having been a cocreator of *Saturday Night Live*), was especially vocal in saying the pilots looked miserably bad.

The opinion from the L.A. crowd was not much different. One of

Ancier's executive lieutenants said, "There was a lot of skepticism about *Michael Richards*. We all thought *Titans* was terrible." But Ancier impressed many, including Bob Wright, with an impassioned plea for *Titans*, saying this was the kind of sexy, guilty-pleasure show that NBC desperately needed to change its momentum.

The pressure on NBC only increased that spring as the cast of *Friends* used the impending end of their contracts as leverage to seek a monster payday. Nobody really believed the show would not return, but the negotiations were certainly delicate.

One NBC Burbank executive, called into a meeting about the negotiations, was surprised by who was *not* there. "Where's Garth?" the executive asked. Sassa made a bit of a joke of it, but he said, "He's not invited because we can't trust that he'll keep it confidential."

The executive knew that Garth had gained a reputation for being less than discreet, letting little bits of information drip into the show business community. But this seemed remarkable: The president of NBC Entertainment was not in a meeting about the future of his most important show because there were fears he could not keep a secret. The executive was expressly told not to reveal anything of the meeting to Ancier.

By the time the talks got down to the wire, Ancier was back in the loop. His mission was to perform an elaborate charade in which he devised two fall schedules, one of which did not include *Friends*. (He inserted another comedy, *Just Shoot Me,* at 8 P.M. on Thursday.) He then had to convince the cast's agents—as well as NBC staff members who were close to the actors—that he was serious. So Ancier asked the NBC marketing department to prepare a batch of promo spots that essentially told the audience to tune in for the final episode of *Friends*. Then he told the cast's agents that the promos for the final show would start running during NBC's coverage of the NBA on the Sunday afternoon before NBC's Monday upfront announcements.

The deal closed at 3:30 A.M. Sunday morning. The actors, who had been demanding $1 million an episode, had to settle for $750,000.

The renewal of *Friends* meant Sassa and Ancier would have a far happier upfront presentation the next day. Unfortunately, they still had to sell the advertisers on their crop of new shows. A couple of comedies, *Tucker* and *Daddio,* looked awful, even in the carefully selected highlight clips. Ancier had to admit the *Michael Richards* pilot was a mess, but it was on the schedule anyway, with the promise that it would be totally recast (except for Richards) and reshot.

As for *Titans,* when NBC played clips from the new series, the advertisers howled with laughter—but this one wasn't supposed to be a comedy. In one scene, the show's vixen, played by Yasmine Bleeth, had to reveal to a love interest the awful news that both her parents had been killed in a car crash; but she did it flashing a totally incongruous come-hither smile.

The mood inside NBC soured. Bob Wright was upset; the sales department complained that there was nothing new the advertisers wanted to buy. Almost everyone's anger was directed at the Sassa/Ancier team.

As bad as the upfront week was, by the end of the month, the news was worse. On May 31, CBS introduced *Survivor* and electrified the nation. Wright's prescient urgings about getting into this reality business had not spurred any real action. And now CBS had a raging reality hit.

Still, in their staff meetings in Burbank, Ancier and Sassa both continued to disdain the notion of reality programming. "Garth openly said this is not something that's going to stay," one NBC executive said. "Even after the success of *Millionaire* and *Survivor,* he was saying this is a summer quirk. This isn't going to last."

By mid-June, rumors were spreading that Sassa's job was in trouble. They were denied, but it was true that Jack Welch had grilled Sassa intensely during an internal NBC management meeting. Welch wanted to know why the network had failed to see the reality train coming. Ancier and Sassa told the press in July that they had misjudged the public's interest in the genre and would soon be pursuing reality entries of their own.

The first they chased was a quasi-S&M Dutch import called

*Chains of Love,* in which one woman would be linked (literally) to four men for a week to decide which one she would like to date. Ancier called it "a relationship show." But as much as they wanted to jump-start their own reality efforts, NBC's program department was astounded at this overripe choice. One executive said, "We can't do this; this is NBC."

As CBS and *Survivor* laid waste to the summer, with the clear indication that more was on the way, the stakes piled up higher for NBC's own fall lineup. Sassa and Ancier badly needed something to stick.

Sassa decided he needed outside advice. At Turner, when he was looking for a new organizational approach, he had called in a strategic management consultant named Stephen Baum. That summer, he turned to him again.

Baum staged a series of meetings with the NBC management team in Burbank. First he observed them in regular meetings, sitting in circles and talking. Then Baum watched the managers interact with one another during routine business days. Sassa's goal was not to target anybody, but simply to devise a new management strategy for the group.

When Baum had finished his work, he went to Sassa to report. "You don't have a strategy problem," he told Sassa. "Your biggest problem is Garth." Baum listed the issues with Ancier's management style and how it had affected the running of the office. "This guy is going to bring you down," Baum said in his report.

NBC's fall schedule was almost precisely the wipeout internal critics had predicted. *Tucker,* whose pilot about a horny teenage boy featured no fewer than five erection jokes, was an absolute embarrassment. *Michael Richards* opened to big ratings as the *Seinfeld* fans flocked to see their old favorite, but they hated what they saw and left in swelling droves as the weeks went by.

*Titans* was a painful flop—painful to watch, painful in its results. It became celebrated for delivering the season's most mocked line of dialogue, from a young floozy to a naval aviator: "As usual, you smell like jet fuel and Old Spice."

Randy Falco, who ran the business side of NBC in New York, said everyone at the network had been on board with trying a serialized prime-time soap. "But that wasn't a try," Falco said. "That was awful. That was an embarrassment."

. . .

Even with the woeful new additions, NBC retained a lot of strength in its schedule. Through a combination of special episodes, schedule maneuvers, and the preemption of most of the sludge, NBC managed to edge out ABC in November to win the first sweep month of the season among its prized 18-to-49-year-old crowd. No one in Burbank was allowing themselves to be deluded, not with the collapse of just about every new show; but a win was a win, and NBC scheduled a conference call with reporters at the end of the sweep to mark the occasion.

Sassa and Ancier repaired to the NBC conference room along with Mitch Metcalf, the scheduler who had replaced Beckman. The sweep achievement got short shrift in the questioning. Several reporters asked Ancier about his standing with NBC, and when he expressed confidence that everything was fine, one reporter decided to run that past Sassa. What about the rumors some people were hearing that Garth was on his way out?

"Here's the trick to that question," Sassa began, the kind of line that pricked up the ears of every reporter. But he blathered on about how at Turner they had always to deal with rumors about being purchased and the rule was not to comment on such questions. "So, from a company point of view, you can't be out there saying support or no support or whatever, because sometime in the future, under different circumstances, you can't play that game of publicly being out there, because the absence of your answer may be an issue."

No one had a clue what Sassa was talking about. The reporter, confessing that he could not parse the meaning of that, asked what exactly Sassa was trying to say. "I'm not going to comment on any specifics," Sassa said. "We never have commented on people in the past, and we won't do it in the future."

Inside the conference room in Burbank, smoke from the train wreck circled the room. Ancier, sitting next to Sassa, had no idea what this meant for him. They got off the call as quickly as they could. Ancier, visibly upset, went back to his office; Sassa fled to his, trailed by the network's PR staff. Inside the office, Sassa, usually a cool customer, looked shaken. "I completely fucked up," he said.

They all knew the press would hound them now on Ancier's status. The PR staff needed to know how to answer the flood of questions. "I don't want to lie," Sassa said. Then he concluded, "Tell them he's staying."

He wasn't, of course. Ancier traveled to New York the next week for NBC's annual holiday party. He went to see Bob Wright on a Friday morning and confronted him. "Look, I'm a big boy," Garth said. "I've been doing these jobs a long time. I have a contract. I'll play it any way you want me to play it. I am a mature adult. I'm not going to embarrass the network. So I think we have to figure out a plan for what we're going to do here. And if I'm not going to be here, we should talk about it."

Wright was reassuring. "No, there's no problem at all," he said. "Nothing to worry about." Wright did not want this situation brought out into the open right as NBC was throwing its holiday party. The last thing he wished to do was embarrass Ancier, whom he still liked. But he had concluded that Garth had simply become too withdrawn to do the job.

Ancier skipped the party that night. He wasn't sure what to think. But it wasn't as though there was an obvious candidate out there to replace him.

· · ·

The following Wednesday evening, Kassie Canter, the network's top PR executive, got a call from Steve Battaglio, a reporter working for a short-lived Internet site called Inside.com. He said he had a tip that Ancier was out, as well as even bigger news: Garth was being replaced by Jeff Zucker, the executive producer of the *Today* show.

Canter tried to put him off, saying she had no confirmation of that but that she'd get back to him.

The news was true, but NBC was not ready to announce it, chiefly because nobody had told Garth Ancier. When Sassa was informed that Inside.com had the story, he told his PR staff to start writing up the necessary releases, which would be sent out the next morning—after he broke the news to Garth.

Sassa was angry about the leak, because the deal with Zucker was not yet finalized. He assumed the information had seeped out of the NBC news division, either because Zucker had told some of his *Today* staff—most logically, Katie Couric, whom Jeff was close to—or else Andy Lack, the president of News, had put out the word. Sassa suspected that Lack saw Zucker as a potential long-term rival in the NBC hierarchy and wanted to derail him any way he could.

Whatever the reason, Sassa had to contact Ancier quickly that morning, December 14, before Garth heard it through whatever was about to be posted on Inside.com. The trouble was, nobody could find Garth. Ancier had moved into a temporary residence while his home was being remodeled and nobody seemed to have his phone number. After some frantic searching, he was finally located. Sassa told Garth he should come in—immediately.

The news did not come as a total surprise to Ancier, who had been hearing rumblings—and naively dismissing them—from a friend on the *Today* show. "Katie is talking about how you're toast," the friend said. And now he was.

At first, Ancier reacted to the decision with an equanimity that some of the staff found remarkable. He actually told the PR staff that he wanted to participate in the press conference discussing the change.

But as the emotion of the day settled in, Ancier amended that stance. He got several calls from industry friends who expressed their own outrage at how Sassa had hung Garth out to dry. Ancier begged off the NBC press call but said he would talk on his own to a number of reporters.

Sassa introduced Zucker by saying NBC needed a "fresh perspective" in the entertainment job. He also said, incongruously, that the decision to oust Ancier was "not about the programming." Instead, while calling Garth a friend and great human being, Sassa alluded to Ancier's weakness in certain "administrative duties" and said they had come to an understanding about making this change.

Ancier, who would no longer call Scott Sassa a friend, nor even speak to him again, dismissed any notion that he had an understanding with Sassa. Nor did he agree with the assessment of his performance. Referencing the disputed 2000 presidential election, which had been settled by the Supreme Court only days earlier, he noted that he had just led NBC to a sweeps-month win in November. "I feel like Al Gore the other night," Ancier said. "I accept the decision of the Supreme Court, even though I strenuously disagree with it."

Ancier at least walked away with the biggest payday of his life. Having won the November sweep, he got the bonus NBC always paid to its entertainment chiefs for being number one those months. And, because he had left the WB with real reluctance, he had written his NBC contract well. Ancier not only got the full amount NBC owed him, but all his options in GE stocks were vested. He wound up selling GE at its high point and emerged from the wreckage of his eighteen months at NBC with millions in his pocket. It helped salve the pain a bit, as did eventually landing back at the WB.

Sassa streamed praise on his new entertainment president, saying, "Jeff Zucker understands what NBC stands for in terms of urban, smart shows"—even though Jeff had never programmed, developed, or even read a script for a prime-time show in his life.

More tellingly, Sassa noted that Zucker had been part of a "very valuable team that makes a lot of money for the company." He mentioned Bob Wright as having endorsed the choice, understating the reality by a considerable margin.

In both New York and Los Angeles, NBC executives knew how highly Wright regarded Zucker, then just thirty-six, and the spectacular job he had done in news.

Zucker, confidence flowing freely, said he expected his *Today* experience, especially in terms of spotting cultural trends, would translate well to the entertainment job. He called himself "an outsider from the inside," a term that aptly summed up how he would come to be seen in L.A. And if any of NBC's West Coast executives had missed this reassertion of power by the East Coast corporate guys, that comment clued them in for sure.

"I think that can benefit all of us," Zucker said of his outsider status. "I know what's important to the success of a prime-time schedule, and I can provide a fresh set of eyes to look for that."

Inevitably, reporters went after NBC's soft underbelly: no reality shows. Sassa emphasized how Zucker's news background "has more of a bent toward reality programming."

Zucker wasn't arguing with that, but he was going to Hollywood, after all, where all those writers, directors, and actors lived. "The key at the end of the day is smart, well-written comedy and drama," he said. "That's where we will put our emphasis."

As always where Jeff Zucker was concerned, skeptics were not in short supply.

·  ·  ·

On Monday, December 19, four days after his appointment was announced, Zucker flew to Los Angeles to meet with the NBC entertainment staff for the first time. He was uncharacteristically nervous, not because he thought he might fail, but because he was about to deal with the new and unknown.

Zucker had barely stepped off the plane when he got a special welcome to Hollywood from Leslie Moonves. That morning CBS announced that, starting in February, it was scheduling its second edition of the colossal hit *Survivor* on Thursday nights at 8, right smack against NBC's last remaining comedy powerhouse, *Friends*. It was the most aggressive challenge to NBC's supremacy on that night in almost twenty years.

Jeff Zucker got the message right away. "Les Moonves sucker-punched me," he said.

# CHAPTER FOUR

# THE TRIBE HAS SPOKEN

In the summer of 1999, Conrad Riggs, a young television business affairs executive who, on a hunch, had chucked his career as a cog in the corporate end of the business to hitch his fortunes to an obscure young producer, was calling every person he had ever met at any network—except ABC. His business with ABC had recently come to a frustrating end.

Riggs was scrambling, trying to fan the embers of a flickering idea that had obsessed his employer, a British émigré named Mark Burnett, for more than two years. The concept was for a completely new kind of television show, one Americans had never seen before. He and Burnett were both convinced it could be a ticket to enormous success in the business, if only somebody would take them seriously enough to back it financially.

They had already been close, ever so close, with ABC. Riggs had even started a negotiation with that network the previous spring, the first step toward a deal that would have placed the show on ABC that summer. Four years earlier, before Burnett had acquired the American rights to the idea, ABC had kicked the tires on the show, only to allow it to drift away as the network dithered over its cost and prospects. This most recent rejection had been especially galling for Burnett and Riggs, because ABC had closed down the deal after committing to a different summer show from another British producer.

But Riggs, like his boss, remained a true believer in this idea, and its potential to transform not only their careers but the careers of whichever network executive finally had the guts to commit to it. Riggs held no grudges; he understood that business was business. But he firmly believed that the ABC executives, no matter how happy they were with that other series, had made a mistake they would eventually come to regret, bitterly.

At the moment, however, Riggs could not afford to waste any time rehashing the disappointment at ABC. He was near the end of his network contact list. He and Burnett had made the rounds of executives at both cable and broadcast networks, in some cases more than one time. They needed to find somebody new, somebody who would come at their idea without preconceptions.

On Riggs's list was the name Doug Prochilo. Riggs remembered Prochilo as an acquaintance from days when they each worked in the business affairs department at Disney. Now, Riggs knew, Prochilo was the personal assistant to Anita Addison, the head of the drama department for CBS. Prochilo was not exactly a ticket to the inner circles of CBS, but it was a connection, and Conrad Riggs needed a new connection in the worst way.

. . .

That same summer Ghen Maynard was, basically, a nobody at CBS. A young executive in the drama department, he didn't even have an office at the CBS headquarters in Los Angeles. All he had was a cubicle in what CBS called "The Bullpen," a warren of desks and partitions arranged outside the offices of the real executives.

Maynard's location was of such little consequence that his nearest colleague was not a fellow development executive but a personal assistant, Doug Prochilo. The two of them sat outside the door of Anita Addison, who was also Maynard's immediate boss. Prochilo and Maynard talked frequently, as office mates do; Prochilo was impressed by Maynard's passion for television and his interest in advancing his career in the business.

In the midst of a conversation one day, Prochilo told Maynard he might be getting a call from an acquaintance named Conrad Riggs. Prochilo described Riggs as a go-getter business executive, though he was not really sure where Riggs worked now. In any case, he said, Riggs was out looking for somebody, anybody, who might listen to an idea for a new show, and Prochilo had offered up Ghen's name. That all sounded interesting enough to Maynard, who wanted to be more active in developing shows.

"Sure, have him call," Maynard said.

Riggs phoned a few days later. He explained to Maynard that he worked for a producer who wanted to pitch an exciting idea for a new kind of TV show. Riggs sketched out the premise in a couple of sentences. The show was going to take a bunch of people, regular people, not actors, out on an island and strand them there. And then they were going to vote each other off one by one. Riggs did not mention anything about what had transpired at ABC, or how many other places had checked out the idea already—and passed.

Ghen Maynard was thirty. He had been in television for less than two years. Mostly he had been involved with standard-issue CBS-style dramas like *Judging Amy* and *Family Law*. The show Riggs was describing sounded nothing like that. Which was just fine with Ghen Maynard. His interest was piqued.

Riggs asked if his client, an independent producer named Mark Burnett, could come in to CBS and pitch the show formally. Maynard agreed to try to set it up—which he knew meant running it by a superior. Before Burnett came in, Riggs suggested, maybe Maynard should take a look at the show Burnett had been producing for the Discovery Channel, a high-adventure competition called *Eco-Challenge*. Riggs would send a tape.

Maynard had never heard of Mark Burnett or *Eco-Challenge*. But when he watched the tape, he was immediately impressed by the quality of the production, the visual style, and the skillfully edited storytelling. Now he was eager for his meeting with Mark Burnett.

For a pitch, Maynard couldn't sit a producer in his little cubicle, so he went to a next-level executive, Rob Kaplan, who arranged for

Ghen to borrow an unused office. That's where Maynard met Mark Burnett for the first time—on July 27, 1999—and listened to Burnett's utterly compelling pitch.

Everything about it, from the first words out of Burnett's mouth, struck Maynard as wildly original. First there was that accent—Burnett's East London dialect made him sound almost Australian. At thirty-nine years old, Burnett seemed much younger; he was extremely fit, appropriate for a guy who worked on endurance competitions. Then there was his enthusiasm; he clearly had a passion for this project. More than that, he had a vision. Burnett described a show that would have the epic look of a Jerry Bruckheimer movie.

The payoff for Maynard was Burnett's explanation of how his concept could play out as a microcosm of society, with type-A leaders, cliques, and other confrontational group dynamics. It was the smartest thing Burnett could have said. What Burnett was outlining sounded remarkably like the kind of experiments Maynard had studied and found fascinating at Harvard, where he had majored in social psychology. He at once foresaw how the show's setting and premise might resonate with an American audience. The idea of being stranded would have immediate cultural and literary reference points, from *Robinson Crusoe* to *Swiss Family Robinson* and every lost-at-sea film ever made. The show would evoke the near-universal feeling of being lost, whether as a child separated from his parents in a supermarket or a driver who takes the wrong turn in the boondocks. And the rejection element would be totally familiar to anyone who had been cut from a school team or had been laid off by the company.

The vote-out notion appealed to a mean streak in Maynard, who was sick of television's happy-smile endings. Here people would literally be sent packing. The casting also was a promising element; it could be targeted to every audience segment in America. Maynard knew how important that was to CBS, the one network that had a prerequisite of including older people in its casts.

Maynard, a fan of shows like *Felicity* on the WB and *The Real World* on MTV (one reason a show with real people rather than actors did not faze him), was not in synch personally with the CBS audience. He did not regularly watch a single show being broadcast by his own network. But Maynard was convinced there had to be a way to find a show that would capture the fancy of people his age without sending CBS's core audience of retirees fleeing to the History Channel.

This project, which Burnett was calling *Survivor*, sounded like it could be that show.

But Maynard was still a nobody, at least in the sense that he had no authority to buy a show on his own. And his brief experience in the world of network television told him that Burnett's outsider status was going to be tough to overcome. Most deals were made with producers with established track records. Newcomers almost always ran into a "no" somewhere in the decision-making process, because executives would say: "We don't know this guy; let's pass."

Adapting his social psychology training, Maynard had been observing the mechanics of decision making in television, where eight or ten executives would often gather in a room with no one willing to step up and take a risk. He associated the process with something he had studied called the "unresponsive bystanders theory," which posits that if you're lying in the street half dead, you're more likely to be helped out if just a few people are in the vicinity than if you are surrounded by a crowd. With a lot of people present, there is a tendency to conclude: Well, no else seems to be helping, why should I?

In TV, Maynard noticed, a big group in a conference room kicking around an idea meant that it was impossible for an individual to step up and claim personal ownership. But a young executive, with no reputation at all, could grab an idea and run with it. Which is what Ghen Maynard intended to do.

It wasn't easy. The reaction to the show at the executive level just above him was predictable: Who is this guy? What kind of show is this with no writers or actors? It seemed to Maynard that some television executives were almost conditioned to think: *Okay, what's the reason I'm going to pass on this?*

But Maynard realized that, in this case, the opinions of next-level-up executives were irrelevant anyway. The only thing that mattered at CBS was the opinion of one executive. Maynard had to present the idea to Leslie Moonves.

Moonves already knew Maynard a bit, because he made it a point to suss out his new young executives. At Maynard's first big pitch meeting, Moonves had waited for the producer to leave and immediately asked: "Ghen, what do you think?" Maynard had not been shy about speaking up, and Moonves had encouraged him to bring ideas to him. Les recognized that the young guys on the staff were out talking to the other young people, and that's how breakthroughs happened.

Maynard got himself on Les's calendar. He went in fully prepared, with a budget analysis and Burnett's tape of *Eco-Challenge*— useful, Ghen concluded, for demonstrating that this producer could handle a rugged production without anyone getting killed. But Les quickly devalued the benefits of the *Eco-Challenge* tape. "Never heard of it," he said.

Maynard plowed ahead, laying out with enthusiasm the details of the premise: island, real people, challenges, vote-out, million-dollar prize. Moonves, as always, listened politely; but Maynard had almost lost him at hello. Les didn't say it out loud, but he decided a few minutes into Ghen's speech that what he was hearing was a really stupid idea. When Maynard was finished, Moonves said, abruptly, "Ghen, this is CBS. That's a cable show."

Les did not exactly kick Maynard out of his office, as he would later say when praising Maynard for his tenacity. But he said no— flat no; and a no from Leslie Moonves almost always closed the book.

But Maynard could feel in his gut that this idea was much more than another cable show. He was convinced that the networks had to start learning from cable anyway, taking so-called niche ideas and finding ways to expand them for bigger audiences. The next step, he concluded, was to find some kindred spirits to back him in another go at Leslie. The best choice, he was sure, was Kelly Kahl, the top

CBS scheduling executive. Inside the network, everyone knew that Kelly Kahl had, as one colleague put it, "big smarts and big balls." Those traits had brought him close to Les, who had enormous trust in Kelly. And, like Maynard, Kahl was a generation younger than the boss.

Maynard talked up the idea in the halls over the next week, before he finally laid it out for Kahl. Kelly's reaction seemed favorable, if tepid. Maynard already sensed that he could get only so far talking up this idea himself. The best way to impress Kahl was with Burnett.

Kahl had liked Ghen's broad-strokes description of *Survivor*, but when Burnett turned up at CBS to pitch Kahl, he brought the idea to a new level. Kahl came away from the meeting thinking this was about the craziest idea he'd ever heard, one that as a scheduler he could not see playing at any time except in summer. But he found it intriguing, and it sure seemed to him an idea worth bringing back to Leslie.

Kahl and Maynard began gathering reinforcements. Chris Ender, the top PR executive, immediately saw the press potential: imagine all those local articles about contestants from all parts of the country. Marc Graboff, a business affairs executive, loved the concept as well. Even the CBS sales department weighed in favorably. JoAnn Ross, one of CBS's chief sales executives in New York, was entranced with the idea from the start. So was Bill Cecil, the West Coast sales chief. Burnett had demonstrated his savvy about the show's business opportunities; he talked about the possibilities for giving certain advertisers the right for their products to be seen in the body of the show itself. Burnett had done the same thing on *Eco-Challenge*—every first-aid kit, for example, contained Tylenol, and the cameras caught the often-exhausted competitors going for the painkiller a lot. Maybe thirsty *Survivor* contestants could be seen downing bottles of Coke.

With a growing list of backers, Maynard and Kahl decided the time was right to go for broke; they would convince Moonves to take the pitch from Burnett.

• • •

$M$ark Burnett walked into Leslie Moonves's office on November 24, 1999. He recognized the importance of the performance he was about to give, but his nerves were steady, his pulse calm. That was his style: bravado or bust. He had been through the network dance with this show many times before without success, but he had always kept any feelings of self-doubt locked up and hidden away. He wasn't about to let them escape now.

Accompanied by his CBS supporters and Conrad Riggs, Burnett took the floor in front of Moonves. He did not open as most producers would, with a description of the format and how it would work week to week. Instead, Burnett told a story, as though spinning a yarn around a campfire.

Imagine what would happen if a plane went down, said Burnett, and the survivors were caught in an adult version of *Lord of the Flies*. Burnett sketched the characters, giving them fictitious names and personalities. He described the events of the first episode, starting with what the opening credits would look like, through the establishment of the camps, the two tribes, the challenges, the "tribal council," all the way through to the vote-out and the farewell comment by the evicted tribe member. It was all precisely detailed and highly visual, right down to a scene he described of the characters walking barefoot in the sand at the water's edge.

Most of his listeners, even those who had heard the pitch several times, were enthralled. Les Moonves at least *looked* enthralled. As he finished, Burnett pulled out a couple of visual aids: two mock magazine covers, one from *Time* and the other from *Newsweek*. *Survivor* was featured on both of them, under headlines trumpeting it as a national phenomenon.

The only person in the room not completely swept away was Moonves, but he always hid his cards well. Moonves said the idea sounded great, but he did not commit to buying it. The big problem was that Burnett was looking for a commitment not just to make a pilot, but to shoot an entire series. Economically, that sounded like a big risk. As the meeting broke up, Moonves told Burnett that he and his people would talk it over.

With Burnett gone, Moonves made his reservations clear. How, he wanted to know, could CBS give this thing a thirteen-week run, at something just short of $1 million an episode, and not risking losing the bundle if America didn't get it? There was no money in the budget for such an expensive summer play; and while it was on, CBS would be losing the revenue from the repeats of the show it replaced.

Moonves sent his troops away. They continued to meet and soon hatched a new plan. The solution they offered Moonves seemed simple enough. What if CBS and Burnett could convince a certain number of advertisers to sign on to the show sight unseen? Burnett was an awfully convincing pitchman, they all agreed, and he had those "product placement" tie-ins to throw in.

Moonves was still dubious, but this was a no-harm, no-foul arrangement. "Look, if you guys can figure out a way to pay for this," Les said, "go play in your sandbox."

Burnett hit the road with CBS sales executives Joe Abruzzese and JoAnn Ross and wove his hypnotic tale for advertisers like Reebok and Target stores. They started securing sponsors. The group guessed that they needed eight or nine full sponsors to cover the nut, which consisted of the approximately $800,000 an hour CBS said its time was worth, plus Burnett's production budget for the show, which he put at $750,000 an hour. Burnett himself would receive $35,000 for each episode, not an especially high fee at all.

The unusual nature of the presale of commercials—which made *Survivor* more or less a "time buy"—created the need for an unusual contract. The two sides decided to form a partnership called The *Survivor* Company, owned half by CBS and half by Mark Burnett. The company would purchase thirteen hours of time in the summer from CBS.

Under the terms of the contract, should the show go to another cycle, CBS could either sell the time outright to the company again, or take all the commercials and sell them itself, in exchange for paying a license fee to Burnett. The fee was hard to determine, however, because no one could predict how the show would do. Some at CBS thought *Survivor* might only be good enough to merit renewal as weekend daytime sports programming, for slow periods between football and basketball seasons. That would involve a much lower fee than another prime-time run. The two sides decided to include a simple clause in the contract saying that in future deals the license fee would be negotiated "in good faith."

About a month after Burnett and the sales team went into action, they were only one sponsor short of their goal. *Survivor* had become a virtual no-lose play for CBS. The sheer determination of the group of executives who had backed *Survivor* impressed Moonves, and no matter how the show performed now, CBS would not lose a cent. Besides, it was a kicky idea; Moonves had come to agree with his "guys" about that.

"Go ahead and pick it up," Les told Ghen Maynard. At CBS only Leslie Moonves could green-light a show, and he had just given the OK to something only dimly recognized at that point as a "reality show." ABC had its unscripted *Millionaire* show on the air; but Moonves knew that was just a new iteration of an ancient television format, the quiz show. Fox had its crude, if usually popular, reality specials, like *When Animals Attack* and *World's Greatest Police Chases*; but Moonves didn't see the business heading hell-bent in *that* direction.

CBS was committing to something no one in America had really seen before on network television: a prime-time show with no actors, no script, no writers, but still a drama, a story being "performed" by people out of real life. This was either going to be a brave new world for network television or the dark night of its soul; but whatever it was going to be, Leslie Moonves had opened the door to it.

Maynard and Kahl gave the news to Burnett together. Shrugging off the bravado for a moment, the producer was thrilled almost beyond words. Almost, because he found enough words to thank his CBS backers. Burnett had been chasing this dream for more than two years and had suffered rejections from every network, some of them twice, as well as from several cable channels. Burnett's belief in *Survivor*—and himself—had never wavered. Now Leslie Moonves believed in him too.

• • •

Absolutely nothing in Mark Burnett's early life set him up as a television producer or showman of any kind. An only child of blue-collar parents who worked for a Ford Motor plant outside London, Burnett did well in school but liked being what he called "a tough guy" too much to go to college. He became a soldier. And not just any soldier. Burnett signed on to the elite British Parachute Regiment, made famous in the book and film *A Bridge Too Far*.

Burnett saw plenty of action, first in Northern Island dodging IRA bombs, and then in the Falkland Islands War in 1977, where in one battle Burnett saw twenty-four men from his company killed, and another ninety-three wounded. "It was real stuff," as Burnett assessed it. "Horrific but, as a young man, in a kind of sick way, exciting."

At the end of his commitment, Burnett heard about a former colleague who was recruiting ex-military types for an assignment in Central America. Thanks to his mother's instincts that this "security job" in Los Angeles (he had lied to her) sounded troubling, Burnett chucked it and decided instead to find work in L.A.

He was twenty-two. He had six hundred bucks in his pocket. His only contact, Nick, had landed a job as a chauffeur and set Burnett up for an interview. Burnett was hired as a driver and part-time nanny for $125 a week. Of course, he got to live in a Beverly Hills mansion with fifty channels of TV.

While on that job, Burnett was out one day toning himself on a run along North Beverly Drive, wearing only a pair of tight shorts emblazoned across his fit butt with the Union Jack. A Cougar convertible full of funny old English ladies pulled up. They jumped out and swarmed over him, sure he was some notable British actor lad. The moment was pivotal for Burnett. It gave him a glimpse of what fame meant in this town.

After a succession of nanny positions, Burnett landed one for a client in Malibu who steered him to other opportunities, like selling T-shirts on Venice Beach. Burnett was in the middle of pursuing a new project, marketing credit cards for L.A.'s huge Hispanic mar-

ket, when he went to a Hollywood party with a friend who had a
minor film job at Columbia Studios. The young beauties at the party
could not have been more bored when Burnett talked up his credit-
card idea; but when his friend mentioned he worked in films, they
were enraptured. Awash in jealousy, Burnett made up his mind to
find a more creative outlet for his talents and ambition.

At about that time, he saw a newspaper article about the Raid
Gauloises, a French-produced, coast-to-coast endurance race
staged in New Zealand. Burnett had his epiphany. He would establish and market a televised race in some forbidding locale, taking
people to the edge of exhaustion and physical danger for a big
money prize.

That Burnett came up with such an idea was hardly remarkable;
that he accomplished it was close to astonishing. Burnett had
absolutely no television experience when he managed to sell the
idea of the race to MTV in 1995.

The first *Eco-Challenge* show, in April 1995, was no ratings
smash for MTV, but it was a sensational calling card for Mark Burnett as a first-time producer. It was visually gripping stuff, well shot
and well edited. ESPN contacted him immediately and asked him to
stage another race for its X-Games event that same year. Later, Burnett sold the event, first to the Discovery Channel and then to USA
Network.

He had tried pitching it to the broadcast networks first, but all
he got from that was one useful contact, a Fox executive named
Lauren Corrao. She mentioned to Burnett that he might want to
meet another Brit named Charlie Parsons, who was going around
L.A. with an idea called *Survive,* about people being stranded on a
desert island.

Burnett had never heard of Parsons, a well-known producer in
England, but he liked the sound of *Survive.* Burnett learned that the
project was being considered at ABC, under yet another Brit, an
executive named Michael Davies.

At that moment, Davies stood somewhere in the middle of the
transatlantic cross-currents that were slowly washing onto a British

programming concept American shores called "reality television." Davies had been working for Walt Disney's television production company, Buena Vista, since 1992, trying to find a way to sell some of the less conventional, and less expensive, program formats that were working in England and Europe. At one point, Davies brought his studio bosses an idea for an interactive game show. The executives laughed at him; no game show was ever going to work on network television in America. "We do sitcoms and dramas and newsmagazines," they told him.

Moving up to the head of something called "alternative programs" at ABC, Davies continued to advocate new show ideas, including *Survive*. Davies, a friend of Charlie Parsons, got ABC to commit a pittance of $130,000 to developing the concept, mainly consisting of constructing a toylike model of an island. The project fizzled out, though not before Lauren Corrao called Davies, furious over losing a crack at bringing the show to Fox. She told Davies that if he ever stole her idea for hiring Mark Burnett to produce the show, she would file a suit.

Burnett harassed Davies for months, pressing him to set up a meeting with Parsons. Finally, at a Hollywood party, Davies introduced the two men. Parsons and Davies hit it off, but it took long negotiations before Burnett acquired the American rights to *Survive*.

Parsons had already managed to sell *Survive* to Swedish television, and that version, called *Expedition: Robinson,* became a huge hit, though with a couple of downsides. The production was lowbrow and tawdry; worse, the first contestant voted off the island wound up committing suicide.

Shortly after Burnett acquired the rights, the show's title became *Survivor*. Conrad Riggs noticed one day that a newspaper's television grid listed a show on the Discovery Channel called *Survive*. Riggs scribbled the "or" at the end and Burnett agreed they'd go with *Survivor*.

Under any title, nobody wanted the show. Burnett struck out first with his partners at Discovery, then at several other cable outlets. He went to the networks next (reversing the normal process) and got nowhere at Fox, CBS, and NBC. But suddenly, thanks to Davies, interest perked up again at ABC.

Several Disney executives expressed interest, including Andrea Wong, who worked in Davies's department; Lloyd Braun, who was then in charge of Disney's Touchstone studio; and Steve McPherson, Braun's number two at the studio. Wong, pursuing the same strategy that CBS would later, sought advance deals with advertisers. Encouraged, Conrad Riggs started his negotiation with ABC.

But timing, and network politics, intervened. It was just at this time that Michael Davies acquired a tape of a game show that was making noise in the U.K. But Davies had fallen out of favor at ABC, because of an ill-considered pitch he had made for a wild, misogynistic comedy pilot called *The Man Show*. Davies said, "It essentially killed my career at ABC, it was such a high-profile miss." (It went on to become a sizable hit for the Comedy Central cable channel.)

Davies was so on the outs that Jamie Tarses, then ABC's top program executive, expressly ordered him to keep his mouth shut at a meeting on future programming. Michael Eisner, as was his wont, went around the room asking people for new ideas. When he reached Davies, the executive had no choice but to speak up. Remembering that Eisner had asked about reviving game shows like *The $64,000 Question*, Davies said he had a tape of a similar show that was building huge audiences in Britain. He reached in his briefcase and handed Eisner the British version of *Who Wants to Be a Millionaire?* Eisner said he'd take a look.

The next day, Davies got an e-mail from Eisner saying, "I'm not sure if I'm embarrassed to say this, but I loved this."

Going all-in on the project, Davies quit his ABC job and signed on as executive producer of the American *Millionaire*. ABC had not said they would buy the show, but Davies was told to produce a pilot.

Davies selected Regis Philbin as host and flew him to England to shoot on the set there. It was an egregious flop. Philbin, a television natural in the United States, could not connect with the British audience. Still, all was not lost. Davies came in with a budget for an eleven-episode run of *Millionaire* for a *total* of $1.7 million. ABC could have spent more on a test pattern.

One of the ways Davies managed to keep the costs so low was to assign himself a producer's fee of $0.00. He gambled that the show would be a hit and that he would make up his financial loss later. As it turned out, Davies did not make a cent on *Millionaire* until the following January. Even after *Millionaire* was a summer smash and returned three nights a week in November, landing as the number-one-, two-, and three-rated show during that sweep month, Davies still had not been paid. He had the hottest show on television and had never been poorer in his life—until Lloyd Braun, the Touchstone studio chief, turned up in January and wrote Davies a check for $500,000 as an advance against profits.

With *Millionaire* off and running, ABC lost interest in Davies's other project. The network passed on *Survivor* for a second time. An exasperated Conrad Riggs was soon on the phone to his acquaintance Doug Prochilo at CBS.

• • •

In the months before *Survivor* went on the air in 2000, whatever reservations Leslie Moonves may have had about the show were long gone. He was touting the network's bold vision in jumping into reality TV. "What's happening is people are realizing you need to be different," he said. "You can't go with the same old meat and potatoes anymore. You've got to shake things up. And clearly people are realizing it's a big world out there and shows really can come from the other side of the Atlantic."

Chris Ender had worked magic with the press, creating a steady undercurrent of anticipation about the show—who might be in the cast, which location might be chosen, what the heck was going to happen to the people on that island. Ghen Maynard took up direct responsibility for the show. He was the executive with the relationship with Mark Burnett, and he and Burnett collaborated closely. They discussed the format in terms of drama: Every act break had to end on either a moment of conflict or jubilation, or a question that would be answered in the next act.

CBS was conscious of the fact that it was creating an all-new template in writing the contracts with would-be participants in shows like these. As a result, the network's legal department went into overdrive to ensure that CBS was fully indemnified against all contingencies. The contract included clauses warning what animals a contestant might be attacked by, including (but not only) monkeys, gorillas, snakes, wild boar, and crocodiles. CBS was not responsible for things like flood, lightning, typhoon, and avalanche. The program executives found the contract hilarious. When one would read sections of it out loud, the group would collapse into hysterics.

But the lawyers had reason to worry, especially after the mystery man on Fox's *Who Wants to Marry a Multi-Millionaire?* special turned out to have been the subject of a restraining order filed by an ex-girlfriend.

CBS ordered all-encompassing background checks and psychological tests for its fifty finalists for *Survivor.* The network flew all of them into Hollywood, put them up in a hotel, and called them in for interviews at all hours of the day or night. Some were awakened at 3 A.M. and pressed to answer tough questions about their personalities. The point was to see how they reacted under stress. Burnett wasn't looking for milquetoasts. He wanted people who would mix it up. Conflict was essential to creating drama.

Maynard thought they learned a lot about their candidates this way. "A lot of these people were inspirational," he said. "Some of them were frightening." Many made extremely strong first impressions. Among them was Richard Hatch, the openly gay contestant who challenged the producers from the start by walking around naked on the island. "I honestly felt Richard was a dick," Maynard said. "Very smart. But definitely we went: Oh, people are going to hate him."

Which, of course, was not a bad thing. "You need villains," said Maynard.

Moonves, widely regarded as the best casting executive at CBS, was brought in as the closer. He looked at tapes of the finalists and found almost all of them disturbingly unlikable. In person, though, Les found the group promising. He got a charge out of the process; he always would. Casting reality shows wound up being one of Moonves's great kicks, even when one would-be entrant, responding to a question about his attitudes toward gays, called Moonves a "big homo." Completely comfortable in his own heterosexuality, Moonves cast the contestant anyway.

Moonves's excitement about the project continued to grow after it started production. Maynard went off to Malaysia for the first several weeks of the shoot. He quickly sent back a section of tape that Les could present at an event called the "mini-upfront," when the networks described their roster of projects in development to the advertisers. In 2000, CBS held the event in New York at the Ed Sullivan Theater, home of David Letterman's show. Starting with a long helicopter shot of a tropical island showing a long spit of sand, the clip introduced the host, Jeff Probst, walking the beach and describing the contest about to take place. The advertisers were clearly jazzed.

Maynard stayed on the island, Pulau Tiga, for the first four episodes. Needed in L.A. for the start of pilot season, he took the long flight back, winding up in the CBS parking lot where he had left his car. He was half asleep, but he couldn't help himself. He went into the building, carrying a batch of rough tapes from the initial shooting.

"Do you want to see some stuff?" Maynard asked Moonves. Les gathered a group, including Chris Ender and Nancy Tellem. They dropped everything and watched for forty minutes. Les couldn't take his eyes off the screen. When Richard Hatch revealed he was gay, Les was awed. "This is fascinating," he said.

•   •   •

CBS scheduled the premiere of *Survivor* for 8 P.M., Wednesday night, May 31, 2000. It was after the close of the May rating sweep, which ensured that the show would be facing only minimal, if any, original programming. CBS had no real idea what to expect from a show like this. But the buzz was everywhere.

ABC certainly could hear it. In a surprise, last-minute maneuver, deliberately made so late that CBS could not alter its own schedule, ABC announced it would air a new edition of *Who Wants to Be a Millionaire?* to go head to head against the premiere of *Survivor*. It was a blatant effort to cripple the new show before it could get out of the gate.

Moonves and his team were pissed. "You would think that ABC would accept their victories and not have to go out and try to stop someone else from having a victory," Moonves said. Stu Bloomberg, one of the heads of ABC Entertainment, responded, "Why not do it? It's a competition. We obviously don't want them to get on the air and get traction."

Was ABC's motivation to blunt *Survivor* derived from the fact that ABC had not once, but twice, passed on the opportunity to own the show itself? That suggestion was inevitable—and hard to dismiss.

CBS executives swallowed hard and geared up for a ratings beating on that first night, hoping *Survivor* would not be too damaged by the *Millionaire* gambit.

The night of the premiere, all the top CBS executives were in Las Vegas for an annual meeting with the owners of the network's affiliated stations. Moonves was scheduled to address the group on Thursday morning, soon after getting the early ratings.

Several of his "guys," including Kahl and Ron Scalara, the head of the promotion department, were so keyed up they couldn't sleep. They stayed up all night gambling, hitting some of the bars, and psyching themselves up. Kahl realized what *Survivor* could mean for CBS: It was probably the best chance for the network to appeal to viewers under thirty-five years old that he had seen in his tenure there.

The group assembled in Moonves's room early: The first ratings would be in about 6 A.M. Vegas time. Everyone stood by with Black-Berries at the ready, like gunslingers spoiling for a shoot-out. The first numbers came in: ABC a 10.8 rating; CBS a 10. When the numbers were broken down, ABC had 16.8 million viewers; *Survivor* had 15.5 million.

Moonves had wanted to win, of course, but numbers like that for a summer show were in every way spectacular. And it got better. When the breakdown for age groups came through, *Survivor* had beaten *Millionaire* in every category of younger viewers: 18 to 49, 18 to 34, even—stop the presses—teenagers. CBS had a show teenagers wanted to watch.

The *Survivor* premiere was the most-watched show CBS had had on any Wednesday night in more than two years, summer season notwithstanding. Moonves and his staff began high-fiving wildly. They heaped praise on everyone who contributed, with special mention for Chris Ender, who had masterfully orchestrated the advance publicity. A couple of hours later, Moonves stood up in front of the affiliates and said, "I have some interesting news from last night. It's the best news we have seen in years."

That was only the beginning, of course. One week later, *Survivor* crushed ABC's second attempt to derail it with another edition of *Millionaire*, not only drawing more viewers overall but wiping out the game show in the younger audience categories. ABC's move had proved to be monumentally boneheaded. Its hit game show suddenly looked vulnerable, shorn of appeal to young viewers—and ABC had already announced it was going from three editions of *Millionaire* a week to a mind-boggling four in the coming fall season. The two big British imports came together for a moment that summer and then flew past each other like elevators going in opposite directions—taking their networks with them.

A short while after the premiere, Kelly Kahl was back home in Wisconsin taking a driving vacation through the state with his dad. He flipped from station to station on his car radio, amazed that all any of them wanted to talk about was *Survivor*. As Chris Ender had predicted, local newspapers began giving saturation coverage to the various contestants from their area, printing their pictures and stories of their lives as though they were movie stars. *Survivor* was all over the Web, too, with endless guesses about the winner of the game, a fact that CBS guarded like the nuclear code.

Even the other networks had to acknowledge the phenomenon. At NBC, the producer of *Today* caught on fast and started booking the contestants voted off the island, even though they had already appeared on CBS's morning show (which was getting a ratings boost itself). Some NBC executives complained that he was only promoting CBS, but Jeff Zucker argued that *Today* could not ignore a cultural phenomenon of this magnitude.

Neither could *Time* and *Newsweek*. They both put *Survivor* on their covers, using pictures remarkably similar to the mock-ups that Mark Burnett had brought to his first meeting with Moonves.

Morale at CBS soared. Moonves himself achieved both professional and personal high points. Walter Cronkite called with congratulations, saying, "You've brought the luster back to CBS." But the best compliment came from his own fifteen-year-old daughter, who told him, "Dad, my friends are now excited about this show on CBS." Les never thought he'd hear that sentence from one of his kids.

•   •   •

Not long into the run, CBS began talking about bringing *Survivor* back as a regular-season entry. "We could have another *Survivor* ready by January," Moonves said only two weeks after the premiere. Burnett was already touting the Andes, Africa, or the Australian outback as possible new locations.

But Les had more immediate plans to cash in. He wanted to order two more hours of the show, thus adding plenty of additional commercial revenue. He reasoned that this could be done by adding a recap show in the middle of the run and an hourlong reunion of the cast after the finale. The commercials for these new hours certainly could be priced far higher than what the already spoken-for shows had been able to ask. In addition, Moonves wanted to squeeze two more commercial units into the existing shows, taking the commercial load from eighteen units to twenty. New advertisers not already in the series would now pay a premium to get in.

All fine, Les was told by his business and sales staff—except he understood, of course, that this additional commercial time was actually *owned* not by CBS, but rather by The *Survivor* Company— that is, the combination of Mark Burnett and CBS that had been created to sell the sponsorships in advance. "Remember?" they gently reminded Les. "That was how it was possible to get this show made in the first place."

What this meant was that Les could add all the commercial units he wanted, but 50 percent of the net profit of those sales, as well as 50 percent of the net profit from the two additional shows he wanted to produce, was, Moonves was told, going to go to, uh, well, that guy named Burnett.

The news struck Moonves like a mallet blow to the forehead. Those in the room observed a sight not unlike what the Romans must have glimpsed on a morning 1,921 years earlier when they looked over at Vesuvius.

"What? What do you mean I'm sharing ad revenues with Mark Burnett?" Moonves exploded.

An effort was made to explain how the deal had been made, a deal Les had apparently blessed back before production began. Moonves remained aghast.

"Who the hell is Mark Burnett that he gets 50 percent of my ad revenue?" Moonves demanded.

The money involved was considerable. The two new episodes of *Survivor,* plus two added commercials in the episodes left in the run, added up to about $20 million, surely well beyond Mark Burnett's wildest dreams. Burnett would get half. Without the new elements, he stood to make only a total of $455,000 on the show.

Moonves was enraged not so much because of Burnett's big payday, but because the deal violated what he considered a sacred principle: You never share a cent of ad revenues. If this utter unknown Burnett was going to get half of the commercial take, what was Moonves going to tell John Wells, or David E. Kelley, or Dick Wolf, or any other hit makers when they knocked on his door asking for the same? This was allowing the inmates to run the asylum.

After going over the deal again and again and thinking through the angles, Moonves put in a call to Burnett, who was in Manhattan doing publicity for the show. Burnett was in a cab in midtown with Conrad Riggs. Les got on Mark's cell and told Burnett of the plan to sell these extra commercials, acknowledging that technically Burnett was supposed to share in the revenue. But that wasn't how network television worked, he explained. CBS was going to do its normal thing and go out and sell them and keep that additional revenue.

Riggs could only just get the gist of this from Burnett's side of he conversation, but he got the feeling Mark was slightly confused and might be about to say yes.

"No, Mark, goddammit, time out," Riggs said. "Put him on hold, tell him we'll call back. Tell him the line went dead, you can't hear him anymore."

Burnett told Moonves he'd call him back. Then he and Riggs went over the way the deal had been set up—and how they had counted on the possibility of a financial windfall if more commercials were ever sold. Maybe not this much, but, hey, a deal was a deal. "They can't really do anything about it, bro," Riggs told Burnett.

They knew Moonves would be pissed, but they let him know they expected their share of whatever new commercials CBS sold.

That left one other negotiation unsettled: What would be the deal for a second edition of *Survivor*? Moonves asked his business-people if the original deal now meant that he had to split the ad revenue 50/50 with this guy on the second cycle of the show.

No, they told him, the good news was that they had built into the deal the option of switching to a license fee—they could pay Burnett, as they would any other studio or producer, a per-episode rights fee. Fine, said Les, what's the fee? Well, see, that's where the unusual nature of this contract came into play again, they told him. Nobody really knew what a show like this might be worth, so the agreement just stipulated that a license fee would be negotiated in good faith.

Les looked like he would pop a vein. "You mean I don't have a license fee already set? And this guy can now hold us up?"

Not exactly, Les was told. There were certain limits. CBS owned half the show, so Burnett could never shop it to a different network. And if they hit an impasse in the negotiations, they could take it to arbitration. Moonves surely did not want some outsider getting into

THE TRIBE HAS SPOKEN

his business and trying to set a license fee—especially if the performance of this show was going to be a once-in-a-lifetime success for CBS.

With deadlines looming for new casting and preproduction on *Survivor II,* Moonves held out as long as he could, publicly disavowing any agreement that sounded like revenue sharing. A trial date was set for arbitration. The standoff went literally to the last minute.

Whatever his level of outrage about the unique position Burnett had maneuvered himself into, Moonves did not want to risk alienating this obviously talented producer. *Survivor* had become, in a summer run, the most potent programming weapon Les had ever had, reaching an audience of an astounding 51 million people for the finale—more than the Oscars, more than anything else that had appeared on television in years, with the exception of the Super Bowl.

The final negotiation started on the steps to the arbitrator's office in L.A. Moonves stopped Burnett and Riggs going in and said, "What can I do to settle this?"

Burnett and Moonves went off to a side room and began to thrash it out. The process went on for hours, with the two men emerging at intervals to talk over the details with their business advisers. Almost a full day ticked by. Finally, they settled on a big license fee for Burnett, just under $1 million an episode—but no revenue sharing. "It's just semantics," Burnett said. "I just want to be paid well."

Riggs came out of the rugged day of negotiating with even greater respect for Moonves's abilities. "He's the smartest creative-and-business guy in television," he said. "If I ever had a mentor, I'd want it to be Leslie." Nobody talked about hard feelings. "It's just about the fucking value of the show," Riggs said.

# CHAPTER FIVE

# REALITY ... WHAT A CONCEPT

Some months after *Survivor*'s spectacular run on CBS, Mike Darnell, the impresario of reality television for the Fox network, shared the stage on a reality-TV discussion panel with Ghen Maynard of CBS. Darnell was in his customary uniform: black T-shirt, black jeans, cowboy boots, his black, unkempt hair framing his delicate face in tendrils of black curls. With his slight frame, barely five feet tall, Mike was quite a visual contrast with the squarely built, business-suited Maynard. After the event concluded, Darnell walked up and shook Maynard's hand. "I have to thank you, because you saved my job," Darnell said.

It was true that *Survivor* revived interest at Fox in reality television, and the Darnell oeuvre specifically, at a time when he had been exiled to television Siberia. But it is unlikely that Darnell was ever really close to losing his job. Mike had important patrons at Fox, starting at the very top with Rupert Murdoch, the chief of News Corporation, Fox's parent company. Like some others at Fox, Murdoch saw Darnell as an irreplaceable asset, an instinctive genius of the extremes in human diversion. Though Mike appalled some who worked with him, exasperated others, and made almost everyone at Fox a little nervous about what he might come up with next, Darnell was protected by his mystique. No one wanted to be the executive who pushed Mike Darnell out the door just before he came up with the next spectacular, talked-about, headline-making reality idea.

Still, Darnell had been sidelined for months before *Survivor* aired, a victim of his own cause célèbre smash, *Who Wants to Marry a Multi-Millionaire?* Darnell experienced the Mt. Everest and Death Valley of his career within days of that show's broadcast in February 2000.

Darnell had gotten the idea for the special at his wife's cousin's wedding in Parsippany, New Jersey. Watching the ceremony, Darnell connected people's fascination with weddings to the sudden, unexpected (to Mike certainly) popularity of ABC's *Millionaire* game show the previous summer.

"I kept thinking: Why is this show working? Because winning money is a huge American dream," Darnell said. "And I'm sitting watching another huge American dream, which is getting married. What's bigger than that? Getting married to a wealthy man."

The two-hour special Darnell concocted with producer (and good friend) Mike Fleiss was singularly outlandish: a beauty pageant among single women vying to marry some unseen guy just for his money. The show and its plus-sized success was the talk of the nation, page one of numerous newspapers (including the *New York Times*), the lead sketch on *Saturday Night Live,* and an endless topic of hand-wringing by feminists on the state of the American woman and by sociologists on the state of American culture.

A day after the prodigious ratings landed (they went up exponentially each half hour, indicating that women all over the country were frantically dialing each other up, saying: "Are you watching *this*?"), Darnell was already planning a special on the happy couple returning from their honeymoon and talking about a reverse special with a rich woman picking out a guy to marry.

Then the bad news started. First, questions were raised about just how rich Rick Rockwell, the multimillionaire bridegroom, really was (he had some real estate holdings but had been a local comedian in San Diego who moved into motivational speaking). Then a

Web site, The Smoking Gun, posted a restraining order an ex-girlfriend had filed against Rockwell.

Sandy Grushow, the head of the Fox television studio and network, called Darnell immediately. "Hey, what's this about this guy beating up his wife or something?" Grushow asked.

Darnell replied, "Oh, that can't be true." He explained that they had done an extensive background check, but of course, now that the couple was coming back from their "honeymoon," they would ask Rockwell about it.

Mike Fleiss got word of the issue while riding in a limo on the way back from the airport. Confronted with the information, Rockwell explained that it was a nine-year-old incident and, besides, it was a total exaggeration: He had only let some air out of the woman's tires.

Fleiss called Darnell with the bad news. "Looks like it's true." Darnell immediately phoned Grushow. "I guess it's true," he told him, apologizing for going back only seven years on the guy's records.

"Well, that's game, set, and match," Grushow said. The special was instantly canceled. No more *Marry a Millionaire* shows of any kind.

With the press howling about Fox's irresponsibility, Grushow went further; he announced Fox would never again do any of the reality specials that Darnell had made famous. "They're gone; they're over," Grushow said, defining such specials as "anything that is exploitative, that reeks of desperation, anything that's merely out for ratings."

Darnell was upset, of course, but not so much by Rockwell's lack of complete candor as by Grushow's reaction. "It was handled horrendously, quite frankly," Darnell said. He did not think Grushow should have been apologetic; instead, he should have just said, "We did our best; we're standing by our television show."

Grushow did none of that, and Darnell had never felt more isolated at his network. Still, it wasn't like no one had noticed those rating numbers.

Less than a week after the special, in the midst of the firestorm of criticism in the press about Fox's lax supervision and the degrading nature of the show—and, by extension, all of "reality TV"—Darnell got a call from someone he did not know: Scott Sassa of NBC.

Sassa expressed his sympathy for what Mike was suffering—not from the press, but from his own management. "Grushow is hanging you out to dry," Sassa said. Darnell was hardly going to disagree with that. Sassa suggested they meet for a discreet lunch.

A few days later, Darnell went to the apartment Sassa was renting in L.A. for what Mike suspected was going to be a serious discussion about joining NBC. Darnell had no intention of trying to show NBC he was somebody he wasn't. He showed up in full rebel regalia—yellow jeans and yellow snakeskin boots.

That didn't faze Sassa. He already had Bob Wright's blessing to go after the guy who had scored that massive ratings coup. Here was someone who could get NBC into the reality game overnight. So what if he was a little strange-looking?

"They're totally disrespecting you," Sassa told Darnell. "You don't have to work for them anymore. You should just walk in there and tell Grushow you quit. We'll hire you and pay you much more money."

Darnell told Sassa how much he appreciated the offer and that he was going to talk it over with his wife. Sassa knew at once that Darnell was going to say no. He seemed bound to Fox, despite all the grief Grushow was giving him.

Some of Mike's colleagues concluded that Darnell feared emerging from the protective cocoon of Fox, where his carefully constructed maverick persona had been embraced, even coddled. If he signed on for the more formal business structures he knew existed at the other networks, would he be able to blow off meetings, keep agents waiting for hours, hold all his plans close to the vest until the last possible minute? Not likely.

At least one Fox coworker thought the conflict with Grushow was a turning point of sorts for Darnell, "sort of like when Anakin became Darth Vader." It was in this period that Darnell began sniping behind the scenes at Fox's scripted shows, trying to undercut them even before they got started, the coworker said. "He was trying to convince people that the network was always on the precipice of failure and that only his stuff would save us."

More than ever, Darnell turned "insular" (Mike's own word for it), relying on his wife, Carolyn, a public relations professional, and the small band of assistants in his department (many at Fox called them Darnell's "posse," a characterization that Mike did not disagree with) to protect him against the animus he believed was coming from Sandy Grushow.

Even before the special, Darnell had sensed nothing but friction in his dealings with Grushow. The Fox entertainment boss had publicly denigrated the whole genre of programming that Darnell had brought to Fox, all those highly rated, talked-about events, from *When Animals Attack* to *Outrageous Behavior Caught on Tape* to *World's Scariest Police Chases*. Grushow had come to the network disavowing them all, saying Fox needed to clean up its act and concentrate on developing high-quality scripted shows. "I, personally, would rather fail with quality than succeed with garbage," Grushow said at a press conference.

Darnell knew whom Grushow was talking about with that garbage crack. He had his own opinion of Grushow, saying, "Of course, Sandy found it very easy to fail with quality."

Failure was one thing Darnell could not abide. He lived and died by the ratings, not by what anyone wrote or said or thought about the quality of his shows. He once told a Fox colleague, "It's best not to have an opinion about a show until you see how big the ratings are."

• • •

Size was always a predominant factor in Mike Darnell's life. He simply did not grow, not like other kids did. He started small and stayed small—tiny, really. He lived in Philadelphia, son of a policeman, obsessed with television from an early age. At ten, a talent manager saw him singing ("Joy to the World"—the "Jeremiah was a bullfrog" version) at a Police Athletic League event and told Mike he

could make it in commercials. Eventually, that led to a long career
in child and juvenile parts (size again). His parents moved to California with him, the family then, and always, remaining close.

Darnell worked in television, finally landing a regular role in a
Saturday morning kids' show on NBC called *Big John, Little John.*
Even at twenty, Darnell continued to audition for child roles,
because he was still no more than five feet and about ninety
pounds. One day at yet another lineup to read for parts, he casually
asked a fortyish actor what he did when he didn't have an acting job.
The man said he waited tables. Darnell felt a chill run down his
spine. That was not a prospect he wanted to contemplate at age
forty. Darnell never went to another audition.

Instead, he took a job in a bank and worked his way through Cal
State Northridge. Carolyn Oberman, his longtime girlfriend (they
were neighbors as kids), had landed a job with the Emmy Awards,
and that only encouraged Darnell's desire to get into the business
side of TV.

He landed an internship at KTTV, the Fox station in L.A., which
eventually became a full-time job. It was mostly low-level stuff in
the news division, and Darnell didn't even like news. It took him
eight years to find a way out. Mike finally forged a relationship with
Barry Diller, then the head of all of Fox's operations, who liked the
kid's energy. Diller found a spot for him with the Fox network in the
specials department.

It was hardly something that excited him. Fox was doing music
specials with Queen Latifah and *Rock and Roll Skating.* Darnell
couldn't stand it. One day a producer came in pitching a show
called *Encounters.* He said he had video of an "alien autopsy." This
sounded more like Darnell's language.

And damn if the fifteen-minute tape did not look like somebody
carving up an alien. Darnell asked the guy when the tape was made,
and he told him "supposedly 1949." Mike asked him if he could val-
idate the date. The producer came back and said the tape was from
either 1949 or 1969.

Close enough for Mike. To protect the network from assaults

from science nerds, Darnell titled the show *Alien Autopsy: Fact or Fiction?* and let it rip. It attracted almost 12 million viewers. Fox reran it five more times. The thing was ratings catnip. Darnell fabricated a show called *World's Greatest Hoaxes* and used it again.

Nobody in television in the mid-1990s loved what he was doing more than Mike Darnell. He was flabbergasted when he chatted with other network executives and they would say, "I don't watch a lot of TV." Mike lived to watch television, and to make television.

In 1996, Darnell was put in charge of the department as vice president of specials. Within a few months, he blasted one out of the park with *When Animals Attack,* an assemblage of video footage showing reindeer trying to stomp hunters and the like. The timing was fortuitous, because later that same year, a new executive moved in to take charge of Fox Entertainment.

Peter Roth had been at the 20th Century Fox television studio, so he was well aware of the problems at the network. Fox had failure all over the schedule at that point. David Hill, the executive then in charge at Fox, wanted Roth to turn things around quickly. The worst problem was a black hole on Monday night where two failed comedies had been. Roth did not know Mike Darnell, but he called him into his office and asked, "What have you got?"

Darnell told him about a couple of specials he had in the works, *When Disasters Strike* and *World's Greatest Calamities.* Roth nodded. "Okay, those are on the air in the next four weeks. And I want *When Animals Attack 2.* Whatever you've got; the harder the better."

Darnell had found a kindred spirit. In the next year, Mike churned out an astonishing sixty-eight specials, including such memorable shows as *Busted on the Job, Outrageous Behavior Caught on Tape, When Stunts Go Bad,* and *World's Deadliest Swarms.* In November 1997, he put together *Breaking the Magician's Code: Magic's Biggest Secrets Finally Revealed,* which laid bare the rudimentary mechanics behind most of the magic tricks audiences have seen for a lifetime. It was the perfect mix of fascination and outrage.

The special inspired howls of protest from magicians all over the country, who complained that Fox had violated a sacred trust of show business in betraying the magician's art. Darnell lapped the protests up—other than being somewhat concerned when his father almost got into a fistfight with an amateur magician. The furor only helped the numbers. The magic special was Darnell's biggest hit yet.

Peter Roth certainly wasn't complaining. He would call Darnell almost every week with the question: "What else you got?" And Darnell would unspool a list of what Roth called "magnificently odd, outrageous, obviously commercial ideas." Roth also made it a point to call Darnell's home every Tuesday morning at 6 A.M. as soon as the first ratings results were in. Every time it was a big score, Roth would scream into Darnell's answering machine: "MDTV!" What Roth cared about was winning, and when Darnell had a hot special on, Fox invariably won that night.

Roth began giving Darnell free rein. "He was as autonomous as anyone who ever worked in TV," Roth said. "Go off and bring those shows to me. I didn't care how things were done. I wanted to win." The decision to unfetter Darnell from any real supervision would lead to worrisome consequences down the road.

Even in the early days, not everyone at Fox was as blinkered as Peter Roth about the potential downsides of Darnell's unchecked run. The sales division, for example, generally despised the Darnell specials; they considered them lowbrow crap, impossible to sell for good rates because the audiences that most liked them were young, male, and either unemployed or poorly paid. Many advertisers, especially the elite ones, did not want to be associated with this kind of material.

Roth put his personal pride in check when it came to Darnell's output, thinking rather of the needs of the company. One day when Roth was out with his wife and mother-in-law, the subject of *When Animals Attack* and other outré Darnell specials came up. Roth's mother-in-law wondered why people "keep putting these terrible shows on." Roth looked sheepishly at his wife, who told her mother, "Mom, that's *him*."

Roth had some real success at Fox, but like several top executives before and after him, his tenure was short. The heads of Fox

Entertainment seemed to come and go in congressional-year cycles. Mike Darnell was the constant. He became the figure who most stood for the Fox "brand." That was never absolutely defined, but from the beginning it encompassed words like "youthful," "edgy," and "antiestablishment."

Roth himself put Darnell's face on the Fox brand. "He embodied the spirit of what Fox was supposed to have been: daring, distinctive, and different," Roth said. "That's what's to be expected when you watch Fox. As much as anybody, Mike was the true maverick of the company."

Darnell himself cultivated that image, as Scott Sassa was to learn. Darnell affected a persona. He was habitually late for meetings, if he showed up at all. He blew off agents and producers if he was busy. He virtually never returned a phone call. His hair was always long. He never wore suits, instead sticking to his T-shirts, jeans, and cowboy boots. Not that he needed them to stand out; he knew his height made him automatically unique.

How this actually affected Darnell was a matter of some debate inside Fox. Certainly, Mike himself often made reference to his size, deflecting some of the criticism tossed at him by saying his height made him a target for derision. Some of his coworkers thought he reveled in his unusually small stature and used it to his advantage; others thought it had left him with psychological scars that at least partially accounted for his interest in the darker, more cynical side of human nature.

"There's a real paranoia there," one longtime Fox executive said of Darnell. "He's a real enigma. Part of it is he's such a diminutive guy. He will tell you he's not a dark person, try to convince you that's not where his life is. Yet it manifested itself in his editorial judgment. Part of the reason he became what he became was because there were so many people in his life who either actively encouraged him or failed to discourage him."

Chief among these, according to this Fox executive, were "people like Rupert, and David Hill and Peter Roth, who were so desperate for ratings that they didn't much care where they came from."

Another executive who spent several years working with Darnell called him "the delinquent child of the Fox Network," and said, "A lot of it is purely for image. It's one thing if you can back it up. He's a P. T. Barnum kind of guy. He has no interest in making good television. He doesn't think good television is why people watch TV. He thinks it's all about the concept and the gimmick—and he's not 100 percent wrong."

Darnell knew he was identified as an exploiter of base instincts, but he thought it was an unfair characterization. He saw himself as a colorful rogue, not some dark prince of programming, less a schlockmeister than a shockmeister. "I like to twist things," he said. "I like to get a reaction out of people. I like the audience to go: What? What are they doing? But in a way that shocks you, but generally doesn't turn your stomach."

Still, some stomachs had to be turned by the 300-pound tumor in a woman's abdomen that was a highlight of Darnell's *Guinness Book of World Records* show. Or the guy who pissed in the dough he was using to make rolls for a lawyers' convention in *Busted on the Job*. Or the groom who puked at his wedding on *Shocking Behavior Caught on Tape*.

And those moments were only from the Darnell canon that did get on the air. Some of his ideas were too much even for Fox. For one proposed show, Mike wanted to sink a ship at sea live—it proved too costly. For another, he tried to get a stuntman to actually parachute from the stratosphere in something he was titling *Space Jump*. Some Fox lawyers balked because it seemed there really was a good chance of killing the guy.

Most infamously, Darnell came up with an idea to crash a 727 (Mike originally wanted a 747) jetliner into a mountain or in a desert (after the pilot had bailed out, of course). Darnell planned to fit the plane with numerous cameras that would capture the disaster in all its destructive glory.

This idea had a good deal of traction inside Fox before some spoilsports spoke up. Jon Nesvig, the head of sales, often had deep concerns about the Darnell specials because so many advertisers resisted going near them. Nesvig pointed out that on the plane-crash show, there was no way to know in advance what sort of accidents might be in the news the night of the special.

Other Fox executives brought up the possibility of battles with environmentalists. What if the crash started a fire, or killed some helpless wildlife?

Darnell believed he saw a way around all these issues. Though he initially envisioned the crash show as a kind of thrill ride (how else would a viewer get to experience an airline crash and actually sort of enjoy it?), he suggested Fox counter the opposition by presenting the crash special as a "public service" show on air safety. Darnell noted that NBC's newsmagazine *Dateline* had broadcast a lot of automobile crash tests. Surely airlines did the same with planes.

That proposal didn't fly, and neither did Mike's 727. In general, though, Darnell was allowed to push the limits with impunity. He managed to get all manner of shocking and offensive activity onto the air, under the rubric of animals and people doing outrageous things when a video camera happened to be around. It seemed to some at Fox that Darnell had no self-regulator and there was no line that couldn't be crossed in the cause of seizing an audience.

On one edition of *Busted on the Job*, David Hill, the chairman of Fox Television, was asked to make the call on just how far Darnell could go. He said yes to a scene of an employee relieving himself in his boss's coffee. But no to a scene where a female executive interviewing a male applicant was called out of the room, and the male job applicant got up, walked over, and sniffed the chair where she had been sitting. It was a surefire talk-about moment that Darnell had edited into the show at the very last minute. Hill ordered it pulled.

Mike squeezed it into a later show.

·   ·   ·

Before the British reality imports hit, Mike Darnell lived in the oddity department of television. His material was treated with utter disdain everywhere but Fox. At NBC, Don Ohlmeyer frequently predicted Fox's next trick would be to broadcast video of Buddhist monks immolating themselves in Times Square.

Darnell later railed at the hypocrisy. He pointed out that NBC paid a big price to steal away Bruce Nash, one of Mike's prime outrageous-video producers, giving him his own series, and in Nash's first show for NBC a zoo worker got his head stuck up an elephant's ass. "I couldn't get that piece on Fox!" Mike said. That was true; NBC's compromise was to eliminate the *squish* sound effect Mike used when he tried to get the unfortunate elephant man onto one of his specials.

But the *Millionaire* game show and especially *Survivor* opened the eyes of American television executives to a whole new programming genre, the reality *series*, and that was an area Darnell was uniquely positioned to exploit. Fox was suddenly saying "Hey, Mikey" again.

Nobody at Fox mentioned the fact that Mark Burnett had pitched *Survivor* to Fox long before he found a home for it at CBS. Nor did they especially want to remember they had put Darnell on double-secret probation for the *Who Wants to Marry a Multi-Millionaire?* fiasco. They simply wanted their enfant terrible to get back in the game as quickly as possible.

Sandy Grushow, who had succeeded David Hill as the man in charge of all of the Fox television operations, was way out on a limb, having decried the "garbage" associated with Darnell and complained that it had tarnished Fox's image. He had never seen Darnell as a team player. Grushow felt Mike sucked up every drop of available credit for his successes and openly courted the press to enhance his personal reputation. Darnell was a fabulous interview subject, wildly colorful and controversial, and unashamed of any of his sideshow attractions. He got more ink than any other Fox executive, including Grushow. But eventually the press got to be too much. Fox's public relations people were under strict orders not to put Darnell on the phone with any reporters unless Grushow himself approved.

By the time *Survivor* got on the air, Grushow had installed another management layer between himself and Darnell, adding Gail Berman as president of entertainment. Berman knew Fox had to get some juice out of its reality division, and that meant cranking up Mike again.

Berman was game for that assignment. In her first week on the job, she arranged a meeting with Darnell. He arrived at her office with a long sheet of ideas for both series and specials. As he described them to Berman, her head began to spin.

*Surprise Wedding* (reluctant grooms are fooled into facing an audience of 1,500 people, with their girlfriends insisting that they marry on the spot); *I Want a Divorce* (soon-to-be-divorced couples compete for their assets); *Hotel Getaway* (a couple's prize trip to a resort is sabotaged by bad food, horrible service, and obnoxious fellow guests); *Love Cruise* (barely dressed singles date each other on a sailing trip and vote losers off one by one); and *Temptation Island* (longtime unmarried couples test their relationships on an island filled with great-looking singles whose goal is to bust up the romances).

Berman was amazed and just a bit alarmed at some of the ideas. One in particular gave her the willies, *Space Jump.* When Darnell finished his rundown, she had one admonition for the executive newly under her supervision: "No one dies on my watch," she said. "Let me be really clear about that, Mike."

Once they had that understanding, Berman felt free to tell Darnell that some of his ideas sounded terrific. She thought *Love Cruise* did not sound any wilder than "what you'd see at your local temple—like a singles weekend at Grossinger's." And she was truly charged up about the prospects for *Temptation Island.* Berman said, "Who wouldn't watch that?"

Fox scheduled *Temptation Island* for January 2001. Grushow, having denounced Darnell's shows only nine months earlier, was at pains to explain his quick return to glory.

"We work in a dynamic business," Grushow said. "Things change. . . . We never said we were getting out of the reality business. Everyone is trying to react to audiences' having a huge appetite for this kind of programming."

And after all, what were the odds that another one of Darnell's programs would be hit with a scandal?

Berman didn't want to calculate those odds, especially not with a show that was openly inviting howls of protest about the ethos of setting out to tempt committed (though unmarried) couples into infidelity. After Fox announced *Temptation Island,* the press bombarded the network with questions about whether they were sanctioning prostitution. To Mike's delight, the show was already "extraordinarily controversial." He knew he had a hit on his hands.

That didn't erase Berman's concerns. She took it upon herself to double-check the backgrounds of all the participants in *Temptation Island.* As president of Fox Entertainment, she had hundreds of scripts to read, actors to audition, and pitches to listen to. But she personally went through every application of every contestant who had been approved by Fox's risk-management team to appear on *Temptation Island.*

Berman knew their family backgrounds, their interests, what they liked for breakfast. Nobody was going to slip anything by Fox this time.

Three episodes into the shooting at a resort in Belize, but well before any part of the series had reached the air, Berman got a call before dawn one morning from an agitated Mike Darnell.

"We have a big problem," Darnell said.

Berman's blood ran cold. She thought of her first conversation with Darnell, and how he had cutely sought to calm her fears about fatalities by having a special pillow made for the couch in her office. Embroidered on it were the words "No one will die on my watch."

Berman said, "What's the problem, Mike?"

"It seems that two of the contestants on *Temptation Island,* Taheed and Ytossie, have a child together." Taheed Watson and Ytossie Patterson were an attractive African-American couple from Los Angeles. They were the most colorful personalities of the four couples in the show, thanks to their constant bickering and emotional outbursts.

Berman did not flinch. "No, they don't," she said.

"Gail, are you not listening to me?" Darnell said. "I just got off the phone from the producers. I know what the story is."

Berman still insisted he was wrong. Darnell became frustrated. Why was she arguing this point that he knew to be true? So she told him about how comprehensively she had gone through all the contestants' backgrounds. She was sure she would prove to be right.

Obsessed with establishing the truth, Berman left for the office almost immediately. When she arrived, it was still very early. She went right to the background books, which were where she had left them, right behind her desk. She pulled out the file on Taheed and Ytossie.

There it was, in the questionnaire: "Do you have a child? Do you have a child together?" In both cases, the couple had each answered no.

Satisfied, Berman knew she had been correct. She called Darnell back. "Mike, we don't have a problem," she said. "I checked all this myself. I am so sure of this. I checked everything and everyone. They don't have a baby."

"Gail, they lied," Darnell said.

Berman, a mother of twins, was still incredulous. Who would lie about having a child? No one would lie about that.

But confronted during the show's taping, the couple had already admitted it. Later, they claimed they had told the producers the truth in advance and had been advised, because the producers were desperate to have a great-looking black couple on the show, that acknowledging the child was "the wrong answer." First time back from the *Marry a Millionaire* fiasco and Fox had been caught again failing to check out thoroughly a reality contestant's background.

And it wasn't as though the information would have been hard to obtain. The *Los Angeles Times* reported that it took only a matter of minutes to research the couple online, using only their first names, and find notice of a paternity suit that had been filed eighteen months earlier.

This time nobody at Fox was apologizing for negligence. Instead, they decided that kicking the couple off the show presented an exciting opportunity; it could be used as a point of "drama" in the series. This might be just the kind of controversy that "MDTV" thrived on. Darnell had every reason to believe this would be good for a bounce in the ratings—which, then and always, was what Mike Darnell was all about.

News of the latest Fox reality scandal broke the same day that the first episode of *Temptation Island* hit the air. The show pulled in more viewers than the opening episode of *Survivor*. Episode Three, when Taheed and Ytossie were tossed off the show, complaining and wailing, was the highest-rated show of the series.

The rehabilitation mission of Mike Darnell was in full sail.

· · ·

On a busy sound stage in Hollywood in late December 2001, Mike Darnell found himself pressed for time. It was almost 10 P.M. and Darnell, surrounded by his staff, had only a few weeks to get his next show produced, edited, and ready to broadcast. Darnell could not afford delays because he had to ensure that *his* show, *The Chamber,* did not get beaten onto the air by ABC's show, *The Chair,* which was, in almost every respect, precisely the same concept.

Darnell had liked *The Chair* when it was pitched to him a month earlier. He had told the creator, Julie Christie (not the actress, but a producer from New Zealand), that he wanted it and would be aggressive in the bidding. *The Chair* was definitely Mike Darnell–style television. Ostensibly a quiz show, it was more like a survival test with contestants locked into a chair, where their heart rate and other vital signs would be monitored as they were asked questions and were subjected to distracting and often threatening stimuli, like flames, fireworks, or even the occasional surprise appearance of an alligator.

That sounded like Darnell's specialty, traffic-accident television: shocking, controversial, sure to outrage some quarters of the media, and just as sure to get viewers talking. But he hadn't won the rights to *The Chair.* He lost in the bidding to ABC. No matter. Dick Clark Productions was quickly signed up for a Darnell version of the premise, with some added thrills thrown in. Darnell called his version *The Chamber,* and if that conjured up instant word association with "torture chamber," so much the better.

Or as Darnell himself put it, "I wanted it to sound frightening."

Beyond the usual coterie of staff that trailed Mike, he had invited a few of the other executives from Fox Entertainment to the taping, including Gail Berman and Preston Beckman, now Fox's top scheduling executive. Darnell's wife, Carolyn, was at his side, as she most often was.

Fox and ABC were already sparring nastily over the provenance of the two shows, and Christie, the creator of *The Chair,* had actually filed suit, claiming Darnell had stolen her idea. This was nothing new for Darnell and his network. CBS had sued the year before over a show called *Boot Camp,* which had all kinds of elements reminiscent of *Survivor.* And ABC had cried foul in 1999 when Darnell came up with *Greed,* a game show with numerous touches, like lighting and sound effects, that seemed to be direct lifts from *Who Wants to Be a Millionaire?*

The *Millionaire* creators thought about suing, but didn't. And CBS regretted having done so on *Boot Camp.* (The network wound up settling and paying court costs of about $250,000.) Darnell learned quickly a lesson he would apply again and again: Ideas in reality television were almost completely uncopyrightable. A little twist on the notion and, presto, you have a new reality. Such tweaking became a Darnell specialty—and of course only fed the notion among certain of his critics that "twisted" was just the right word to describe him and his taste in programming.

*The Chamber* promised to be Mike's pièce de résistance. He and his team had devised something that looked a bit like a cage from an S&M movie. It featured a chair that resembled "Old Smokey" from Sing Sing, with similar straps to tie a contestant down.

The game was played akin to *The Chair*—or perhaps the Salem witch trials. The contestant would be asked general-knowledge questions while being rotated over flames as though being roasted on a spit, raising the temperature in the chamber to 150 degrees.

For other questions, blasts of frigid air would rake the contestant—usually attired in a tank top—lowering the temperature in the chamber to 20 degrees. In addition, water would be hosed on the contestant's face, which, if done right, formed icicles on lashes and nose hair.

All the while, the chair was being rocked violently, as the contestant was shocked by electrodes strapped to various muscles, causing involuntary contractions. All this for the princely sum of a thousand dollars for each correct answer.

The format had already proved too much for the original host, a young sports announcer named Matt Vasgersian, who walked off during a run-through. One production staff member called it "a pig of a concept."

But in the storied tradition of the business, the show was going on. As he took stock of the setup during the taping, Preston Beckman concluded that Darnell was clearly trying to thrill the audience into thinking Fox might actually kill someone on television. Beckman helpfully suggested that maybe they ought to pull an ambulance up next to the chamber as an ominous on-set presence, and maybe have the people who strapped the contestant into the chair wear black rubber masks—executioner-style.

Beckman was trying to have some fun with the show, but Carolyn Darnell was wary. The discussion ended quickly anyway, because on stage a contestant seemed to be in some duress during the roasting-on-a-spit segment.

Berman, the top executive on the scene, was understandably alarmed, especially when it became clear there had been a malfunction in the chamber and the contestant apparently could not get out. Technicians sprang into action, but it was some moments before they could free the contestant or cut off the searing heat.

Berman, highly regarded inside Fox for her creative instincts, which had been honed in serious theater in New York, was not accustomed to scenes like this on Broadway. "Please don't die, please don't die," she whispered, rocking back and forth.

It took only another minute for the contestant to be freed. No harm done—though not much help either, as it turned out. *The Chamber* had one week of heavy viewing by the rubbernecker audience, then dropped like a stone and was quickly yanked off the air.

Nobody was overly troubled by the scare on the set. It was just another moment when a Fox executive in charge of Mike Darnell had reason to be short of breath.

# CHAPTER SIX

# MY FICKLE FRIEND, THE SUMMER WIND

L ate in the summer of 2000, a critical decision was looming at CBS: What do we do with *Survivor* when it comes back in the regular television season? As powerful as the show had been in the summer, CBS recognized it might simply have caught lightning in a bottle, and maybe against first-run competition it would not be the same phenomenon.

That September, Leslie Moonves convened his senior staff to talk about upcoming scheduling issues. The meeting took place in the CBS conference room, dominated by a big magnetic scheduling board containing the night-by-night lineups of the networks, with shows in various colors. The conversation quickly drifted to some general musing, along the lines of "All right, what do we do?"

As this conversation flowed, Kelly Kahl, without saying a word, stepped up to the board. His back to everyone, he reached up to Wednesday night at 8 and removed the yellow strip with *Survivor* printed on it. With his other hand he lifted the drama *Diagnosis: Murder,* the show with the oldest audience in television, off of Thursday night at 8, and slapped *Survivor* there—right next to the strip labeled *Friends* on NBC.

When Kahl had switched shows around in the past, he usually could hear discernible "Hmmmm" sounds behind him. This time he heard nothing: dead silence. He did not turn around right away, because he was waiting for the feedback. Nothing. Kahl started to get a bit nervous. Finally, he turned, knowing exactly where to look first. Moonves was staring at him with an expression Kahl interpreted as "Are you kidding me?"

Immediately, the room exploded in protest. Joe Abruzzese, the head of sales, looked like he might have a seizure. "You're killing me here," he said. "I mean, *Survivor* is huge on Wednesday. You move it to Thursday, you're going to be taking a lot of money out of my pocket." Abruzzese, more than almost anyone else at CBS, knew the enormous value of *Survivor*. It had brought in no fewer than nine advertisers who had previously never bought a single commercial in a CBS prime-time show, marketers like Budweiser and Reebok and even the U.S. Army. Now Kahl wanted to put all that at risk?

"We're still not going to win Thursday," someone else said. "We'll be able to dominate Wednesday if we leave it there."

Moonves quieted the room. He did not offer an opinion, as he almost never did in the scheduling meetings. He liked to listen to all the arguments, picking them apart with questions, before he made a decision. He wanted to hear what Kelly had to say.

"Boss, if we don't attack Thursday now, we never will," Kahl said. He did not think it was even a question that CBS should do this. "These things come along, what, every ten years, twenty years?" Kahl said. "If you've got the golden hammer, you've got to use it. For profitability, to make any kind of inroads on NBC, to be a real player, to be a real network, we have to do this. How are you a real network on Thursday night if you're ten ratings points behind? We can be a real network or we cannot."

The speech did not quell all the protests. Nor did it totally sell Moonves. For one thing, *Survivor* was just a single piece of the night, not an entire Thursday strategy. For another, this kind of risky play was antithetical to Moonves's slow-and-steady strategy in rebuilding CBS. It was brick by brick, not Molotov cocktail by Molotov cocktail.

But Moonves also knew that CBS owned the rights to the Super

Bowl the following January, which meant a guaranteed giant audience for whatever CBS chose to broadcast immediately after the game. *Survivor* could be kicked off on Super Sunday night, right after the game, so the first new episode would get a surefire launch, with plenty of promotional reminders that it would now be playing regularly on Thursdays.

Moonves knew he would have some sleepless nights making this decision, but Kelly's words stuck with him: "We can be a real network or we cannot."

Still, a nagging issue remained. *Survivor* might be the hottest thing on television in a decade, but it was just one hour. That was not enough to take on the Goliath of NBC Thursday nights. If Moonves was truly going to charge up that hill with Kahl, what on earth was he going to use at 9 P.M. to hold on to that massive *Survivor* audience, an audience of younger viewers that CBS had nowhere else on its schedule?

Les could have polled the room that day and found no answers; but one executive, his head of drama development, Nina Tassler, was sitting there, unbeknownst to her or anyone else at CBS, with the solution already in her hands.

• • •

Eleven months earlier, on a late October evening, Tassler, winding her way down the hill on the valley side of Laurel Canyon Road, pulled up to the light at the busy intersection with Ventura Boulevard. She was on her way home after another long day of dealing with the demands of a network development season. By this point, Halloween week, Tassler had listened to between 300 and 400 pitches for new hourlong drama series from producers and writers all over Hollywood. She had selected the ideas she wanted to turn into scripts, and was feeling the relief of coming to the end of her busiest time of the year. Tassler was feeling drained by the volume of work; she was plumb exhausted.

As Tassler waited at the light, her cell phone rang. The call was from Jonathan Littman. Tassler knew Littman from her days working in development at Warner Brothers studio, when Littman had held a similar position at the Fox studio. Now Littman was the top television executive for Jerry Bruckheimer, the celebrated maestro of action movies like *Beverly Hills Cop* and *Top Gun,* who wanted to branch out into TV series production.

"I got a great pitch you have to hear," Littman said when he got on the line. "Even if you don't buy it, Nina, it will be by far the most entertaining pitch you've heard all year."

This was not a message that Tassler wanted to hear, not less than a week from November. "Jonathan, I can't," she said. "You know where I am with my schedule. I'm closed. I love you, Jonathan. But you know where I am right now."

Littman was not deterred. "Honestly, Nina, the writer is so entertaining, and you'll love the idea. Just hear it; please, please, I beg you. Just hear it."

Tassler's development slate was finished. Her budget was basically used up. Jonathan was a friend, though, and a good development executive, so Tassler said wearily, "What's the idea?"

"It's a forensics show," Littman said.

Tassler's ears perked up. For most of her life she had been a mad fan of the creaky, pedestrian NBC series *Quincy,* in which Jack Klugman played an L.A. medical examiner. Tassler loved nothing more than a good autopsy, and she seldom missed shows like *HBO Autopsy* and *A&E Investigates.*

Still, her deadline was imminent and most of her money was spent. "Jonathan, I don't know," Tassler said before adding resignedly, "Well, who's this writer?"

Littman explained he was a new talent. "But I promise you it will be entertaining. You must, must, must hear this pitch."

Tassler let out a sigh. She knew CBS did not have a forensics-based show among its candidates for pilots. "Okay," she said, still presuming this would be an unproductive sideshow. She resignedly booked the appointment for the following week. This lowered the prospects even further for the idea's ever making it onto the CBS schedule, no matter how "entertaining" the pitch was.

Littman turned up a week later accompanied by a balding young man in glasses, dressed all in black. He looked baby-faced to Tassler, but not scared. If anything, he looked revved up and ready for action.

Littman introduced him as Anthony Zuiker. They all sat down, Zuiker perching himself on the very edge of Tassler's couch, like a predator about to spring. Zuiker slowly removed his glasses, shut his eyes, and began to speak.

"I'm going to tell you a story about the world of forensic medicine," Zuiker said. Using his hands like an orchestra conductor, creating a rhythm of story and character detail, Zuiker sketched out a police division called a Crime Scene Investigation unit, based in Las Vegas and headed up by a laconic but charismatic scientific investigator named Gil Grissom. The unit solved crimes by the intricate examination of forensic evidence: blood-spatter patterns, bullet fragments, loose hair and fibers, DNA residue on cocktail napkins, and so on.

As Zuiker described the crime scenes and the methods used by the unit, he got more and more worked up. He laid out a plan to include what he called "snap-zoom" scenes inserted into the film, which would use animation and other techniques to show in detail things like bullets penetrating tissue, or bones breaking under the pressure of a collision. Zuiker accompanied these descriptions with his own sound effects: "Chuh, chuh, chuh." His hands never stopped gesturing, signaling the progression of the story. By the time Zuiker wrapped up, he was literally bouncing up and down on the couch with excitement.

Nina Tassler watched the performance with increasing interest—and awe. She was completely hooked. In the language of the television business, Tassler bought the pitch "in the room." She was excited by the idea and Zuiker's clear passion for it. "Go write a script," she told him. "And write fast, because I have to have a first draft before Thanksgiving."

The show was coming to her this late, Littman explained, because they had had to go to ABC first. That network had had first crack because Bruckheimer's production-company deal was with Walt Disney, the owner of both ABC and the Touchstone television studio, which was to be the financial backer of *CSI*.

Tassler could not remember commissioning a first-draft script this late, and from an unknown writer, no less. Of course, she knew that, sooner or later, the show would have to get the OK from Leslie Moonves.

•  •  •

As he had with George Clooney, Moonves often picked out actors whose styles he particularly liked and then tried to find a television series to fit them. For some time, Les had been impressed with the work of a somewhat obscure actor named William Petersen, identifying him as a sure television star if only he could convince him to read a script and take a series role. Moonves had personally chased Petersen for almost eight years, going all the way back to his days running Warner Brothers.

Unlike Clooney, Petersen already had a movie career, having been in films like *Manhunter* (in which his cop character caught a killer named Hannibal Lecter) and *To Live and Die in L.A.* To Moonves's experienced eye, Petersen's low-key, controlled performances looked ideal for television.

Over that eight-year span, Moonves arranged a yearly meeting with Petersen and his representatives. His question was always the same: "What do I have to do to get you to do television?" Petersen was polite but not interested. Finally, in 1998, Moonves was convinced he had found the perfect role, in a series version of the classic Western *The Magnificent Seven*. Moonves made his pitch: "Billy, you want to do the Yul Brynner part?"

He got a surprising answer. "No, but there is a Western I'd like to do."

This was at least progress. Moonves asked which one. Petersen told him: *Have Gun, Will Travel*. Nothing could have been better for Moonves. CBS owned the rights to that classic series; Petersen could play Paladin, the gun-for-hire San Francisco sophisticate. CBS would do it.

Petersen backed out a short time later. Frustrated, Moonves came up with a new plan. CBS would sign Petersen to a holding deal, one that would not commit the actor to anything. But he would be paid a fee simply to listen to pitches from Nina Tassler. "The good news," Moonves told Petersen, "is that if the script we bring to you is bad, you don't like it, we're going to have thirty more to show you, all leading roles."

Petersen agreed to this no-lose concept—money for nothing if CBS found no role he liked. The deal was on the books at CBS when Nina Tassler was developing shows that fall. But she had found nothing she believed was suitable for William Petersen—until Anthony Zuiker walked in the door.

The lead character in *CSI*, Gil Grissom, was solid, bright, determined, something of a loner, but deep, soulful, altogether inscrutable. It sounded like a Billy Petersen role. Tassler knew she had a $1 million holding deal with a prominent actor sitting there generating nothing in return for CBS. Closing out that deal was extra incentive to find something the actor might spark to.

The same day that Tassler sent Zuiker off to write his first draft of *CSI*, she contacted Petersen's closest representative, Cindy Chvatal, Petersen's longtime friend and partner in his production company, High Horse Films. "There's a writer that I really think you and Billy should meet," Tassler told her. "He's kind of wacky, but you may like him."

When Petersen met Zuiker at the Beverly Wilshire Hotel, they hit it off over their mutual Chicago backgrounds and fondness for the Cubs. The two men talked for four hours, Zuiker pitching away, with his sound effects and his vivid tales of the science of crime-scene investigation, spinning around the room like a dervish. Petersen loved him. He walked out of the meeting and immediately told Chvatal: "This is what we're going to do."

Billy called Moonves with the good news. Les, who had not been in on Zuiker's pitch, was a bit nonplussed. "What? Crime-scene investigation?" Moonves said. "You mean the fingerprint guys? You're gonna dust for prints? That's gonna be your show?"

Petersen assured him he was truly passionate about this idea, and especially about the quirky young man who had created it. "I believe in Anthony Zuiker," Petersen said.

•   •   •

Anthony Zuiker's personal story was unlike any other—and yet emblematic of many odd but compelling tales of television talent appearing out of nowhere and breaking through, thanks to a burst of true originality.

In 1996, when he was twenty-six years old, Zuiker, already a bust at a brokerage firm, was making $8 an hour driving forty-second-long tram rides between the Mirage Hotel and the Treasure Island Hotel in Las Vegas. He did not believe he was fated to live out his life so meaninglessly. Zuiker had earned two degrees at the University of Nevada, Las Vegas, one in philosophy and another in communications. He knew he was smart and talented. From a young age he had exhibited a gift for imaginative, colorful writing.

When he was fifteen, he wrote a poem for his barber to send to an estranged girlfriend. The barber got the girl back; Zuiker got free haircuts for a year. Later, he wrote a letter on behalf of his stepfather, a maître d' for Vegas hotels, which led to a $300-a-week job writing letters for executives. Zuiker was nineteen at the time.

An only child, he found ways to amuse himself, like inventing all kinds of sports board games that could be played with dice. In high school he developed another talent, extemporaneous speaking. He competed in debate and won state-level prizes.

None of that helped him after college. Zuiker found himself at loose ends. The brokerage job didn't last. He hurt his back lifting bags as a bellhop. To make a few extra bucks, he came up with goofy ideas for billboard advertisements, like the time he sold a Vegas sex shop on the idea of a billboard featuring three inflatable women dolls, with the tagline "Picking Up Airheads Just Got Easier."

Zuiker was always writing—an actor friend, Dustin Abraham, asked him to write original monologues he could use at auditions— but nobody was noticing. Zuiker found himself sinking into despair, driving a tram, in the middle of the night, full of miserable people who had just lost more money than they could afford. Zuiker felt close to breaking mentally. In his darkest moments, he found himself asking God why he had been given these unusual talents if he was never going to get a chance to use them.

And then, out of the blue, a Hollywood agent called. He had heard Zuiker's friend, Dustin Abraham, performing a highly original monologue about a horse race and had asked the actor who wrote it. So how about it? Did Anthony believe he could write a screenplay?

Zuiker, so out of it in terms of show business that he thought William Morris was a cigarette company, had no clue about how to write a screenplay. But this was the chance of a lifetime. He bought books by Syd Field on the basics of screenwriting. One of the first things he took away was the admonition: Write about what you know.

Zuiker, whose mother was a casino pit boss, came up with a story about a young addicted gambler who takes a job as a runner for a gangster. The agent promised little, only to send Anthony's spec script, *The Runner,* around to a few places.

The next day, the agent phoned with news: He had an offer for $35,000 from an independent producer. To a guy making $8 an hour and praying for some way out, the offer sounded like a gift from heaven. Zuiker snapped it up, unaware of just how cheap his price of escape had been. Later, as the script got around, it attracted an offer from a studio for $1 million.

The script was golden for Zuiker anyway. He got a new agent and a manager out of it, and more than that, a calling card. In the next several years, Zuiker got other offers and made some money; he even wound up pitching a movie idea to Leonardo DiCaprio. Leo loved him, and briefly committed to the film before backing out.

The film business began to frustrate Zuiker, because his scripts were not getting produced. Now married, he needed to keep paying the bills. So when Jerry Bruckheimer's office called saying they liked the voice in his scripts and wondering if Anthony had any ideas for television, Zuiker jumped at the chance to set up a meeting. Not that he had any ideas. Zuiker watched little conventional television, his tastes running to harder-edged fare on HBO and anything having to do with hip-hop.

But his wife, Jennifer, had a favorite show that intrigued Zuiker. It was *The New Detectives: Case Studies in Forensic Science* on the Discovery Channel. Here were tales of detectives using strands of hair and drops of blood to solve decades-old cases. Zuiker's creative juices began to bubble.

He set off to do research, arranging to spend time with crime teams working out of the Las Vegas Police Department. The cops were extremely generous to the likable kid, taking him along to crime scenes and even involving him where they could. At one crime scene, with the suspect still at large, the team collected evidence in a bedroom. One detective handed Zuiker a comb and told him to run it through the carpet to collect hairs and fibers.

Zuiker attacked the assignment with his usual enthusiasm. When he came to the bed and lifted the skirt, he was met by a pair of red-rimmed eyes—and a sudden swipe from long fingernails intent on scratching out his own eyes. Zuiker leaped up, calling out, "Geez, I'm just the writer!" As the cops rushed to his defense, flashing guns, pinning the suspect down, and slamming her into handcuffs, Zuiker was convinced: "Oh, this is for sure a show."

Jerry Bruckheimer agreed. At their meeting, he was taken by the infectiousness of Zuiker's energy, his "verbal assault" as he pitched his stories. Bruckheimer set up a meeting with the Touchstone studio.

Steve McPherson was newly installed as head of Touchstone and was eager to get product from Bruckheimer's company onto his development slate. He had never heard of Anthony Zuiker, but he was certainly willing to hear a pitch from this new voice.

When he did, McPherson was taken aback—in a good way. Zuiker did his one-man show, flying around the room, making noises, pulling fake guns. It was wildly entertaining. McPherson thought he was fantastic—and that his idea sounded even better. Here was a show that could tell separate stories every week, meaning it might repeat well, like NBC's *Law & Order*. McPherson committed Touchstone to producing *CSI* and set up a meeting for Bruckheimer and Zuiker with ABC, the studio's sister company.

As famous as Jerry Bruckheimer was for his action films, he had done no television and he was coming into ABC accompanied by a writer without a single television credit. Still, Zuiker wove his pitch magic for a group of executives from the ABC drama department, jumping around the room, leaping on furniture, and bringing his characters to vivid life.

ABC passed.

No real explanation was given. Nobody said Zuiker came on too strongly, or the idea seemed too formulaic, or too male, or too much like something else they had in development. McPherson concluded that they simply didn't get it. They passed.

Zuiker was crushed; more than that, he was embarrassed—and angry. Nobody had ever rejected a pitch from him before, and this one had already engaged a great filmmaker like Jerry Bruckheimer. In reaction, Zuiker decided to start up his own production entity, and he had a name for it: "Dare to Pass." If anyone asked about the name, Zuiker explained, he would always point to his *CSI* experience. "Dare to pass on me and this is going to show up somewhere," he said.

Thanks to Jonathan Littman's aggressive wooing of Nina Tassler, *CSI* now had a chance to show up on CBS.

• • •

Tassler got the first draft of *CSI* in early December—later than she or the network wanted. As she read it, she was struck by its fascinating elements and Zuiker's arresting writing. But she struggled to get through the scientific detail. She still loved the idea, but it was going to need rewrites, and that meant more time. After a third draft, she deemed it ready and sent it up to Moonves. Les could tell now that this was far more than Billy Petersen taking fingerprints, but he was not immediately sold. He could not quite see the show in the draft. He tabled a decision on whether to go to pilot.

Tassler wasn't discouraged; this was often Moonves's process.

But time again was pressing. At the next staff meeting, Moonves grilled Tassler about how strongly she was backing the show; where she saw it fitting on the schedule; did she believe it had legs? He also wanted to be assured that someone experienced would be hired as a showrunner if *CSI* got past the pilot stage.

Bruckheimer was another factor. He made successful but expensive films; how did that translate to television? It was certainly a big positive that Petersen had attached himself to the script, but Moonves had questions about the "snap zooms" of bullets entering bodies. What was that going to look like on screen?

After the meeting, Tassler made a cover-all-bases insurance move. In her pile of scripts that Moonves had already approved to go to pilot was a glossy new legal drama called *Hopewell*. It was created by an outstanding talent, René Balcer, who had written numerous great episodes of *Law & Order*. And it had a strong male lead, the lawyer in the center of the piece. Tassler sent the script off to Petersen, to make sure, as she put it, "that there was no buyer's remorse."

Petersen had not the slightest doubt. He read *Hopewell* and then faxed off a letter to Moonves to repeat in strong terms how passionate he was about *CSI*. This was the show he wanted to start his career in television. He would not choose another.

Moonves got the letter and called in Tassler. He told her that he was impressed with Petersen's passion for the show; and if he picked it up, would Tassler promise to stop talking about her damned *Quincy* all the time? She agreed, and Les gave the go-ahead to shoot a pilot of *CSI* as the very last project picked up that development season.

Tassler was thrilled. But they were already deep into February and dangerously close to not being able to deliver a pilot in time for consideration on the fall schedule. It was going to be a race against the clock, and Tassler could hear the ticking in her head.

•   •   •

Every decision on *CSI* was made breathlessly. Thankfully, the star was secured and Marg Helgenberger—another Moonves suggestion—slid easily into the costar role. Moonves, involved as always with virtually every important decision on every single show, was less happy with another bit of casting, a young actress named Chandra West. "She looks a little too beautiful," he said. "What's she doing here?"

Moonves was more concerned about finding the right director. Given Bruckheimer's movie connections, the expectations were high. Bruckheimer first approached Tony Scott. who had directed numerous films for Bruckheimer, including *Crimson Tide*. Scott was interested, but he had committed to shooting a commercial. The negotiations went on for weeks. All the while, Tassler was watching the clock in growing panic. Soon enough, the panic was real; Scott fell through.

In desperation, Bruckheimer suggested a director named Danny Cannon. All Cannon had done of note was the film *I Know What You Did Last Summer 2,* not a credit likely to inspire Leslie Moonves. And Les was not impressed. But Bruckheimer, who had a reputation for identifying emerging directing talent, argued that Cannon had a sense of style and shot great film. It was so late, Tassler told Moonves they simply had to start or lose the project. Les agreed to let Cannon have the job.

Shortly after shooting began, Moonves was back with another question: Where was the showrunner? Surely no one was putting a neophyte like Anthony Zuiker in charge. Les always wanted an adult in charge, or else his network's dollars were likely going through the shredder.

Tassler reached out to Carol Mendelsohn, a producer who had spent years working on *Melrose Place*. The content of the new show could hardly have been more different, but Tassler didn't care. Mendelsohn knew how to run a show.

When a rough cut was assembled, Tassler and the show's producers met in Bruckheimer's office to screen it. Tassler was disappointed. The story still remained confusingly dense, and just a bit too grisly for her taste. The opening scene, in which Grissom minutely examines the maggots on a corpse's body to determine how long he's been dead, was especially strong stuff. Tassler suggested some edits, which Bruckheimer promised to make.

When Touchstone tested the pilot, the results were promising, though they also included comments about how graphic some scenes were. Tassler liked the new edit, but it didn't matter much. She had no time left. She had to screen the pilot for Leslie now or there would be no time left to make changes if he insisted on them. It was so late, already into April, that Moonves had no openings left on his overpacked schedule for a regular screening.

Tassler, in her early forties, an attractive, petite woman with deep stores of energy and a buoyant, outgoing disposition, tended to be obsessive about screening her pilots at optimum times. She wanted to make sure the hour was ideal, everyone in the room was relaxed, the coffee was freshly brewed. But, like everything else with *CSI*, there simply was no time left to wait for a Kodak moment. Tassler was forced to squeeze in the screening of *CSI* during Moonves's lunch hour.

They ordered in deli. A small group of executives grabbed sandwiches, pickles, and coleslaw and settled themselves into Moonves's huge corner office. Tassler made everyone as comfortable as she could, but she still didn't like the setup. Lunch was distracting; Les's office was distracting. But there was nothing more she could do. She popped in the tape.

The opening scene of the pilot was an impressive aerial shot of Las Vegas by night, which cut to a hand holding a gun and loading bullets in the chambers. The scene intercut shots of the Vegas strip. Then a taped voice began to read what sounded like a suicide note ending with, "I love you, Mom," followed by a gunshot.

So far so good, as far as Tassler was concerned. Moonves seemed engrossed.

The scene shifted to the outside of a suburban home and a police SUV pulling up. A plainclothes detective, perhaps speaking for the expectations of the uninformed in the audience, piped up, "Here comes the nerd squad." And there was William Petersen as Gil Grissom, making his way into the house. He and his partner located the corpse in the bathtub, and Grissom, clinically opening a metal suitcase and putting on glasses, noticed a key bit of evidence: maggots, fat, disgusting maggots, crawling on the body.

At the precise moment the insects appeared on screen, Tassler heard the crunch of Leslie Moonves's teeth biting into a forkful of coleslaw. *Oh, my God,* she thought. *This is a disaster.* The next sounds she heard were audible "ughs" and "oofs" coming from Moonves's direction.

Afterward, Moonves was stoic, not mentioning the maggots right away. He called it an interesting piece, but he had some notes, beginning with what he said was "the change we have to make at the head of the picture." That's where the maggots were. He also found the storytelling unclear.

When Moonves spoke to Steve McPherson a short time later about where the show stood, he told him the show was just too graphic. "You guys have to dig deep and redo this thing," Moonves said.

Tassler knew what all this meant. Time was almost up. The last changes were going to be so late, the pilot might not even be finished in time to be screened in New York prior to setting of the schedule. Whatever happened with *CSI,* Nina Tassler knew it was surely going to come down to the very last minute.

· · ·

By the time the CBS crew arrived in New York in May 2000, they had a pretty good idea of what the big shows on their coming schedule were going to be: a comedy called *Bette,* starring Bette Midler, and an ambitious remaking of the classic television drama *The Fugitive,* being produced by Arnold Kopelson, who had made the hit movie remake starring Harrison Ford. (Ford wasn't going to be in the series, of course—Tim Daly, late of the NBC comedy *Wings,* was taking the role.)

But Moonves never officially set the CBS schedule until the last minute. He wanted to take full advantage of CBS's positioning in upfront week, after both NBC and ABC had played their cards. Les could then make adjustments if need be. No show was absolutely guaranteed a spot on the schedule until the night before Les's appearance at Carnegie Hall.

On the tentative schedules that Moonves had kicked around with his aides before they left Los Angeles that weekend, *CSI* was nowhere to be found. As Tassler had predicted, the show arrived too late to be screened with the other CBS pilots in New York. It had only been seen at a last-minute screening on Friday. Those who did get the chance to see the reedited *CSI*—which to Moonves's specifications now included a plotline killing off the character played by Chandra West—had decided it was vastly improved and was now, in Tassler's words, "a schedulable show."

*CSI* had also scored well in the hurried testing CBS's research department had put togther. Still, as the CBS entertainment team flew to New York, *CSI* did not seem to be a front-runner for the schedule, or even much of a blip on the scheduling radar. The door of opportunity was barely open.

On Monday evening, Moonves met with his top executive staff in a big conference room at the CBS "Black Rock" headquarters on Sixth Avenue. They all knew NBC's official schedule at this point. CBS could countermove with impunity. The plan that evening was to move *JAG*, a military drama that had been playing on Friday nights, over to Tuesday. That freed up Friday at 8 for CBS's big play, *The Fugitive*. Three other new dramas were on the scheduling board at that point. *CSI* was not one of them.

Amid all the CBS executives in the room that night was an interloper. Phil Rosenthal, the executive producer of CBS's big comedy hit *Everybody Loves Raymond*, had taken up his by-now customary place among the group doing the last-minute scheduling analysis.

Rosenthal was there in a special capacity: Leslie's gag man. A former standup, Phil knew how to manufacture jokes for any occasion; he knew how to get an extra laugh by making a joke a "leaner," which he defined as "an old Jewish bah-*bum*-bump joke." From the very first year *Raymond* was on the schedule, which coincided with Moonves's first year at CBS, Les had enjoyed Rosenthal's keen dissection of the fundamentals of humor. He invited Phil to sit in on the planning for his upfront speech that year, and toss him a few lines where he thought appropriate.

Rosenthal's lines hit so big with the crowd at Carnegie Hall that Les decided on the spot that he wanted Phil around every year to add a few bah-*bum*-bumps to his speech. Rosenthal loved doing it, not just because he was a natural tummler at heart, but also because he had come to regard Moonves so highly. Les had given *Raymond* a big chance in its first year, moving it to Monday nights behind the only comedy working on CBS at the time, *Cosby*. That move, risky at the time, had made Phil Rosenthal a hugely wealthy man, and he would always be grateful to Moonves for that. But he also liked Les, and had become so close to him that he thought of Les as a kind of a professional father (though they were only about a decade apart in age). So his annual jaunt to New York to help pump up Les's speech became a kind of command performance.

The CBS staff was accustomed to having Rosenthal around. "He was a big player on the team every year," said Chris Ender. Rosenthal loved being with the gang who sat together checking out what NBC and ABC had said during their upfronts on Monday and Tuesday and deciding how hard to come back at them.

Some of Les's other "guys" accepted Rosenthal into Les's inner circle at the upfront. His position became stronger than ever one year when Les asked Phil to check out the clips of the new series that were going to be used in the presentation—cut-downs, as they were known.

At first, the idea was to get the opinion of someone who had not seen the actual shows about whether the chosen clips were too long. That evolved into questions about whether the clips worked in selling the idea of the show. Finally, Rosenthal started being asked what he thought of the actual shows.

Not everyone was comfortable with this arrangement. Rosenthal had no stake in what got on the air or not—his show was already on, and was a hit. Who was he to offer an opinion on somebody else's show, an opinion that could potentially change some writer's or star's life?

That Monday in 2000, Rosenthal was still hanging around in case Les wanted him to juice up his presentation. It was getting late, and Phil complained to one executive that he was getting hungry. Rosenthal was so into food that he displayed a different meal on camera at the end of every episode of *Raymond*—and here he was in New York, ready to go to a great restaurant, and Les wouldn't let him get the hell out of there.

Moonves, apparently still unsettled by something about the schedule, looked around for Rosenthal. "Hey, Phil, I want to show you this thing," he said. The whole room came to attention. All eyes went to Rosenthal.

Moonves told Rosenthal he wanted him to see the cut-down of the show CBS had slotted for Fridays at 9, something called *Homewood P.I.*

Moonves started up the cassette. The premise of *Homewood P.I.* was apparent within a minute: a fortyish former New York cop had retired to the suburbs with his lovely family, only to be pressed into solving local crimes with the help of his three teenage children. It was a crime show trying to be a comedy. The star was a very familiar television face, Tony Danza. In one scene, Danza interrupted the rock-music cacophony of his teenage son's garage band, grabbed the microphone, and walked down his driveway singing an ersatz-Sinatra rendition of "The Summer Wind."

When the tape ended, Moonves asked Rosenthal: "Okay, Phil, what do you think?"

Rosenthal hesitated for a half second. Then he said: "Isn't it enough with this guy, already?" The comment had the rhythm of a punch line. But Rosenthal got no laughs from this room.

"Hey, this is not appropriate," one executive said. Several others, including some who clearly had a vested interest in the Danza show, spoke up saying how upset they were by this uncalled-for comment.

Moonves quieted the room. "I asked him," he said. He turned to David Poltrack, the network's longtime research guru. "How did it test?" he asked.

Poltrack consulted his sheaf of data. "Tested very well." Les nodded, taking the information in without comment.

One of Les's "guys," observing Moonves, guessed that the boss had Carnegie Hall on his mind, questioning how the audience would respond to the Danza clips. If they had the same reaction as Rosenthal, would that undercut CBS's presentation? Would CBS get laughs it didn't intend?

Murmured criticism of Rosenthal's presumptuousness still filled the room. Moonves shushed them all. Then he started to look around on the conference table and the floor, where cassettes of edited cut-downs were stacked up. "Where is it?" Moonves said to no one in particular. "Where is that other thing that I liked?"

Someone reminded Les that the schedule had been all but settled. He waved the comment off, finally locating the cassette he wanted in the pile at his feet. Turning back to Rosenthal, Moonves said, "Just look at this," and he slotted the tape into the machine.

A new cut-down appeared, all fast movement and dark colors and kicky effects. "Now, this I would watch," Phil Rosenthal said as the scenes from *CSI* flashed by. "This is cool."

More muttered protests circled the room. At least one other executive agreed completely with what he had heard Rosenthal say. He couldn't speak up, however, because he feared the supporters of *Homewood P.I.* were ready to turn on anyone critical of their show—and besides, it still was not clear what the boss thought.

Moonves turned to Poltrack again. "How did this one test?" he asked him. Poltrack went back to his data. "Really good, a little less than Danza." Poltrack did not want to say too much, because he had already indicated at some earlier meetings that he liked *CSI*—and he knew, as did others in the room, that Moonves sometimes suspected Poltrack had an agenda, based purely on research.

Moonves lifted his hands to his face, less a nervous gesture than an indication that he was trying to make up his mind. Many of those in the room had seen Moonves roll things around this way, but when they looked over at Rosenthal, they saw something different. He was no longer hungry or impatient; he was just plain angry.

"You just told me you like this *CSI* show," Rosenthal started yelling. "Here's a thing you're telling me you like. Don't you have the right to put on one that you just like?"

Moonves, who never believed in snap decisions about anything, and certainly not the schedule, just nodded and told Rosenthal, "I hear you. I hear you. I've got a decision to make."

As Rosenthal left for his long-delayed dinner, one of CBS's inner-circle executives could not believe what had just happened: An outsider had interfered—at Les's request—with CBS's sacred scheduling ritual, and Moonves had clearly given him as much say, more really, at that moment, as any of his actual staff members. The executive did not blame Moonves, who was simply using all available resources before making his decision, but the fact that the process had come down to this astounded him.

The next day when the group showed up for the final session, just prior to their official announcement of the new fall schedule, they saw *CSI* on the board for the first time. There it was, on Friday night at 9, in place of *Homewood P.I.* An L.A. executive, who believed Moonves had made the right move, thought: *Maybe it was enough with that guy already.*

• • •

Everyone involved with *CSI* had reason to be elated, but the tale took a new twist only two months later. CBS got word that its 50/50 business partner on *CSI* wanted to pull its investment out of the show. The partner was the Touchstone studio, owned by the Walt Disney Company, which also owned ABC. Moonves immediately smelled a rat. He was convinced that the Disney management could not countenance cofinancing a show that might turn out to be a hit on CBS.

Nor was he wrong. Shortly after the start of production, Steve McPherson at Touchstone started to hear grumblings about the show from his Disney superiors. The message, McPherson said, was: "Oh, wait a second. That's going to cost a lot; and it's on CBS—not ABC."

McPherson exploded. Here he was heading a studio allegedly trying to do business all over town and his bosses were pulling the plug on a show in production just because it was going to be on a network they didn't own. What better way to vitiate the production company and turn it into a joke all over Hollywood? Moonves wasted no time driving home the point, telling the *Wall Street Journal,* "Any network that expects to get a show from that company is out of their minds."

McPherson, believing he was putting his career on the line, screamed loud and long—and futilely. Disney pulled its money out of the series.

That left CBS Productions holding the bag for all the show's costs. Every network series is produced at a deficit—usually between $300,000 and $800,000 an episode—in the hope that it will become a hit and throw off hundreds of millions in syndication. But assuming all the costs means accepting all the risk of loss if the show fails, and most series do. That's why networks tended to take only half interests in shows. They would happily split half of the rare huge payday from a hit in exchange for half the loss on all the flops.

Tassler feared that Touchstone dropping out meant CBS might pull the plug on *CSI.* She heard ominous rumblings of panic. The network scrambled to find another backer. The show was offered to production entities all over Hollywood. Even NBC Productions was given a shot at it. They all took a look at the pilot. No one bit. The odds that this expensive-looking drama would ever return a profit sitting on Friday nights at 9 on the gray-haired CBS network seemed as forbidding to most business affairs executives at other studios as a half-lame long shot at the Irish Derby. Not even Paramount Television, a sister division to CBS thanks to the network's acquisition by Viacom, would consider helping CBS out on this one.

Moonves realized he had to look beyond Hollywood—way beyond, as it happened. He decided to call Peter Sussman, the chief executive at a Canadian production company called Alliance Atlantis. The company had coproduced a successful miniseries version of *Joan of Arc* with CBS the previous year. Moonves pitched Sussman on the value of becoming a partner in a weekly series.

His timing, as it often was, was perfect. Sussman had been pondering how to get his company into the series business, and here was an invitation to join a show that already had a spot on a network schedule. Sussman watched the pilot. He was impressed. He saw "a good show, well made." To Sussman, what was appealing about *CSI* was not really the innovations of the "snap-zoom" scenes. "We liked it because it was a core genre," Sussman said. "It was a murder mystery."

Moonves's call offering a half stake in *CSI* turned out to be the most financially significant conversation Peter Sussman would ever have in his life.

● ● ●

In the fall of 2000, NBC's coverage of the summer Olympics from Sydney, Australia, delayed the start of premiere week for every network. Most of the heavily promoted new shows did not get on the air until the first week of October.

CBS made no secret of the shows it expected to break out. During that long buildup to the start of the season, CBS pounded at viewers with promotional messages on behalf of *Bette* and *The Fugitive*. The latter was launching on October 6. Numerous articles in the press covered the network's effort to revive this television classic, but reviews for the new version were mostly mixed.

In oh-by-the-way addenda to the *Fugitive* coverage were comments about the other new show CBS was launching the same night, *CSI*. They were mostly along the lines of "yet another crime series." Some critics respectfully acknowledged the show's interesting take on crime solving, but expectations were clearly low. Maybe, if a lot of people watched *The Fugitive* at 8, enough of them would stick around at 9 for this other crime show to make it viable.

As they always did with premieres, CBS executives woke up early the following morning—even though it was a Saturday—to get the first word of the ratings. Kelly Kahl got up at six and made a call to a CBS ratings hot line. He heard the number for *The Fugitive* and it sounded good, if not quite great. Probably would translate to about 13 million viewers. Not bad at all. And oh yeah, what about *CSI*?

When he heard the numbers, Kahl froze in astonishment. This

was going to translate to more than 17 million viewers. *CSI* had beaten *The Fugitive* in its first week on the air? With virtually no promotion?

Kahl dialed Chris Ender, who he knew would already be up and checking the numbers. When Ender answered, the first words out of Kahl's mouth were "Holy fucking shit!"

Steve McPherson got up a little later. Unlike the CBS staff, he did not have much interest in the numbers for *The Fugitive*. But having lost *CSI* to Disney's narrow-minded competitiveness, he was curious about how the show had fared. When McPherson read the ratings on his computer, the list only gave the totals by network and hour, not by program. As he looked at how CBS's numbers grew from the 8 o'clock hour through the 9 o'clock hour, McPherson concluded that he had missed something. He dialed Jonathan Littman at home.

"What happened, Jonathan?" McPherson asked. "CBS wound up doing a two-hour premiere of *The Fugitive*? I thought you guys were going to be on last night."

"We were on," Littman said. "Those aren't numbers for *The Fugitive* from 9 to 10. Those are *our* numbers."

"Oh my God," McPherson said. "This is amazing."

• • •

By the end of November, *CSI* was the undisputed hit of the new season. It was piling up Friday-night ratings that no network had seen in years: 20 million, 21 million viewers. Even more impressive, it was pulling in more young adult viewers than any other show on the network.

Kelly Kahl had noticed. The numbers he was seeing from *CSI* had only one comparison among recent CBS programs: *Survivor*. And what about his go-for-broke plan about attacking NBC on Thursday night with *Survivor*? It was still swirling around in Leslie's brain.

One of the key objections, Kahl knew, to challenging NBC's Thursday stronghold with *Survivor II* was that there was no strong follow-up show to take advantage of its huge audience. Up until now, what could CBS place behind *Survivor*? Episodes of *Diagnosis: Murder* with its audience of refugees from Lawrence Welk?

Now there was this completely unexpected gift from the ratings gods. Could CBS risk undoing the strength it was building on Friday night to put its two new high cards back-to-back on Thursday?

Kahl wanted the answer to be yes, but he needed some backup. He approached David Poltrack. Could Poltrack do a little of his mumbo-jumbo research and predict what kind of number *CSI* might do if the network moved it to Thursday behind *Survivor*?

No one at CBS was ever quite sure how David Poltrack ran his special research operation in Las Vegas, but Poltrack, perhaps the most aptly named executive in television history, was always generating fascinating, if occasionally dense, studies of the television audience. Here he took a special interest because of his early support for *CSI*. In short order, he had some statistics for Kahl to look at.

"I think we can do a 14 share in the 18-to-49 audience with *CSI* on Thursday," Poltrack told Kahl.

"David, you're crazy," Kahl said.

But any number close to that was worth chasing. Kahl believed he had the second piece he needed to sell his high-risk, high-reward plan to Moonves, a plan finally to mount a Thursday-night attack on Fortress NBC.

≥ CHAPTER SEVEN ≤

# SUPERSIZE ME

Jeff Zucker had not planned on his first formal encounter with the NBC entertainment staff in Burbank to be a crisis meeting. But it couldn't be helped. Les Moonves had already announced his intention to come after NBC on Thursday nights with the double-pronged assault of *Survivor* and *CSI*, and Zucker knew he could not simply sit there and take it. NBC had to have a response—though what that response might be, he had no clue.

As he walked into the big conference room down the hall from his new office, prepared to lead his first 9:30 A.M. staff meeting, Zucker was hoping someone on the staff might have a bright idea. He could only wonder: *What have I gotten myself into?*

The staff settled into their seats, all eyes on the new guy. This was Zucker's show. Scott Sassa, still the president of NBC West Coast, and Zucker's boss, was not in the room.

After he greeted everyone, Zucker got right to the point. NBC's Thursday was under attack, and it was serious. Zucker knew as well as anyone the power of *Survivor*. He had documented its stunning cultural impact the previous summer every week on *Today*. Now CBS was relaunching the show in the strongest possible spot, immediately after the Super Bowl. Once the second edition of *Survivor* was up and running on Thursdays, in the first week of February, the vote-out half hour especially was sure to be a super-magnet for viewers. And NBC was hardly prepared to defend itself. The network had once again failed to insert a potent—or even viable—comedy in the half-hour slot behind *Friends*.

Up on the big scheduling board at the front of the room, everyone could see the name of the show still residing there: *The Weber Show* (originally called *Cursed*). Nobody believed that misbegotten comedy, starring the barely known Steven Weber, was going to cut it against this kind of competition. If they couldn't come up with something to help out *Friends*, NBC was going to get steamrolled from 8:30 to 9. That would damage *Will & Grace* at 9. In the ultimate nightmare, NBC could lose Thursday night to CBS.

"We can't just sit by," Zucker told his troops. "We can't just stand pat. We gotta fight back."

The list of comedies available as backup entries impressed no one. If Garth Ancier had had a better comedy in development, surely he would have used it instead of *Cursed*. Had *Michael Richards* shown any sign of life on Tuesday, it might have been an alternative to move to Thursday, but that show had flopped ignominiously in a matter of weeks. NBC still had one other power-hitting comedy, *Frasier*, but that was holding up Tuesday night all by itself. Saving Thursday at the expense of getting wiped out on Tuesday made no sense to anybody.

The plain truth was that Zucker, now thirty-five, had arrived in Burbank at a moment of high anxiety. NBC's fall season had been nothing short of a disaster. When added to previous years of indifferent to pathetic program development, Zucker was left holding on to a few vines with his hind end dangling over a deep ravine. How many years were left of *Friends* and *Frasier* anyway? The studio owners of those shows were already stepping on NBC's neck with their license-fee costs. If something else even close to their level of appeal were in the pipeline, NBC might have been able to play chicken with the studios over those fees. But the whole industry knew NBC was caught with its programming pants down. It was pay up or be exposed in public.

For years NBC had been getting by on Thursday with two strong comedies, *Friends* and *Will & Grace*, one just-acceptable comedy, *Just Shoot Me*, at 9:30, and the still invincible (but unconscionably expensive) *ER* at 10. That was enough to keep those advertising premiums—the NBC version of crack—piling up. It was, that is, as long as the competition kept rolling over like submissive puppies. Suddenly, CBS didn't have its paws in the air anymore; it was up and growling. NBC had shrugged off years of woeful comedy development because it still ruled Thursday with the good shows it had left. Now the day of reckoning was at hand.

Zucker looked at the scheduling board and threw out an idea. "Why don't we just make our good shows longer?"

From the looks of incredulity that greeted him around the conference table, Zucker could tell that he had just uttered something so naive, so totally out of it, that he should be shamefaced. But that wasn't in his nature. He pushed on.

"I don't see why we can't expand some things. Why don't we just do a big McDonald's-type thing and supersize it?"

Zucker was spitballing at this point, but as the words came out, he couldn't imagine what might be wrong with the idea. Except, of course, that he could tell from the averted eyes and deathly silence all around him that most of these people listening to him were drawing a quick conclusion that this new guy was either stupid or delusional, and the network was in way bigger trouble than anyone had dreamed possible.

"Look, I mean, I love *Friends*, you know?" Zucker continued. "I can't get enough of *Friends*. So why wouldn't I want to watch ten or fifteen minutes more of it?"

Nobody was going to contradict the new boss overtly. But no one on the staff thought this half-baked caprice made the least bit of sense. As they filed out of the room, one executive expressed the prevailing opinion: "The guy is off his rocker."

More than anything else, that initial meeting stirred up questions about Zucker's complete lack of Hollywood experience. Here he was coming from that morning show in New York, where obviously he could move pieces around any way he wanted. But this was Hollywood, and television shows came packaged as half hours or hours. "Morning Boy," as some took to calling him, clearly did not get it.

Zucker blithely went on pursuing his idea. If he was going to pull this off, *Friends* was the key, so his first approach had to be to Warner Brothers, where the hit comedy was housed. Zucker put in a call to Peter Roth, chief executive at the Warner studio—Moonves's old job.

Zucker ran the concept past Roth, happy that he was not doing it in person since he was certain Roth's expression would have signaled that he, too, thought this new guy was nuts. But Roth always had a taste for bold strokes, and he did not dismiss Zucker out of hand. He told him, "If you really want to try this, the only way it's going to happen is, you gotta come over here and talk to the creators and the cast."

So in his first week in Hollywood, Jeff Zucker journeyed to the set of *Friends* to meet the most recognized stars in television: Jennifer Aniston, Courteney Cox, Lisa Kudrow, Matthew Perry, David Schwimmer, Matt LeBlanc. The creators, Marta Kauffman, David Crane, and Kevin Bright, still with the series since their first deal with Moonves, joined them. Sassa and Roth accompanied Zucker. But this was Zucker's white elephant; he was going to have to sell it all by himself.

Zucker's pitch was part appeal and part pep talk. He made it clear that NBC needed to stand up to CBS. They had to fight back with their best weapons. It was important for him personally, yes, but also for them, the creators and cast of television's biggest show, not to allow this upstart to come in and take over their home, Thursday night.

Was it such a big deal? Zucker wanted to know. Didn't every taping run long and need to be trimmed? "Is it really any extra work?" Zucker asked. "And if it is, wouldn't it be minimal?" There were going to be financial considerations, of course, but that wasn't what this was about. This was about being competitors. He appealed to the show's pride: *Friends* was the top dog in TV. Would they take this challenge lying down?

Zucker was new in Hollywood, but here he was on familiar ground. What was required here was a fierce competitveness and some clever manipulation of existing assets—more or less what he had been doing for years running *Today*. There he frequently had had to play with the elements to wring out their maximum value. "Supersizing" was essentially more of the same.

While he waited to hear if the *Friends* team would sign on, Zucker approached *Will & Grace,* a much easier task because NBC owned the show through its in-house studio, NBC Productions. The top executive at the studio, Ted Harbert, ex–head programmer at ABC and a longtime Hollywood insider, had reservations. His first reaction was simply "No, we can't do that, there would be issues with the guilds"—meaning the actors, writers, and directors unions. Zucker argued that could be worked out. *Will & Grace* was going to supersize if NBC needed it to.

Zucker was not much worried about the third show, *Just Shoot Me,* figuring everyone involved was thrilled just to be on the air, and if NBC decided it needed some extra-long episodes from that series, they would go along happily. Everything hinged on those power players from *Friends,* because they still ruled Thursday night.

A short time later, Zucker got some good news. The *Friends* group was up for the game: They agreed to give it a go, at least for two weeks.

Zucker looked around for other potential weapons. He was well aware that *Saturday Night Live* was having one of its periodic break-out seasons, largely because of Tina Fey and Jimmy Fallon, the new team on the "Weekend Update" segment, and the hilariously versatile Will Ferrell.

Lorne Michaels, the executive producer of *SNL,* was one of Zucker's best friends at 30 Rock in New York. When Zucker had been considering taking the Burbank job, Michaels had been one of the people who counseled him. Now Zucker had a proposal for Michaels: If *Friends* could play at 40 minutes for a couple of weeks in the February sweep to blunt the launch of *Survivor,* could Lorne back that up by supplying 20 minutes of original *SNL* material—a sketch with Ferrell and a "Weekend Update" segment with Fey and Fallon—so NBC could avoid using *The Weber Show* altogether?

Michaels never liked to overexpose his show in prime time, but, counterculture veteran that he surely was, he was also an NBC loyalist at heart. Michaels agreed to give it a two-week shot.

Zucker had his "Supersize Thursday" for at least the first two weeks of the face-off against *Survivor.* By the time NBC announced the move on January 16, Zucker had gotten *Friends* to go for all four sweep episodes at 40 minutes. He had only two *SNL* segments to fill out that 8-to-9 hour. A week later he solved that problem, adding a 20-minute special of *Friends* outtakes, hosted by Conan O'Brien, in the third week, and a simple 40/40/40 gimmick the final week of the sweep, with each of *Friends, Will & Grace,* and *Just Shoot Me* running an extra 10 minutes.

Zucker announced the changes as an effort to try to survive. But he clearly relished the buzz that his "supersize" gambit was creating.

"Why should we roll over?" Zucker said. "I still expect *Survivor* to do boffo in the ratings, but at least we're trying to do something different."

NBC had its matchless promo department, headed by John Miller and Vince Manze, pump up the volume on behalf of "Supersized Thursday." The performance more than justified the hype. NBC held its own against the assault of *Survivor II* on opening night, with *Friends* trailing the nationwide phenomenon by only a few million viewers and just one rating point in the prized 18-to-49 audience. *CSI* was potent, but the *SNL* special held up competitively as well. And *ER* came on strong enough at 10 for NBC to still win the night with something to spare.

As the month went on, it became clearer that Zucker's semi-baked gimmick had been a brilliant counterstroke for NBC (and something of a precedent for network television, which would see virtually every hit show "supersized" in years to come). Thursday night was safe—for now. But, as with many of the moves Zucker made in Hollywood, this one would eventually be criticized as a fan dance rather than real forward progress in developing a new generation of hits.

On the day he publicly christened the move as "supersizing," Zucker added a comment that revealed what the move—and he himself—was all about: "These are fun games to play," he said.

·  ·  ·

Even before he loved the competition, Jeff Zucker loved the heat. Born on Homestead Air Force Base near Miami (his father was a doctor in the Air Force), Zucker grew up in the sun.

Disdaining team sports, both because of his size (he was almost always the shortest kid in his class) and because he liked being responsible for his own individual performance, Zucker played tennis year-round. School was no problem at all. Zucker could get an A falling out of bed. But he had no interest in following his dad and being a doctor. His passion was journalism. He edited the paper in junior high and three years in high school, where he was also class president sophomore, junior, and senior years.

He was intrigued by Miami's local television news, fascinated by the precise timing of the anchor's lead-in to the taped report that followed. Then there were the Dolphins. Zucker started attending every home game in 1972, when the Dolphins recorded an undefeated season. Zucker was seven; he thought his home team simply never lost.

College was a foregone conclusion: Harvard. So was his first stop on campus: *The Crimson*. He gravitated to sports, thus beginning the pattern of his life: first sports, then news. His sports editor was a senior named Michael Bass—and a connection was established.

Zucker moved up to sports editor himself in his sophomore year, setting him up for what only Harvard could call a newspaper editor: "president" of *The Crimson*. Sports editors did not usually get that position. Zucker, of course, did. He was thrown into the natural rivalry between *The Crimson* and *The Harvard Lampoon*. The *Lam-*

*poon* liked to mess with the uptight *Crimson* guys, and that year they managed to steal the president's chair (Zucker's, that is) right out of The Sanctum (as only Harvard could label the upstairs of *The Crimson*'s offices).

Zucker, playing into the hands of his tormentors, tried to press charges. That resulted in his first meeting with the *Lampoon* editor, a gangly wiseass redhead named Conan O'Brien, who was being led away in handcuffs the first time Zucker ever laid eyes on him. "I was mostly at *The Crimson* and he was mostly at *The Lampoon*," Zucker said. "So he had to be an asshole."

Senior year the Harvard thing to do was to apply to law school. Zucker dutifully did, getting accepted everywhere he applied—Columbia, NYU, Virginia—except Harvard, the only place he really wanted to go. At the time he was shocked to his toes, but later he called it the biggest break of his life. Zucker had kept in touch with Michael Bass, who, after his own graduation, had landed one of the all-time great television entry jobs. He was hired in 1984 to be the researcher for ABC's coverage of the summer Olympics in Los Angeles. It was a job with a storied history, because many of those who held it, including Dick Ebersol of NBC, went on to significant careers in television. Bass wangled a spot for Zucker that summer in the research room.

NBC had won the rights to the 1988 games in Seoul, and the production team needed a bright kid to fill the role of researcher for that Olympiad. Zucker's name came up. He took the job on his graduation day from Harvard in 1986.

Zucker spent the next two years traveling, interviewing every significant coach and athlete in the world. By the time the games started, he knew more about the Olympics than anyone else in Seoul. His writing impressed the producers, who assigned him to be the writer for the network's late-night coverage, anchored by Bob Costas.

As he had throughout his life, Zucker shone under pressure. He hit it off so well with Costas that he picked up the distinctive rhythm of Costas's speech. Zucker also worked with a number of other on-air NBC performers, including Maria Shriver and Jane Pauley.

Back in New York, Costas, who emerged from Seoul with his star greatly enhanced, asked to see Zucker. He handed him a bonus check out of his own pocket. Costas also offered him a job on NBC's Sunday NFL pregame show. Zucker resisted, because it was half a day's work on only sixteen Sundays.

Then Jane Pauley contacted him. She, too, had been impressed with his work in Seoul. When he told her he was unsure of his next step, she introduced him to the executive producer of her show, *Today*, a guy named Marty Ryan. All Ryan had to offer was a fifty-two-week job as a vacation relief writer—essentially a full-time fill-in. Ryan had no expectations the kid would last beyond that.

Zucker showed up at *Today* in January 1989, totally unaware that the place was about to implode. He had been there only three weeks when news that Bryant Gumbel had written a scathing memo about the deficiencies of the staff, including Marty Ryan, and especially the weathercaster Willard Scott, leaked to the press. The ensuing furor engulfed the show. Zucker, twenty-three, wondered if the place was always this insane.

Over the next several months, *Today* became the nation's leading gossip story, with Marty Ryan forced out, then Jane Pauley apparently pushed aside for a younger woman, Deborah Norville. Every move NBC made was an exploding cigar.

Zucker simply threw himself into the work. He was young and single, with no social life, so he had no problem working all night. News kept breaking—Manuel Noriega in Panama, the fall of the Berlin Wall, Boris Yeltsin standing down tanks in Moscow. Zucker was around at night to set up the next day's coverage. He had already eased his way into a permanent, quasi-producing job. Now he was literally booking guests and planning segments of the show, all on an unofficial basis.

The impressive work he was doing lifted his profile inside the show. When NBC, trying to find a way through the chaos, decided to create an opportunity for a promising young woman reporter, naming her *Today*'s national correspondent, Zucker became the logical choice to be her personal producer. He attached himself to Katie Couric.

As he had with Costas and Pauley, Zucker immediately impressed Couric—helping her sound smart and look good on the air. Then Zucker got a feeler from one of his other contacts from the Seoul days. Maria Shriver was about to start a prime-time magazine show called *Yesterday, Today, and Tomorrow*. Shriver steered Zucker into an interview with the NBC executive in charge, Sid Fetters. After the interview, Fetters told Shriver he wouldn't hire Zucker because he was too young.

That meant Zucker was still working with Couric when she was called in from the road to begin a trial run as a host on *Today*. It was 1991, and Zucker got a fancy new title: supervising producer. He was twenty-five.

Tom Capra, a longtime local news executive (and son of the famed film director Frank), had just taken over as executive producer. In the control room each morning, Zucker could not help but notice the strange lack of communication between Capra and the show's hosts. When the hosts would be looking for direction from the producer, Capra sat mute. The director, Bucky Gunts, began looking for somebody to take charge. Nothing was happening. Zucker recognized a vacuum when he saw one, as well as an opportunity. He started to speak up, jumping in with the proper instructions, like: "We'll go to Bryant after the break, and then Katie will intro the segment on the Pentagon." Gunts began taking his lead from Zucker.

A weird kind of kabuki drama invaded the *Today* control room: Capra sat in the executive producer's chair but said almost nothing during the telecasts. Zucker would stand behind him and make every call. NBC ended the charade nine months later, officially naming Zucker executive producer on January 14, 1992—the fortieth anniversary of *Today*. He was twenty-six.

Maria Shriver called Sid Fetters with a question: "Is he still too young, Sid?"

Zucker did so well so quickly that he and NBC's management both got an inflated idea of just how much he could handle. A little over a year later, Michael Gartner, then president of NBC News, named Zucker executive producer of NBC's *Nightly News with Tom Brokaw*—while keeping him on as EP of *Today*. It was insane to think even a brilliant young talent like Zucker could pull off that double bill—and equally presumptuous of Zucker to believe he was capable of doing it.

"It was arrogance and stupidity," Zucker admitted later. "It was crazy. It wasn't fair to Tom. It wasn't fair to Katie and Bryant, or to either show or either staff."

Zucker began behaving badly, flying off the handle, screaming at his support staffs, ordering people fired for any perceived shortcoming. He was losing control of himself. But he was already the golden boy of the news division. No one had the guts to speak up and tell Zucker to get ahold of himself—and his ego.

Almost no one. Jack Welch, the chairman of GE, called in periodically to check on how Zucker was doing. Welch had already formed a bond with the young hotshot producer. He had noticed how much better the *Today* show was doing under the kid, and he would call and offer congratulations. Sometimes the archconservative Welch would send in funny faxes, accusing the show of turning into *Pravda,* advising Zucker to stop being so liberal. But that was all in fun.

About eight weeks into this ludicrous experiment, when Welch asked how he was holding up, Zucker confessed that the grind of doing both shows was killing him. He asked Welch which of the two shows he should limit himself to.

"You should do the *Today* show," Welch told Zucker. "It's more important to us."

Zucker parked his hubris and went back to the show he loved. *Today* staged a ratings comeback almost at once. Zucker had a few bumpy moments, including a detour into producing a prime-time magazine show, which Zucker despised. The experience left him briefly at a loss, and he listened to an offer from Roone Arledge to jump to ABC to produce its newscast.

Andrew Lack, the NBC News president, came back with a better offer: Come back to *Today,* which had opened its street-level studio in Rockefeller Center. Lack's offer was for Zucker to produce *Today* again for a year, get to it number one, and then move on to *Nightly News.*

Zucker managed the first assignment in a matter of weeks. *Today* took control of the morning audience under Zucker and never looked back. It became one of the most talked-about shows on television, with Zucker introducing a stream of ideas to the show, from the meaty—like eliminating all commercials in the first twenty-two minutes of the broadcast and creating a seriously newsy start to the show—to the sugary—like on-air weddings and outdoor concerts on Friday mornings. Most important to NBC, the show churned out even greater profits, $200 million a year and more. Moving on to *Nightly News* was never mentioned again.

Zucker had *Today* on full throttle, storming to new ratings heights in 1996 during the Atlanta Olympics. He was set to produce election-night coverage in November. That was the plan, anyway.

In October, Zucker began to have strange sensations in his stomach and lower abdomen. His dad thought it was probably nothing but sent him to a GI specialist in New York. He did a few tests.

On October 22, Zucker and his new wife, Caryn, had plans to see an off-Broadway play in the city, *I Love You, You're Perfect, Now Change.* The doctor called just as they were about to leave for the theater. "I've got some tough news for you," he said, getting straight to the point. "You've got cancer."

Zucker buckled. The doctor told him he had a plum-sized malignant tumor in his colon. Colon cancer. He was thirty-one years old, married only four months. Zucker collapsed on his couch, crying uncontrollably.

The surgery was scheduled for October 31. Zucker watched the *Today* show Halloween costume contest (another of his creations) just before he went into the O.R. A couple of nights later, he watched the election night coverage he had been scheduled to produce. That same week, the doctors came to his room and told him the cancer had spread; he would have to undergo chemotherapy. This was unexpected and a huge blow, even to the superconfident Jeff Zucker. He wept again with Caryn.

Zucker never stopped believing he would pull through. But chemo meant nine months of hell. After being away about two and a half months, during which Michael Bass, now his second in command on the show, ran things, Zucker came back to *Today*. The staff greeted him with tears and applause. "No question, he was beloved," Alex Constantinople, the show's PR representative, said.

Zucker had to schedule his chemo sessions for Friday afternoons in order to work most weeks uninterrupted. But that meant a grueling weekend of diarrhea and fatigue. One time he was given too large a dose and he became violently sick and had to be hospitalized for a week.

But he made it through the treatments and bounced back, resuming full command of a show that grew to unheard-of ratings dominance. *Today* began beating the second-place *Good Morning, America* on ABC by as much as 2 million viewers a day, the widest margins ever.

Zucker was scrupulous about getting his health checked out, and during a routine checkup in 1999, again in October, he got some further stunning news. The doctors had found another tumor in what was left of his colon.

This was not a recurrence of the same cancer. It was a new malignancy, a wholly new episode. The doctors told him he had a predisposition to growing tumors in his colon, a genetic defect.

Zucker was now just thirty-four, facing a future of wearing a colostomy bag. He chose another, innovative option. The doctors took out 90 percent of his colon. The other 10 percent they connected so he could still digest and eliminate. It made his digestive cycles extremely fast, but Zucker didn't give a damn about that. He could live with that—emphasis on live.

The health crisis changed Zucker, made him appreciate things that really mattered, like his family, which by this point included a son and a daughter. He still loved to kick ABC's ass in the morning, and he was still volatile in the control room, though somewhat less frequently. And now the fury didn't linger. "Who gives a shit; it's only television" became a favorite line.

Not that he completely mellowed. Zucker never lifted his foot off the competitive pedal. He knew he had built *Today* into a force, and he wielded its power wantonly. His most famous confrontation came in 1999 with the queen of celebrity publicists, Pat Kingsley.

A Kingsley client, Calista Flockhart of *Ally McBeal,* was scheduled as a guest to promote a movie version of *A Midsummer Night's Dream.* But she made clear through Kingsley that she adamantly refused to answer questions about her apparently alarming weight loss. Kingsley called the *Today* bookers and said that unless they promised no weight questions, Flockhart would not appear. Zucker told her *Today* did not accept conditions on interviews. Flockhart canceled.

Zucker retaliated by canceling scheduled appearances of her two costars in the film, Kevin Kline and Stanley Tucci. Kingsley then raised the stakes by reneging on a deal *Today* bookers said had long been in place for the first interviews with Tom Cruise and Nicole Kidman promoting their movie *Eyes Wide Shut.* Kingsley decided to deliver the two stars to *Good Morning, America* instead, saying the ABC show had offered a better deal.

Zucker, now in full dudgeon, called Kingsley and they had a snarling screaming match over the phone. Zucker told the publicist, "If you want to play this game, all your clients are going to be persona non grata on the *Today* show."

That list included some of the biggest names in Hollywood, but Zucker told the staff, "I don't care; we won't book her people." And they didn't, not for the rest of the time Zucker produced the show.

From his perch on top of the ratings, Zucker loved nothing more than to tweak his competitors at ABC. When *GMA* was opening its new studio in Times Square (which Zucker considered a blatant rip-off of the *Today* street-studio idea), Zucker prepared a particularly provocative stunt. He commandeered the Jumbotron screen in Times Square and threw on live pictures of *Today,* which meant that the *GMA* hosts had pictures of the competition playing on the air over their shoulders.

Zucker defended himself against accusations of trying to sabotage a competitor's show by saying, "It was totally for fun. What can I say? I get bored."

Zucker did have a lot of fun at *Today,* but not everyone working for him did. One of his coworkers called his occasional temper tantrums legendary. "Sometimes you would see the immaturity coming through, ripping people and kicking trash cans and firing people. The union guys were always filing claims against him. Jeff was always: 'Fire that audio guy.' 'You're fired, get out of here, I want you off the set now.' He just had no tolerance for somebody who wasn't doing their job."

But the same staff member said Zucker fought for his staff and was extremely considerate of their personal lives. "He had lots of people who would die for him. He fought the company for you."

Midway through 2000, Zucker began to get restless. He had been back at *Today* for his second run for almost seven years. His next logical step would be the presidency of NBC News, but Andy Lack was in that job and entrenched.

So when Leslie Moonves called and invited him to drinks, Zucker was intrigued. He met Moonves at the St. Regis Hotel in midtown. The job being discussed was president of CBS News, a post then held by Andrew Heyward. Moonves was feeling out Zucker's interest before he made an offer. In any case, Zucker was under contract at NBC. Zucker had one conversation about escaping the contract with Ed Scanlon, the NBC executive who handled all the network's big contract negotiations. Scanlon told him it wasn't happening. Zucker, somewhat reluctantly, shut down any further contact with Moonves.

Heading up a news division was now foreclosed as a possibility at two networks, leaving Zucker without an obvious plan of action. He still loved producing live television and would be in the control room again for NBC's 2000 election night. In the weeks before that historically close vote, Zucker got a call that opened up a completely unexpected possibility. Al Gore himself, who had gotten to know Zucker from various appearances on *Today*, called with a feeler: Would Jeff Zucker be willing to consider a post in a Gore administration as press secretary?

When Zucker talked the idea over with some of his colleagues, they had the impression that he was flattered and maybe a little tempted. But the approach never got very far. Zucker indicated he would not accept it.

Zucker led NBC's coverage of the 2000 election and its aftermath. Covering a story that big energized Zucker; but when it finally ended he was at loose ends again, though not for long. Ed Scanlon, who believed Zucker's talents had virtually no bounds, had been quietly plotting Jeff's career. He strategized that Zucker's next move should be to the West Coast, where he could fill in his résumé with achievements for the entertainment side. Scanlon's first thought was to make Zucker head of NBC's in-house production unit, NBC Studios. Sassa was on board with that idea and even interviewed Zucker for the position. But Caryn Zucker quickly short-circuited that plan: She was not in the least interested in moving to L.A. so Jeff could learn how to run a production studio. It was not even an obvious promotion over what he had been doing in New York.

After the election, with the entertainment situation deteriorating, Scanlon began nudging Zucker toward Garth Ancier's job. When he broached the idea, Zucker had an eye-opening moment. "Wow, now that's interesting," he said. The conversations had to remain secret, but Zucker got some guidance from various experienced colleagues, including Dick Ebersol, who had been a personal mentor, and Warren Littlefield, who had firsthand experience to relate.

Zucker's issues with taking the job had nothing to do with self-doubt. He did not lack confidence in himself and his abilities. His big concern remained his wife and children. Caryn still did not want to move to L.A. with two toddlers and live that Hollywood life; she loved New York.

Professional questions were also involved. Was this the job to take if he ultimately wanted a top corporate position at NBC in New

York? Zucker made a call to another executive he knew at NBC and brought up what sounded like his template for making such a move.

"Jeff called me," the executive said, "and his attitude was: I'll do it for three years. Bob Iger did it, why can't I?"

Bob Iger, who had climbed by this point to the number-two position at Walt Disney, had made a similar move earlier in his career at ABC, leaving a corporate job in New York to take on the ABC entertainment division in the 1980s. It had worked out for Iger, even though he never gained a personal reputation as a programming maestro, the way somebody like Brandon Tartikoff had.

The NBC executive whom Zucker called had had a number of dealings with Iger and knew him well. The executive said, "Jeff has got forty IQ points on Bob. It makes sense that he called friends and talked about the Iger model."

By early December, the decision had been made. Bob Wright and Jack Welch agreed to give Zucker the position. The contract details were worked out, and Zucker told Wright and Scanlon that he would love to do the job—for three or four years. Caryn Zucker endorsed the plan, though she still had reservations about moving the family out of New York.

Wright told Zucker he was actually pleased with the idea of a closed-end assignment because he thought that people who held the top entertainment jobs and were tied by background to Los Angeles were too beholden to the town.

• • •

Jeff Zucker came to Hollywood as a blank slate. He had not developed prime-time shows at a network or a studio, as almost every one of his predecessors had. He had produced news shows. No one really had a clue what kind of creative stamp he would put on NBC. The best guess was that he would push to get NBC into the reality game.

Zucker heartily endorsed two reality programs NBC had acquired before he arrived, a wannabe *Millionaire* game show from England called *The Weakest Link,* and a gross-out stunt program called *Fear Factor,* which featured contestants eating everything from sheep eyeballs to pig rectums.

The latter show had landed at NBC as a result of a series of embarrassingly bad decisions. When the success of *Survivor* and pressure from Bob Wright had compelled Ancier and Sassa to jump into the reality genre, they had purchased what, on paper, seemed like the sleaziest of formats, *Chains of Love.*

After months of defending that choice against both internal and external critics, Sassa found himself in the shower one morning, overtaken by a cascading flood of conscience. Sassa concluded that NBC could not degrade itself with a show like this. He came to the office that day and announced that NBC was going to wash its hands of this impending abasement, no matter what the cost.

That position played into the hands of the production company for *Chains of Love,* Endemol, a Dutch entity responsible also for *Big Brother,* the international hit that went to CBS. Endemol could have extracted a huge penalty fee from NBC, but it went for a business solution. Endemol allowed NBC to get out of the deal for *Chains of Love* in exchange for picking up two other Endemol reality shows, one called *Sweet Revenge* (which wound up being called *SpyTV*), and the other *Fear Factor.*

Zucker took a look at the shows and had no qualms about using them. He scheduled both as summer series. *The Weakest Link* held even more promise. Zucker was convinced the dominatrix-styled British host, Anne Robinson, could cross over as an American star.

Of course, NBC had scripted shows in development as well, and Zucker made a point of acknowledging NBC's crying need for new quality hits, especially in comedy, to replace its aging stalwarts. Despite those comments, Zucker was already making enemies. Some abhorred his embrace of the reality genre, a trend that traditional Hollywood resisted because it was costing writers and actors jobs. Others simply disliked what they saw as his attitude that the town should adapt to him, not the other way around.

In interviews Zucker described the television economic system as "just nuts," singling out the entrenched system of Hollywood relationships, where agents and studio and network executives, as well as writers and actors, all seemed to be conspiring to maintain a cost structure that had not changed despite the diminishing power of the networks. "One of the biggest problems with this business," Zucker declared, "is that every year the networks have fewer viewers and yet the industry keeps on doing things the exact same way."

That sentiment branded Zucker as outside the mainstream Hollywood culture, which was built almost entirely on relationships. That was fine with Zucker. Outside the mainstream was not a place he minded swimming. His wife and kids never moved to L.A. He lived in a rented house in Coldwater Canyon and flew home to New York every weekend. If that didn't send the message clearly enough, Zucker put out the word that he had no interest in meeting with most of the agents in town. "Why would I waste my time?" Zucker said.

Much of the posturing came down to Zucker's supreme sense of self-confidence. He had never developed an entertainment television show in his life, but he had no doubt that he could. His was a career built on taking on tasks that challenged others but did not especially challenge him. That was another way he was akin to Moonves. Whatever job in television Zucker took on, he sized up the workforce and concluded he could likely do all their jobs—and better.

And yet Hollywood was different. Collegial, tribal, insular, the town operated more like a club than a profession. You didn't simply step up and push your way into the club; you were admitted—or not. Zucker made no secret of the fact that he was disinterested in the club, disdained the club, and the members didn't like that all.

Agents complained about him; so did writers. There was no schmooze factor with this guy. His attention span seemed permanently locked in *Today* show mode. There were vacancy signs in his eyes when he talked about ideas for shows. His mind seemed programmed not to the entertainment cycle but to the news cycle: What's happening today? What's happening next? What's on the other channels?

After his success supersizing Thursday night, the Hollywood established sized him up and realized that Zucker was smart—scary smart by Hollywood standards. His capacity for sucking up information was clearly prodigious. He was certainly engaging and likable, with all the necessary gifts of a showman: outgoing nature, self-possession, quick wit. No one doubted his skills as a leader. NBC's Burbank unit, long a snake pit of warring interests, was starting to pull together. And Zucker didn't dither on decisions. He gave answers, a quality the business always liked.

But unlike the *Today* show, where Zucker could blow off publicists and stars with impunity because they simply *had* to be on his show, NBC was in no position anymore to snap its fingers and have the best talent come running. Like it or not, Zucker needed to at least dip his toe into the Hollywood game. That was how you attracted the best talent, the talent NBC had to have.

Some of that talent was not charmed by the new guy at NBC. "Everybody complained when they would meet him in his office," one major talent agent said. "Every meeting, he spent all his time looking away from whoever was in there and at the TV sets in his office. He could not take his eyes off that bank of monitors, afraid that something would go by that he would miss, even though one of the biggest writers in television is in there pitching him. They're pitching their hearts out and he's not really looking at them. I got that phone call fifteen times. One writer said to me: 'I'm never pitching that guy again, because he watched television the entire pitch.' He has a very short attention span. You gotta listen to writers tell their stories."

Even Zucker's friends acknowledged that. "He's notorious about not looking at you," one NBC friend in New York said. "He's paying attention, but he's not looking at you. Initially, that can feel quite awkward. He's not a great backslapper. He does it, but I don't think he's the most comfortable in that situation. He's great on the phone, a great phone guy. But if you see him at a party you can be totally put off. Who is that guy? He doesn't give a shit about me."

•　　•　　•

Zucker had only about six months to set up his first development season, not enough time to put a personal stamp on a programming direction for the network. He knew his job was to protect Thursday night, and he needed at least one new comedy to work "in a big way."

Unfortunately, when he got a look at NBC's twenty pilots for new series that spring, he was hit by the usual wave of "what happened to that?" disappointment that attends every network development season. Most of the NBC programming department saw only two viable comedies, *Inside Schwartz,* which added a sports-style commentary to a schlub's romantic aspirations, and a medical satire called *Scrubs.* Zucker liked the first a lot, thought it was a potential hit, but had questions about how commercial the latter might be. He was already forming an opinion that shows shot on film without audience laughter and laugh tracks never became big hits.

Two new comedies hardly satisfied NBC's glaring need. So, despite the doubts of many of his staff, Zucker threw his support behind a third comedy, *Emeril,* a bizarre sitcomization of the life and work of the cable television chef Emeril Lagasse. Zucker wanted to give the show a shot. He saw Lagasse as a larger-than-life personality, and with NBC having so little to start nights off at 8 P.M., Zucker's gut told him to go with a high-profile personality.

"It was Jeff's showman's instinct that led him to *Emeril,*" said Ted Harbert, who produced the show for NBC Productions. "Emeril is a showman. He is attractive to people. People want to see him. Yes, that's true, people want to see Emeril. But people also want to see him in a good show."

Zucker himself pushed to buy *Emeril* after the head of NBC's comedy development, Joanne Alfano, had twice passed on the show. But he wasn't alone. Bob Wright was a fan of *Emeril* as well.

On the West Coast, that was more cause for worry. Harbert saw Zucker as "vulnerable to suggestion." Harbert said the NBC system of picking programs was fundamentally inefficient. "Jeff had a lot of power, but that NBC system of Bob Wright and Randy Falco and the research executives in New York, they get in your hair big-time."

No other network had such an ingrained polarization between their East Coast business operation and their West Coast entertainment operation. Friction seemed to flare up between the two staffs at NBC with every new programming regime. One of Zucker's most important lieutenants said, "That company is run by a lot of people. There have always been a lot of talented people in development, but the company isn't run by the West Coast. You always felt the East Coast thought those knuckleheads on the West Coast don't know what they're doing."

Zucker was convinced that he was the person who could bridge the coastal divide. But even as he gained acceptance among the staff in Burbank, the coastal culture clash continued.

•   •   •

Something else fed the hostile reaction Zucker was attracting in some quarters of Hollywood. His name was *always* in the papers.

Egos in Hollywood being elephantine and delicate at the same time, everyone noticed who was getting written about. And those who weren't resented those who were. Jeff Zucker sailed into L.A. on a tsunami of press coverage, and it never let up. Two forces were at work: a guy with an interesting story met up with a guy who knew the ways of the press better than anyone who had previously held a network entertainment job.

Zucker had the outsider, fish-out-of-water thing going: Could the wonder boy of *Today* conquer prime time? He had the can't-miss backstory of overcoming not one but two life-threatening bouts with cancer. And he was already well connected to many of the reporters on the TV beat by virtue of his long tenure at NBC News.

Zucker was, in fact, a journalist. His professional career had been all about covering big stories. So, unlike the vast majority of his executive competitors, he did not have to fumble around wondering what the press wanted and how best to handle a question. He did not have to call in his PR executives to monitor his calls when a reporter was on the line. He knew how to give a good, made-for-a-lead quote.

His expertise was deep. Not only did Zucker understand the mechanics of journalism, he also understood the *game* of journalism, and especially the pack mentality of most reporters. Stories could be shaped for mass consumption.

His arrival in Burbank would have been a hot story anyway, but Zucker took it to the next level with his play-to-the-crowd cockiness. The saturation coverage Zucker received made some rival executives batty with resentment. One prime example was Gail Berman at Fox. Berman was highly respected for her creative abilities and generally was written about approvingly—though sparsely by Zucker standards. One of her closest Fox colleagues said, "Gail is particularly thin-skinned. She is obsessed with Zucker, and the way he works the press drives her fucking nuts."

Berman aggressively denied having a chip on her shoulder about the press, but she did accuse the "mainstream media" of favoring the established networks—and Jeff Zucker in particular—over Fox.

Zucker himself clearly didn't give a damn about Fox, not at first anyway. He was focused on CBS and Leslie Moonves. "Jeff loved to goad Les," said Alan Berger of CAA, Zucker's former agent and long-time friend. "You poke the stick at the bear to see if he's awake. Oh good, he made a lot of noise."

Moonves poked back, of course. He was awfully good at the game as well. Berger described the jousting in light terms: "I think it's fun for both of them. It's all showbiz. It's great to have two show-men in those jobs." Zucker repeatedly described the various moves and countermoves, like the "supersize" stunt, with a gleeful laugh, declaring it all in fun.

On the Moonves side, it seemed a bit less playful. There was often an edge to Les's comments about Zucker. To his staff and friends, he routinely referred to Zucker as "Zippy." Under his professional skin, Moonves had respect for Zucker (he had tried to hire him to run CBS News, after all), and he often said he liked having what he called "a worthy opponent." But Les had been the undisputed champion of the television industry, and even if Jeff never put one hit show onto NBC, he looked like a serious challenger in the press-coverage department.

Whatever gibes Moonves came up with, Zucker shrugged them off, never taking anything personally. But the rivalry over network leadership was certainly real. Beyond his wildest expectations,

Zucker had the breakout hit of the summer of 2001: *Fear Factor* rode its rats and vermin to monster ratings. Zucker's delight was not in the least tempered by the howls of outrage from the nation's television critics. They moaned and gnashed their teeth over NBC's sellout of its image as the "quality network." They acted as though a national treasure had been violated. Zucker laughed all the way to first place.

The din from the critics would have been deafening had Zucker been listening. Far from being disturbed by his critics, Zucker seemed to court them. When he faced the press that summer, Zucker marched out to Pat Benatar's "Hit Me with Your Best Shot," wearing a bulletproof vest. More showmanship. It got laughs, but Zucker was still grilled about why he was showing people eating sheep's eyeballs on NBC, the network of *The West Wing*.

"Get real," he told the critics. "We're having fun. Let's not take ourselves so seriously."

Zucker *was* having fun, even though Sassa had warned him before the event not to wear the vest. It's a good gag, Sassa told him, but it only invites more shots later—and you won't always be wearing a bulletproof vest.

· · ·

That fall *Emeril* tanked, along with *Inside Schwartz*. *Scrubs* did OK—and the critics liked it, which was becoming something of a kiss of death to Zucker. A couple of dramas worked out: *Crossing Jordan* and a third edition of *Law & Order* called *Criminal Intent*.

By January, *Fear Factor* was back on the schedule as the regular Monday-night-at-8 entry. It would continue to attract hit ratings— and critics' rotten tomatoes—for some time to come.

Taken together, Zucker's first slate of fall shows provided enough new bowling pins for Zucker to continue his successful juggling act, even if he was beginning to have to dance on one leg and wear a blindfold to keep it interesting. NBC had enough headliners left on its bill for Zucker to scratch together another seasonal win for NBC—and with it the comfortable bonus check for finishing first in the 18-to-49 competition.

At season's end, Zucker raised a few more hackles by boasting about all the places across the network schedule where NBC was finishing number one. Though entirely true, it seemed to many of his rivals that Zucker personally had not done a thing—aside from his work at *Today*—to contribute to that success and so he had not earned the right to exhibit such braggadocio.

More tellingly, NBC's winning ratings margin over the second-place network on Thursday nights, which had been a stupefying 228 percent in 1999, had fallen to just 19 percent.

That got NBC's attention—and sent Zucker scrambling back to *Friends*. Though it had started out for sure as the last season for *Friends*, Zucker could hardly afford to face a Thursday against *Survivor* without his best defender. In February, he engineered another expensive renewal of the series. The cast got that $1 million an episode each this time. Everyone swore that this season there would be no more reprieves—it would absolutely be the last go-round for television's biggest comedy.

To go along with that news, *Frasier* was another year older; so was *Will & Grace*. No reinforcements for any of them were in sight.

≥ CHAPTER EIGHT ≤

# "I'VE BEEN THERE"

In the summer of 2001, Marc Cherry, scriptwriter and showrunner, was flat broke, without job prospects, and worried about his impending fortieth birthday.

On a sleepy summer afternoon, Cherry, visiting at his mother's home in L.A., was distractedly watching the TV with her. Cherry had a close, if sometimes awkward, relationship with his mother, a reserved woman from Oklahoma. CNN was on. The news was all about the case of Andrea Pia Yates, a woman from a suburb of Houston, Texas, who had confessed to snapping one day and drowning all five of her children, ages six months to seven years, in their bathtub. The story was so pitifully tragic that Cherry forlornly turned to his mother and said, "Can you imagine a woman being so desperate that she would hurt her own children?"

His mother, Martha, turned to him, took her cigarette out from between her lips, and said dryly, "I've been there."

The response horrified and fascinated Cherry, who had believed his mother—though her marriage to his father was rocky and ended in divorce—had been essentially happy in her life as homemaker. Now, listening to her explain just how many women were beset by this kind of despair, Cherry was struck "on the most primal level" that his own mother believed she had experienced that sort of desperation.

The incident sparked Cherry's imagination. Maybe this revelation could be put into storytelling form. After all, desperation was a feeling he could empathize with himself at this moment in his life. He had not worked in more than a year, a depressing comedown for a writer who had once supervised the huge comedy hit *The Golden Girls*. Nor did the prospects for new comedy work look exciting. There had been between fifty and sixty sitcoms on the air when Cherry started out. Suddenly, there were almost none.

After his last gig folded, his agent, a woman named Marcie Wright, who had represented Cherry throughout his career, becoming one of his closest friends, sent out some of his previous scripts, trying to get him staff work. She got no replies. Not a nibble.

Worse, Cherry realized he was careening toward a crisis—his birthday. Cherry knew all too well how the business worked. Age forty was a point at which television writers had to begin contemplating new careers, because program executives were geared toward attracting young audiences. If a writer admitted to being forty, he could expect to be met by rolling eyes in pitch meetings. Having *The Golden Girls*, a show about senior citizens, as your big credit was only asking for rejection.

Without a regular paycheck, Cherry had been subsisting on $30,000 he borrowed from his mother. Facing this obvious turning point in his career, he knew he had to try something bold—and his conversation with his mother about Andrea Yates was percolating in the back of his mind. What if he could write a flat-out brilliant spec script, something so undeniably good someone would *have* to buy it?

Cherry convinced himself that he had to "write something for the express purpose of showing everyone how fucking smart I am." He decided to "write an HBO show"—something like the ones Cherry himself loved, maybe a "a *Sex and the City* meets *Six Feet Under*."

He kicked the notion around all summer, conjuring characters and situations he could put them in. By fall Cherry had written the "teaser"—the opening scene before the credits—for what he was already starting to call his "opus." At that time, he still expected it would be another half-hour sitcom—that was the form he knew. In the back of his head, he was still envisioning it as the half hour HBO was always looking for to complement *Sex and the City*.

But already this "comedy" was brimming with the kind of edge Cherry had never included in previous sitcoms. In his teaser, a woman named Mary Alice, who also served as the narrator (a touch borrowed from *Sex and the City*), puttered about her house, doing her usual morning chores, before calmly pulling a revolver out of a closet and just as calmly loading bullets into the chambers.

That was the easy part. The days drifted by. Cherry slept late, went to breakfast at Jerry's Deli, read the papers, watched a lot of news, watched Oprah in the afternoons, hit the gym, visited his friends. Somewhere in between all that he wrote a bit, thinking always of *Sex and the City*—and his mother.

One character he formulated, Lynette, surrendered a career for full-time motherhood, which she found overwhelming. (Martha Cherry gave up a career as a fashion designer when she embarked on motherhood in the 1960s.) Another character, Bree, he described in the script as a porcelain-skinned, red-haired beauty of extreme buttoned-down temperament (a description that would have easily fit Martha Cherry).

By this point, Marc Cherry knew he was writing in a form he had never tried before, a one-hour filmed show. All his half-hour sitcoms had been shot on videotape. He was determined to make his opus elegant, full of subtle humor, not jokey but filled with irony.

His characters, as broad as they were, seemed viscerally real to him. That was because his inspiration, as it had been in many things, was Martha Cherry, a woman who was never less than lady-like and "hated things to be unpleasant."

·   ·   ·

Marc Cherry was born in Oklahoma in 1962, but he was raised mainly in southern California. His father worked in oil, so the family relocated a lot. Cherry went to fourth grade in Hong Kong and seventh grade in Teheran. For Cherry and his two sisters, life was full of odd family drama, "tinged with people saying the most amazing things to each other," Cherry said.

As a kid, Cherry always sang and performed. When he got to college at Cal State Fullerton, he majored in musical theater, and landed a spot in an Up With People–type group of cheerful crooners called The Young Americans. (The group's official history boasts the information that "in the 60s we were able to help solve some of our nation's problems that occurred between our youth and the 'establishment.' The Young Americans helped bridge 'the generation gap.'")

Cherry was set on a career in show business as a performer, but the very day he won his Actors Equity card he was struck by a burst of self-realization. With looks like his, he concluded, "I'm a young character actor. I need to do something until I age."

He and his best friend, Jamie Wooten, were always funny at parties; they set out to try comedy. It was a heady time to be young sitcom writers in L.A. Hundreds of jobs were available. After submitting a spec script, Cherry and Wooten got hired on *The Golden Girls,* then a hit for NBC on Saturday night. In two years they had moved all the way up to showrunners for the series, a critical credit for young writers.

When the series ended they first supervised an ill-fated spin-off, then tried an original series, *The Five Mrs. Buchanans.* CBS loved it, and scheduled it in 1994. It made it through one season, then was canceled. So was the writing partnership. It was the start of a protracted trek through a desert of rejection for Cherry, who had no idea how long—and desperate—the drought would be.

By the spring of 2002, Marc Cherry was devoted full time to writing *Desperate Housewives.* He believed that this was the make-or-break moment for his career. His script was going to be so good, it would have to sell to somebody and revive his name in the business—or else it wouldn't, and he did not want to think about what that would mean.

The television business was churning madly that spring. Leslie Moonves had CBS on the march, tenth of a rating point by tenth of a rating point, climbing toward the top; Jeff Zucker had arrived to inject pizzazz and palaver, if nothing quite hitlike, into NBC; Fox's programmers were scrambling to forge an identity—and find some profits—as onetime hits like *The X-Files* and *Ally McBeal* faded into memory; the top managers of Disney and ABC were groaning under the weight of repeated failure.

And reality television was everywhere, terrifying everyone who worked in the creative end of the business.

Oblivious to all of this, Cherry obsessively wrote and rewrote his script, doing little else. Finally, in August 2002, he believed the opus was ready to be seen. Marcie Wright, who called her agency The Wright Concept, contacted people she believed would be most likely to give it a fair look, people who might remember Marc's reputation as a comedy writer. After all, it *was* funny. So she sent it off to comedy executives at a batch of networks: CBS, Fox, Showtime, and, of course, HBO.

When executives at these various networks received the script, with no introduction or context, they did not know what to make of it. "It was twice as fat as normal," Cherry said. "And it wasn't laugh-out-loud joke, joke." The rejections came back quickly: Thanks. The writing is really outstanding, but not for us.

Cherry was devastated. Which overdue bill was he going to pay with compliments about his writing? No one would even throw some cash his way to rewrite the spec.

Marcie Wright did not see the sense in simply sending the script around to more places. They needed an advocate, someone who might bring in other deal elements that might interest a network. She racked her brain and made a call.

In the summer of 2002, Peter Tortorici, who had bounced around the business after being booted from CBS in the coup de Moonves in 1995, was totally independent—and very far from Hollywood. He was ensconced up in Vancouver, Canada, serving as executive producer on a series called *Body and Soul,* a drama about holistic healing, for the values-based but small-potatoes PAX TV network. That meant, as Tortorici put it, they were producing an hourlong drama "for the price of an average family of four's grocery cart."

Marcie Wright called him because she was reaching out to everybody who had had a good working experience with Marc Cherry, and Tortorici, as head of CBS Entertainment, had scheduled his last comedy, *The Five Mrs. Buchanans*.

"You know you were always nice to Marc, you were always a big fan of his," Wright reminded Tortorici. He said he remembered *Buchanans* and Cherry's work well. But that had been seven long years earlier—a couple of careers' worth of time in the television business. Tortorici had heard nothing about Marc Cherry since then.

"He's written something really special," Wright coaxed Tortorici. "What do you think? Would you like to read it?"

This was an easy one. Tortorici, as an independent producer, relied for his livelihood on finding good material. What was there to lose? Sure, he said, send it along.

Tortorici was still in Canada when the script arrived. He read it in his hotel room—straight through. Long before he finished, he had come to a conclusion: *Okay, this is a game-breaker*. What struck Tortorici was the skillfully rendered dark comic tone, which he knew was not on the air anywhere. It felt completely fresh, and it had that sensational title.

He called Marcie Wright. "Look, I think it's brilliant," he told her. "If I can be of any help . . ."

"Well, be of help, then," she blurted out. "Whatever you can do." Tortorici said he would get on it as soon as he returned to Los Angeles.

When he did get back to town a few weeks later, he arranged a meeting with Cherry, who was thrilled to be getting some supportive feedback at last. Tortorici told him, "I'll do everything I can to see if I can set this up, because I think it's great." But Tortorici offered Cherry some insight based on his long network experience. "I think what's going to happen here is that you're going to be met with initial resistance because it's so different."

Tortorici suggested trying to finance the pilot in a nontraditional way. "Any time you're doing anything that's not on the air," Tortorici told Cherry, "no matter how many times they tell you, 'Well, that's what we're always looking for,' it's not." He explained that network executives want something that is not yet on the air—only, *after* it actually is on the air and has proven itself by bringing in viewers.

At the time, Tortorici was also doing program consulting for an advertising firm called Mind Share. The company's executives had begun noodling with the idea of financing shows as early as the script phase. The idea was to gain early advertising advantages as well as potentially an ownership stake in the show if it took off.

Tortorici sent *Desperate Housewives* to the Mind Share group, expecting them to fall as hard for it as he had. They didn't quite. The message came back: We think it's pretty good. Tortorici told them he begged to differ: It was far better than that. Though he would have preferred more enthusiastic backing, Tortorici forged ahead. He made a few calls to network contacts, trying to place the show on his own. He got nowhere.

At that point, on a totally separate track, he and Mind Share made a deal with NBC for a different project, a part-improv comedy called *Significant Others*. That deal at least put Tortorici on a formal business footing with Mind Share—and got him a parking place on NBC's lot in Burbank.

Eating in NBC's commissary every day, Tortorici was well placed to run into the NBC executives and talk up *Desperate Housewives*. One of these was Karey Burke. Burke was heading up one of two development teams that NBC had created. She had survived several executive regimes at the network and now had a position of real authority under Jeff Zucker. If Tortorici could get a green light from her, he and Cherry would be in business.

The deal for *Significant Others* set up a partnership where Mind Share would produce start-up shows for the network at a much-reduced cost, by working off-season and finding lesser-known or out-of-work actors. It was a low-risk deal for NBC. The network would allow Mind Share's creative people to go through the unused, and so far unloved, material in NBC's development bin. If Tortorici found something he liked and NBC agreed on it, Mind Share could proceed directly into production, skipping the pilot stage.

NBC started giving Tortorici stacks of material to read. That was where he had found *Significant Others*. The experience gave Tortorici a handle on the quality of the material NBC was seeing. He quickly decided that *Desperate Housewives* was, for sure, better than anything NBC had in house.

Tortorici went to see Karey Burke with Cherry's script in hand. "Look," he told her. "The stuff you're giving me is good. But I want you to read something I think is even better."

Burke agreed to read the script. That was great news for Tortorici, but he did not know what to expect from Burke. Some development executives took a visceral dislike to any material they had not commissioned themselves. Tortorici needed Burke to give this script a real chance. She got back to Tortorici quickly. "It's fabulous. Let me get it into the system here." Burke added that he might have to follow up with Chris Conti, who was head of NBC's drama department.

Tortorici waited with hopeful anticipation to hear back from NBC. In the meantime, he received another script that NBC was interested in having Mind Share develop, about a psychic soccer mom. Tortorici liked that one well enough to schedule a meeting with Conti, figuring this was an ideal opportunity to bring up *Desperate Housewives*.

When he met Conti, the drama chief was openly enthusiastic about the soccer-mom show and eager to have Tortorici take it to his Mind Share partners. Tortorici was perfectly happy to do that. But then he asked Conti, "What about *Desperate Housewives*? Did you ever read it?"

"Yeah, it's a really good script," Conti told him. "But Zucker will never make it."

Tortorici did not ask why. He knew better. If the network entertainment boss had shut down the idea, there was nowhere else to go. Tortorici simply accepted the bad news and went on his way.

What he did not know was that Chris Conti was lying to him.

What had transpired in Conti's office that afternoon was perhaps the shortest conversation known to Hollywood: "Did you read the script?" "Yes, *loved* it, but just can't use it right now."

Network executives heard up to 400 pitches a year, and read countless more spec scripts. Time was exceedingly precious to them in development season. Peter Tortorici, who was not Dick Wolf or David E. Kelley, nor any other recognizable hit producer at that time, was asking about a script that NBC had simply given short shrift and decided to pass on. Like most executives in his position, Conti was doing whatever he could to get off the subject quickly, to blame someone else, and move on.

The truth was Chris Conti had never read a word of *Desperate Housewives.* And neither he nor Karey Burke had ever put it in front of Jeff Zucker. So he had never read it either.

When *Desperate Housewives* came up at a staff meeting, Conti had noted that NBC already had several female-oriented dramas in development, including a high-profile entry called *Miss Match* (which was to star Alicia Silverstone) and *American Dreams,* a show that the network—and Zucker especially—saw as a high-quality effort. Though Burke had liked *Desperate Housewives* enough to submit it to the group for discussion, she had not sold it with anything approaching passion.

*Desperate Housewives* was brought up at an NBC development meeting with no real advocate in the room. As Ghen Maynard at CBS could have predicted with his "unresponsive bystanders theory," the idea was doomed. The entire development staff knew that Jeff Zucker had frequently signaled that he was reluctant to develop too many shows geared toward women, and that he was especially hesitant about picking up shows with continuing story lines—serials—because they usually could not be repeated.

The bottom line: NBC Entertainment as an institution passed on *Desperate Housewives,* in the same way they passed on hundreds of ideas for new shows every year—a fleeting look and good-bye. The show was in house, in the system, and it even had an advertising company willing to help finance it. *Desperate Housewives* could have appeared on NBC as early as the 2003–2004 season. But it didn't. NBC passed.

• • •

With NBC's message about the show's female appeal ringing in his ears, Peter Tortorici figured *Desperate Housewives* ought to be a slam dunk for Lifetime—cable's "network for women." He had a great relationship with the development executives there because they had once worked for him at CBS. So, with a certain degree of confidence, he sent the script over there. Cable was better than nothing.

Instant rejection. The Lifetime executives said the script was not the "Lifetime brand." Tortorici interpreted that to mean it did not fit some rigid notion of the channel's concept of its "signature programming," which at that point seemed to be shows that "empowered" women.

Stymied, Tortorici ran though other possible options. Cherry himself had reported that a CBS development executive told him the network would reject anything that could be interpreted as "that dark stuff that Les hates." Tortorici could not see the project at Fox—women in their forties, the center of attention on *Desperate Housewives,* probably would seem like old bags on Fox; and the show was less hip than dark and subtle, which he didn't expect Fox viewers would get.

That left ABC. In the past, Tortorici had had no success running spec scripts past Thom Sherman, ABC's head of drama. In his gut, Tortorici still believed *Desperate Housewives* was a hit show. He just could not make it happen.

With great reluctance, Peter Tortorici bowed out of *Desperate Housewives.* He would not be the last television executive to be left with a nasty hangover from a party he missed the chance to attend.

•   •   •

While Tortorici was striking out trying to place Cherry's script, Marc got a call from a friend of his, Robert Kuhn, a screenwriter (*Mickey Blue Eyes*) who was also a client of Marcie Wright. Suspicious about some payments he had failed to receive for a movie project called *Shackled,* Kuhn had done some digging. Over the course of an eight-month-long investigation, he had discovered that not one, but two of his checks had never made it through the offices of The Wright Concept. The amount totaled more than $150,000. Kuhn was convinced that Marcie Wright had embezzled the funds. He counseled Cherry to check his recent payments carefully.

The notion seemed preposterous to Cherry. He had earned so little in recent years, it did not seem possible that Wright could have pocketed much of anything owed to him. Beyond that, he simply could not believe she would do something like that. Not Marcie. Theirs was not a mere business relationship. Marcie was one of Marc's closest friends. He had vacationed with her and her husband. He trusted her in every way.

Still, he made the calls. His only significant paying project since 1996 had been a CBS pilot, *Kiss Me, Guido* (retitled *Some of My Best Friends*). One of the reasons Cherry had so many financial problems was that he had not received as much from that project as he originally hoped. Could there have been another reason for that?

The calls made it clear. Out of payments due to Cherry, Wright had skimmed $79,000—money that could have staved off so many problems for him. This was more than a felonious act; this was a stark, cruel betrayal. The economic loss, painful as it was, almost paled by comparison.

Wright tried to justify her actions by citing her own personal problems, and saying that she believed her clients were her friends who would understand the situation. This did not play at all as a rationale to Cherry, and it hardly salved the gaping personal wound.

"Here I am getting older by the second," he said. "The best thing I've ever written has now been turned down by five different places. I'm borrowing money from my mother. And now my fucking agent is arrested for embezzlement."

His first move, he knew, was to find new representation—if anyone would take him. His lawyer set him up with three different agencies. Cherry was gratified with his first meeting, which went well, but elated by his second. Andy Pattman and Debbie Klein, two agents from Paradigm, a small but up-and-coming Hollywood agency, read *Desperate Housewives* and got it immediately.

Enthused, they met with Cherry and told him they were sure he had a hit show and were avid to represent him. Cherry was thrilled but figured he might as well take the last meeting, just to be sure.

The third agent, well known, took Cherry to lunch. Within seconds, Cherry got the impression he was dining alone. The agent barely looked at Marc, seemed to regard him as a hopelessly washed-up writer, and spent the entire meal checking out the room to see if somebody interesting was coming in.

That evening, Cherry decided he would go with Paradigm. The next morning, before he could call and decline the other two agencies, Cherry's phone rang. It was that same obnoxious agent, calling to tell Cherry he had no interest in representing him—"just too many people on my list right now." Cherry was infuriated that he hadn't had the chance to dump the guy first.

But he was delighted with his new agents at Paradigm. They got to work immediately, strategizing new ways to get *Desperate Housewives* into the right hands. They even put it in front of a couple of movie people, just to see if someone would bite and make it as a feature.

Even if Cherry's finances did not immediately improve, his self-image did. His problem, he told himself, was that his representation had been lousy. Marcie Wright, beyond stealing from him and leaving him broke, had never really made anything happen for him. Within days, Andy Pattman called with a fresh thought: Maybe *Desperate Housewives* had been positioned all wrong. Pattman said, "The problem with this is that you pitched it to all the comedy places and you're calling it a satire. We need to call this a soap opera and sell it as a soap opera."

Cherry was not averse to this idea. He knew his script had elements of a soap, including its serialized storytelling, but he had just never thought of it that way. Paradigm represented another client, a writer/producer named Chuck Pratt. Pratt had been a longtime showrunner on *Melrose Place* (and after that, though no one mentioned it, on *Titans* for NBC). Now he was the showrunner for the daytime soap *General Hospital*.

Pattman told Cherry, "Chuck is going to show you how to turn this into a soap opera."

Pratt read the script and told Cherry he loved it. He was convinced it could play as a prime-time soap. "You don't even have to change much," Pratt said. His one significant suggestion was to play up the show's mysterious elements. Right at the end of the pilot, Cherry had dropped in a kicky note of mystery about why Mary Alice committed suicide. Pratt suggested they introduce the mystery elements earlier.

"You have to let people know there's a mystery part of the show long before the end of the episode," Pratt said.

To Cherry, who had listened to a lot of bad suggestions about how to improve his script, this finally struck the right chord. It was easy to accomplish as well. Cherry fleshed out the characters of Mary Alice's husband and son. And he also invented a teasingly delicious scene early in the pilot where the son finds his father using a pickax to dig through the bottom of their empty swimming pool. As if that wasn't mysterious enough, Cherry threw in a line for the dead Mary Alice to narrate over the scene of the ax ripping though the pool's concrete: "It was the sound of a family secret."

Pratt loved the additions. So did Cherry's agents. Unfortunately, none of it helped in Paradigm's efforts to land Cherry a job on a current show while the agency tried to find a buyer for *Desperate Housewives*.

As the summer of 2002 ended, Cherry remained out of work and flat broke. Somebody, somewhere, with some kind of juice in the television business, was going to have to step up and champion the women on Wisteria Lane.

# CHAPTER NINE

# *IDOL* MINDS

In mid-June 2002, Sandy Grushow, the head of the entertainment division at Fox, was preparing to take his wife on a glorious vacation to Venice. A vacation seemed especially appealing at the moment because problems at Fox were dogging Grushow, mainly having to do with the network's gnawing need to find a breakout hit, the kind of show that whole nights—and executive careers—were built around.

CBS now had *Survivor* and *CSI*. NBC, for all its misses, still had *Friends* and *ER*. Even woebegone ABC had found magic that spring with its cheesy, ersatz romantic hit, *The Bachelor*.

Fox had no card even close to a national phenomenon in its programming hand, unless you counted the new drama *24*, but that series, while wonderfully received by critics, had played only marginally in the ratings. One month earlier, announcing a new fall schedule, Grushow had faced down the grim task of introducing a lineup that for the first time since the mid-1990s did not contain either *Ally McBeal* or *The X-Files*, the two greatest hourlong series in Fox's history. They had finally faded away. In their place Grushow had added a "space western" called *Firefly*, and a new entry from *Ally* creator David E. Kelley called *Girls Club*. Grushow had bought that one even before he had seen a pilot.

To say he was uneasy was understating the point. The network was facing a dicey fall unless something broke in their favor. Speaking with his second in command, Gail Berman, just before he left for Venice, Grushow reiterated the obvious: that the network was at a crossroads, crying out for what he called a "game-changer."

"We better come up with something," Grushow told Berman.

Berman ruefully agreed. Neither could see that something anywhere on the immediate horizon.

Briefly, they discussed the prospects for the little summer show they were about to launch the day after Grushow touched down in Venice. Sandy's hopes were decidedly modest. Maybe the thing would do well with female teens, he said, though surely it was not going to resonate with the 18-to-49 crowd, the one that really mattered to Fox.

Berman had the same general feeling. She said she could see it becoming a "moderate summer success," maybe good enough to be brought back the following summer, something fresh to fill up a few time periods during the summer months.

That would be about the best they could hope for from this show with the somewhat ungainly title of *American Idol: The Search for a Superstar.*

 •    •    •

A little over a year earlier, in April of 2001, a British music executive named Simon Cowell sat at a meeting in Los Angeles with executives from a network he had never heard of, something called UPN. Cowell had never pitched a television show in America before—and the way things were going, he thought he never would again.

The UPN executives who sat across the table from Cowell clearly had no clue who this guy was, and, apparently, even less interest in finding out. Maybe they knew his partner, Simon Fuller, from his leadership of the Spice Girls. Surely, they had heard of them. But then again, as Cowell checked those blank, disinterested faces, maybe not.

No matter. Cowell had enormous faith in the idea that he and

Fuller had for a music-based television show. Fuller was the most successful manager of music acts in the U.K., and he, Cowell, was the most successful artist-and-repertoire man currently working in Britain. They both knew how to launch new singing artists, and now they had an idea for a show that would allow them to utilize their talents on camera.

Despite the wall he sensed going up at the UPN meeting, Cowell never cowed, simply plowed ahead with his pitch. "What this is really about is the American Dream," Cowell told the American executives in his smooth British tones. He laid out the format for the show he and Fuller were calling *Pop Idol* in Britain, describing how exciting this show would surely be. When Cowell wrapped up his comments, the room was stone silent.

At the opposite end of the table, a young woman executive, whom Cowell had identified in his head as the "lippy second in command," seemed to be calculating whether this truly was the end of the presentation or not.

"And what exactly do you think we're supposed to be doing for you?" the woman said dismissively.

"Well, actually, sweetheart," Cowell replied, applying just a dash of acid, "it's more a question of what I could be doing for you."

Again a terrible silence fell. Then the woman piped up: "Well, we'll get back to you."

Cowell had heard that line before—too many times for it to bother him during his sojourn in the United States. He, Fuller, and a third partner, yet another Simon, Simon Jones (an executive with Thames Television), had paid calls to the broadcast networks, to MTV, and to other cable networks. Every single one of them had a free shot that April at landing the show the three Simons were putting on offer. No one showed the least interest, and many of the network executives offered shoulders so cold that Cowell could have chilled his wine on them. Uniformly, they had been, Cowell thought, the worst, most appalling meetings of his life.

One meeting was so bad, Simon Jones had seemed on the verge of walking out and Cowell had kicked him under the table—he was interested in the free dinner the network was going to give them after the meeting. But in one other meeting it was Cowell himself who almost pushed too hard.

As another supercilious network executive tried to put them off gently with insincere pap about how intrigued they were with this project, without any hint of a real commitment, Cowell decided to wind this particular twit up.

"Does that mean you're thinking about it?" Cowell pressed him. "Shall I get back to you in a week? Shall I come back to see you again in a month?"

Cowell wouldn't let it go. He wouldn't let the guy off the hook. As the responses got more and more testy, Cowell thought the executive was going to call security and have him forcibly removed. Cowell let up just in time to make sure he was still able to dine out that night.

If Simon Cowell had needed evidence to prove that despite his extensive credentials in the U.K. music industry he was a nobody in the U.S., the last week had surely provided that. But he was not overly bothered by all the rejection. His show, *Pop Idol,* was still going on the air in a few months in Britain, and if it proved to be the hit Cowell expected it to be, maybe his next meetings in America would go differently.

• • •

The contrast with how *Pop Idol* had been sold in England could not have been sharper. Cowell and Fuller met with representatives of the British network ITV, spent what Cowell estimated was no more than thirty seconds describing the idea, and they had a deal. But of course, the two Simons had enormous reputations in the British entertainment world, and they were entering a market that had already embraced music-oriented reality shows.

In England, the show *Pop Stars,* originally developed in Australia, which traced the formation of a singing group, had engrossed the nation. Another music show, *Fame Academy,* had also done extremely well.

Cowell had been invited to be a judge on the first edition of *Pop Stars,* and at first he had accepted. But he quickly had misgivings about being a person who ran a music label going on television to demonstrate how to put together a group. Cowell thought it was "like a magician showing how you saw somebody in half." He bowed out.

When Cowell got a first glimpse of *Pop Stars,* however, he knew he had made a mistake. The show looked like a piping-hot hit, though he had an instant insight. To Cowell, the attractive part of *Pop Stars* was the round of auditions to select the band members. As constituted, *Pop Stars* had no ending. With Fuller, Cowell conceived a show built around season-long tryouts, with the winner announced at the end.

What Cowell told ITV was, "It will have all the fun of *Pop Stars,* but we can do it better. We can do it a lot harsher than on *Pop Stars,* and the public will vote and choose the winner. And we won't be relying on the music to make the show successful: It will be a soap opera."

Cowell also volunteered himself as a judge, knowing he had the precise expertise called for in selecting a singing star. Fuller and his company, 19 Entertainment, along with FremantleMedia, owned the show. Cowell took no ownership stake, but he did get royalty rights for his label, a part of the BMG music group, on every recording released by an *Idol* performer worldwide. That was the essence of the show's appeal for Cowell.

All he was concerned with was that the right person would win so that he would get access to a good artist. If the show was a hit, so much the better; Cowell's new artist was more likely to sell a lot of records that way.

When Cowell started shooting *Pop Idol* in England in the summer of 2001, the production plan called for four judges to sit in an audition room while contestants trooped in one by one. The judges would discuss each singer after he or she left the room. Nothing more specific was spelled out.

The first auditions took place in Manchester. By the time five or six singers had walked through, sung, and then had their performances rehashed by the judges after they had left the room, Cowell was almost crawling up the walls.

"I'm dying in here," he told the producers. "This is not like a real-life audition." He turned to one of the other judges, the veteran British pop producer Pete Waterman, and said, "We have to actually tell the performers to their faces what we thought. We've just got to tell these boys and girls the truth. They're rubbish."

Cowell had invited Waterman in to work as a judge, expecting him to be the "nasty" one. Simon had known Waterman for years and perceived his reputation to be: a "complete asshole." But Waterman got more "emotional" on the show than Cowell expected (he actually teared up at one performance). Cowell, meanwhile, acted no differently on the air than he did at real auditions—he was cold and distant. And his comments reflected that.

As the show took off after its premiere that October, the British press concentrated on Cowell and his barbed comments. He was the nasty one, the "mouthy" one. The show quickly began to revolve around Cowell and his withering appraisals of the wretched talent being brought before him.

*Pop Idol* was the hit of the year in England. The two finalists both released albums after the show concluded and sold millions. Simon Fuller had two new hit artists to manage; Simon Cowell's label had two huge-selling albums. Their collaboration was a ringing success—and they were just getting started.

•   •   •

Alix Hartley, a British-born talent agent with an expertise in music, who worked for the heavyweight Hollywood talent agency CAA, was a natural to represent her countryman Simon Fuller in the challenge of going back in to the networks in the fall of 2001 and finding *Pop Idol* a home on American television.

Given how both *Who Wants to Be a Millionaire?* and *Survivor* (both conceived by British producers) had emerged as hits in the summer months, CAA's strategy was to pitch *Pop Idol* as a perfect new reality programming vehicle for the summer of 2002. It was light, entertaining, and not very expensive to produce. As an added advantage, having started a fifteen-week British run in October, it would have fully executed weekly editions on tape to serve as the template for the American version.

Andrea Wong, who ran the reality department for ABC, was an ideal target for the CAA pitch. She was aggressively seeking product and had been closely watching the British market in the wake of her network's failure to follow through on *Survivor* when it had been twice in ABC's clutches.

But CAA and the producers of *Pop Idol* ran into a problem that *Survivor* never had to face. Music had already failed in the U.S. in reality formats on two networks, one being ABC. That network had tried a show in 2000 called *Making the Band,* about assembling a boy-band singing group. Though it had a small following, mostly among pubescent girls, the show simply could not cross over into a wider audience. The music format was blamed. Music had become just too stratified, the argument went, to ever build a wide enough appeal in the U.S. to succeed on the scale an American network television show required.

The WB network, which was mainly the network of pubescent girls, tried a similar format the next season, *Pop Stars,* a format derived from the Australian and British models of the same name—only with an all-girl group. It, too, found only a niche audience.

Andrea Wong knew all that when CAA came in touting *Pop Idol.* She passed. CAA met with Jeff Gaspin, the executive Jeff Zucker had put in charge of NBC's reality division. He passed in the room. The agency never set up a formal meeting with Ghen Maynard at CBS's reality division, feeling as though their initial phone call had fallen flat.

That left Fox. The British producers had gotten nowhere in the spring when they tried to interest Fox in *Pop Idol.* But CAA made a new effort anyway. Alix Hartley and Simon Fuller went in to see Mike Darnell.

That October, reality television was again undergoing serious scrutiny in the wake of the 9/11 terrorist attacks. The networks talked a lot about relying on "comfort television," which did not sound like anything Mike Darnell had ever been associated with.

Fuller pitched his idea with fervent passion, and that impressed Darnell. What Mike really liked was the notion that the format would essentially be all audition, complete with a lot of truly woeful early performances. Darnell had never liked the band-making shows once they got past the auditions. Here was a format where the auditions, replete with people making cringe-inducing asses of themselves, would rule.

Darnell, thinking of summer budgets at Fox, wanted to know if the show had sponsorship attached. Hartley told him CAA was working on that very angle. Mike told Hartley and Fuller that they should bring the idea up with Sandy Grushow, the head of entertainment for Fox, and his chief lieutenant, Gail Berman.

When Grushow and Berman heard the pitch, they both had the same reaction: "Ehhh." A talent contest did not sound like inspiring television in the twenty-first century—nor like a breakout hit, which was what Fox had an increasing need for. But both executives knew the network also could use something that might pass for fresh summer programming. The problem was, Fox was out of money. The program budget for the year was exhausted, bone dry.

Grushow told the CAA representatives that Fox was simply not going to pay a license fee for this program—if it was going to get on the air, it would have to be as a fully sponsored broadcast. "We don't know much about this show," Grushow told them. "But if we can get it for nothing, it's sort of a no-brainer."

CAA indicated that of course it could line up sponsors. Fox said come back to us when you do.

CAA believed it could interest one of its clients, Coca-Cola, in becoming a sponsoring entity on the show. But that was a long way from selling out the show before it even got on the air (the exact process that *Survivor* had to go through at CBS).

Gail Berman had enough interest in the idea to check in occasionally with the CAA team to see if they had lined up the necessary sponsors. To the CAA representatives, this was not an indication of a burning interest in their show. "Fox's interest was half-assed," one of the negotiators for *Pop Idol* said. "The network was extremely reluctant. We were running into a brick wall with them."

CAA did not see the show as a monumental expense. It was offering just an eight-episode summer show, nothing that would break a network's budget. But Fox, still citing empty coffers, would not budge off its stand that it would pay absolutely nothing in license fees.

One conversation about the show with Peter Chernin, the News Corporation president who oversaw the Fox network, was especially frustrating to the CAA team because Chernin indicated, jokingly, that the only thing Fox would be interested in for summer programming would be "cheap jugglers."

By this point, early in winter, *Pop Idol* had become the talk of Britain. Fox had made no effort to secure the show, so CAA went back at Andrea Wong from ABC, armed with those mighty ratings from the British run. Wong asked to see a tape of the British show. That was encouraging. A tape was delivered. Wong watched it—and passed again.

The impasse with Fox continued. CAA had not heard from Darnell. Berman and Grushow continued to press for a fully sponsored show; nothing was happening, even with the show's fabulous success in England.

In February 2002, Lee Gabler, who ran the television division for CAA, took a trip to Salt Lake City during the Winter Olympics. He was not especially interested in seeing the games, but Coca-Cola had a major presence in the games as a corporate sponsor. Gabler met with Steve Heyer, who was then president of Coke, and the subject of *Pop Idol* came up.

Gabler pitched the show, with its energy and family-friendly format, as a possible vehicle for a Coke sponsorship. Heyer jumped on it.

Now CAA had one big corporate backer for the project. Coke was not going to buy out all the time for eight episodes, but it was certainly a boost—or at least CAA thought so. When the agency went back to Fox with the news of Coke's participation, Grushow remained reluctant. He told the CAA representatives he was still gun-shy about committing to the show if Fox had to cough up money to cover even part of a license fee.

Even a small fee would matter, Grushow explained, because Fox would have to cover the amortization costs of what it would have made from whatever repeats it would have scheduled those eight weeks. Bottom line: CAA still had no deal for *Pop Idol*.

But even as the frustrating talks with Fox dragged on, CAA was developing a connection that some at the agency believed might play out to their advantage. Back in October, several of the CAA executives had met with Elizabeth Murdoch, daughter of Rupert, at the international television programming festival in Cannes known as MIPCOM. A blossoming relationship took hold there.

With the talks about *Idol* stalled in L.A., the CAA representatives reached out to Liz Murdoch, who ran News Corp's most important television operation in England, the BSkyB channel out of London. That meant she was witnessing the phenomenon of *Pop Idol* first-hand.

Fortunately for CAA, Liz flat out loved the show; she did not have to be sold on it. Hearing that her father's American network had yet to act on making a deal for the U.S. rights, Liz Murdoch decided to give the process a helpful nudge. She called her dad and told him how much she loved *Pop Idol* and how big the show was becoming in England. She urged him to buy the rights for Fox.

Rupert Murdoch put in a call the next day to Peter Chernin, his Number Two at News Corp, and the top decision-maker on all the biggest moves made by the Fox network.

"What's going on with this show *Pop Idol,* Peter?" Murdoch asked him. "It's a big hit in England. I spoke to Liz and she says it's great."

Chernin was familiar enough with the situation to report that their network people had been talking about it with the agency, discussing potential advertising backers. "We're still looking at it," Chernin said.

"Don't look at it, *buy* it!" Murdoch ordered. "Right now."

With those orders ringing in his ears, Chernin followed up quickly, calling Grushow and Berman. He asked them where they stood with *Pop Idol*. They told him they were still waiting for the advertiser sponsorships to come through.

"Just close the deal," Chernin said. He explained the call from Rupert.

"We'll get it closed today," Grushow said.

Grushow thought the command decision from Rupert put Fox in a bad position to conclude a favorable deal—the network did not get any kind of ancillary rights, for example, which he believed the network easily could have extracted had CAA remained desperate to find any American home for the show. With Murdoch ordering the deal to close, Fox could not buck the producers' resistance to surrendering an ownership percentage.

The actual order for the series suddenly changed as well. Instead of an eight-episode summer order, Fox asked CAA for fifteen episodes—the same duration as the show in Britain. The CAA agents concluded that one of the Murdochs, or maybe both, had insisted that the show be done *exactly* as it was in England.

That did not mean Fox would import the British hosts and judges. Fox fully expected to hire figures from the American music industry for those jobs. But after the deal was concluded, and Grushow finally was able to watch a tape of the British version, he told Berman that he was taken by the nastily charismatic British judge. Grushow said the man reminded him of the abrasive American talent manager Sandy Gallen.

Grushow said, "I think as part of the deal, we should insist on bringing this guy over as a judge."

He still could not remember Simon Cowell's name.

·   ·   ·

By the winter of 2002, *Pop Idol* had made Simon Cowell one of the most talked-about cultural figures in England. He was a tabloid newspaper's dream, seen by millions every week on television, saying something outrageously quotable ("You're a disaster"), doing something unconscionably cruel (several young women left the auditions convulsed in tears after hearing Simon's corrosive assessments of their talents), tirelessly promoting his program.

Cowell was pleased when he heard the show had finally sold in the United States, but mildly shocked when he learned that Fox was requesting that he come along as one of the American judges.

Cowell had not planned on turning himself into an international television star; he only wanted to make the show a hit for the benefit of his record label. Toward the end of the run of the British original, Cowell went to talk over the American offer with his bosses from BMG, the media giant that ran his label.

Nobody told him not to do it, but Cowell emerged from that meeting deciding he did not want to continue on the American version. He called up Nigel Lythgoe and Kevin Warwick, two British producers who were going to continue with the show in the U.S., and told them, "You'll have to find another judge. I'm just not interested."

Cowell's concern was that his record company had had all its success in the U.K. and Europe. Though he felt completely qualified to judge British talent, he wondered what right he had to judge American talent. Just to be sure, Cowell contacted his lawyer and asked if he had any contractual obligation to stick with the show if it moved to America. His lawyer said no. "Fine, that means I'm not doing it," said Cowell.

But a short time later a woman in the music business, who was a longtime friend of Cowell's, heard he was passing on the American show and called to ask him why.

"Because it's a lot of my life to give up," Cowell said, adding, "And I have concerns about judging Americans."

"Simon, a good singer is a good singer," his friend said, "whether they're Russian or English or Japanese. That should have nothing to do with your decision."

That observation certainly seemed sound to Cowell. "And you're going to regret it if you don't go," his friend added. "If the show is a hit without you, you're going to think you could have been part of that. And if it isn't a hit, you're going to think that you could have made the difference."

Cowell began to have second thoughts. But another concern plagued him. He had witnessed how American television executives functioned during those hideous meetings in the spring. Some genius at the American network was bound to try to water down the show, and especially his acerbic comments. Cowell would have no interest in a sweetened version of *Pop Idol*. Then Kevin Warwick called.

"Look, Simon, we're going over to produce the show in America," Warwick said. "I will look after your back again. You won't have to compromise what you do. You can be yourself."

"So I can really be the same as I was in England?" Cowell asked.

Warwick assured him that he could. "Well," Cowell asked, "what if it's not a hit in the first two weeks? Will Fox stand by the show?"

"Absolutely," Warwick said. "They've offered us assurances that they will stick by the show, because that's what it might take, a few weeks."

That closed the deal. "Fine," Cowell said. "Let's give it a go, then."

A few weeks later, Cowell arrived in L.A. for his first round of meetings with Fox and the American producer, Brian Gadinsky. Fox had agreed to lease Cowell a house in Beverly Hills while he was shooting the series. Cowell met the real estate agent, who showed him around the house.

"I'm not sure about this show of yours," the agent said.

"Why is that?" Cowell asked.

"Because they've built in a month's break in the lease," the agent said.

•   •   •

At first they considered rechristening it *America's Idol*. Darnell thought that made it sound like it might be about a New York fireman, so he suggested *American Idol*. Nobody wanted "Pop" in the title of an American series, both because—with the exception of Michael Jackson—nobody in the U.S. music business ever used the word "pop" anymore and because *Pop Stars* had been a failure. Darnell, of course, was going to be the executive in charge of the new entry, because as a reality show it fell under his supervision.

Rupert Murdoch, as he often did, sat in on a meeting that winter to go over the development slate for the network. When it came time to talk about reality programs, Murdoch asked about *Idol*. Darnell was ready with his plans for how to execute the format. "Here's what I want to do," he began.

Murdoch cut him off. "You don't change a thing," Murdoch said. "This show works in England. And you're going to make the same show they made in England. The problem with you Hollywood people is you always want to change things and you ruin everything."

No one in the room believed that Murdoch had studied the structure of the British format to determine it was flawless. But everyone knew that he—thanks to the prodding of his daughter—had stepped up to ensure that Fox acquired *Idol*, and that the network would not have it had he not done that. Murdoch seemed to also perceive that whatever lack of enthusiasm had inspired the deliberately vacuous negotiations for the rights to the show was likely still infecting the Fox program people. Murdoch seemed to have the impression that his top Fox executives doubted *Idol* would amount to anything.

No one would think of challenging Murdoch's views, but some Fox executives really did believe the British format had some obvious flaws. For one thing, it had two hosts, which surely made the show seem unnecessarily cluttered. And the four-judge panel invited trouble because it was an even number. If the judges split two and two, the format called for Cowell to break the tie; but that seemed to reduce the number of judges to one.

Fox had not signed Cowell to a contract—at his insistence. He told the Fox executives, "I'll do one season and see how it goes." That was music to the ears of the Fox group, still worried about the expense of this little summer show that had suddenly grown to fifteen episodes. Nobody really knew how the show was going to do. Cowell was still saying that he was not in it for the salary, but for the money that would come from finding another hot artist for his label. Cowell did not even acquire an American agent—not right away.

Fox offered him what, by American television terms, was a pittance. Under the original terms, for his work on the entire first series of *American Idol,* Cowell would be paid about $25,000—total. But he was also unencumbered by an option in a contract for a second season.

On his first day in L.A., Cowell met with Darnell. It was a good match. Cowell loved Mike's edgy sense of humor; it struck him as more of a darker, European sensibility than what he found in most Americans. Darnell also said how much he liked the audition shows in the British version, a sentiment that Cowell completely agreed with.

Cowell believed the audition shows—where his own role as the brutally honest talent evaluator was obviously more prominent—provided great comedy, but also something he called "a look through the keyhole at something people aren't normally allowed to see."

The whole Fox operation impressed Cowell because no one ever attempted to censor him or turn him into a sweetheart of a guy. To Cowell, Fox seemed to be bravely acknowledging that the American audience, like the British, was ready to rebel against what Cowell called "the terrible political correctness that invaded America and England."

For a change, Fox was going to allow the audience to see something that wasn't sanitized. They would embrace the fact that with Simon Cowell doing the judging, "lots of useless people were going to be told that they were useless."

The selection of the other judges went relatively smoothly. When Fox brought in Randy Jackson, the onetime bass player for the band Journey who became a successful producer and A&R man for Columbia Records, Cowell liked him immediately. When Cowell heard that Paula Abdul was also going to be named a judge, Cowell thought that was also a solid choice, given her long career in music in the U.S.

Because the British show had had four judges, Fox kept looking for a fourth, though Cowell thought everyone else they brought in fell into his broad category of "just useless." Again following the

British formula, Fox hired two hosts, Ryan Seacrest, an L.A. radio DJ, and Brian Dunkleman, an obscure standup comic and actor.

Cowell did not meet Paula Abdul until the first round of auditions for the show, which took place in L.A. At that point, no one at Fox had ever even seen the three judges interact. A fourth judge had still not been chosen, but given how much time the auditions were expected to take, the idea was to start with three and, if a fourth was found, add him or her later.

Almost nothing was said among the judges before the first auditions rolled. The petite, delicate-looking Paula seemed quiet and polite to Cowell; big and burly Randy was affable. The first singers came in. They had been screened, of course, and included a healthy mixture of respectable warblers and delusional, tone-deaf screechers.

This was teed up for Cowell, who unleashed his lash on every offending wannabe. He told one girl to get a lawyer and sue her vocal coach. Others he labeled with such terms as "wretched," "horrid," "pathetic." When one kid said he would someday regret all the hearts he was breaking, Cowell dismissed him with the line "You're a loser."

The chorus of put-downs was clearly not what Paula Abdul had been expecting. Several times during the first day, she looked over at Cowell in shock. Cowell took notice. Apparently, Paula had been anticipating the kind of audition American kids usually got: "Oh, you were great, thanks, we'll let you know." Instead, they were leaving either angry or in tears.

After the taping, Cowell cornered Lythgoe and Gadinsky. "I think Paula is going to walk," he told them. "I don't think she's going to want to continue to do the show."

Abdul did not quit. But the relationship between her and Cowell was instantly tense. Their fractiousness on the air in those early shows was definitely not a put-on.

As the auditions moved on to a second round, Cowell remained concerned about how Abdul was going to react to his give-no-quarter style. Just before the taping began, one of the newer American producers came up to him with a long sheet of paper in his hand. He offered it to Cowell.

"What is it?" Cowell said.

"We've written a script for you today," the producer said.

"What do you mean a script?" the befuddled Cowell said.

"We've written put-downs for you, more put-downs," the producer said.

"What do you mean, you've written me put-downs?"

"Well, you're scripted, aren't you?" the producer said.

"No, I'm not scripted," Cowell said, now more appalled than surprised.

"Well, do you want these?" the producer said, offering the list again.

"No!" Cowell said, utterly indignant. Apparently, these people were accustomed to everything being scripted.

After the auditions were completed, Cowell flew home to London. He was confident that the show would make great television. He had no idea if it would break through and be a hit, because he felt he could not predict American tastes the way he could British tastes. But he was more than satisfied with how the auditions had gone. He would return for the live-performance shows after the first few editions of *American Idol* went on the air.

· · ·

One evening, after *Idol* had been commissioned as a summer show but some time before it was set to premiere, Preston Beckman, the scheduler for Fox, got a call from Mike Darnell. He asked if Beckman could come down to his office before he headed home.

Waiting in the office, along with Darnell, were Simon Fuller, Ken Warwick, and Cecile Frot-Coutaz, the executive from Fremantle-Media. Darnell and the *Idol* producers had been kicking around the issue of how the network was going to report the results of the audience voting. In England the show was broadcast early in the evening on ITV; the votes were phoned in and tabulated. A couple of hours later, before the network signed off, the hosts of *Idol* appeared again, gave the results, and announced which of the finalists was going to be sent home.

All this was possible in the U.K. because the entire country was contained in one time zone. "Can we do something like this in America?" Fuller asked.

Beckman had been involved in numerous tricky scheduling assignments in his long career at NBC and Fox, but nothing like this.

"That's just not going to work here," he explained. "First of all, we're only a two-hour-a-night network. We have to hand it off to affiliated stations at 10 P.M. in the East. And besides that," Beckman added, "we have three time zones to deal with, if you don't count Hawaii. Even if we could announce the results the same night, the entire West Coast would not have a chance to vote. The voting would be over before the show even started at 8 P.M on the West Coast."

This dilemma had simply not occurred to anyone before. The producers looked at each other quizzically. *Idol* had a built-in audience-vote element. That was the climax of each week's show: the contestants sang, the audience voted, somebody was eliminated. There was no way to do *Idol* without the vote-out.

"Okay, so maybe the West Coast doesn't vote, then," Darnell said.

Nobody jumped at this idea—other than out of its way. "Mike, are you nuts?" Beckman said.

Beyond the fact that such a concept would mean a huge chunk of potential viewers would have no stake in the outcome, cutting off the voting before 10 P.M. Eastern time would also mean that the results would be all over the Internet before the show even aired on the West Coast.

"What else can we do?" Fuller asked Beckman. "Can we announce the results in a morning show the next day?"

Beckman informed Fuller that Fox had no network morning show. He thought for a second. "Really the only thing I can think of is that we have to do a second show every week."

More puzzled looks appeared. Nobody had contracted for a second show—and what would it look like even if they did one?

Beckman warmed to his idea. "The one thing we have going for us is that it's summer," he said. "We have the time. We could do a second show the next night."

When he left, the *Idol* producers were deeply engaged with Darnell, discussing the possibility of a second weekly show.

Grushow and Berman, meanwhile, were evaluating what was involved in staging mass auditions of walk-in volunteers in numerous cities around the country. It seemed like a hugely complicated undertaking, something that nobody in Mike Darnell's reality division had ever had to handle before. Like some others, they—especially Grushow—had questions about the unconventional style of Darnell and his staff, who often seemed to function more as a posse (some called it a cult) than a cadre of professionals. They were certainly a group intensely loyal on both a professional and personal level to Mike, who was loyal right back at them. Their closeness—they tended to travel around the Fox building in a pack—often led to cracks from some of the other Fox employees. The joke in some Fox circles was that Mike made his staffers drink the Kool-Aid before he let them sign on.

. . .

Simon Cowell was back at his day job in London on June 11, 2002. He had music artists, and selling records, on his mind, not *American Idol*. The fact that the show had gone on the air the previous night in the U.S. had completely slipped his mind.

At about 3 P.M. London time, Cowell got a call. It was one of the *Idol* staff members in L.A. When Simon picked up the phone, the guy on the other end was so excited he could hardly speak.

"Simon, this is amazing; it's a hit."

Confused for a moment, Cowell said, "What are you talking about? What's a hit?"

"*American Idol*. We opened last night, and the ratings are going through the roof."

"Fantastic!" Cowell said. "I'm really pleased."

The report was only a slight exaggeration at that point. For its

Tuesday-night premiere, *Idol* was the most-watched show on American television that night, with 10 million viewers; the Wednesday-night edition passed 11 million. Both ranked even better among the young viewers Fox coveted, beating all competition in the 18-to-49 group and, even better, finished first and second for the week on the air among viewers between 18 and 34.

Cowell immediately embarked on a round of publicity, doing fifty interviews with American radio stations in one day alone. Of course, the phenomenon that would soon dominate American pop culture—and set Fox on an unprecedented ratings run toward real competitive balance with the other three networks—was only beginning. Within a matter of weeks, Fox was making arrangements to bring *Idol* back in the regular season, starting the following January—the game plan according to *Survivor*.

*American Idol* would not be only the "game-changer" Sandy Grushow and Fox had been searching for. It would be a business-changer for all of network television.

Simon Cowell sat right in the middle of it all—with no contract and no agent. Alan Berger of CAA, who counted among his clients Katie Couric (and formerly Jeff Zucker), sensed a train was about to leave the station. He went down to the *Idol* set one night early in its run, with the intention of hopping on. Berger waited until after the show finished taping to meet Cowell and introduce himself. The conversation went well. Berger reeled Cowell in as a client.

Berger thought Fox had taken advantage of Cowell by paying him so little for the first edition of *Idol*. But there were mitigating factors. Cowell had not wanted to sign a contract, he told Berger.

"You mean they have no option on you for the next one?" Berger asked.

"No—no options," Cowell told him.

Berger quietly began to anticipate something highly favorable for his client and his agency.

When Grushow approached CAA about signing Cowell for the second *Idol* that January, Berger started the bidding at $250,000 an episode. Grushow blanched. He asked if Berger was out of his mind.

"Sorry, you have no options," Berger said. "I have a little leverage here; that's the way it goes."

Grushow told Berger, "We can do this show without him." Berger, stunned that Grushow would be willing to take such a risk on his breakout show, saw that position as a throw-down. Essentially, he and Cowell decided to wait till next year.

Fox offered Cowell $40,000 to $50,000 an episode for the second go-round of *Idol*. Berger said they would settle for that figure, but only if there were still no options in the deal for a third session. Berger and Cowell were betting that the series would still be flying after a second edition.

The night of the first-season finale of *Idol*, Berger met with Cowell and told him he had won an agreement for one more series of *Idol* shows—but still with no options to commit him for the future. Cowell smiled at his agent and said he thought this was a great situation.

"It is," Berger told him.

After the second edition of *Idol* scored the biggest ratings of any show on American television in the 2002–2003 season, Alan Berger got word that "marching orders" had come down from the top of News Corporation: Cowell needed to be locked up with a long-term deal.

Soon after, Simon Cowell signed a contract with Fox committing him to three more editions of *American Idol*. He was to get $8 million for each year, making him Fox's highest-paid star.

And Cowell was already hatching plans to make much, much more.

# CHAPTER TEN

# AN UNOPENED PACKAGE

I n the summer of 2003, Lloyd Braun, the chairman of ABC Entertainment, was on an annual vacation with his wife and four kids in Hawaii, getting a little R&R from the ratings wars. The sun was warm, his golf game was solid, and his family was healthy. So Lloyd had nothing serious to complain about in his personal life.

But it was not the best of times in Braun's long show-business career. Trained as an entertainment lawyer, Braun had represented, among others, the *Seinfeld* creator Larry David (Lloyd's name famously turned up on a recurring *Seinfeld* character, who wound up becoming deranged). Braun subsequently held senior executive positions, first with Brillstein-Grey Entertainment, where he played a role in the creation of *The Sopranos,* and then with Disney, where he became head of the Touchstone studio. In 1999, when Disney combined the studio and network operations, Braun landed at ABC.

Now, more than three years into Braun's watch, ABC was continuing to sink in prime time, still trying to recover from the bone-headed decision to cut the network's development budget after its game show *Who Wants to Be a Millionaire?* became an unexpected smash in the 1999–2000 season.

ABC's bosses at Disney had decreed that the game show must run first three and then four times a week, thus ensuring that the audience would be utterly sick of it within eighteen months. ABC had been much criticized at the time for running *Millionaire* into the ground, but in retrospect it looked as though the game-show phenomenon was about to flame out anyway, so Disney might have been wise in its impatient greed, squeezing $300 million or so in profits out of the show while it was still popular.

The lame-brained part had been paring the entertainment-development budget to the bone, under the bizarre assumption that ABC would not need nearly so many new shows now that it had *Millionaire* filling four hours of its prime-time schedule a week. If the show was being flogged to an early death to take advantage of its short shelf life, why was Disney also shutting down the assembly line of new products that would surely be needed once *Millionaire* left town?

ABC made only a pitiful eleven pilots in the 2000–2001 season. Networks often made more than thirty. ABC's entertainment division thus went out to meet the onslaught from the other networks post-*Millionaire* virtually unarmed. The result was a bloodbath that was taking ABC years to recover from. Of course, it might have helped had ABC picked up either *Survivor* or *CSI,* both of which the network had first crack at before they landed at CBS. Now these shows were slaughtering ABC's hapless entries on Thursday nights.

Braun had hung in at ABC Entertainment, matching up with different partners, first Stu Bloomberg and now Susan Lyne. Braun got along well with both of them; it was trying to live with the upper management at Disney that taxed him. He chafed under what he considered micromanagement, especially by Bob Iger, the Disney president, who earlier in his career had held Braun's position and never stopped inserting himself in the entertainment department's operations. Iger and the Disney chairman, Michael Eisner, had said on numerous occasions that they were going to take a personal hand in fixing ABC. To Braun and other executives at the entertainment division, that meant Eisner and Iger were making all the key decisions and keeping a tight rein on every budget. Braun and Lyne could not commit to any significant expenditure—like green-lighting any show—without first running it past the Disney budgeteers.

After several showdowns with Iger, Braun was getting worn down. That was one reason it felt so good to get away with his family to the Big Island. Given how things were going, Braun had reason to wonder how much longer he would be working at ABC's entertainment offices in Burbank. A big hit show might help; two would be better. But finding a hit had become almost excruciatingly difficult at ABC, where decision making was like an endless parlor game of "Mother, May I?"

Braun's frustrations had reached a peak a few months earlier. In March, Mark Burnett had walked into Braun's office, accompanied by his business chief, Conrad Riggs, to pitch a new reality series. Anything by Burnett was going to be a hot property, given his success with *Survivor,* and Braun was obviously salivating at the prospect of landing him for ABC.

Burnett sketched out an idea similar to *Survivor,* except the new jungle was going to be the business world. He called the new show *The Apprentice.* A group of young go-getters would compete for a job with a prominent business executive. The idea by itself excited Braun, who told Burnett it was one of the best reality ideas he had ever heard. Did Burnett have someone in mind for the mogul?

"I've just signed Donald Trump," Burnett said in his matter-of-fact way, his voice barely rising above a whisper.

Braun's face went white. "You have a deal with Trump?"

"Yes," Burnett said. "And by the way, we understand you guys tried to make a deal with Donald last year."

It was true. Braun had personally tried to sign Trump for a reality show. But Trump, as conscious of his super-exposed public image as any man alive, had found ABC's proposed format uninspiring. The network wanted camera crews to follow him around as he interacted with politicians and contractors. To Trump, that sounded like too much of an intrusion into his daily life—as well as a stupid idea.

But Donald had liked Braun personally, called him a great guy, and when he made his deal with Burnett he strongly suggested that they hit ABC first. Trump thought ABC sounded ripe for a quick sale.

He was right. Braun could not contain his interest. "I want the show," he told Burnett and Riggs excitedly. "I'll commit to it right now." He asked Burnett for an exclusive negotiating period.

Burnett made clear to him that no deal could be closed in the room. He was determined to take the show to CBS and NBC to gauge their level of interest. But he wanted Braun to know that ABC had first crack at making an offer, and the sooner they came up with a proposal the better their chances were of closing the deal.

Braun assured Burnett he was intent on making this deal, and that ABC would bid first to close out the others. They exchanged handshakes, even hugged a bit, and Burnett left.

But Lloyd Braun had a problem; he had no authority to make the deal. It was sure to cost between $15 million and $20 million up front. That was considerably beyond the budget Braun had to play with. Braun and Susan Lyne had to take any deal above $100,000 up through the convoluted chain of command at Disney; that involved Bob Iger, of course, and his trusted friend and lieutenant Alex Wallau, the president of the network, and ultimately Michael Eisner himself. The actual negotiation with Burnett would have to be handled by Mark Pedowitz, the head of ABC's business affairs. The follow-up on Burnett's show was completely out of Braun's hands.

Conrad Riggs did get a call from Pedowitz soon after the meeting, asking what the terms would be. The initial request was $1.2 million an episode for fifteen episodes guaranteed—a total commitment of $18 million. Pedowitz said he would call back. He did, only a day later. ABC's counteroffer, he said, would be $800,000 an episode for six episodes guaranteed. That was a commitment of only $4.8 million. ABC was cutting Burnett's terms by almost three-quarters.

Riggs said to Pedowitz, "You know what, that's a different show. This is our show; this is what it's going to cost. Thank you very much. If you change your mind, call me back."

Burnett later said the experience soured him on presenting ideas to ABC. "I honestly get a sick feeling in my stomach going over there," he said. "It's awful going over there knowing it's going to be so hard for them to make a deal."

ABC having effectively passed on yet another potential hit, Burnett made his way to CBS and NBC, places where the men in charge of entertainment had the power to commit to deals and execute them. As soon as he heard the pitch for *The Apprentice,* Jeff Zucker had a similar reaction to Braun's. He wanted to buy the show before Burnett could leave the room. The difference was that Zucker was able to accomplish it.

• • •

As Lloyd Braun was licking his wounds on the beaches of the Big Island that summer of 2003, Tony Krantz, a former CAA agent turned television producer, was hanging up his latest production shingle on the Warner Brothers studio lot in Burbank. Krantz started up the company, which he was calling Flame TV, after leaving Imagine Entertainment, where he had worked on shows like *Sports Night* for ABC and *24* for Fox.

Like most executives who fell under the heading of "nonwriting producers," Krantz could only start up his business by finding good material. If a writer had a hot idea or a promising script, Krantz could provide services to see it to fruition, services like development help and ultimately production money from his studio. In his exclusive deal with Warner, whatever shows he developed would be the property of the studio, which would try to place them with the right network.

Krantz believed he had an eye for good writing; more than that, he believed he had the experience to develop nascent concepts and help shape them into shows a network would want to buy.

One day that summer, Krantz's top development executive, Nina Lederman, turned up in his office with a question. Would Tony be interested in reading a spec script that had been talked up to her by a friend? The friend was a television comedy director named Dennis Erdman who worked with Darren Star, the creator of *Sex and the City.* This was not Erdman's script, Lederman pointed out. He had pitched Nina on behalf of a friend of his, a writer named Marc Cherry.

Lederman said Cherry's name had rung a bell. "Remember that script we took a look at last summer, *Desperate Housewives*? And we weren't sure about what it was, whether it was a comedy or not?"

Krantz had a faint memory of it. His impression, he recalled, had been that it wasn't yet a finished product. But he had thought it had something appealing about it. Now, Lederman told him, Cherry and his agents from Paradigm were trying to pitch it around as a soap opera, not a comedy. Erdman was attached, too.

Sure, Krantz said, let's look at it again.

Paradigm sent the script over. As Krantz read, he found it far more polished than the earlier version. It felt fresh. Not that he didn't think it could use a little input. He sent his reply back to Paradigm: We like it a lot; we want to develop it.

This was the best news Marc Cherry and his representatives had gotten yet about *Desperate Housewives*. Krantz was an unabashed Hollywood insider. He was a known producer with solid credits; he had a production deal with one of the biggest TV studios in Hollywood; and he knew absolutely everybody in town. If he attached himself to the show, it stood a good chance of being picked up by somebody.

Cherry and Dennis Erdman journeyed to Krantz's office for the first of what were to be numerous meetings. Krantz made it clear that they were in the discussion stage; no deal had been set. Cherry understood and was more than willing to participate. He even offered to do whatever rewrites were agreed upon for free. After all, everything else he had written on *Desperate Housewives* to that point had been for free.

Krantz was extremely complimentary about the show—best of all, from Cherry's point of view, Krantz really got it.

"I want you to know that I think this script is really funny," Krantz said. "I've talked to everyone on the staff here and told them this is such a great project and a great script."

"Thank you so much for saying that," Cherry replied effusively. "And I just want you to know that I am nothing if not collaborative. I am just so happy to not be by myself anymore and to have great people working with me." Cherry went on in this vein, emphasizing his experience working with teams of writers and producers, how flexible he was, and how well he understood the process of working together amicably.

"You are just going to find me so amenable to your ideas," Cherry concluded.

"That's great," Krantz said. "Because the first thing I wanted to say was, I'm just not sure about this title."

"You change the title, I walk off the project," Cherry fired back.

The rest of the room was taken aback.

Then Cherry smiled and explained that he, sort of, was only kidding. But he just wanted to make the point. "This is a fucking great title."

Krantz sought to explain himself. "Marc, I'm just concerned that the title will appeal to only 50 percent of the audience."

"What do you think might be better?" Cherry wanted to know.

Krantz said, "Well, how about *The Secret Lives of Housewives,* something like that?"

"Uh, no," Cherry said. "It's *Desperate Housewives*. Thank you, though, for the thought."

Krantz backed off immediately. He had been worried that men might be turned off by the title (though at least one participant in the show thought it might catch men's fancy because it sounded a bit like the title of a porno movie).

He had some other ideas, though, and they sounded much better to Cherry. In the draft of the pilot that Krantz had read, Cherry ended the episode with his Susan Mayer character, the dizzy but appealing divorced housewife of the central foursome, kissing her new crush, Mike, the handsome but mysterious neighborhood plumber. Krantz suggested that having the two romantic leads kiss already in the pilot was giving too much away. "You've got to delay that," Krantz told Cherry. It was a note Cherry respected—and used.

Cherry estimated that by the time they finished the development work he had altered about 15 percent of his original draft. The biggest change was tonal. The show was still comedic. But with the help of their soap expert, Chuck Pratt, it could be pitched to networks as a soap opera.

Krantz was totally gung-ho now. He was ready to push *Desperate Housewives* aggressively through the necessary channels at Warner Brothers. Kranz first sent it off to the studio's drama department, expecting a quick nod to go ahead.

Instead, he met with a collective "so what?" From Krantz's point of view, this was simply a case of unimaginative development staffers not getting what the script was all about. He would have preferred that they be enthusiastic about it, but he didn't really care.

Krantz had a 100 percent exclusive production deal at the studio; that meant he could not take this project elsewhere, and so if he insisted that this was the project he was pursuing, Warner Brothers had to back him, subject only to a financial agreement with the creators. At that point, Krantz regarded Warner Brothers as "the bank" and nothing more. The only thing remaining was the deal itself.

Krantz approached the Warner Brothers business affairs office with a contract that contained mostly conventional elements: They would ask a network for a license fee of about $1 million an episode. The studio would then make up the routine deficit, which, depending ultimately on cast and production costs, would likely hit a range between $500,000 and $800,000 per episode. Cherry would be credited as creator and executive producer. Pratt would be an EP. Krantz would take an EP credit as well and the fee that went with it, which would come out of the $1.5 million or so cost of each episode. Nothing unusual.

There was just one other thing. Paradigm wanted a 3 percent package fee per episode. This in itself was also relatively standard in the TV business. Agencies that supplied the key components of a show—usually the creator/producer, along with perhaps a key piece of casting and/or a director—always asked for a package on a series. Packages were the lifeblood of the agency business because of the potential for big payoffs, especially down the road. If a show became a hit and an agency had the package, it would mean profits in the tens of millions, at least. Packages meant cash up front, cash in success, and big cash in syndication if a show made it that far.

Agencies took the package percentage in lieu of charging their client or clients a commission, so they were good deals for the talent, if not the studio. In most cases, a package was supposed to mean exactly that: The agency supplied a package of elements—the writer, a couple of stars, the director. But sometimes an agency could successfully demand a package when it was offering only the key element, which in television, a writer's medium, meant the show creator. Every big-name creator, from Dick Wolf (*Law & Order*), to Steven Bochco (*Hill Street Blues*), to Aaron Sorkin (*The West Wing*), got their agencies package fees.

In this case, Paradigm was asking for a package fee for delivering Marc Cherry. Warner executives wanted to know why. Why were they supposed to pay this 3 percent fee, which, based on a $1 million license charge, would work out to $30,000 an episode, to secure the services of a writer who was, as one Warner executive bluntly put it, "as cold as a mackerel at that point in his career"?

There was more to the resistance than that, however. The Warner executives involved in the negotiations, which included Peter Roth, the hugely experienced television executive who had moved to the top job at the Warner television studio, and Bruce Rosenblum, the head of business affairs, argued that they had the long-term interests of the studio in mind.

Paradigm was not, to Warner's way of thinking, a packaging agency. It was a small operation, and in this case it was delivering only this writer—far from in demand, Warner would emphasize in the talks—who had a spec script. If Warner acquiesced, its executives believed, they would have every small agency in Hollywood demanding a package every time they had a writer whose show Warner wanted to produce.

Krantz's deal had hit a serious snag. He pointed out that Warner was already getting a load of benefits for free. Cherry had written the script for nothing. Now he had done numerous rewrites for nothing. All the development work that Krantz's team had done during multiple meetings had not cost the studio a penny. And they were also getting Chuck Pratt, a second Paradigm client, a seasoned soap-opera production talent, in the deal. That, to Krantz's mind, was easily worth the price of a package.

"If this was CAA or Endeavor," Krantz told Roth and Rosenblum, citing two of the biggest agencies in town, "you'd pay this fee, and you know it."

The Warner executives did not dispute that. But they argued that those agencies would have delivered a real package, not one writer who had not had a significant credit in a decade. Krantz knew he was also fighting against the utter lack of enthusiasm for the project that the studio's drama staff had expressed. Peter Roth, who had often demonstrated great taste in material, had not even read the script. He made it clear to Krantz that he wanted to keep the issue of the quality of *Desperate Housewives* separate. He simply could not set a precedent by giving a package in this instance. That was why he had not read the script.

Krantz, seeing his opportunity slipping away, tried some creative approaches: He could divvy up some of his own fee in some way to account for part of the package. Paradigm could defer some of its package fee, receiving it only if the show was a success. Warner Brothers made it clear that the dispute was not about the breakdown of the money; it was about the notion of committing any money at all to this fee, which would become a point of reference for every small agency in every negotiation henceforth. Warner Brothers simply refused to do it.

Krantz kept at it, trying new formulas. By now, he had fallen in love with the project; he was convinced it had all the elements to be a career-altering hit, exactly the kind of show a producer would regret losing for the rest of his career.

But Paradigm was getting antsy. Time was starting to run out in development season. Andy Pattman, the agent who had signed Cherry for Paradigm, thought he had a way to get the script to Touchstone, a studio affiliated with ABC through their common ownership by Disney. Pattman gave Krantz an unofficial two-minute warning: Close the deal or he was going to have to give Touchstone a shot.

Tony Krantz knew he could not stay with the project if it went to Touchstone or any other studio. He was exclusive to Warner Brothers. Wherever the show ended up, he knew he would get nothing for the development work he and his staff had done, no credit at the end of every episode, no ticket on the ride to success if there was one.

Time ran out. Warner Brothers would not compromise. *Desperate Housewives* would not be a Warner Brothers production, which it could have been for a fee of only $30,000 an episode.

After hearing the news that the deal was dead, Krantz went to his office and found a bouquet of a dozen red roses on his desk. They were from Marc Cherry. His note said he was embarrassed at how it had all turned out and he apologized. But there was nothing he could do.

There was nothing Tony Krantz could do either, except wait and see if he would someday be watching *Desperate Housewives* on the air.

• • •

Another frustrated man, Lloyd Braun, sat in a beach chair in Hawaii, trying as hard as he could to relax—but thinking always of some way to resurrect ABC, if that was possible under the claustrophobic top-down management structure that Disney had imposed.

That evening, Braun and his family ventured down to the beach for the hotel's clambake, an annual event. Braun was distracted. The previous night, he had watched the TV broadcast of *Castaway*, with Tom Hanks. Now he sat down in his beach chair, with his plate of clams and corn on the cob, and stared out at the ocean, thinking of the themes in the film: a plane disaster, isolation from society, the feeling of being utterly, hopelessly lost.

*I wonder if there could be a way to do a television series like that?* Braun thought. People obviously were drawn to stories like this, shipwrecked souls washing up on a remote island. Look at *Survivor*. It was a gimmick, but the broad theme was the same. What if there were some way to combine *Survivor* with the elements of *Castaway*?

Braun believed he had the makings of a pitch tumbling around in his head. So he tried the idea out on the only people around him at the moment, his wife and kids. They agreed it had possibilities. His teenage daughter Charlotte was especially enthusiastic. Braun filed the idea away in the back of his brain and let it go for the moment.

• • •

Every year the entire ABC management team, from entertainment executives, to lawyers, to business executives, even publicity executives, met for what was called a retreat. It was designed to generate fresh ideas for the network—as well as suggestions about how to improve ABC's existing shows.

This year one executive new to ABC took it as a message about the fortunes of the company that the meeting was being held not at some tony resort but at a company-owned hotel at Disney's California Adventure, the latest Disney theme park in Anaheim. The hotel, the Grand Californian, looked like a huge log cabin. The only perk offered was the chance to cut in on the lines to the rides.

The group of about fifty initially met in a big banquet room. The weekend's schedule was broken down into various "exercises" designed to generate stimulating interaction among the disparate executives. The assembly was broken up into groups of eight. Each group was to choose a leader, who would head up a discussion that would kick around ideas for new shows submitted and narrow the ideas down to three: one drama, one comedy, one reality show. The three would then be nominated for discussion when the large assembly got back together.

To the new executive it seemed like one more indication of how disjointed the programming process at ABC had become. Perhaps because no one seemed definitively in charge at ABC, with a clear point of view—the way it was at CBS, for example—it seemed to this executive that it was only through some bloody process that anything at all got on the air at ABC. Why should anyone be surprised that only the least objectionable or provocative ideas made it through?

In his group, Lloyd Braun had a few half-thought-out notions he was going to throw into the mix. But he knew they were all lame.

Instead, when his turn came, Braun found himself talking about the only idea he really liked.

He began by explaining how much he had liked the movie *Castaway*. "What if it was a whole plane of people," Braun said, "and we make the plane crash look totally real? It's all real. Then the group that survives the crash has to form its own little society on the island. But we make it all real."

Braun even had a name for the proposed show, a title he had been thinking of stealing for some time from a short-lived NBC reality show. The show featured teams of young people, dropped in a remote stretch of Outer Mongolia, who had to find a way to get to the Statue of Liberty. "We can call it *Lost*," Braun said.

Braun's group, not surprisingly, chose his idea as their drama suggestion, and so it was presented by the group moderator when all the groups reassembled to discuss their selections. But Braun's moderator had barely started describing *Lost* when Lloyd jumped in and began excitedly explaining the show. "We really should do this," Braun said, taking up the role of advocate.

The idea of *Lost* did stir some genuine interest. It certainly wasn't another cop show set in L.A. But dissenters spoke up quickly. Wouldn't it feel like we were trying to do a scripted *Survivor*? someone asked. Someone else mentioned the potentially dread comparison to *Gilligan's Island*. And there were questions about how many stories you could tell based on this premise.

Braun defended his idea forcefully, saying that the counter to all the questions was to make the show real. Not a contrived reality like *Survivor*; not a ridiculously heightened reality like *Gilligan's Island*. Put the viewer into the real situation, Braun argued, and the stories will flow.

Several members of ABC's drama department were not taken with the idea. It seemed to have limitations that could only be overcome by exceptional execution—and how many shows were exceptionally executed? But they realized that with their division head advocating the idea so vocally, there was a fair chance it was going to be pursued.

That night at dinner, Thom Sherman, the head of ABC's drama department, sat down with Susan Lyne, Braun's partner in running ABC's entertainment division.

"You know what?" Sherman told Lyne. "One idea I really liked was Lloyd's. Sounds fresh."

# CHAPTER ELEVEN

# *FRIENDS* TO THE END

To the consternation of his critics and competitors, Jeff Zucker could not contain his self-satisfaction about NBC's network dominance entering the 2002–2003 television season. NBC had cemented its hold on Thursday night again, so all did seem right with NBC's world.

The turnaround had mostly been accomplished on the strength of a stirring comeback by *Friends,* which, thanks to a creative renaissance, had countered the once formidable challenge of CBS's *Survivor.* The reality show was still strong, and it continued to give NBC problems at 8:30; but *Friends* was again the show generating all the buzz, thanks to some sexy and romantic plotlines, mainly involving the show's most glamorous performer, Jennifer Aniston.

Zucker decided to hand the precious spot after *Friends* to his most promising new comedy, *Scrubs.* He still had his doubts that a quirky comedy shot on film with no laugh track (and beloved by kiss-of-death critics) would emerge as a knockout hit. But it was worth putting *Scrubs* to the test to see if it could develop wide appeal.

Zucker had a new hope for Thursday at 9:30: a comedy from the team that had brought NBC *Will & Grace.* This one, *Good Morning, Miami,* was about a hotshot young producer of a morning television program. The cynics who said Zucker favored it mostly because he had been a hotshot morning television producer *from* Miami had a case. The show was hopelessly lame.

But for Zucker the best news was that, so far, nothing Leslie Moonves had tried had made a serious dent in *ER*'s ratings. Zucker was confident NBC's critical Thursday-night supremacy was in no danger—yet.

Other scheduling pieces were clicking into place. *Fear Factor* was a soaring hit on Monday nights, driving Zucker's critics in the press to ever-greater heights of hair-pulling, mouth-foaming outrage. The third edition of the *Law & Order* franchise, *Criminal Intent,* was building nicely on Sunday, and the other two editions were stalwart 10 P.M. hits on Tuesday and Wednesday.

Overall, the picture had brightened considerably in Zucker's eighteen months on the job, allowing NBC to continue, and even extend, its hold on first place in the 18-to-49 ratings and the huge advantage in revenues and profits that went with it.

NBC had it all working, as Zucker was so fond of telling the press. The *Today* show was still the master of the morning; Jay Leno and Conan O'Brien and *Saturday Night Live* gave NBC a triple-threat late-night franchise no other network could touch. NBC, once the subject of endless rumors that General Electric would put it on the auction block, was now a bigger profit center than any other GE division.

But under all the bluster, Zucker had a few genuine concerns, mainly about what was going to happen when he no longer had *Friends*. As had happened twice previously, NBC had gone an extra mile the previous winter and secured the ever-more-in-demand cast of *Friends* for one more year.

Zucker got the deal done for a license fee of $7 million an episode. That was then. Zucker started the new season in September 2002 knowing that *Friends* was gearing everything up toward an end date the following May.

In October, Zucker was in New York along with his friend and top business affairs executive, Marc Graboff, for a round of budget

Courtesy of CBS

Leslie Moonves, chairman,
CBS Corporation.

Courtesy of CBS

Kelly Kahl, chief program
scheduler for CBS.

Courtesy of CBS

Mark Burnett, creator of
*Survivor* and *The Apprentice*.

COURTESY OF CBS

Nina Tassler, president of CBS Entertainment, with Anthony Zuiker, creator of *C.S.I.*

COURTESY OF CBS

Dan Rather, the CBS news anchor, after his final newscast.

COURTESY OF LLOYD BRAUN FAMILY

Lloyd Braun, former chairman of ABC Entertainment, with his family in Hawaii.

COURTESY OF THOM SHERMAN

Thom Sherman, former head of drama for ABC.

COURTESY OF MARTHA STEWART LIVING OMNIMEDIA

Susan Lyne, former president of ABC Entertainment, now president of Martha Stewart Living Omnimedia.

COURTESY OF ABC

Stephen McPherson, president of ABC Entertainment.

COURTESY OF ABC

Marc Cherry, the creator of *Desperate Housewives,* with the cast of the show.

Mike Darnell, head of reality programs for Fox Network.

COURTESY OF FOX BROADCASTING CO.

COURTESY OF FOX BROADCASTING CO.

Simon Cowell, star of *American Idol.*

Courtesy of Fox Broadcasting Co.

Preston Beckman, chief
scheduler for Fox Network.

Courtesy of NBC

Bob Wright,
chairman of NBC.

Courtesy of NBC

Jeff Zucker, CEO of NBC
Universal Television Group.

COURTESY OF NBC

Martha Stewart, host of *Martha*.

COURTESY OF NBC

Donald Trump, star of
*The Apprentice*.

COURTESY OF NBC

Conan O'Brien, host of
NBC's *Late Night*.

COURTESY OF NBC

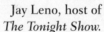

Jay Leno, host of
*The Tonight Show*.

COURTESY OF NBC

Kevin Reilly, president of
NBC Entertainment.

COURTESY OF NBC

Steve Carell and the cast of *The Office*.

COURTESY OF 20TH CENTURY FOX TELEVISION. ALL RIGHTS RESERVED.

(L-R): Ethan Suplee as Randy, Nadine Velazquez as Catalina, Eddie Steeples as Darnell, Jason Lee as Earl, and Jaime Pressly as Joy in *My Name Is Earl*.

meetings with the NBC brass—mainly Bob Wright and Randy Falco. The meetings tended to go on interminably, but this time Zucker had some big issues that had to be discussed urgently. Yes, it was *Friends* again.

Zucker and Graboff laid out the situation. In discussions with Warner Brothers the preceding spring, after concluding the deal that brought *Friends* back for a ninth season, Peter Roth told NBC that nothing short of a fully loaded and unlocked Brinks truck would bring *Friends* back for a tenth year. This had nothing to do with artistic concerns; it was all about the studio losing any substantial financial interest in extending the show.

The explanation came down to syndication revenues. As all studios do with hit shows, Warner Brothers had marketed the repeats of *Friends* aggressively, selling them to local stations around the country for big prices and collecting upward of a mind-boggling $3 billion. But stations do not need endless numbers of repeats to fill out their schedules. Once a show is on for eight or nine years, it has accumulated between 175 and 200 episodes. No station needs more than that to run them throughout the year. At the prices Warner Brothers had demanded for *Friends,* stations simply had no interest in adding more episodes.

The stations had been obligated to continue buying whatever fresh episodes were produced through the ninth season. But the studio had no more deals with stations after that. That meant the only monetary value Warner Brothers had in *Friends* was whatever NBC agreed to pay for each episode.

With its $7-million-an-episode license fee, *Friends* was the most expensive show per half hour in television history. NBC had at one time paid Warner Brothers $13 million an episode for *ER,* but that worked out to *only* $6.5 million per half hour.

Incredibly, even at that bloated price, Warner Brothers was still producing *Friends* at a deficit: Apparently, $7 million an episode—or a yearly fee of $168 million for the twenty-four episodes NBC ordered—gets eaten up fast when each of six cast members takes $1 million out of the kitty every week and the creators, writers, and directors—not to mention all the other costs—swallow another huge chunk.

When Peter Roth informed Zucker what it would cost NBC to tag on yet another year of *Friends,* it sounded like the ravings of a would-be Croesus. Zucker told Roth it wasn't going to happen and to plan for the definitive finale at the conclusion of season nine.

Then Zucker went back to his office and dispatched Graboff to investigate the claims Warner Brothers was making about having no financial incentive to continue the show for another year. Graboff came back with a surprising message: "Shockingly enough, Warner Brothers was telling the truth; there really isn't much value, if any, to them in syndication for a tenth season."

Zucker delivered that message—and the figure—to Wright at the NBC budget meeting in October: NBC would have to pay a heart-stopping $10 million an episode to keep *Friends* on the air.

Zucker also brought along a recommendation: NBC should pay up.

It had become painfully clear to Zucker, as it had to most everyone else at NBC, that *Friends* was the linchpin to holding on to Thursday night. The network had tried for years to find a comedy to replace it, and nothing remotely close was on the horizon. By this time, in mid-October, it was depressingly apparent that the comedy-development team had struck out again. *Good Morning, Miami* wasn't going to fill *Friends's* shoes with anything but sand. As for *Scrubs,* it was looking more and more, as Zucker had expected, like a niche hit, unlikely to ever expand beyond the core audience who loved it.

A *Friends* deal for $10 million an episode—or a migraine-inducing $240 million for the year, essentially wiping out the entire annual profit of the *Today* show—would strain the NBC prime-time profit machine. But only a bit. Zucker figured that NBC could still package other shows with *Friends* in its ad sales and book some money that way. The alternative was to go into an upfront in May without any "must-buy" comedy to offer advertisers on Thursday night, endangering the huge premiums that NBC always relied on.

For twenty years NBC had been able to find the next hit to keep its Thursday winning streak going. Sustaining that run had inspired NBC to inventiveness in programming and scheduling, moves that had transformed network strategy and even the way Americans watched television.

The departure of *Friends* would bring on an inevitable crisis, and NBC wanted to—had to—put that off as long as possible. For Bob Wright, institutional memory came sharply into play. He knew NBC had peeked into the abyss of a total wipeout of its Thursday-night comedy franchise once before, only to be saved at the very last minute by the bizarre combination of a buried treasure and Whoopi Goldberg's love life.

At that time, in 1993, NBC tried mightily to keep the only Thursday show working at the moment, *Cheers*, alive for one more season. The effort failed when the show's star, Ted Danson, quit to run off with Whoopi. Out of that trauma came a miraculous comeback, however, because NBC was able to plug an under-the-radar Wednesday-night show called *Seinfeld* into the Thursday-at-9 slot long occupied by *Cheers*.

Bob Wright, aware of the history, knew NBC simply could not afford a collapse on Thursday, the night it had used to rewrite the economics of the television business. The breakout of *Cosby, Hill Street Blues,* and a string of other NBC hits had been timed fortuitously to coincide with a surge of demand from advertisers to buy time on Thursdays.

The buying frenzy was driven initially by the movie studios, all of which came to the same conclusion: Heavy television advertising on Thursday was critical to pumping up the box office. Studio films regularly opened on Fridays, and more and more they depended on huge opening weekends.

Other advertisers quickly realized the value of Thursday night as well. With young viewers steadily abandoning television on Friday and Saturday nights, Thursday became the last time to reach them. So fast-food companies wanted in. Soda-pop makers wanted to reinforce their brand before weekend leisure activities. Car dealers knew they sold most vehicles on the weekends.

NBC's Thursday shows appealed especially to young, urban viewers with good incomes. This was an idyllic match for ad buyers. NBC had millions of these highly desirable customers committed to turning up on Thursday night, so it began charging advertisers a premium to lock up some of its scarce commercial space. Starting in the early 1990s, more than 40 percent of NBC's total revenues were pouring in from Thursday-night commercials.

All those facts and figures were in Bob Wright's mind when he gave Jeff Zucker the approval to offer Warner Brothers $10 million an episode for one last injection of *Friends*. Wright, who had become the premier business executive in television over his long tenure supervising NBC, was no slouch in terms of programming savvy. He did not have to be told that NBC currently had nothing on its schedule that could pass for a pale shadow of *Seinfeld*. Nothing on any other night was going to ride to the rescue on Thursday night this time.

Zucker and Graboff flew back to L.A. on a morning in late October. They had a meeting set for that afternoon with Peter Roth and Bruce Rosenblum of Warner Brothers, along with the *Friends* creative team of Marta Kauffman, David Crane, and Kevin Bright, and their agent, Nancy Josephson of ICM.

When the two NBC executives landed, they called the Warner executives and told them they wanted to come to the lot a half hour early and meet with them, along with Josephson. Zucker said he had "something important to discuss" and he didn't want to do it in front of the show's creative team.

In the Warner offices, Roth and Rosenblum looked at each other and had little trouble guessing that this had to be about a bid to keep *Friends*. But what could NBC do? Roth wondered. He concluded that the only way Zucker could possibly incentivize everyone involved was to pay such an extraordinary license fee that the series would become a serious loss leader for the network. It did not make a lot of business sense, but Roth and Rosenblum were certainly eager to hear what Zucker had to say.

At the meeting, Zucker got right to the point: "Last year when we asked you what it would take to secure a tenth season of *Friends*, you told us how much it would take. We're here to tell you that we do want a tenth season and that we are prepared to pay that exact amount: $10 million an episode."

Roth and Rosenblum were stunned. They had given NBC a figure where it would legitimately make sense to extend the show one more year—and Zucker had gone right to that figure. First offer.

The excitement in their reaction was palpable. Graboff thought the Warner executives might actually leap up and high-five each other and Nancy Josephson might kiss Zucker. Then everyone pulled themselves together. The Warner side brought up the potential reluctance of the creators and cast, who might already be "emotionally prepared" for the series to end. After all, didn't Jennifer Aniston want to get more seriously into movies?

Zucker and Graboff sensed where this was heading: a request for even more money—this was Hollywood, after all. Zucker shut down that line of conversation immediately, saying, "We are giving you the number you guys previously said you would take." There were not going to be any bump-ups, not to stroke Aniston's ego or for any other reason. The Warner side got the message and backed off.

As soon as Zucker and Graboff left, Roth and Rosenblum sat down to discuss the offer, which Roth found stunning, exquisite, and remarkable. More than that, the executives acknowledged that the bold bid clearly meant Zucker's need for the show was overwhelming. This was Warner's network partner coming out and saying it needed the studio to push for this show to go on and it was willing to pay an enormous price to accomplish that. "Jeff is our partner here," Roth said. "We can't *not* support this."

For Roth the unexpected NBC offer had additional impact, because it had the potential to alter a plan he had been working on for months, a means to keep some of that golden *Friends* revenue stream flowing.

• • •

After the end of the previous *Friends* negotiation, with Warner Brothers laying down its $10 million ransom note, Zucker planted a seed with Peter Roth. In a social conversation, Zucker kicked around the notion of what NBC and Warner might do in terms of a spin-off to *Friends*.

In the conversation, Roth and Zucker had come to the same conclusion: The one potential sequel they could foresee would be a show with Matt LeBlanc reprising his Joey character with a different supporting cast of characters. The perfect model was *Frasier,* in which a popular supporting player from *Cheers* was sent off to a different city to head his own show—with spectacular results.

Roth firmly believed Matt LeBlanc was coming into his own. At the start of the series, he had been considered the cast's weak link, more a comic device than a character. His Joey character would come into a scene, say something mind-bendingly stupid, get a quick laugh, and the scene would go on from there. He seldom drove any story line, because there simply wasn't that much to do with him. And LeBlanc did not seem an overly gifted actor.

The first time that the *Friends* cast held out for a big raise, Warner and NBC had considered dumping LeBlanc from the cast rather than pay him the same rate as the other, far more valuable actors.

But in more recent years the writers had fleshed out the Joey character, increasing his role in the show. The audience responded. Joey's popularity soared, particularly when the plot called for him to fall for Rachel (Aniston). In 2001–2002, Joey had a breakout season.

Roth had also developed a personal bond with LeBlanc. He found him to be smart, engaging, and really a good businessman about his career. The plan in the fall of 2002 was for Roth to pitch LeBlanc personally on the idea of continuing Joey in his own series, starting in September 2003. He met LeBlanc for dinner at an L.A. restaurant called Pinot Bistro. Roth let LeBlanc settle in before going at him with the earnest, arm-around-the-back sincerity that was Roth's personal style.

"Matt, I'm here tonight representing both Warner Brothers and NBC," Roth said. "We think you're terrific. We want to do something with you. Let's let tonight be a very loose first conversation that would incentivize you to do another show."

"Sounds all right to me," LeBlanc said.

"Okay," Roth said. "If you could wave a wand and have any show you wanted, what would it be?"

LeBlanc didn't have to think about it. "Well, the one thing I know is that I would not want to play Joey Tribbiani." He also indicated he might prefer to take a year off before he did anything.

This was not what Peter Roth wanted to hear, of course. But he was undaunted. "You know, I'm a student of television," Roth continued. "I have been for thirty years. If you think about *Seinfeld,* each of the supporting actors waited a year and then played a different character in a new show. And that didn't work out for any of them. Whereas Kelsey Grammer stayed as Frasier the very next year after *Cheers,* moved to Seattle, took advantage of the momentum and the popularity that the character had."

Roth wanted to plant that thought and move on. "But you know what—I hear you and we'll talk again."

By the next meeting, a lunch, things had gotten serious. LeBlanc brought his lawyer and agent along. Now Roth revved into a passionate speech.

"Guys, I need your help," he said. "I want a Joey sequel to happen next year. I'm well aware of the risks of a spin-off. I choose to live my life half-full, not half-empty. I believe you could create history here, Matt. I really do. While people can certainly separate Matt LeBlanc from the character, people are in love with Joey. We have to take advantage of momentum. If we wait a year, lethargy will set in. It will never work."

LeBlanc was still cautious. He had the most to gain by setting off on his own, but he also had the most to lose if he made a wrong choice. The talks went on. Finally, in September, Roth arranged another dinner at Pinot Bistro. This time LeBlanc said words Roth wanted to hear: "I'm open to it."

In the following weeks, Roth approached Kauffman and Crane, more or less as a courtesy. He knew they would not want to continue on a Joey sequel. But he needed their blessing to go on using the character they had created. They agreed and began talking about which members of their writing staff had the skill to bring off the new show. Kauffman and Crane recommended Scott Silveri and Shauna Goldberg, a writing team—and romantic partners in real life. Roth had them lined up and thinking about a format for the *Joey* show, with *Frasier* as the prototype.

These talks were well under way when Jeff Zucker turned up with his $10 million offer. Roth shut down the work being done on *Joey*. The spin-off would still be there after another year of *Friends*—and would likely even benefit from a year of gestation.

•   •   •

Zucker followed up his gambit at Warner Brothers by scheduling a big meeting with the myriad representatives—managers, agents, lawyers—of the six-person *Friends* cast. NBC was going to be paying the full costs of the show—at $10 million an episode, Warner Brothers would finally not need to deficit a cent—so nobody from Warners had any reason to be involved in the negotiations with the cast. Zucker put Graboff in charge.

He began by putting the same offer as the season before on the table: $1 million per star for each of twenty-four episodes. NBC also set a deadline to close the deal of early December—knowing full well somebody would try to stretch that out.

In most of the previous five-act negotiations with the *Friends* cast, David Schwimmer had played the Hamlet role, always unsure, expressing reservations about going on with the show, about staying too long, about needing to do other things in his career. In general, the most amenable stars were Courteney Cox and Jennifer Aniston. That's what Graboff expected to encounter again.

This time it was just the opposite. Schwimmer—whose forays into "other things in his career" had mostly fizzled—was happily on board early. Cox, on the other hand, was instantly resistant. Graboff and Zucker could not quite grasp what her objections were; she seemed to be trying to be difficult for the sake of being difficult. But it seemed resolvable.

Aniston, however, had NBC genuinely worried. With her Rachel character having given birth at the close of the preceding season, and then becoming confused about which guy she really loved, Aniston had sincere questions about the future story lines for Rachel. She also had the most promising shot at a film career. With her marriage to movie icon Brad Pitt, Aniston was now also the highest-profile star in the *Friends* firmament.

As always with the *Friends* negotiations, it was all for one and one for all, so NBC could not hope to break one star off and still have a show. After much wrangling, Aniston finally agreed to at least the concept of one more season, but she would only agree to participate in twelve episodes. That wasn't going to carry NBC through a full season of Thursday nights. NBC still pushed for twenty-four.

The haggling went on. Zucker himself got on the phone several times with the cast members. NBC tried to break the impasse by attempting a compromise: It dropped its order to twenty-two episodes, then twenty. Still Aniston would not come to terms.

With the deadline looming NBC made a final offer of eighteen episodes, the minimum it felt it could stretch out to a full season's run. Aniston generously deigned to say yes—as did the rest of the cast.

Of course, some financial issues remained. Things got sticky again.

At 3 P.M. on Friday, December 20, the last business day before the holiday season (when all of Hollywood shuts down tight), Roth got word: The deal was off. NBC was walking away. The negotiations had broken down over—what else?—money. Roth went off to the Warner Brothers holiday party that evening depressed. He was convinced it was over.

As it happened, Friday was taping night for *Friends,* so the cast was at the sound stage working. Roth periodically interrupted the partying at the Warner offices to take a call about the talks. The only good news he heard was that Kevin Bright was offering himself as arbiter, but the prospects still seemed dim.

The NBC executives were feeling exasperated, but not defeated.

The cast members (through their agents) were pushing for the moon: they wanted to be paid for twenty-four episodes even though they would now only shoot eighteen. They were asking for bigger trailers, use of company planes, the Hollywood works. Zucker and Graboff realized that if they were ever going to conclude a deal, it couldn't be this way, with concession after concession. They were being bled dry. They were going to have to reach deep and send a message.

So at 3 P.M. Zucker and Graboff put out word that they were walking away. The demands were too much. Zucker sent a note to Bob Wright, saying, "We tried, but we couldn't get a deal done." It sounded like a concession speech, but it wasn't. It was an all-out game of chicken.

Graboff stayed in his office late into the night, wondering if the *Friends* side would cave—and condescend to take the fortune that NBC was laying at their feet. At the same time, on a stage not far away in Burbank, during breaks in the taping of the episode, the cast convened in what they called their "clubhouse" and sent messages out to Kevin Bright, who would periodically call Graboff and update him on where things stood. The agents no longer seemed to be involved.

With NBC threatening to take its money and go home, it became clear to the *Friends* cast that they could agree to scarf up their $18 million each, or walk away and leave that boodle on the table. At 11 P.M., the call came. The cast would accept NBC's last offer—with one modification. One of the eighteen episodes had to be a clip show; the stars essentially insisted on getting $1 million apiece for a show they didn't work on at all. NBC gave in.

Peter Roth, home from his party at this point, got a call telling him it was all going to work out after all.

NBC would get a final season of Thursday nights under the safe-keeping of its ten-year-old hit comedy; Warner Brothers would collect the biggest haul ever doled out for a half-hour television series, $180 million; six comedy actors would walk off with more cash for seventeen weeks of work than Chaplin made in his career; and Jeff

Zucker would get one last chance to make his bones in Hollywood by finding a real hit he could stick his name on.

Back to the wall, Zucker would somehow have to find the show that could hold on to Thursday night, the most valuable piece of real estate on television, the house that *Cosby, Cheers, Seinfeld,* and *Friends* built.

CHAPTER TWELVE

# GIRLS' SHOWS

**B**y the summer of 2003, a kind of fatalism pervaded the gloomy halls of ABC Entertainment. Nothing the network added to its schedule, whether good, like the glossy action drama *Alias,* bad, like a time-travel drama called *That Was Then,* or ugly, like the egregiously leering reality series *Are You Hot?,* had been able to ignite even a flicker of a spark.

The entertainment division's beleaguered leaders, Lloyd Braun and Susan Lyne, seemed to be grasping at any new program strategy that floated by. First, they emphasized the return to ABC family values by introducing a raft of family comedies, some of which, like *My Wife and Kids* and *8 Simple Rules for Dating My Teenage Daughter,* offered encouraging early hints of success. But this strategy came just as network comedy in general was losing mass appeal. Worse, starting in January, both those comedies had run into Fox's two-night-a-week steamroller, *American Idol.* The promising newbies were all but smothered in their cribs.

Braun and Lyne next veered toward a reality-glutted schedule, inspired by the only reliable ratings hit on ABC's schedule, *The Bachelor.* With so many holes to fill, Braun and Lyne plugged in offerings like *Extreme Makeover,* with its icky tales of cosmetic surgery. They tried *I'm a Celebrity, Get Me Out of Here,* a bald-faced rip-off of *Survivor,* only starring low-wattage names nobody wanted to see. They even reached below the belt for *Are You Hot? The Search for America's Sexiest People,* which featured babes and studs in mini bathing suits being scrutinized for cellulite.

The reality pandering did not work on any level. Ratings were still lousy and sales worse, because advertisers steered clear of that low-rent programming, even when the ratings were good. It wasn't great for PR, either. The lurch away from the family strategy toward the likes of *Are You Hot?* was so extreme that Lyne was compelled to admit, after the show had been canceled, "The minute Lloyd and I saw it on our air, we were uncomfortable with it." So was everyone else.

Inside ABC, people wondered how long it would be before the Disney managers became irretrievably uncomfortable with the people running the entertainment division. The staff generally liked Braun and Lyne and sympathized with the difficulties they had running the place when their strings were constantly being pulled by Disney's managers. No one thought the system for finding shows was working, or even had a chance to work.

"You couldn't say that there was a person at the top that had a strong point of view and was determining the schedule that I could divine," said a senior ABC Entertainment development executive.

Braun would have liked to have been that person, or maybe that person with creative input from Lyne. But that was clearly not the way things worked at the Walt Disney Company. Even when a hit idea sashayed up and propositioned ABC, as *The Apprentice* had, and *Survivor* had, and *CSI* had, and even *American Idol* had, ABC always seemed to trip over its feet, get the stammers, or keep its wallet in its pocket too long to consummate the deal.

• • •

In that same summer of 2003, Thom Sherman, the head of the drama department at ABC, hosted a standard development meeting with representatives from the Paradigm agency—not because he was expecting them to have much for him. He wasn't. But it was ABC's policy to meet with all the agencies during development season, just because you never knew when a long shot might come in. Matt Bedrosian, a Paradigm agent, was running the meeting for his group.

In the midst of his rundown of projects, Bedrosian said, "We have a script we really like from this guy, Marc Cherry, who used to write on *The Golden Girls.*"

Sherman could not help himself. He rolled his eyes. Long experience led to a rote reaction: *It's a spec script. That probably means it was a pitch that the writer couldn't sell anywhere so there's probably something wrong with it. It probably isn't any good.*

Bedrosian wasn't quite finished. "And it's called *Desperate Housewives.*"

"Well, that's a great title," Sherman said, honestly impressed. He did not express any further interest. He still had no idea if the script would be good, but he had to admit he loved that title.

Bedrosian continued down his list; Sherman forgot about the conversation entirely.

A couple of months later, Sherman saw Bedrosian's name on his call sheet. When he called back, Bedrosian said he was checking in because he remembered that Sherman had been excited about the title of this spec script they represented, *Desperate Housewives,* and it was now in shape to be read. He added that his colleague, Andy Pattman, was also sending the script over to ABC's affiliated studio, Touchstone.

At the Touchstone offices on the Disney lot, not far from where Sherman worked, Stephen McPherson, the studio chief, had taken Pattman's call at about the same time. The agent, who considered himself a buddy of Steve's, asked McPherson if he remembered Marc Cherry. Sure, McPherson told him, from *The Golden Girls.*

"Great. Well, Marc has a script I think you should see," Pattman said.

"Oh, great, a new comedy from Marc. Okay," McPherson said.

"Uh, no, it's a drama," Pattman said.

"Uh—a drama? From Marc Cherry?" McPherson said, a bit nonplussed. "Well, okay. Send it over."

Inside the ABC offices, Thom Sherman got the script from Bedrosian, and set it aside. He would read it at home that night along with several others. Sherman still expected absolutely nothing to come of it. This was, after all, nothing more than a spec script from a writer he had never heard of, who apparently had generated no significant credits since *The Golden Girls,* which had gone off the air a long, long time ago.

That night, Sherman settled in to read. He picked up *Desperate Housewives* with all the enthusiasm of a man setting out on after-dinner chores, like washing the dishes or letting out the dog. His attitude changed before he finished the first page. Sherman was captivated. When he put the script down less than an hour later, he was amazed: This was one of the best scripts he had ever read.

The next day, Sherman decided to give *Desperate Housewives* to a couple of his staff members—Heather Kadin and Julie McNamara—to get their reactions. Sherman did not tell the women how much he liked the script.

That night, Kadin took *Desperate Housewives* home, read it immediately, and was astonished at the quality of the writing. She would strongly recommend that Touchstone buy the script.

Julie McNamara, married to a busy TV writer named John McNamara (who had written *The Fugitive*), put off her reading until she was ready for bed. She tucked herself in, arranged the pillows behind her head, picked up *Desperate Housewives,* and commenced.

Of all the executives who had read the script—and it had been dozens by that point—no one loved it more than Julie McNamara. From the first page, she loved it. Beginning to end, she loved it. McNamara usually approached new material from a business perspective, trying to guess how a show would fit it into a genre the network needed. This was not like that. This was the pure pleasure of being transported by superior storytelling. McNamara knew that she as a consumer, not a television professional, would be addicted to *Desperate Housewives.* McNamara did not want to change a scene, a character, a word of Marc Cherry's script. All she wanted to do was make it a series.

The next morning, McNamara came to the office full of excitement. She found Sherman and Kadin together and gave her report. "I absolutely love this script," she said.

Kadin seconded that, and Sherman agreed, though with more restraint, saying he liked the script enormously.

The next morning, Sherman decided to jump into action early. From home around 6 in the morning he sent off an e-mail to Steve McPherson. At that point, Sherman had no clue what McPherson thought of the *Desperate Housewives* script, though he was aware from Paradigm that a copy had been sent over to Touchstone. In the subject line, Sherman typed in "Desperate Housewives." His message to McPherson—copied to Steve's two top Touchstone development lieutenants, Suzanne Patmore and Josh Barry—was straight to the point: "I LOVE THIS! What's the deal with it?"

When he got to the office a few hours later, Sherman had a reply message from Josh Barry. It read: "Glad you like it. We think it's cool too. Great voice, huh?" The message went on to say: "Warner Bros. wants it also, but Paradigm is saying they should be able to deliver it to us."

Sherman was encouraged by the message, though it further convinced him that McPherson and his Touchstone team had read the script a couple of days earlier and had been waiting to see if ABC was interested before stepping up and shelling out any money to buy it. His instincts were confirmed about an hour later when he got an e-mail from McPherson. The one-line message read: "It is ours if we want it."

For Sherman this did not mean that *Desperate Housewives* was good to go. He saw it at that point as a promising piece of development. Touchstone, confident now of ABC's interest, would buy the script. Then they all would meet with Cherry; they would talk it through. After that the script would go on the stack that Sherman and his staff would present to Braun and Lyne closer to the time when they had to decide which scripts to shoot as pilots. It made no sense to Sherman to go hog-wild about a show this early. But when he spoke later that day with McPherson, they agreed they both were high on this project. McPherson said he would commit the money to getting it off the market right away.

That same day, Monday, September 15, Marc Cherry got the call from his agents: Touchstone was buying *Desperate Housewives*. All the work, the rewrites, the endless supplication to production companies, studios, and networks had finally paid off. Marc Cherry was a paid writer again.

Four days later, Cherry got a check for $79,000. It was not for the script. Marcie Wright had accepted a plea bargain in the charge of embezzlement, which required that she make restitution to her clients. The Touchstone check arrived the same week. Cherry, who had been ankle-deep in debt for so long, stepped back for a moment. "Okay, that era of my life is over," he said to himself. "I'm okay for a while."

. . .

Later that fall, Cherry went to ABC to meet with Thom Sherman, whom he did not know. He realized this was going to be a session where the network would give him their suggestions for changes they would like to see in the pilot, and maybe some casting ideas. They certainly would want to know where the story was going. Cherry wasn't worried about that. He had had ample time through the show's long incubation to come up with a detailed outline of how the first season would play out.

Cherry arrived at Sherman's office, ready to work. He even had a notebook. "Marc, I've read the script a couple of times now," Sherman said. "I just don't have any notes."

That never happened to a writer in Hollywood. Executives *always* thought they had brilliant ideas to contribute—otherwise, why were they employed in these high-paying jobs? But Sherman, a pleasant, bright guy in his mid-thirties, said he could not think of a thing that needed to be changed. Cherry had such a singular vision, Sherman said, and had written in such a distinctive voice.

They did talk casting and other elements. Cherry laid his out plan for the first season's plot. It all sounded good to Sherman, who

said they would be back to him when the script moved up the executive chain.

After assessing some other scripts in development, Sherman
decided they should waste no more time and deliver *Desperate
Housewives* to Braun and Lyne. Lyne was key, because this show
ought to be in perfect synch with her personal sensibilities. Sherman dispatched Heather Kadin and Julie McNamara to do the job,
especially counting on Julie to convey her extraordinary ebullience
about the script.

Kadin and McNamara marched into Lyne's office script in hand.
"You must read this today, Susan," McNamara said. "Don't take it
home. Don't save it for the weekend. You have to stop what you're
doing and read it today."

Lyne had the impression that McNamara and Kadin were going
to camp outside her office until she cleared the decks and read the
thing.

Lyne's take was almost the same as that of all the other ABC
executives who had read it; she was highly impressed. But Lyne was
slightly more cautious. She understood the passive-aggressive management style that prevailed at ABC under Disney. Second-guessing
was endemic, and with so many superiors all wanting a say, you
could not make any move without a degree of hesitance. Lyne loved
the script, but she had a pressing question: "What happens next?"

Lyne wanted to meet with Cherry to hear him lay out his story
lines for the series. Sherman said he would set up the meeting. In
the interim, McNamara and Kadin talked to Lyne about how perfectly the *Desperate Housewives* script had fulfilled both her and
Braun's two development goals. For Braun, the mantra had become
"make it different." Here was a show that was like nothing else on
the air.

For Lyne, hitting the bull's-eye meant finding a concept that
qualified as a "girls' show." This had been Lyne's mandate for the
development department for two years. At a series of lunches with
Kadin and Stephanie Liefer, the head of ABC's comedy department,
Lyne and the others had lamented the fact that there were few or no

shows that drew them hungrily to the set each week. All of the women watched *The O.C.* on Fox; that was it.

Liefer particularly decried the mass invasion of crime procedurals in prime time. The women knew that Steve McPherson at Touchstone was emphasizing procedurals in a big way. It made sense. That's what people were watching, including women. And Steve had a personal stake in chasing after a procedural franchise. He had lost out on *CSI,* a show he had loved and backed, when the Disney managers ordered Touchstone to pull out of its investment in the show.

But Lyne believed that the glut of cop shows shortchanged much of the young female audience that craved intricate, character-based, relationship shows with lots of hot (implied) sex—shows, Lyne said, that "women love to talk to their girlfriends about the next day." Nobody articulated that crying need better than Stephanie Liefer at the "girls lunches" in the Disney commissary.

"All my shows are gone," Liefer said in mock anguish at one of the lunches. "All *my* shows, the shows I would go home to watch." First Fox had ended *Ally McBeal.* Then HBO had terminated the best "girls' show" of them all, *Sex and the City.*

For two development seasons, Lyne had directed work on a concept called *Gramercy Park,* a splashy New York–based soap about nannies, the rich people who hired them, and their romantic entanglements in the city. It never panned out. ABC's development team, constantly looking for what became known in office shorthand as "the show that Stephanie would watch," had even suggested concepts to involve Candace Bushnell, the columnist who inspired *Sex and the City.*

One of ABC's most maddening frustrations was the inability to find a show at 10 P.M. on Wednesday night that could retain the big female audience that flocked to *The Bachelor.* In the fall of 2003, ABC had tried a stylish drama about a woman U.S. marshal in Miami called *Karen Sisco.* But its numbers were disappointing; it, too, squandered the big *Bachelor* audience.

McNamara and others thought *Desperate Housewives* might fill that slot successfully. They approached Libby Hansen, an executive in ABC's reality department, and asked if she would read the script with an eye toward judging its compatibility with *The Bachelor*.

Again the response was encouraging. Hansen liked the show a lot. "The only thing I might say is: Will it be young enough for the *Bachelor* audience?" The women protagonists in the show were, after all, well beyond the mid-twenties group that made up the core audience for *The Bachelor*.

That response finally did generate a note for Marc Cherry from ABC. Maybe in his backstory for the character of the former model, Gabrielle, he could move her age down to late twenties or early thirties. Cherry had no problem with the suggestion.

When Cherry and Chuck Pratt showed up at Lyne's office, they knew they faced a critical meeting. They had to sell Lyne on their plan for future episodes of the series. At the time, Cherry had no idea that of all the executives in television, none was as likely to identify with the characters in his story as Susan Lyne, a svelte, elegant platinum blonde in her early fifties, who favored striking ivory or pastel suits.

Essentially, Cherry was pitching, except this was not just a concept, it was a whole series. He filled in character details and started weaving stories about where these women were headed in season one. It was all there: Lynette's issues with mothering and the impact of a new baby on her marriage; the ongoing affair between Gabrielle and her teenage gardener; the crumbling marriage between Bree and Rex; Susan's oft-frustrated romance with the mysterious plumber, Mike, who linked up to the show's central secret about the dead Mary Alice.

On the spur of the moment, Cherry and Pratt came up with a scene about Bree and Rex going into marriage counseling. Bree did not want people to know. Then, Cherry said, warming to the idea, Rex blurts out the secret at a dinner party, enraging Bree. To get back at him, Bree reveals that Rex cries when he ejaculates.

The off-the-cuff joke drew big laughs from the ABC executives. Cherry made a mental note to write the idea down in his notebook as soon as the meeting was over. That piece of dialogue would later become, Cherry acknowledged, a "seminal line" in the show's first season.

By the time he was wrapping up, Cherry knew he had Susan Lyne in the palm of his hand. When he outlined the show's central secret, concerning the shocking family scandal behind Mary Alice's suicide, Cherry hit the concluding surprise so well that Lyne gasped out loud.

Cherry concluded that when a president of a network entertainment division gasps in shock at your story line, you've moved onto the A list. He was less sure about Braun, who still seemed hesitant about *Desperate Housewives*. Cherry suspected that Braun was fixated on getting his own baby, *Lost,* on the air.

Shortly after the meeting, Sherman told Cherry that Braun had asked if they could mount the show as early as the following summer. That was certainly an indication that Braun had taken a positive interest. ABC had not even ordered the shows to go to pilot yet, but Sherman said he had received authorization (and money) for Cherry to write two more scripts. "Just to get a jump on things," Sherman said.

As promising as this was, it was no picnic for Cherry, who had committed to spending late November and early December writing on a benefit for a friend. With the holidays to follow, he wondered how he could crank out two more episodes by January.

In mid-December, Lyne and Braun held a strategy session. It might make sense, they agreed, to order a few things to pilot before everyone left for the holidays. This was unusual because Bob Iger, who still tightly supervised the entertainment division, had told them that he did not want them to order any pilots until all the scripts were in. That way, ABC would not lay out money for a pilot only to suffer buyer's remorse later if a better script came in.

In other years, Braun and Lyne could not order even a single pilot on their own. All those decisions—and they tended to be torturous—went through Iger. But with the Disney company in the middle of a fight with board members Roy Disney and Stanley Gold, and the Comcast Corporation making noise about buying the company, both Iger and Michael Eisner were totally preoccupied. Braun and Lyne were left to pick up the pilots on their own.

If this was going to be their only chance, they decided to go for it. There were six or seven shows they really liked, and it was time to give them pickup orders. The first show, they agreed, would be *Desperate Housewives*.

Lyne went off to call McPherson and tell him that one of Touchstone's scripts was getting an early pilot order. When she returned, she recounted that McPherson had expressed a bit of surprise. "This is the first thing you're picking up from me?" Steve said.

Lyne was amused. Although McPherson had made it clear that he really did like *Desperate Housewives,* he had given her the impression there were other shows in development that he liked more. She wondered whether Steve had doubts that the show would make it onto the schedule. Or maybe it rankled him ever so slightly that *Desperate Housewives* had merely landed in his lap. This was not a show that Touchstone had developed. In essence, the studio had done nothing but write a check.

"I don't think Steve could entirely divorce himself emotionally from that fact," one of the executives involved in the development process said. "He was happy that ABC had responded so positively, but, as a person, for him it was hard that it didn't come from his shop."

Lyne and others also suspected that McPherson might have some legitimate concerns about the genre of the show. It was far from a procedural. This was a serial drama geared toward women, and character-driven, female-oriented dramas were treacherously difficult to execute.

As Heather Kadin put it, "Every year you tried a show like this and the tone was crucial, because if you didn't hit it perfectly the show was awful."

But it was much too early to worry about the show's long-term prospects. Much could happen between the pilot and the time the network put the schedule together for the upfront.

In this case, much would turn into mountains.

•   •   •

In the middle of the maneuvering to get *Desperate Housewives* up and running, ABC's drama department began the effort to turn Lloyd Braun's minimalist idea for a show called *Lost* into a script—at least to the extent of spreading the word that ABC was kicking around this notion of a group of people stranded on some uncharted island. Aaron Spelling's production company responded quickly, saying that one of its writers, Jeffrey Lieber, had been interested in developing a show with just such a premise.

Lieber came in and pitched his idea to ABC. It started with a plane crash, which set up a *Lord of the Flies* sort of situation. ABC hired Lieber to write a script. Braun saw his idea emerging as a dynamic, fresh drama. But when Lieber's script arrived, nobody at ABC liked it at all. Braun, who read it in a coffee shop at the La Quinta resort over the Christmas holidays, was appalled right from the start: Lieber, or somebody, had dumped his compellingly commercial title and changed it to *The Circle*. Braun found the script flat and uninspired, beginning to end.

Thom Sherman also thought the script was pedestrian, too "on the nose"—the show-business expression meaning literal. He suggested to Braun that they give the writer three weeks for a revise.

Braun disliked the rewrite even more. Sherman had to agree. He concluded that this final disappointment would likely be the end of Braun's big idea, at least for this development season. But he had not taken into account how much Braun had personally staked on this project.

Braun called Sherman to his office. "I'm going to call J. J.," he said.

Under any other circumstances, Sherman would have laughed out loud. He and Braun had a standing joke: Whenever a promising idea was sabotaged by a lackluster script, either he or Braun would say: "Let's get J. J. to rewrite it."

That was how highly they regarded the writing talents of J. J. Abrams. He was already represented on the ABC schedule with the critically praised—though marginally rated—*Alias*. Previously, he had created and written *Felicity,* the briefly hot youth series for the WB. Braun had developed a close relationship—a personal bond, really—with Abrams, regarding him as the freshest creative mind he had encountered in his years in television.

It was not a universally held opinion. Some executives, notably the Disney president, Bob Iger, had soured on Abrams over his handling of *Alias,* a show some had hoped would be the hit to turn around ABC. Iger thought Abrams had wrecked the promising series by emphasizing convoluted plots at the expense of romantic story lines for the show's strikingly sexy star, Jennifer Garner. Lyne lost count of the number of times that an exasperated Iger had told her, or e-mailed her, that she had to fire Abrams off of *Alias.*

Neither she nor Braun would consider doing such a thing. Iger and the Disney boss, Michael Eisner, accused them of "coddling talent." Now Braun wanted to coddle Abrams right into his pet project. He was already out on a long limb with Abrams. When Braun was at Touchstone, he had signed Abrams to an exclusive deal: four years for $20 million. All Abrams's new shows would go to the Disney studio.

But Abrams had not generated any new shows aside from *Alias.* As the deal's term wound down, Braun felt like he had counted on much more from J. J. He told Abrams he thought he had been shortchanged. Not to get even one other pilot "does not feel morally right to me," Braun said in the meeting. He conceded that with just a few months left on the deal, there was no way contractually to force Abrams to come up with another show idea. Still, Braun had asked Abrams to go home and think about it.

Abrams did. He returned in a couple of weeks with an idea about bounty hunters called *The Catch*. His deal with Braun was up, but Abrams went off to work on it on trust.

Now, with *Lost* in jeopardy, Braun called Abrams again. When the writer came in to talk, Braun acknowledged that Abrams was deep into *The Catch,* which Abrams was only doing because of his personal debt to Lloyd. "But I want to tell you that I have this new idea that I'm crazy about," Braun said, "and we've totally screwed it up. In your hands, I know it would be a hit."

When he heard the concept, Abrams was intrigued but clearly reluctant. He told Braun he was still consumed with the bounty hunter pilot. Lloyd pressed him, saying they could hire another writer to handle the heavy lifting and J. J. could just supervise. Abrams agreed to think about it, but, to Thom Sherman at least, it seemed possible that J. J. was merely paying lip service to his friend Lloyd.

About a week later, Abrams called, saying, "The good news is I've thought about it and I have some ideas; the bad news is I've thought about it and I have some ideas."

Braun wanted to hear any ideas. Abrams said he had two main thoughts. The first was that just having a bunch of people trying to create a society on a desert island after being stranded by a plane crash was not a series. "To have a series," Abrams said, "something is wrong with the island. The island has to be a character. Something is keeping the characters in constant jeopardy."

Braun knew Abrams's fondness for science fiction, and he liked adding a hint of sci-fi, in theory; but he told Abrams it would be better if it were more science fact. Whatever malevolent force existed on the island, it should seem plausible in real life, so the show would not become campy or preposterous. Abrams agreed.

The writer's second insight had to do with the structure of the series. The show had to be about the people, so it should not start with the plane crash. That was the opening to a B movie, Abrams said. Instead, in the first scene the crash should already have happened, and we should see the characters and events unfold in flashbacks. That way we can set up a storytelling form that will allow us to get off the island and into the backstories of the cast.

Braun thought this was a stroke of genius. It expanded the show's possibilities enormously. And it would eliminate the most significant objection people still had: that the show would become limited and claustrophobic after only a few episodes with the cast cooped up on an island.

Seeing that Braun was all but jumping out of his skin, Abrams tried to tamp down the enthusiasm a bit. He told Braun this was definitely not something he could write by himself, not on such short notice. "You guys really do have to find somebody who can take up the brunt of the writing," Abrams said.

With the holidays over, it was already incredibly late to be starting a pilot script, never mind trying to find a writer for one. Heather Kadin, who had worked on *Alias* and knew Abrams as well as anybody on the staff, had an immediate idea. For months she had been whispering the name of Damon Lindelof in Thom Sherman's ear—saying he was a great writing talent waiting to be discovered. Kadin had read Lindelof's quirky one-act play about time travel called *Ollie Klublershturf vs. the Nazis.*

When he heard the name, Sherman remembered that he had been impressed by Lindelof's work on a cop show called *Zone 5.* Sherman had not even wanted to make the pilot, but Ted Harbert, the old ABC entertainment chief, then an independent producer, was its main backer, and Harbert still had stores of goodwill at ABC. Harbert had been so passionate about the pitch, and the script was so cheap—only $55,000—that Sherman had agreed to make it. When Sherman read the script, he knew he had been right in the first place—it was not a series. But he agreed that Damon Lindelof was a talent.

With the help of a CAA agent, Tony Etz, ABC set up the meeting. Lindelof, it turned out, was an *Alias* addict as well as a sci-fi freak. He and Abrams held a three-hour meeting and hit it off at once. They shared the same concept for *Lost*—adventure, lots of characters, and a dollop of sci-fi. In a few days, Lindelof and Abrams were back at ABC with an outline, sketching out the new story, starting with an arresting opening image of a man waking up in the jungle not knowing where he was, and introducing the menacing unknown force on the island.

Braun took the material home on Friday night. He was over the moon about it. The next morning, Braun took his daughter Charlotte to her riding lessons in Malibu. While she rode, he stopped in to see an old friend, Marc Gurvitz, who lived next door to the riding academy. Gurvitz had been a talent manager when Braun worked at Brillstein-Grey.

"You see this, Marc?" Braun said, brandishing the outline, as Gurvitz greeted him. "This is *ER*. This is the best show I've ever seen." He told Gurvitz he was ordering a pilot of the show just off the outline—"even though it probably will mean the end of me at ABC."

Only four days after Lindelof first met with Abrams, Braun was committing to a pilot based not on a script, but on an outline. This amounted to a hugely risky move, almost unprecedented, but there was no other way to get a pilot up and running in time to be considered for the new fall lineup. ABC had to go on faith.

Susan Lyne supported Braun, but agreed with his assessment of the risk; the move looked like an invitation to a beheading. This was committing to a pilot on a wing and a prayer. It was apparent to anyone who read the outline—and knew Abrams's production history— that this pilot was going to be extravagantly expensive. Not only would it have to shoot entirely on some junglelike location, but it required a spectacular special-effects-laden air crash and a life-size wreck of a fuselage. And as Braun continued to insist, it had to all look real.

Abrams compounded the financial worry with his frenetic casting process. As the search for actors went on, the number of speaking parts kept growing. ABC was getting reports: Abrams is bringing in Korean people and big fat guys. Then he wanted a Paris Hilton type. The cast—and the cost—kept mounting, reaching more than twenty speaking parts.

The script was arriving act by act. The whole process was insanely unorthodox, but the pages themselves were riveting. Even Lyne, who started off as a cautious supporter, became hooked when she saw the quality of the work Abrams and Lindelof were turning in.

One scene stopped all the participants in their tracks. At the end of Act II, the writers suddenly and shockingly killed off the apparent protagonist, Jack. This was the character that the reader—and later viewer—would identify with. He was suddenly wiped out. Even though it was wildly creative and original—like Janet Leigh in *Psycho*—it was simply too jarring. Bob Iger, who was reading the script by this point, gave a note in the strongest possible terms: The writers must reconsider killing off Jack. They did.

One important player who was not an instant fan of *Lost* was Steve McPherson, whose studio was on the hook for this runaway train of a project. He told Braun and Lyne and several other executives that he hated everything about the show. Although most of the staff disagreed with that assessment because the quality of the work they were seeing was so good, some understood why McPherson might be objecting. The project was messy and unmanageable. It was risky, expensive, and in a format that demanded viewers watch every week or be "lost" themselves. That was what had happened on *Alias*. Worst of all, the show—a serial—was surely not going to be easily repeatable, which made the costs even more onerous.

But whatever resistance the project met, Lloyd Braun seemed determined to overcome it. One executive on his staff decided that Braun had decided to go all the way on *Lost*. He had staked his career at ABC on this pilot, and he was going to live or die by the way it turned out.

. . .

Marc Cherry's career, in the meantime, had moved off the critical list. He got the word on his first day back from the Christmas holidays that ABC was ordering a pilot. He had been expecting this news, of course, but he was no less thrilled, thinking: *Oh, good, I'm not going to die broke.*

As the series' principal showrunner, Cherry was immediately under the gun. He set up a production office and began building a staff. At the same time, the script was sent out to the various talent agencies so they could line up their actors, writers, and directors for possible assignments.

Within weeks, Cherry started hearing an amazing buzz around town. He had been through the process of getting a script picked up for a pilot before, so he knew the difference between pro forma comments like "Oh, we liked your script and we may have a client interested in it" and what he was hearing now: "This is the best script of pilot season." Every time he heard it, his reaction was a genuine "Really!"

Heather Kadin was hearing the same thing. It was the script every writer in town wanted to work on. That didn't really surprise her. She knew the town was filled with what were known as "character writers," people who liked drama based on character development as opposed to the action of the weekly plot. These writers had been sidelined for years in the rush for procedurals that had swept the networks. Now suddenly there was a pilot going into production that was all about characters—and women characters at that.

Marc Cherry had his pick. He enjoyed one particularly satisfying moment. The big-time agent who had ignored him at lunch and rejected signing him called up, trying to be jolly.

"Well, I guess you didn't need me to represent you," he said.

Cherry did not appreciate the levity. He had been vulnerable, and this guy had hurt his feelings badly. A short time later, the agent sent over a batch of scripts from writers he represented. Cherry promptly dumped them in the trash. It was his little moment of revenge.

The momentum behind *Desperate Housewives* continued to build. The script made it into the hands of some of the best-known fortyish actresses in Hollywood. And ABC and Touchstone said they were willing to step up and hire a feature director for the pilot.

P. J. Hogan, an Australian best known for the 1997 Julia Roberts film *My Best Friend's Wedding,* was just coming off a big-budget holiday film, *Peter Pan,* which had bombed at the box office. Hogan was available, and ABC sent him the script. He, like so many others, was delighted by it.

Hogan met with Cherry and complimented him extravagantly on his script. That pleased Cherry, but he was somewhat intimidated by the notion that a feature director was deigning to work on his little labor of love.

The two men spent their first day together scouting locations. They drove around tony L.A. neighborhoods in a minivan. Cherry, a big guy, was stuck in the back of the airless van and feeling claustrophobic. He thought he might be carsick at any time. So he said little during the trip. They ended up at Hogan's house, to go over his analysis. Hogan began giving notes to Cherry: what image he wanted to open with, what sort of interiors he expected.

Cherry, thinking this was the typical television collaboration, responded with some suggestions of his own. Hogan reacted coolly every time Cherry spoke up. Cherry began to suspect that Hogan expected the kind of writer-director relationship he had experienced in features, which often amounted to lackey and master. But here Cherry was more than the writer: He was the executive producer and showrunner. In TV, that gave him rank well above the director.

Cherry did not challenge Hogan and agreed with many of his notes. Two he did think were "so fucking stupid they would make my head explode." But he did not voice his objections to Hogan yet.

The next day, Cherry learned that Hogan had up and quit, declaring that Marc Cherry was impossible to work with. One of the Touchstone people confronted Cherry, asking him, "What the fuck did you do to P. J. Hogan?" Even his own agents asked him how he had managed to offend this guy so thoroughly in one day. Cherry explained the miscommunication, saying that he had simply taken Hogan's notes as suggestions, not orders. He argued that he himself was "a lovely guy" who would not set out to unhinge his director one day into production.

The episode totally pissed Cherry off. He was just getting his career back on track, and this conflict, which he felt he in no way instigated, had made him look like an asshole in the eyes of his studio and his network—and apparently even his agents. Cherry resolved to fix that impression as soon as possible.

That task was made a lot easier by the quick assignment of Charles McDougall, who had directed numerous episodes of *Sex and the City*. He and Cherry hit it off immediately, erasing any ill impressions left by the odd contretemps with Hogan.

With his director locked in, Cherry turned to the matter of casting—in many ways, the be-all-and-end-all decision. No matter how good the script, nothing derailed a TV project more quickly and completely than lousy casting.

The advantage *Desperate Housewives* had from the beginning was that actresses all over Hollywood were practically crawling into Touchstone on their bleeding knees to audition for these meaty, mature women's roles. Television had always been a women's medium, with almost every show attracting more women viewers than men. But as the networks became fixated on reaching young adult audiences, roles for women over forty became almost as rare as they were in the movies. Most women in series television had to be young and beautiful, and the roles often went to complete unknowns. Aside from CBS, the networks tended toward making new stars rather than recycling old ones.

But *Desperate Housewives* demanded experienced actresses, both because of the age of the characters and because the performances required a fine balance between drama and black comedy.

Cherry felt he had the goods to demand that every actress audition; nobody, no matter how big a name, would be offered a part without first being seen by the producers. And the names lining up were major. ABC floated Mary Louise Parker for the Susan role, and she considered it before declining. Then Calista Flockhart of *Ally McBeal* flirted with the same role. In her case, ABC, contradicting Cherry's dictum, said she would not have to read for it; it was hers. She also passed.

Dana Delaney, who had been in several series, most famously *China Beach,* for which she won two Emmys for best actress, was the redhead everyone wanted for Bree. Delaney auditioned once for Cherry and McDougall at the Touchstone offices. ABC was perfectly willing to make her an immediate offer, and Cherry, impressed, did extend the offer. But Delaney, having been in *Pasadena,* a Fox series she considered similar and which had quickly failed, decided she really didn't want the part after all. Cherry even called Delaney at home and tried persuading her to change her mind—as did her own agents. Delaney, with the plum role all hers, still passed on *Desperate Housewives.*

Sharon Lawrence, who had gained attention chiefly as Dennis Franz's wife in *NYPD Blue,* pushed hard for the Bree role and almost got it. Cherry liked the way she read his comedy rhythms, but she didn't really evoke his mother, and that's what Cherry was looking for.

Julia Louis-Dreyfus was interested in the Susan part. With her enormous *Seinfeld* fan base, she would have been a coup for ABC, but some of the casting executives wondered if Julia, who seemed to have endless stores of gumption and self-determination, could be convincing as the fragile, damaged Susan. "We needed someone a little broken to be Susan," Kadin said.

Cherry actually cast his youngest housewife first. Gabrielle was specifically a Hispanic woman who had been a model, leaving Cherry with relatively few options. Rosalyn Sanchez wanted the part and was suitably Hispanic and gorgeous. But she retained enough of an accent for Cherry to worry that she would sound out of place on Wisteria Lane. Eva Longoria had no trace of accent and looked spectacular, though at twenty-eight she was even younger than the part Cherry had already aged down. Longoria was the first actress signed for the pilot.

Roma Downey, the red-haired Irish actress and onetime star of *Touched by an Angel,* came in and read for Bree, as did Jeri Ryan. Jeanne Tripplehorn and Alex Kingston also came in and read for parts. None got past the audition stage.

The first week the script had been out for casting, agents for the highly regarded Felicity Huffman called and said she was interested in the part of Lynette but would accept only an offer. She would not audition. ABC executives, who remembered how brilliant Huffman had been in their much-praised comedy *Sports Night,* were all for offering the role to Huffman outright, but Cherry insisted she come in and read. Eventually, Huffman's agents talked her into it.

Huffman's audition wowed Cherry; she grasped the role immediately and far outshone anyone else they had seen for the part. When Cherry and Touchstone told ABC they were leaning toward Huffman, ABC said it did not need her to read again for the network. The problem was, four other actresses were scheduled to audition the next day, and until Huffman's deal was actually signed no one wanted to cancel them.

Huffman signed ten minutes before the first actress walked in to audition the next day. Cherry felt he could not insult the four other women by telling them not to bother, so he and the other casting executives sat through the readings knowing they were pointless because the part was already gone. Cherry hoped the actresses would not be offended if they found out later.

Nicollette Sheridan provided a memorable moment. The actress, more famous for her sexually charged look than her deep reservoir of acting ability, unaccountably asked to audition for the part of Bree, the highly tailored, uptight control freak. Sheridan strode into the audition room dressed in what she believed was the requisite pearls-and-pumps Bree look. Her reading became, for anyone in the room, one of the legendarily bad auditions of all time. Cherry thought she was particularly dreadful. The scorching hot Sheridan was so clearly not Bree she was not worth listening to for more than thirty seconds.

So he was astonished when he noticed McDougall rush up to talk to Sheridan afterward, as he did every time there was an actress who clicked for him in a part. Cherry watched McDougall chatting up Sherdian and thought, *Okay, Charles, you must want to fuck her, because there's no way she's getting that part.*

The director had not really lost his mind. From the moment Sheridan walked in, and despite the ludicrous pearls, McDougall had been thinking of the part of Edie Britt, the trampy neighbor who had a few scenes in the pilot and whom Cherry had envisioned as, at most, a recurring character, seen every five to seven episodes. McDougall asked Sheridan if she would like to try out for that part instead.

"Oh, you want me to read the slut?" she said, laughing. "No problem."

That audition she nailed in one try.

Marcia Cross had chased the part of Bree aggressively from the beginning. The actress, best known for the role she had played seven years earlier in *Melrose Place*, displayed a passion for Bree, as well as an implicit understanding of the character. Cherry loved that about her, and the casting executives at ABC were ready to sign. But

Cherry held off committing to her. Still flirting with Sharon Lawrence, he almost lost Cross.

Cherry had no problem with Marcia's acting; if anything, she was too good. With her delicate features, almost vermilion hair, and her exquisite ability to display a crumbling facade, Cherry thought Cross didn't merely resemble his mother. At times, watching her perform, he thought she *was* his mother. Maybe, he worried, Cross was going to cut just too close to the bone.

After considering Lawrence again, Cherry bowed to the inevitable. Cross looked born to play Bree.

From the beginning, the ABC executives had seen Susan as the fulcrum role in *Desperate Housewives*. Most of the name actresses who pursued parts in the pilot focused on that character as well. Considering the level of talent already turned away, the ABC executives had built up great expectations for the actress who ultimately won the part.

When Cherry announced that Touchstone was bringing over Teri Hatcher, some of the ABC executives were flummoxed. This choice seemed to indicate a radical shift in direction, perhaps a wild shot in the dark. But by that point, thanks to Steve McPherson, Hatcher had already had three cracks at auditioning for Cherry and the others at Touchstone.

McPherson, who like Moonves was always trying to spot undiscovered or underused talent, had spent several months trying to develop comedy roles for Hatcher. McPherson had seen photos of her on a camping trip with her six-year-old daughter, and decided that the forty-year-old Hatcher was not a fading glamour girl, but was actually a single mom who clearly had many unexplored sides to her personality.

McPherson invited Hatcher to test for a situation comedy called *Hot Moms*. She didn't get the part, but her comic timing impressed several of the executives at the network.

That effort only further convinced McPherson that Hatcher had untapped talent. He suggested that she take a look at *Desperate Housewives*.

After reading it just once, Hatcher, like many other Hollywood actresses, lusted after a role in the show. "It was one of the best-written things I had ever read, including movies," she said. "It was just perfect, a perfect script."

McPherson mentioned Hatcher's name to Cherry and the other *Housewives* producers as a potential Susan. Despite their skepticism about her ability to pull off such an emotionally turbulent—and yet funny—role, Cherry's team agreed to take a look at her.

The first time Hatcher came in amid all the heavyweight actresses he was seeing, Cherry thought she was OK—good, not great. She didn't blow him away. But neither had anyone else.

So Hatcher read for the part again. This time Cherry thought: *You know, she's pretty darn good.* They had Hatcher audition a third time. Cherry's evaluation went up again: Now Hatcher's effort was very good, certainly among the best Susans they'd seen.

Finally, Touchstone informed the ABC drama executives that they were bringing Teri Hatcher over to read for Susan. One of the top ABC executives said the reaction at the network was a collective "Teri Hatcher? Oh, please."

•   •   •

Teri Hatcher's tale was so familiar, it was all too easy to write her off as another burned-out case. The scenario had played out so many times before in Hollywood: Sexy young thing of limited range ages past her sell-by date and can't get arrested.

The big heat in Hatcher's career had come a full decade earlier when she signed on to star as Lois Lane in the ABC semihit *Lois & Clark.* But the show had burned out quickly and left the air back in 1997.

That was the year Hatcher's daughter was born and she was willing to shelve acting in favor of her personal life anyway. A woman of unusual intelligence (especially for an actress), Hatcher had never intended to enslave herself to show business. Her career had been one of those classic flukes from the start.

In 1985, set to start a semester majoring in math at the California Polytechnic Institute in San Luis Obispo, Hatcher, who hadn't even planned on trying out, won a part in a dance company that appeared as background in the ABC series *The Love Boat*.

After a little lark, Hatcher intended to go back to Cal Poly and then start a career as a high school math teacher. But the *Love Boat* gig led to an agent; the agent steered her to auditions, and Hatcher, a stunning brunette, got a lot of work—in shows like *MacGyver*, *L.A. Law*, and *Murphy Brown*.

Her career-making turn came in a guest role on a *Seinfeld* episode titled "The Implant," written by Peter Mehlman. Hatcher plays Sidra, a new Jerry girlfriend, whom Elaine dismisses for having surgically enhanced her eye-catching breasts. After accidentally stumbling into the naked Sidra's breasts in a sauna, Elaine suspects she was wrong. Jerry, obsessed with learning the anatomical truth, tries to induce Sidra into a moment of revelation. But when Elaine shows up at Jerry's apartment, Sidra recognizes her as the woman who grabbed her breasts to break her fall at the gym. Outraged, Sidra calls Jerry and Elaine mentally ill for pulling such a stunt and heads for the door.

Hatcher departs with an exit line that ranks among the most memorable delivered during the run of the classic NBC comedy: "And by the way . . . they're real, and they're spectacular!"

(Ten years later, just after her debut on *Housewives*, Hatcher told Charlie McCollum of her hometown *San Jose Mercury News*: "Now they're just real.")

The talked-about *Seinfeld* episode helped Hatcher land the role of Lois. But after her daughter was born, the offers dried up. The only attention-getting work Hatcher landed was in a series of commercials for Radio Shack in which she played the fictional wife of the ex–football player Howie Long. Hatcher's career continued to wither.

For years, people assumed she was really married to Long, but her husband in real life was the actor Jon Tenney. With her reputation starting to trend toward "has-been" status, Hatcher began having trouble even getting into auditions. Then she went through a bruising divorce.

In the months before the *Housewives* audition, Hatcher descended into what she called "some pretty sad places." Fearful that she might not actually be able to pay the mortgage on her home in L.A., Hatcher dissolved emotionally one day, falling in tears onto her kitchen floor. She later described her fragile psychological state.

"I failed at marriage. I don't have a career. I might lose my house. I don't have a man." With no consciousness of how her life would inform the part she so badly wanted, Hatcher said she was overcome by "that really desperate feeling, when you feel like you can't see the light at the end of the tunnel."

Despite her striking beauty and "spectacular" assets, Hatcher had had a lifelong struggle with insecurity. Now she was about to read for a role she recognized in every particular: a single mom, angry with her ex-husband, crying out for love, and vulnerable to the core.

•   •   •

Hatcher tried to lower expectations in her first audition by telling Cherry and the other producers that she was not "this glamorous whatever anymore." She was misapprehended on two counts. They weren't looking for that; but it was still in there anyway. By the time Hatcher got to ABC, Cherry was already in her corner, but he knew she would have to convince the doubters at the network. He wrote a new scene, one that ABC had not yet read. Hatcher was going to include it in the audition. Susan would knock on plumber Mike's door with the intention of asking him on a date, only to discover that Edie Britt was already there.

Facing a skeptical row of ABC executives, still lovely, still starlike, but clearly more vulnerable, Hatcher gave an inspired audition. Every line reading, every gesture, every nuance was spot on. The executives laughed in all the right places; they even laughed at the way she flipped her hair. When she got to Cherry's new scene, with Susan thrown by finding Mike with Edie and frantic to find some way to explain herself, Hatcher hit Cherry's laugh line with consummate timing: "I've got a clog in my pipes."

The room exploded with laughter. Cherry knew Hatcher had

them then. Hatcher herself called the audition "truly an out-of-body experience," the best performance of her life.

Heather Kadin, who sat in on the audition, had been one of the skeptics. When Hatcher walked out, she had no doubts left. "We found the heart of our series," Kadin said.

. . .

By the time *Desperate Housewives* was ready to begin shooting, Susan Lyne was its outspoken champion at the network. Thom Sherman had been serving that function, but in February things changed. Lloyd Braun called Sherman down to his office and, ominously, closed the door. Braun told Sherman that J. J. Abrams was about to start up his own production company and needed an executive to run it. "I and he both think it should be you," Braun said.

Sherman was flattered, but he pointed out that he was not really looking to switch jobs, that he loved working at ABC for Braun and Lyne. "And we love having you here," Braun said. Then he paused.

"Are you telling me I should take this job?" Sherman said.

"Look," Braun said, dropping his voice to a whisper. "I don't think I'm going to survive this season. They are going to need scapegoats. There is going to be a list of scapegoats and you're going to be at the top of that list, because we both know we haven't had any hit dramas."

Sherman assumed the "they" in question were mainly Bob Iger and Michael Eisner. Thom had been instrumental in acquiring *Desperate Housewives* and was a big backer of *Lost,* but both those shows were just unesteemed pieces of development at this point.

Giving up supervision of *Desperate Housewives* just as it was getting off the ground was not an easy call for Thom Sherman. But if he was going to be ousted anyway . . . This way he would be with Abrams just as *Lost* was starting up shooting.

Sherman told Braun: "I'm in."

. . .

When the dailies from *Desperate Housewives* started to come in, Cherry got a call from Braun, congratulating him on how the show looked. That made Cherry feel even better, but he still believed Lyne was his "secure champion" in the ABC hierarchy.

Lyne was getting excited by the show's chances. She even began thinking about where it might fit on the schedule. There was always that Wednesday-at-10 spot, but already the ratings for *The Bachelor* were softening. Maybe that wasn't the only place for a show like this.

Lyne remembered all the points Stephanie Liefer and her other women lieutenants had made about how much they missed their "girls' shows," especially *Sex and the City*. That show had drawn women by the millions every Sunday night at 9. HBO had found nothing similar to replace it. Nor did any other network have a dominant show on Sunday night at 9. Women were obviously still hungry for a series just for them at that hour. Why not give them a dose of *Desperate Housewives*?

Lyne told her staff: "We should grab that *Sex and the City* audience by the throat and not let them go."

# CHAPTER THIRTEEN

# "YOU'RE FIRED!"

**A**s the television season reached its midway point in January 2004, Leslie Moonves wore the look of a general who could not have been more confident of his position. The troops he had so painstakingly put in place were gaining ground on all his adversaries. Even better, every one of those adversaries was facing disarray, of one sort or another.

ABC was barely competitive, even in the fall, when it could count on big numbers every week from *Monday Night Football*. Now that the regular season was over, ABC had yet another night of woefully weak programs to drag its ratings average down. Moonves did not see much of a threat from ABC on any night of the week.

Fox was different. They were not to be underestimated. The previous spring, *American Idol* and the preposterously successful *Joe Millionaire* had given the network a huge boost. Fox had almost overtaken NBC and claimed first place in the 18-to-49 competition, which would have been an embarrassing blow to NBC and Jeff Zucker. But that surge was due primarily to a flash-in-the-pan gimmick, and not based on the strength of Fox's core schedule.

To Moonves, the new season was already proving that out. Fox had been unable to maintain the upward momentum of the previous spring. Its new schedule was a complete wipeout, especially the lame effort to re-create the *Joe Millionaire* magic. The public completely rejected *Joe Millionaire II*.

Fox did luck into perhaps the best run of postseason baseball in history, with a seven-game playoff series involving both of the sport's long-suffering sad-sack franchises, the Red Sox and the Cubs. Fortunately for Moonves and the other Fox competitors, both teams lost and that kept the World Series numbers from reaching the stratosphere. Instead, Fox was back to a bunch of shows people really didn't want to watch throughout the rest of the fall. As for the rest of the season, sure, *Idol* was coming back. But how many hours of that could Fox put on the air?

And then there was NBC, Moonves's perennial nemesis. What a teetering house of cards that was beginning to look like. NBC had performed yet another massive belly flop on Thursday night. The most touted new comedy of the season, *Coupling,* had already been driven off the air, not by viewer indifference but by outright viewer hostility. The audience hated the show.

That left a gaping hole at 9:30 Thursday for NBC. *Friends* was only half a season away from retirement. What was NBC going to do to save its once-mighty Thursday? The program coffers were bare. Thursday was tilting hard toward CBS.

Moonves was prepared to seize the day—or night in this case. *Survivor* was ready to storm its way back to the top that February with an "all-star" edition, featuring contestants from previous runs. That was sure to juice up the numbers. Moonves also thought he had some good new program weapons that fall. The new comedy *Two and a Half Men* was looking strong on Mondays; another cop procedural, *Cold Case,* had already made a mark on Sunday; and people even were talking about his Friday-night drama, *Joan of Arcadia,* which had God as a recurring character.

All that and a Super Bowl on CBS in January. How much better could things get? Moonves thought the stage was set for CBS to sweep the prime-time field.

• • •

Tom Freston wasn't much of a sports fan, so he had little interest in the Super Bowl in January 2004. But Freston, the hugely successful head of the MTV Networks cable empire, had a connection to this one, Super Bowl XXXVIII in Houston, because MTV was producing a star-intensive halftime show. CBS, MTV's corporate partner—both were owned by the Viacom Corporation—was the broadcaster. That meant Freston could have hit town and cruised through a few of the lavish parties, then sat to watch the game in a luxury suite with Leslie Moonves, the CBS boss.

The NFL had eagerly sought out MTV's participation because the league recognized it needed to stay relevant to young men. Three years earlier, MTV had put on such a smash halftime show that the ratings had been *better* for halftime than for the game among those younger viewers.

Freston himself had nothing to do with putting on the show. He had assigned that job to his MTV executives, headed by Judy McGrath and Van Toffler. They had experience staging huge events like this; every year they put on the Video Music Awards and the MTV Movie Awards. Twenty minutes of singing and dancing at halftime would surely prove no problem for them.

Unlike Moonves, Freston never felt the need to supervise every detail of an event himself, because he was not a programmer in his gut. He was an expert marketer and an inspiring leader to his staff, and despite being fifty-seven, he had a genuine feel for the changing tastes of the youth culture. Freston happily delegated assignments like this to his MTV team. He wasn't needed in Houston.

Of course, Freston was an American citizen, so he did watch the Super Bowl, the first half anyway, in his apartment in New York. He had been briefed on the halftime show, which sounded like standard MTV fare: performances by singers Nelly and Kid Rock, with a big finale, a duet from Janet Jackson and the red-hot Justin Timberlake.

The game itself was reasonably entertaining—a tight contest in which the New England Patriots led the Carolina Panthers 14 to 10 at the half. Just before the break, Freston heard the phone ring. His wife, Kathy, answered. Moments later, she rushed into the room, informing Freston that her father, who lived in Atlanta, seemed to be having a stroke.

The couple spent the next several hours phoning people, trying to line up hospital care and get an accurate diagnosis. The situation was not settled until 1 A.M.

By then Freston had long forgotten about the football game, the halftime show, and anything but his wife's concerns. When things finally calmed down, Freston realized he had not been in touch with any of his troops down in Houston. It was late, and he guessed they were all out celebrating. So he called Van Toffler, the MTV president, at his hotel and left a message on voice mail.

"Hey, Van," Freston said. "It's Tom. I just wanted to tell you I know you worked really hard on the halftime show and I just wanted to congratulate you on the great job you guys did."

Then he hung up. Freston did not bother to put the television back on. The evening had just been too hectic. His wife had learned her father actually had a brain tumor. All in all, it had been a tough evening at home.

A short while later, the phone rang.

"Man, where have you been?" Toffler said, his voice ragged. "Hello? You thought that was great? Tom, haven't you been watching the news or anything?"

Freston described the emergency at home, then Toffler explained how horribly wrong MTV's show had gone, with Janet Jackson and Justin Timberlake performing an unrehearsed stunt where he ripped half of her bustier off, briefly revealing Jackson's right breast—for more than 100 million people to see.

Freston knew this was trouble. MTV was going to catch hell from every religious group and every conservative social critic in America, not to mention the NFL and Les Moonves. "What is the NFL saying?" Freston said.

"You know what's funny?" Toffler said. "When I got back to my room, I had a gift basket there from Tagliabue." Paul Tagliabue was the NFL commissioner. "The note said: 'Great job, I loved it.' He obviously had sent it in advance. You know, if I could just collect my voice mail messages and my fruit baskets, this would be a really good job."

The fruit was mostly being thrown *at* MTV over the next few days. Freston had actually underestimated the furor. Jackson's stunt—

which Timberlake described famously as a "wardrobe malfunction"—was decried as symptomatic of the sewer that popular entertainment had become, with MTV the chief purveyor of the sewage.

Nobody really believed the carefully choreographed disrobing was an accident, not with Timberlake singing the lyric, "I'll have you naked by the end of this song." The complaints about the show only escalated from there: Kid Rock's lyrics had been offensive and Nelly had spent most of his performance flagrantly grabbing his crotch.

CBS was on the hook mainly because the offending material had appeared on its stations—broadcast stations, licensed by the federal government. Unlike cable, these stations came into *every* American home. And of course this was the Super Bowl, the all-American event designed to appeal to everybody, including kids and grandmas. CBS even got filleted for selling some of its price-gouging advertising minutes to Cialis, the Viagra competitor, which presented a new commercial during the game extolling its product's ability to correct erectile dysfunction for up to thirty-six hours. The pro-forma product warning included the startling message that if men should experience an erection lasting for more than four hours, they should seek "immediate medical care."

MTV and CBS spent the next weeks apologizing to the world; but only CBS faced a heavy fine from the Federal Communications Commission. The chairman, Michael Powell, seized the opportunity to grandstand on behalf of upholding morality in television. Still, Moonves did not blame Freston. He told Tom that he understood that "Jackson fucked both of us." He also told Freston he was pissed off that his own network people had not stepped in during rehearsal when they saw how licentious the show was going to be.

Moonves had every reason to "go supernova"—as Kelly Kahl might have put it—given how ugly the situation got for CBS. But Les stayed cool under fire. He disavowed the act. He defended his network. And he prevented any internecine fragging inside Viacom. If showing such a steady hand made him look better to the Viacom top management, Mel Karmazin and Sumner Redstone, that was a nice fringe benefit.

One thing Moonves's tempered reaction ensured was that his relationship with Tom Freston remained collegial. They had never been close, but the two men were familiar enough with the inner politics of Viacom to recognize they had been placed on parallel tracks and handed running shoes. Nothing good was going to come from making the competition overt.

Besides, they were both members of the notorious Havana Seven.

•  •  •

Freston and Moonves barely knew each other when the two men climbed aboard the private jet for a flight to Havana in February 2001. They had been at the same company since 1999 when Viacom assumed control of CBS. Freston, who enjoyed traveling to exotic locales almost as much as he enjoyed transforming MTV into the most recognizable music and youth culture brand in the world, had helped organize the trip to one of the few places in the world he had not seen. (Before going to MTV, Freston had run, among other businesses, a clothing import enterprise out of Kabul.)

Freston threw out the idea at lunch one day to a couple of his closest show-business friends: Brian Grazer, partner of Ron Howard in Imagine Entertainment (and Oscar-winning film producer), and Jim Wiatt, the head of the William Morris talent agency. "Come on, guys. Let's go on a trip together; let's go to Cuba," Freston said.

Both men were game. Wiatt extended some other invitations, and Freston himself asked his best friend, Bill Roedy, who ran MTV's international operations. Wiatt said he wanted to invite Lorne Michaels of *Saturday Night Live*. Sure, Freston said, bring Lorne.

Michaels then mentioned the trip to his good friend Brad Grey, the talent manager, and Brad told Freston he would like to bring along his own friend, Les Moonves. Eventually, Graydon Carter, the *Vanity Fair* editor, joined the group, while Michaels dropped out.

Brad Grey arranged the private jet; Freston himself secured the necessary permits from the State Department to visit the otherwise off-limits nation of Cuba. A contact in L.A. helped Freston acquire cultural-exchange permits for the seven men.

Once on the ground in Havana, the group took chauffeur-driven 1953 Chevy convertibles to their hotel, which was the old Nacionale, once the headquarters for Meyer Lansky and other famed names from the gangster era. Brian Grazer insisted on staying in the Lansky suite.

While the others lolled at the hotel, after an evening of night-clubbing, Tom and Les hit the city together. Moonves's still-excellent Spanish was invaluable. Freston met with the minister of culture, trying to set up shows for his networks.

All the men agreed that the trip was fabulous. It was topped off the last night with an extravagant show at one of Havana's still-spectacular nightclubs. At about 2 A.M., the moguls heard several military vehicles pull in at the club's entrance. An imposing figure in a medal-festooned military uniform climbed out and walked straight over to the Americans' table.

The officer identified himself, then told the Americans that he wanted to speak with them outside. The group had little choice but to leave the club with the officer.

They gathered outside on the gravel parking lot, anxiously waiting for an explanation. The officer said to them, in English, "El Commandante would like the pleasure of your company at lunch tomorrow at the presidential palace."

The Americans looked at each other briefly before Brian Grazer, famous for his spiked hair that made him look a bit like he'd just stuck a finger in an electrical socket, spoke up.

"Well, that's a nice offer," Grazer said. "But you know I'm afraid that we won't be able to make it. We're flying out tomorrow morning."

The others started shuffling nervously. Brad Grey was near paralyzed with nervousness that Grazer might have just come off as rude enough to get them all in serious trouble. But the officer was unperturbed.

"It's very important to El Commandante that you visit with him tomorrow," he said, "and have lunch in his company. I'm sure it will be arranged so you gentlemen can leave later in the day."

Again Grazer piped up. "You know, I really have things I've got to do . . ."

At that point Moonves, his jaw set, turned to Grazer and said, "Brian, shut the fuck up!"

The group had a lovely lunch with Fidel Castro the next afternoon at the Palacio de Revolución. Castro talked about the entertainment business with some knowledge, indicated he was an enormous fan of *The Sopranos* (on which Grey served as an executive producer), and teased Grazer about his electric hairstyle. The Americans found Castro fascinating.

The trip exceeded all their expectations. When they got home, they talked about taking another trip together.

But one member—always suspected to be Graydon Carter—was a little too enthusiastic and leaked some of the details to the *New York Post*, which ran an account of the meeting with Castro on its Page Six gossip page, under the headline "Castro Butters Up Media Moguls."

That was enough provocation to enrage the virulently anti-Castro Cuban expatriates in Florida, a group that only months earlier had been instrumental in delivering the contested state to George W. Bush, swinging the presidential election in his favor. When a group with that kind of political juice complains, it usually gets action. The Bush White House delivered.

The Treasury Department launched a formal investigation. The seven executives were interrogated about the trip, where the money for it came from, what planes they took to get there, what they did on the island, whom they spoke to. The investigators declared that the permits Freston had secured were worthless. They were intended for artists—not for trips by moguls. For this kind of boondoggle, as the investigators seemed to regard this trip, the men should have secured "research permits."

The executives, some of whom (like Moonves) were known to be active in Democratic politics, suspected a Republican administration was serving them up as political piñatas in an effort to curry favor with the Cuban population in Florida. Whatever the motivation, the judgment was nasty: The men had broken the law. Each was fined the maximum $55,000.

Appalled and embarrassed, the executives hired a legal expert who eventually helped them whittle down the fines to about $5,000 a man—though the legal expenses for each exceeded $10,000. The case took more than two years to adjudicate.

It was more than ever a bonding experience, however. Each member of the group got T-shirts that read "Free the Havana Seven." And a couple of years later, in an act of defiance only a media heavyweight might think of as appropriate, the same group journeyed together to Rio de Janeiro and proved their mettle by staying in the best hotels and having another great time. But when they took a boat trip up the Amazon, they ran into a ferocious storm that almost killed them all. That was the last journey of the Havana Seven.

But it left Freston and Moonves with a close professional relationship. They were very different personalities, and neither had much time for friendship, nor for stabbing each other in the back. "We'll get around to that later," Freston would joke.

• • •

The same January that Freston and Moonves were testing their Havana-forged relationship with the CBS Super Bowl fiasco, Preston Beckman sat in his office at the Fox network on a quiet Thursday afternoon, contemplating the various moves and counter-moves to be made in the prime-time scheduling game. He had already heard Jeff Zucker's announcement that NBC was going to change its Thursday-night lineup, moving its nascent hit reality series *The Apprentice* to a permanent place on Thursday night at 9 P.M. That meant the show would no longer be competing with the Fox ratings monster, *American Idol*—more evidence of the unassailable status of the Fox hit. But to Beckman, the NBC move was more meaningful. It underlined the increasingly assailable status of his former network.

As he considered the move's implications, Beckman got a call from Warren Littlefield. Warren was both a friend and a former NBC colleague from the days when they both helped NBC rule prime time.

"May NBC rest in peace," Littlefield said. "It's over."

Beckman agreed. He had been saying for years that NBC under Zucker was pursuing a destructive strategy of manipulating the schedule instead of rejuvenating it. Zucker was essentially rearranging the drapes while the house was on fire, Beckman thought. Sure, Zucker had paid a fortune and kept *Friends* on the air one last season, but where was *his* hit series that would preserve the great NBC "Must-See TV" tradition?

Both Beckman and Littlefield concluded that the *Apprentice* decision was symbolic: The last pillar of the old NBC juggernaut had crumbled and the network had been forced to abandon its long-time Thursday-night strategy of four comedies leading into the best drama the network had on hand.

That plan had worked for NBC since 1984. Now, NBC was admitting it did not own four strong comedies that it could line up in a row on Thursday nights; that, instead, it needed to insert a hot (but who could say for how long?) reality series to keep from being overrun by CBS.

"You know what?" Littlefield said. "Take a minute and remember everything we did, everything we achieved. We had two decades of dominance."

Littlefield was speaking for the Old Guard, a group of NBC executives who had led the entertainment division to that position of unchallenged ratings success and profits in the 1990s. Beckman had stayed in touch with most of them: Don Ohlmeyer, who had run NBC's West Coast entertainment operation; John Agoglia, the chief deal-maker who had been in charge of business affairs; and others, some of whom still worked in NBC's Burbank offices and communicated quietly with Beckman. They all had the same reaction. As Ohlmeyer put it, "There is no vision of what NBC is supposed to be anymore. It's just a collection of programs."

Nobody disputed the fact that Zucker's hands were tied. What was he going to do to counter CBS's growing strength on Thursdays? Stick with a lineup that had two peak performers, *Friends* at 8 and *Will & Grace* at 9, but two duds in the half-hour slots? At 8:30, he had the estimable but marginally popular *Scrubs,* which was already getting battered by the second half hour of *Survivor.* At 9:30, he had essentially a black hole, after his latest great comedy hope, *Coupling,* the unappealing sexcapade import from Britain, fizzled out.

Zucker, in truth, had agonized over the Thursday-night decision. He recognized the implication of breaking up the NBC comedy lineup, and he realized he could no longer hide the fact that NBC lacked the weapons to hold off Moonves. And it was clear that *The Apprentice* would have been wasted on Wednesdays against *Idol.*

The Trump reality series already had strong buzz. But NBC had premiered it to best advantage, giving it a two-week run Thursdays after *Friends,* where it could inherit a big audience. Then it had slid the show over to Wednesday, where it had gotten knocked around by *American Idol.* The estimates from NBC's research department showed that, unlike the Wednesday run, *The Apprentice* would continue to grow if it played on Thursdays. Zucker knew he needed to maximize whatever chance *The Apprentice* had to become the big hit show that had so far eluded him. He made the move, couching it as a bold step into a new future for NBC. "If you play by the old rules, you will be left behind," Zucker said.

But the decision had less to do with rules than reality. Zucker had no bullets left in the NBC comedy gun. That development itself spoke volumes about what had happened to NBC, not merely on Zucker's three-year watch but all the way back to 1998, when the network's once flush pipeline of comedies had begun to dry up. It was also the best evidence yet that the entire sitcom genre was flatlining.

The only network boss not to pull an oh-fer in comedy since the turn of the century was the reliable Moonves, who had used his ongoing hit, *Everybody Loves Raymond,* to launch the increasingly popular *Two and a Half Men* on Monday nights.

All through the 1990s, NBC had followed its solid on-the-hour comedies with plug-ugly entries like *Fired Up, Built to Last, Men Behaving Badly, Jenny, Encore, Encore,* and *Conrad Bloom.* The list went on and on.

A few stuck around for a while: *Suddenly Susan, Veronica's Closet, Third Rock from the Sun.* None ever became a hit, though *Third Rock* came close for a time. Throughout most of the nineties, NBC had such hot shows on Tuesday and Thursday nights at 8 and 9 that whatever it shoveled into the following half hours was more or less guaranteed strong ratings—at least until the viewers realized what they were being served. Comics in L.A. had taken to calling those NBC nights "the shit double-decker sandwich."

Beckman had a less derogatory, but equally telling, metaphor. He called them "walk the dog" shows. Viewers got up, did chores, ate a cookie, packed the next day's lunch, or yes, let the dog out, anything to tune out NBC's lame half hours.

"We started to get a little full of ourselves," Beckman admitted. "We started to believe we could put anything behind those shows and we'd have a top five show."

But when the television comedy business went sour, NBC's fortunes went south. The 2003–2004 season confirmed that the comedy drought was for real.

"Have you laughed at a sitcom once this year?" asked Jon Mandel, the chief executive of MediaCom, which bought time for clients like Procter & Gamble and Mars candy bars. "Something has happened to television comedy," Mandel said. "It's like they sucked the creative juice out of anybody who was ever good at writing television comedy."

By early February, ratings for *The Apprentice* on Thursday nights started to soar. Donald Trump was suddenly the hottest name in television—as he was pleased to point out to anyone who was listening. His tag line—"You're fired!"—as he lowered the boom on the latest failed high-achiever, became one of the most-awaited television moments of the week. (Trump even filed an application with the U.S. Patent Office to trademark the expression.) It began to look like *The Apprentice* might actually be enough to sustain NBC's Thursday-night winning streak for this season—and maybe more to come.

Zucker dropped any shred of defensiveness about his move. It now looked as if dumping comedy for reality might be the way to go.

"No comedy has hit big since *Will & Grace* six years ago," said Zucker. "Right now, to a lot of these young viewers, comedies just feel artificial."

But nobody in the business missed the significance of what was going on at NBC. "If there was ever a watershed moment in the business, this is it," Lloyd Braun said. "This is NBC walking away from its greatest strength, from the thing that made its name for twenty years."

• • •

The success of *The Apprentice* drove NBC's rivals to their usual fits of gnashing of teeth and rending of garments. Not only had the network seemingly pulled its ass out of the fire at the last minute, but NBC had done it with Donald Trump, of all people. With the exception of Braun and Moonves, few of NBC's competitors had seen Trump as an audience draw. Braun had already tried to put Trump into a reality show, so he sensed the real-estate mogul might have some fascination for viewers. Moonves just believed so strongly in Mark Burnett's ability to outproduce anyone else in reality TV that he expected Trump's show to score.

No one had doubted *The Apprentice* more than Mike Darnell at Fox. Burnett had pitched him the show, though not with quite the same élan he used at the other networks. Burnett had sent Conrad Riggs to Darnell's office while he himself called in the pitch over the phone. Burnett said he was under the weather that morning. It felt like a cursory pitch to Darnell, who was not swept away by the idea. He halfheartedly ran it by the sales division. To his surprise, Darnell heard that all three of his competitors had immediately put bids on the table. Fox was out—not that Mike cared much. Donald Trump did not seem like a television star to him, and a show about the business world, filled with elitist Harvard MBAs, did not fit Darnell's view of what Americans wanted to see on television.

It was no wonder that Zucker felt like this time he had a significant advantage over his Hollywood rivals. Like every other New

Yorker, Zucker had seen Donald Trump in action for years, often in huge letters across the front pages of New York's tabloids—the "wood," as it was known. "I knew what a genius this guy was at self-promotion," Zucker said.

Trump did not let Zucker down. Midway through its first year, *The Apprentice* became a runaway hit, with more than 20 million viewers a week and spectacular numbers among the young adults NBC lusted after. Even better, most of that group was well-heeled. *The Apprentice* had the biggest complement of affluent young viewers in television.

That meant a lot to NBC, which was relying ever more heavily on its appeal to wealthier viewers—defined as those in households with more than $75,000 in income—to add premiums onto its advertising. *The West Wing* once boasted the best audience profile in terms of income, but the show had started to fade after the departure of its brilliant creator/auteur, Aaron Sorkin. Beyond saving Thursday night from the Moonves invasion, *The Apprentice* was picking up the slack among those deep-pocketed viewers.

Trump himself was happy to help to thwart Moonves—at least for a while. The two men had once been on good terms but had a serious falling-out over Trump's Miss Universe and Miss USA beauty pageants, which had been broadcast by CBS. Trump felt Les first gave the shows short shrift, then insulted him by not picking up the options on the pageants—which Trump then sold to NBC.

Burnett had pitched *The Apprentice* to Moonves, who bid aggressively. Trump preferred that Les not get it because of the "Miss Universe" episode. The conflict started to get ugly when Trump publicly called Moonves "the most overrated man in television."

Few in the business ever took on Leslie Moonves, who had developed an almost godfatherlike persona in the industry. But that only emboldened Trump. "I deal with the toughest fucks in New York," Trump said, dismissing any trepidation about taking on Moonves.

Moonves, who did not like being called overrated, called Trump privately and asked politely if he would back off. "Donald, let's get along," Moonves said.

Trump appreciated the sincerity of the approach, saying, "It's very nice of you to call me this way. And you know what? That's fine with me. Because you called, I'm not going to say things like that anymore."

Moonves was appreciative. But at that moment, nobody was more appreciative of Donald Trump than his friends at NBC. On Trump's next birthday, the first call he received in the morning, offering best wishes, was from Jeff Zucker. A few minutes later, Bob Wright called. When Trump's then fiancée, Melania Knauss, rolled over in bed to wish him a happy birthday, Donald said, "Sorry, honey, you're late."

A short while later, Trump got a call that underlined what it meant to have a hit television show. Trump had never met the General Electric chairman, Jeffrey Immelt, even though he had a deal with GE Capital to build an expensive building on Park Avenue. When Immelt called, Trump naturally expected Immelt wanted to talk about the building.

After Trump told Immelt what a great job he was doing as Jack Welch's successor, Immelt said he would love to meet with Trump to have lunch or to play golf.

"Great," Trump said. "So then you're happy with the job we've done on the Park Avenue building?"

"Building? What building?" Immelt said. "Are we doing a building together?"

"Yeah," Trump said. "It's a tremendous success, on Park and Fifty-ninth."

"Oh, well, no," Immelt said. "I was calling to tell you how happy I am with the job you're doing on *The Apprentice*."

Trump calculated that whatever the new building was worth, it was peanuts compared to what *The Apprentice* was making for GE's network, NBC.

• • •

Over at Fox, Mike Darnell swore that missing the call on *The Apprentice* had no impact on his approach to his job. But it was just one in a series of wildly charging swings of fortune he encountered that television season.

*American Idol,* however much or little it was under Mike's control, had emerged as the most powerful program on television. As Fox planned to unleash the third edition of *Idol* in the winter of 2004, the network had every expectation that its powerhouse ratings performer would continue to sweep away everything opposing it on Tuesday and Wednesday nights—and whatever additional nights Fox could squeeze it onto the air.

Darnell had hit another ratings peak a year earlier with one of his most clever "twist" shows: *Joe Millionaire,* a rip-off of ABC's *The Bachelor.* When his friend Mike Fleiss complained, Darnell insisted that *The Bachelor* was merely a riff on the original Fox hit *Who Wants to Marry a Multi-Millionaire?*

*Joe Millionaire,* with its cynical twist exposing women who were willing to fake romance to land a millionaire, bore all the distinctive Darnell markings. It married the faux romance of *The Bachelor* to a new hoax-is-on-the-contestant gimmick. Evan Marriott, the Joe of the title, was actually a lug who made only $19,000 a year in construction work. The girls who threw themselves at him thought he had inherited $50 million.

*Joe* was an unmitigated smash. For its seven-week run it was viewed by young women for its romantic trappings and by young men for its sniggering mockery of the contestants. *Joe Millionaire* got the full reality treatment: endlessly covered in every tabloid, talked about on all the syndicated showbiz TV shows, and hyped by every radio talk DJ in America. Its finale attracted a stupefying 40 million viewers.

Combined with the monster numbers racked up by *American Idol,* Fox had a double bill of reality blockbusters that almost drove the network to its first-ever season's ratings win. The fact that both shows came from Darnell's shop only furthered Darnell's legend as the boy genius of reality TV.

But, as usual, for every bull's-eye, Darnell sprayed wild buckshot all around the general vicinity. *Celebrity Boxing* (highlighted by Tonya Harding TKO-ing Paula Jones) scored good numbers, but for critics at least, landed even further below the taste belt than usual for Mike. The same was true of *The Glutton Bowl* (grotesque eating contests), except the ratings weren't much.

*Man vs. Beast* (featuring forty-four dwarfs in a tug-of-war against an elephant—close decision for Babar) was a rosy little hit, in spite of (or perhaps because of) protests by some animal-rights groups. But *Married by America* (five singles introduced to a batch of supposedly eligible marital candidates who let viewers vote on whom they should marry) was a thoroughgoing embarrassment. It captured few viewers and offended many.

The FCC intervened, voting 5-0 to fine Fox $1,183,000 for indecency—$7,000 for each television station on the Fox network. The main prosecution exhibits—in a show that aired at 8 P.M., no less—were scenes of a Las Vegas bachelor party that included two strippers spanking a man clothed only in his briefs, a topless lap dancer straddling a guy, and another topless dancer allowing a guy to lick whipped cream off her body. All the nudity was pixilated, but that only left *more* to the imagination. Fox protested the fines, saying nothing was indecent.

Then, in April of 2003, Darnell tried another variation on the *Bachelor* theme, a number called *Mr. Personality*. A single named Hayley got to pick the man of her dreams—scary ones apparently—from a bunch of guys wearing *Phantom of the Opera* masks. The ratings started strong but faded fast. At least the show gave Darnell a chance to commiserate with Monica Lewinsky, who served as host. Mike and his wife went to dinner with Monica and shared stories about being assaulted by the tabloids.

After *Mr. Personality* failed, Darnell and his team were compelled to try to resurrect *Joe Millionaire*. Those 80 million eyeballs were impossible to resist. A second edition was taped and slotted for fall 2003. Fox kept the gimmick ultrasecret, though it turned out to be everyone's first guess: The new women were foreigners who thus would not have seen the American original. But making fools of women with accents did not play like making fools of American women. The show tanked.

Nothing was more painful to Mike Darnell than a barrage of bad overnight numbers. *Joe Millionaire 2* was the worst. Fox ran the show on Monday night; its ratings were pathetic from the start—then they got worse. Mike, so obsessive that he almost never slept the night after one of his shows premiered, staying up until he could get the first ratings from the Fox telephone hot line, always took bad results personally. As he often did when one of his shows flopped, Darnell wanted to walk away, abandon the baby, simply get it off the air so the failure would be less public.

"I don't know if I can wake up next Monday and hear those numbers again," Darnell told colleagues.

Gail Berman tried a stealth operation to install someone she could trust inside Darnell's reality unit. She plucked a well-thought-of executive from Fox's diversity-hiring unit, Wenda Fong, and moved her to Mike's department. Her assignment was to put the convoluted *Idol* audition process into some kind of order. Some Fox executives believed Darnell despised this intrusion into his domain and tried everything he could to elbow Fong out. But Darnell insisted that he was comfortable with Fong and welcomed her—acknowledging that if he thought she didn't fit in he would have shut her out and forced her to leave.

One new Fox executive, arriving from a competing network, observed Darnell's activities for a while and asked why information on Mike's shows was received so late, and why even the top entertainment executives never seemed to know what was in a Darnell show until the last minute.

A more senior executive tried to explain. Darnell would announce that he had the best show ever, but it wasn't ready to be seen. He would insist on the best possible time period, but he wouldn't allow the show to be promoted for fear the competition would rip him off. He would maneuver around Grushow or Berman or whoever was in charge of the division by flaunting the support he had from "upper management."

"This is unbelievable," the new executive said.

"Welcome to Fox," the senior executive said.

The amazing thing, the longtime executive told the newcomer, was that rumors were always floating about some other network trying to hire Mike away. "That's the dirty little secret," the veteran executive said. "If Mike pulled at any other network what he pulls here, he'd be fired."

Still, offers, like the ratings for Darnell's stronger shows, kept rolling in. After he turned down Sassa and NBC, Mike had a feeler from ABC that went nowhere. But that wasn't the end of it. Inside ABC, Michael Eisner continued to mention Darnell's name frequently, saying to ABC's entertainment team that the network needed somebody like Mike Darnell with hot creative ideas. The ABC executives wondered how Eisner could square Darnell's material with the company's lingering devotion to the Disney image of family entertainment.

By the time Mike heard from his lawyer that Disney was sniffing around to determine if he would be interested in meeting, Darnell had extended his contract with Fox. He knew the network would never let him work for a rival—even if he had wanted to leave, which he clearly did not.

•   •   •

Mike Darnell was not coming to ABC, but one executive was leaving. Lloyd Braun was fired at the end of March. It was almost a ritual sacrifice at that point. The ABC entertainment chief was unalterably estranged from the Disney bosses, especially Bob Iger. At a Bear Stearns investor conference earlier that month, Iger had made his intentions clear by never even mentioning Braun, only Susan Lyne.

"We made a big change two years ago when we brought Susan Lyne in," Iger had told the conference. "Our job right now is to support her, to give her both the time and room to perform, and I think that's critical. I believe in Susan strongly, and I think she has the goods to turn it around."

Braun had been telling colleagues and friends he was ready to be out from under the oppressive leadership of Disney, so the ax falling hardly came as a shock. When the word came down, Braun was in Hawaii watching J. J. Abrams film the pilot for *Lost.* By then he had already taken significant steps to leave an extravagantly expensive orphan on Iger's doorstep.

With its elaborate plane crash, the enormous cast, and the remote tropical setting, *Lost,* with Abrams directing, was turning into something much closer to a movie than a television pilot. As the dailies came in, the ABC entertainment staff was blown away by the quality of the footage they were seeing—even as the Disney executives were blown away by what it was costing. The bottom line kept creeping upward.

At the Touchstone studio, Steve McPherson had been alarmed by the ballooning numbers almost from the beginning. The head of production for the studio, Barry Johnson, was supervising the budget and sending McPherson honest estimates. McPherson thought they were gigantic. The pressure was mounting, making everyone at the studio nervous. McPherson heard Johnson's top-end estimate grow from $6 million to $9 million, then $12 million. The pilot would run more than an hour, a troubling prospect for a show that was bought on the basis of an outline.

McPherson finally went to Braun. "Lloyd, this is getting really expensive." He balked at picking up deals for some of the ever-expanding roster of actors. Then he suggested that they reevaluate the commitment to making the show.

Braun, already convinced that McPherson hated his pet project, reacted like a parent whose child was in jeopardy. He bridled. Then he took action: He told McPherson he was yanking him off the project. Braun said he would take over himself as the studio executive responsible for *Lost.*

Braun technically had the authority to make this move, because McPherson and the Touchstone studio still reported to him. But it was another in-your-face provocation to the Disney management. Here was Braun throwing the studio chief off a project and taking control of it himself, a project he clearly had his own personal reasons for pursuing. As for McPherson, with this move he knew that the credit—and responsibility—for *Lost* were all on Braun. Lloyd was the guy spending all the money; he was running the project; he would be taking the hit.

The prodigious costs made the show an even bigger target. Michael Eisner told ABC executives he couldn't see *Lost* being anything more than a miniseries. Everyone at ABC Entertainment knew that Iger had blamed Abrams for ruining the promising *Alias*. Braun reported to Lyne that Iger had dismissed *Lost* to him, calling it "a colossal waste of time, energy, and money."

McPherson's view filtered out to the staff, including one member who said, "Steve hated, hated, hated *Lost*. If it had been his decision, he never, ever would have put it on."

Braun could not miss the sound of knives being sharpened. He knew they would soon be pointed at him and his favorite show. Without anyone knowing, Braun began scouting the business for possible other patrons if Touchstone shut *Lost* down.

But by late March, when Iger told Lyne he was finally moving Braun out and bringing in Anne Sweeney from Disney's cable television division to run ABC, the *Lost* pilot was well into production. Killing it at that point would mean swallowing a whale-sized outlay of cash.

•   •   •

A few weeks earlier, at a series of meetings with advertisers known as the mini-upfront, *Lost* had given its first sign of promise, intriguing many in the group. But it was clearly second in terms of buzz to another ABC drama, *Desperate Housewives*. Lyne brought out Teri Hatcher and several of the other actresses to pitch the show, leaving many of the advertisers genuinely dazzled.

Lyne had already decided that, if the pilot turned out to be as good as she expected, she would push as hard as possible to slot *Desperate Housewives* on that Sunday night at 9.

The question for Lyne was whether she was going to have the power to advance the shows she liked in whatever new regime Disney installed at ABC Entertainment. The appointment of Anne

Sweeney seemed to Lyne like one of the sounder moves the company had made in some time. She hoped it would streamline the labyrinthine and maddening decision-making process.

"You couldn't get a marketing budget okayed," one entertainment executive said. The chief business-affairs executive, Marc Pedowitz, told colleagues he was close to quitting. Lyne, who considered Pedowitz her buddy, was unnerved by the prospect of losing him just as she took over full control of the entertainment division.

Iger told Lyne he wanted her to stay on but that he was considering hiring a young ESPN programming executive, Mark Shapiro, to run program development under her. Lyne liked Shapiro, considered him smart and energetic, though she had heard of his King Kong–sized ambition.

But Lyne wanted to warn Iger about something else. "You need to know a few things here," she said. "Some of our really key players are deeply unhappy." Iger could hardly have been surprised by that observation.

"There are two people who I'm really concerned are going to leave, and you really need to meet with them," Lyne said. "One is Marc Pedowitz and the other is Steve McPherson."

Iger was grateful for the intelligence. It was early April. He knew he had to move quickly to reshape the division in advance of the screenings of pilots and selection of new shows.

Assured her position was safe, Lyne stepped aside while Iger took action to form his new team. The talks with Shapiro did not go well. He overplayed his hand with Iger, demanding to run the division himself. Shapiro told Iger he wouldn't report to Lyne. But when Iger talked to McPherson and Pedowitz, he heard the same thing.

Iger decided he could do without Shapiro. But he had to agree with Lyne: He really ought to keep McPherson and Pedowitz.

On April 19, Iger told Susan Lyne he was giving her job to Steve McPherson, with Marc Pedowitz taking over the studio. Lyne felt like she had been poleaxed. All that talk of backing had vaporized in a matter of days.

In describing the rationale for ousting first Braun and then Lyne, Iger pointed to ABC's continuing occupation of the prime-time ratings basement. "I felt that, given the performance, change was necessary," he said.

Pressed about his ringing endorsement of Lyne at the investor conference only a month earlier, Iger disavowed those comments, saying, "I was obviously just reacting to the moment."

On her way out of the job she loved, Susan Lyne remembered what one of her friends who had first worked with her at ABC and then at Fox had told her:

"At Fox, your brothers and sisters want to kill you all the time. At ABC, the parents are totally dysfunctional, but the kids bonded."

# CHAPTER FOURTEEN

# *LOST* CASES

In the spring of 2004, edging his way toward an exit from Hollywood, Jeff Zucker once again had reason to appreciate his knack for exceptionally fortuitous timing.

Zucker had put a plan of succession in place at NBC Entertainment the previous June when he recruited Kevin Reilly, a highly regarded programmer from the FX channel, who had been responsible for two of the biggest series hits on cable, *The Shield* and *Nip/Tuck*. Zucker had installed Reilly as his top development executive, finally elbowing aside Karey Burke, the latest scapegoat for NBC's chronic failure to find the next *Friends*.

Following NBC's acquisition of Universal in December 2003, Zucker received his own promotion to president of the NBC entertainment, news, and cable group. Zucker then elevated Reilly to president of entertainment, clearing the way for Jeff, after the deal won government approval, to segue back to New York for a top corporate job at NBC.

The promotion, beyond giving him supervision of NBC News as well as all of NBC's entertainment cable channels, would put him into the direct line of succession to Bob Wright, tied (more or less) with Randy Falco, the top business operator at the company. Not that Wright was showing any interest in stepping down. He had bristled at an earlier GE move to establish a successor, when Jack Welch had designated Andrew Lack as Wright's heir apparent. That had not sat well with Wright, and, after an exercise of corporate muscle-flexing, Wright had succeeded in showing Lack the door—or, more accurately, the elevator shaft.

The new arrangement was more to Wright's liking, though he pointedly said at the time of the promotions for Zucker and Falco, "An heir like the Andy Lack thing? This is not that."

With the completion of the Universal acquisition set for May 2004, Zucker had only one piece of unfinished business: one more season of development and scheduling for prime time. Then he could leave the day-to-day running of the place to Reilly.

Maybe Hollywood had proved more of a challenge than he originally expected. And maybe it had been more of a struggle to keep the baying hounds of CBS, ABC, and Fox away from the top dog, NBC, than he had hoped when he arrived. But Zucker was winding up his third full season and NBC was going to finish first again. Who could quarrel with that kind of success?

Not that Zucker had to look far for an answer. All he needed to do was read the press clippings. There the caviling critics pounded away at him, howling as ever in righteous indignation that NBC, in its unseemly quest to win in the ratings, was still serving up reality effluvia like *Fear Factor* and *Average Joe*. To make matters worse, Zucker had failed to show proper respect for certain critical darlings, like an artsy cop show named *Boomtown*, which Jeff bounced around the schedule and then canceled.

The critics had company in their hostile assessments of Zucker. His competitors never ceased lobbing maledictions at him—always off the record, of course. Rival executives would whisper through gritted teeth about how Zucker was getting by on a shoeshine and a smile, that he had delivered nothing of real value to NBC in his three years running entertainment: no *Survivor*, no *CSI*, no *American Idol*, no breakout hits of any kind.

"I was surprised at all the old-school, down-the-middle stuff they were doing," said a producer who once worked for NBC Entertainment. "They were doing *Whoopi* and John Larroquette, all these old-style 1970s shows that were not sophisticated in the way NBC audiences had gotten used to."

Whoopi Goldberg and John Larroquette both had sitcoms on NBC that season, shows that Zucker had held out as promising examples of NBC's new direction in comedy. They were indeed old-fashioned and uninspiring, and despite Zucker's indefatigable efforts to promote them—he even moved *Whoopi* to Thursday night at one point—they both were heading toward cancellation.

Both failing shows had been developed on Karey Burke's watch, and they added up to one more season of empty returns on NBC's comedy investment. Burke was seen in some quarters at NBC as an all-smiles/no-moves executive who had put nothing but bricks in plenty of shots in development. Zucker never disparaged her, but eventually agreed with several assessments, including Bob Wright's, that he probably should have looked for fresh blood sooner.

Some staff members who had worked with Burke believed she was being unfairly condemned for sins being committed by others. "Karey is really talented," said the NBC executive-turned-producer. "She had so many bosses in a five-year period, from Ancier to Sassa to Zucker, and she had to teach them about the business. Then you had the East Coast NBC people always figuring they could do the job better. But you know what? The fish rots from the head down."

All the talk of NBC rotting and Zucker flailing missed an important fact: NBC was going to finish the season first again. And Zucker was only too happy to point that out. "We are so much stronger than anyone expected us to be," he said.

Upon hearing comments like that, Zucker's detractors stepped up to the bar en masse for a round of gall. That Zippy had managed to pull out yet another season, even after lame shows like *Coupling* and *Whoopi*, left them all choking down the bile. At CBS, Moonves's official reaction was tempered, though pointed. "Of all the shows Jeff introduced last fall, only one, *Las Vegas*, is going to be back," he said. "We'll have six shows returning."

Of course, NBC had not introduced shows only in the fall. The one launched in January, *The Apprentice,* had made all the difference. "Who knew that the replacement for *Friends* would be Donald Trump?" Zucker said with usual aplomb.

*The Apprentice* had indeed saved NBC's bacon—meaning the Thursday-night revenue haul—and everybody in the industry knew it. Moonves, surveying Zucker's overall tenure in Hollywood, graciously called him "a terrific executive," but added, "He didn't have the greatest of runs at the entertainment division. *The Apprentice* came along just in time for him."

Just in time, no doubt. Donald Trump in for Jennifer Aniston. It had worked out so well that Zucker chided himself for his earlier doubts. "Nothing was bigger than moving *The Apprentice* to Thursday," he said. "It changed the entire equation."

That, it surely did. The equation for NBC on Thursday night had been two hours of comedy for two decades. Two plus two equaled billions. Now Zucker was saying the old equation didn't add up anymore. "Just because it's been comedy for twenty years doesn't mean it is written in stone that it has to be comedy," he said.

Like a quarterback who threw a Hail Mary pass into a stiff wind for the game-winning touchdown, Zucker saw the insertion of *The Apprentice* on Thursday night as a transformative moment. Who was going to say now that Jeff Zucker had never added a breakout hit show to NBC's schedule? Donald Trump was a national phenomenon. His face was everywhere. The show swept to the number-two spot in the 18-to-49 ratings, behind only *American Idol.* Best of all, it hit the sweet spot of the NBC audience: a show all about rich, grasping, young people in New York City made for a perfect appeal to young professionals with six-figure incomes.

Zucker had visions of revenue dancing in his head that spring as he sketched out his plans for the first NBC season without *Friends* in a decade. Pursuing his Donald-as-Jen theme, Zucker estimated that NBC could possibly be *better* off in the fall of 2004. With two rounds of *The Apprentice* planned for the coming season—or thirty-four hours' worth, vs. the seventeen half hours of *Friends* NBC had been able to broadcast in its last season—Zucker expected four times as many high-rated hours of programming.

Imagine if NBC *improved* its Thursday-night numbers the year after *Friends* departed. How big a coup would *that* be? How shocked would the TV world be with that development? That April, the prospect of such a turnaround had Zucker so jacked up that he boldly called NBC's development "the best in years."

At the center of his optimism was the anticipated addition of two comedies. One was a cartoon from the animation maestro of the Dreamworks studio, Jeffrey Katzenberg. Featuring talking lions from the Vegas act of Siegfried and Roy, *Father of the Pride* so excited Zucker that he called it "as good or better than any new comedy on any network."

And then there was *Joey*. The pilot thrilled Zucker. "A spin-off that was two years in the making has turned out incredibly well," he said.

Zucker was so enthused about *Joey* and its chances to be a true replacement for *Friends* on Thursday nights at 8 that he had decided to run the pilot at its full length in his May upfront presentation.

"We have *Joey* and *Father of the Pride* to introduce," Zucker said. "If I had nothing else but those two, I'd feel great."

         •    •    •

That same April, Marc Graboff got a call at his NBC office that threw him. And not much threw him anymore.

Graboff, the head of business affairs for NBC, had observed the machinations of television deal-making close up at two networks, first CBS and now NBC. He had grown accustomed to the often preposterous demands of actors and their agents, relishing the few times that a network would actually stand up and play hardball. Like the time Debra Messing, Grace of *Will & Grace,* tried to hold out for more money. The producers came up with a plan to test her resolve. They suggested a new opening for the season. Will (Eric McCormack) would open a door and say: "Hi, Grace, did you change your hair?"— and Minnie Driver would be standing there. Messing signed quickly.

But for Graboff, this call from Lloyd Braun was something altogether new. A former executive at a competing network was on the phone, trying to assess NBC's potential interest in a pilot, one that was still on the books at his old shop.

Graboff knew that ABC had finally forced Braun out a couple of weeks earlier. Graboff also knew that Lloyd was on extremely friendly terms with Jeff Zucker. Whether or not that was what inspired the call, here was Braun pitching NBC on picking up an unfinished ABC pilot, something called *Lost*.

Braun sketched out the premise for Marc and sold it hard as something truly extraordinary, perhaps the best thing he had ever been associated with. Braun did not go into his deep personal involvement with the show's creation.

From Graboff's perspective, the pitch was unusual in every way. ABC had not even passed on the show yet, and here was a former ABC executive out trying to sell it elsewhere?

Braun told Graboff, "There's no passion for it at ABC or at Touchstone." He said he was confident that nobody at ABC or Disney had any clue what they had in *Lost*.

Naturally, Graboff asked: Why, if the show was really as good as Lloyd was saying it was, were the people who owned it so cool to it?

Money, Braun told him. The pilot was extraordinary, but it was also lavishly expensive—upward of $12 million for two hours. Graboff blanched at the price. Instantly, he thought of a better word for it: "ridiculous."

Still, it was not his role to accept or reject material. Zucker or Kevin Reilly would have to make that call. But how was NBC going to get a look at a pilot that was still in postproduction at the studio owned by Disney—which also owned ABC?

Braun said he could lay his hands on a rough cut and then manage to use some back channels to get it to Kevin Reilly. If NBC's executives liked what they saw, maybe they could get themselves into second position to pick up the show if ABC passed on it—much the way CBS had picked up *CSI* when Touchstone passed on it.

The situations were not exactly parallel. ABC passed on *CSI* as a pitch, not a pilot. Having already produced the pilot of *Lost,* ABC could, if it wanted to, have what is known as "two bites" on the project. Even if the network decided not to pick it up for its fall schedule, it could still hold on to it through the television midseason, preventing anyone else from buying it.

The difference with *Lost* was the massive expense. If another network stepped up and was willing to cover that cost, Braun suggested, the notorious tightwads at Disney would surely be tempted to rid themselves of this bloated extravagance. Braun told Graboff he firmly believed he could pull this off if NBC offered to buy the pilot. "There is no way ABC is going to hold on to a show this expensive if they can get it off their hands."

Braun did not disclose that this was not his first attempt to find a home for his orphaned project. A month earlier, before his exit from ABC, Braun had quietly made a lunch date with Peter Roth and proposed that Warner Brothers buy into *Lost,* then just starting production in Hawaii.

"They don't believe in it," Braun told Roth. "It is not being supported by ABC and Touchstone because of the extraordinary cost." He added, "I'm not sure I'm going to be at ABC to see this thing through." Braun explained that the pilot was shooting in Hawaii and he feared Disney might shut it down at any minute.

Roth was always in the market for great material, and he loved the work of J. J. Abrams, so he was intrigued enough to hear Braun out. Braun swore he could deliver the project if Roth and Warner Brothers bit. He still oversaw the Touchstone studio; he said he believed he could transfer the project if another studio was willing to foot the bill. Braun even showed Roth a *Lost* script so Roth could at least get a sense of the promise that Braun was touting. To Roth it seemed Braun was willing to do whatever it took to save his vulnerable project, to the point of literally risking his job.

Impressed by Braun's passion, Roth took the project to others at his studio. But the discussion was brief. The Warner executives had to wonder if Braun could really speak for his Disney bosses. And even if Warner bought into the show, how could they be certain they would get control over distribution?

Roth gave Braun the news. He had read the script and enjoyed it. But Warner would not pursue a deal.

That decision killed any prospect that Braun could ensure his favorite got made while he was still at ABC. As Braun explained it to Graboff in his phone call, since he had left ABC word continued to filter back to him that *Lost* was being dissed inside the Disney/Touchstone axis. An initial screening of the rough cut of the pilot had not gone well, ABC insiders had reported to Braun. The word was that the decision makers still seemed to be focused either on relegating the show to a miniseries format or else shelving it entirely.

That accounted for the call to NBC. Graboff said he would wait to hear if Reilly or Zucker wanted him to go back to Braun with an offer.

A short while later, an agent friend of Kevin Reilly's got a strange request from Lloyd Braun: Would he drop a cassette of *Lost* into Reilly's home mailbox—in the dead of night if necessary?

While he waited to hear what might come of all this, Marc Graboff pondered Braun's proposal and found it more and more far-fetched. He concluded that ABC/Disney would never simply hand over a finished pilot, no matter how expensive, without some way to protect itself from another disaster like *CSI*. The Disney guys would surely insist on that Hollywood staple, "schmuck insurance," Graboff decided. NBC would not get it clean.

Graboff never heard if Reilly had been unimpressed by the pilot, or simply passed because of the impossibility of the whole enterprise. Internally, he never heard anything more about *Lost* at all.

*Lost* remained at Touchstone and ABC. If it didn't get on the air there, it wasn't getting on the air anywhere.

•  •  •

No such machinations impeded the progress of the *Desperate Housewives* pilot. Marc Cherry grew more confident as the shooting went on, though he was concerned by the sudden departure of Susan Lyne, whom he had considered the show's greatest champion. Thankfully, he concluded, Susan had been replaced by Steve McPherson, who as studio head had stepped up and bought the spec script.

Of course, the show would now have to survive the annual gauntlet known as testing. Before network executives sat in their cloistered rooms and decided the fate of television shows, they played the pilots in screenings for anonymous audiences all around the country. Cherry, like most show creators, regarded this rite as the last refuge of cowardly program executives. Most series creators believed the programmers should have been willing to anoint shows based on their own creative instincts.

Cherry took it upon himself to visit an ABC research facility in L.A., just to get an idea of how his precious opus was going to play. That mainly involved reading the cards filled out by the test audiences and listening in on focus-group interviews. What he learned was hardly surprising. Women liked the show more than men, many of whom rejected it simply because it fell into the category of soap drama.

Cherry totally soured on the process when the woman in charge of the testing that day approached him with a suggestion. "You might want to think about testing this title, or even changing the title," she said. "I think it's going to alienate women."

Nothing could have pissed off Cherry more than somebody trying to change his title. He did not take seriously anything else the woman said, dismissing her later as "some fucking feminist, who just hated the word 'housewives' and just thought it was denigrating to women."

· · ·

On April 21, Stephen McPherson formally took over ABC's entertainment division, a job previously held by two people, Lloyd Braun and Susan Lyne. He had all of twenty-nine days to sort through the entire roster of development, pick the most promising shows, cancel the failing and marginal performers, build a new schedule, and wrap it all up in a smooth, confident presentation to a theater full of advertisers and the press in New York. If that wasn't pressure enough, McPherson had to deal with the squeeze being imposed on the company by its long history of failure. ABC owed advertisers about $100 million in make-good ads—free commercial time awarded to advertisers for ratings shortfalls from what the network had guaranteed.

None of this fazed Steve McPherson. He had pushed for the job, after all, having first been invited to work as the number two under Lyne. McPherson was thirty-nine that spring, fresh from five years running the Touchstone studio, where he had maintained a close but mercurial relationship with Braun before he left. But then, *mercurial* was a word frequently used in the same sentence with McPherson—along with other words, like *no-nonsense, hard-charging, brilliant, moody,* and *volatile.* At Touchstone, McPherson was known for everything from making an impressive commitment to diversity in hiring; to comforting the cast of 8 *Simple Rules for Dating My Teenage Daughter* after the shocking death of John Ritter; to occasionally reducing female staff members to tears.

His background was highly unusual for a top network program executive. McPherson had not grown up watching sitcoms every night—unless they were in French. Steve's father was the headmaster of the American school in Paris, and from age eleven until college, the few American shows he got to see were six months late. He watched the soap *Dallas* that way, with J. R. Ewing dubbed, comically, into French.

In college at Cornell, McPherson gravitated to political science, though he dabbled in theater. He did make a future career friend on campus, however. One of his fraternity brothers was Kevin Reilly.

After a stint in commodities trading in New York and a failed romance, McPherson decided to chuck it all for a shot in show business. His pal Reilly worked as a Hollywood publicist and told McPherson to come out, get a job somewhere, and get started.

McPherson took a job as a glorified gofer for Tony Thomas (son of Danny), a principal at the production company of Witt Thomas Harris. Glorified, because McPherson got to drive Thomas around and read scripts left in the backseat, while also getting Thomas's shirts pressed and picking up balloons for his kids. Still, the job exposed McPherson to the business at a time when Witt-Thomas was producing the hit sitcom *The Golden Girls.* On the job, McPherson had occasion to meet, casually, one of the show's writers, Marc Cherry.

McPherson's career started to take off when he landed a development job under Warren Littlefield at NBC. At first considered an uptight Wall Street type, McPherson soon won over the clubby NBC crowd with his intensity and straight-shooting style. Karey Burke thought he was such an "excellent person," she insisted he date her sister.

Already there was whispering about McPherson's moodiness and occasional flare-ups of temper. But he fit in well with the macho style that prevailed at NBC in the 1990s. Once, at a press party in Pasadena, McPherson and other NBC executives met with reporters around the pool at the Ritz-Carlton. McPherson and Flody Suarez, an outgoing former NBC publicist who had segued into programming, were enduring the dull affair together when Littlefield wandered up.

"You know, these parties get really boring," Littlefield said. "Nothing ever really happens."

Suarez had an idea. "I dare you to jump into the pool," he said to Steve. The dare became a bet. Suarez put up $250; Littlefield had $145 on him. They needed to round it off, so Steve Levitan, the creator of *Just Shoot Me,* kicked in the other $5. The bet was McPherson would not jump into the pool in his suit and swim a lap.

With the press watching, McPherson strode to the pool's edge, removed only his shoes, and dove in. He did the full lap. Suarez thought it was bending the rules a bit to have removed the shoes, but McPherson got every cent of his $400.

When McPherson was named head of Touchstone and then of ABC Entertainment, his longtime colleagues had no doubt he could do those jobs. They knew he was creative, smart, had a strong point of view, grasped the business well, and had good relationships with the agents and managers. The only question about McPherson concerned his temperament.

The portrait of a volatile guy who had periods where he simply couldn't be talked to dogged McPherson, to the point where he thought it was becoming "a tactic to put me down or something, people saying, 'Oh, he's got a temper.'" But his temperament *was* talked about.

"What I mainly experienced was a sort of shutdown quality," one midlevel ABC entertainment executive said. "There were definitely times when, even if you were passing in the hallway or whatever, you could barely get an acknowledgment." The hardest thing to deal with, the executive said, was the "sullen version" of McPherson. "You couldn't read him and you couldn't generate a response of any kind."

A more senior ABC executive, who was impressed with McPherson's talents, said the most uncomfortable part of dealing with Steve when he was at the studio was the occasional phone call when he disagreed with an ABC decision. "You guys better fucking be careful about the way you do your business," the executive recalled McPherson saying.

"We used to call him 'purple Steve,' because when he got angry he would get so red in the face," the executive said. "And there were times when he would get so sullen he would literally mumble."

At one point, an ABC executive approached Braun and told him, "There is way too much time in the company being spent managing Steve. It's just a problem." The executive knew Braun and McPherson were close. But the situation seemed to demand some kind of action. Braun reported back that he had had a heart-to-heart with Steve, who had promised to work on the mood thing.

To balance the stormy side of his personality, McPherson had a wild, fun-loving side, as exemplified by his dip in the Ritz-Carlton pool. Thom Sherman, who knew McPherson from his days at ABC drama when McPherson ran the studio, said, "If you go out drinking with him, he's the greatest guy ever. When we would go to New York for the upfronts, Steve would be the first one ordering shots at the bar. And I'd be right with him, going shot for shot."

Flody Suarez said McPherson was noticeably intense, but no more than he had to be. "It was a terrible time to be at Touchstone," he said. "Steve was like the sanest guy in a crazy house. I'm sure he was frustrated. It's the easiest thing to say he's intense. But I never saw volatile."

McPherson said of his reputation for tempestuousness, "I think there's something to it and there's some overboard. I think I'm a really passionate guy. I tell the truth, and a lot of people sometimes don't like to hear that."

McPherson acknowledged that he was running Touchstone at a time of enormous frustration for the studio, beginning with the calamitous decision to give away *CSI*, a show that would have made the reputation of anyone involved in its conception. "I'm a much more open book than a lot of people," McPherson said, "maybe that's the emotional side of it."

McPherson certainly had to keep his emotions in check that spring if he was going to salvage something out of that bodies-on-the-floor development season at ABC. With less than a month until the upfronts, it was far too late for him to order up any new pilots; he would have to go with whatever Braun and Lyne had selected. Fortunately, many of those pilots had come from the Touchstone shop, so Steve was intimately familiar with them.

He liked a few, especially the procedural shows—Steve was always looking for something to match his lost gem, *CSI*. A new cop drama from Steven Bochco, *Blind Justice*, about a sightless detective, was among McPherson's favorites, though Braun and Lyne had supported it only as a way to get a final, cheaper year out of Bochco's veteran police show, *NYPD Blue*. McPherson liked another action show about the Secret Service and one drama about teenage boys' obsession with sex called *Doing It*.

And then there was *Lost*. McPherson had long before made clear that he was no fan of the project, which was beginning to look more and more like *Moby Dick*, the elephant version. The reports of its mounting costs were giving the entire company agita. Faced with a price tag climbing toward $12 million and beyond, McPherson wondered what the heck he had in this pilot: A ninety-minute opening episode? A two-hour movie?

Braun, the project's real daddy, was gone. Everyone from Bob Iger on down had complained of disturbing flaws in the original script, like killing off the Jack character at the end of Act II. McPherson had cited that to the producers as his biggest objection as well. Mainly, McPherson continued to have doubts that effective stories could be told on a continuing basis with this premise. It just seemed so limiting. And it was a serial, always problematic for a network looking to find a long-term franchise, one whose repeats would always be valuable.

McPherson watched the rough cut of the pilot with several other ABC executives in a screening room. When the producers and their agents got a report later, they were disturbed to hear that as soon as the screening ended, McPherson had simply stood up and left the room. He did not participate in the discussion about the pilot. This hardly seemed good news to the *Lost* team, though they should have realized that McPherson, like most program bosses, never showed his cards at screenings.

But that incident, and other reports of bad-sounding karma surrounding his now unprotected baby, stirred Lloyd Braun to contact NBC.

*Desperate Housewives*, on the other hand, held great promise in McPherson's view, though he had some minor reservations, starting with the voice-over narration from the dead character of Mary Alice. She was played by Sheryl Lee—an actress known mainly for playing another dead character, Laura Palmer in ABC's onetime cult hit turned flop, *Twin Peaks*. McPherson's initial thought was to put Bonnie Hunt into the narrator's role; but first he would have to deal with canceling the failing comedy she was starring in, *Life with Bonnie*.

Whoever was selected, McPherson was convinced the narrator issue could be easily handled. Internally at ABC, it was looking like *Desperate Housewives* was a shoo-in for a spot somewhere on the schedule. It certainly didn't hurt that McPherson felt a degree of ownership over *Housewives,* thanks to his early support of Marc Cherry's script.

Even so, some ABC Entertainment executives wondered if Steve was as passionate a supporter of *Housewives* as he was for some of the other Touchstone projects, ones he had had a direct hand in developing. These executives simply felt it was natural for a studio boss turned programmer to favor projects he had nurtured all along the development process, as opposed to one that arrived full-blown as a spec script.

Whatever the depth of his passion for it, McPherson did have a real connection to *Desperate Housewives.* He never had that with *Lost.* After Braun had removed him as the executive in charge, Steve had no personal association with the show. From observation and scuttlebutt around the shop, many ABC Entertainment staff members had concluded that McPherson was gunning for the project.

"We heard that Steve was telling people this is just not going to get on the schedule," said one executive.

And then, suddenly, the mood shifted. At the next meeting about prospects for the new schedule, McPherson began discussing how to figure out exactly what ABC had with *Lost.* While not showering it with love, McPherson was now at least saying, "It's got to go on the air." He was still throwing out ideas, like maybe it could be a six-part miniseries. But he was not talking about tossing it onto the reject pile.

Inside the ABC group supporting *Lost,* no one was totally sure what had happened. It was true that at a screening Bob Iger had made several positive-sounding comments about the quality of the pilot. Some executives had expected Iger to kill it, simply because it had been the favorite of the ousted Braun.

One executive who remained close to Braun had a different take. The executive heard that Braun had called McPherson personally on the subject of *Lost.* Steve did not mention the call to anyone. Braun kept totally mum. But word of the conversation made its way around a very small circle of ABC colleagues.

The version that circle heard was that Braun had taken the extraordinary step of calling in a personal chit. Braun told McPherson how supremely important *Lost* was to him. Just pick it up, he implored, order it as a series, and put it on the ABC schedule, somewhere, someway. Then at least it would have a chance to fly or crash on its own.

About the same time, the testing for *Lost* came in. It was startlingly good. Many in the test audience indicated they would surely watch this show every week. Those who never heard about any call between Braun and McPherson assumed the late surge in support for *Lost* was tied to the great test scores. McPherson later said simply that he saw the testing and the quality of the film and recognized the brilliant storytelling in the pilot. "I think we have something here," he decided.

*Desperate Housewives* had also hit eye-catching numbers in the testing, at least with women viewers. The male numbers, McPherson noted, were lousy, but that was to be expected. He could just imagine that a guy being asked if he would watch a show like this would answer: "No, please, I'm not gonna watch this show." But that didn't mean they wouldn't, especially if the women in their lives committed to never missing it. ABC just had to get the message out about what a distinctive, fun show this was going to be.

McPherson, who had sat around at Touchstone armchair-quarterbacking every promo and grumbling about what he saw as the lame marketing efforts at the network, now had a shot at steering a campaign on his own. He called himself "obsessed with marketing" and was convinced, especially given ABC's abysmal track record in launching new shows, that what the network needed to do was choose a couple of pilots and put all their promotional muscle behind them.

That strategy conveniently coincided with the instincts of Anne Sweeney, the new corporate head of ABC, whose career had been forged in the world of cable, where tight budgets always forced channels to put all their promotion dollars behind a single show, or at most two.

Together, McPherson and Sweeney decided they had to focus all their promotion time and money on the best material they had— and from the testing and their own instincts, that meant *Desperate Housewives* and *Lost*.

McPherson knew now that he had to go all the way with *Lost*— pump it up as much as he could and hope the public would buy into the outlandish premise. But the pilot, which had grown to two hours— partly because of cost, partly because ABC was hedging, thinking it might have to be run off as a two-hour movie—seemed unwieldy to McPherson. Introducing the show in a two-hour format was going to pose a formidable challenge. McPherson thought he had a better idea.

He went to J. J. Abrams, Damon Lindelof, and Thom Sherman, who was now ensconced in Abrams's production company, with a suggestion: Maybe we should split this thing into two separate episodes. All it would take is a little editing.

Initially, the *Lost* producers resisted. The pilot as shot was a cohesive whole; splitting it in two would destroy the continuity— and besides, there was no natural break point. But this was the net- work boss asking for changes, changes that would enhance the show's chances to get on the air. The editing commenced.

ABC's top marketing executive, Mike Benson, got his marching orders from McPherson: Put all your bets down on these two horses, and don't stick to conventional ideas. Benson conceived a saturation campaign. ABC would use Internet postings to create buzz. They would stick messages about *Lost* in bottles and float them onto beaches all over the country. They would buy ads on dry cleaner bags touting *Desperate Housewives*. They would buy radio and cable spots, spending everything that was in the budget.

As he prepared to go into the final scheduling meetings for his first upfront, Steve McPherson had a plan in place. He was going to hitch his star to these two new hourlong shows and ride with them as far as they would take him. He had a firm idea where he wanted those shows to go. Like Susan Lyne, McPherson saw an opportunity for *Desperate Housewives* to seize a disenfranchised female audi- ence on Sunday nights at 9.

By this time Cherry had found a new narrator for the Mary Alice part, Brenda Strong, whose voice was silky and ironic and perfect. One ABC entertainment executive, who had some initial reservations about McPherson's abilities, gave him full credit for fine-tuning *Desperate Housewives*. "The part Steve is really good at is when the project is 90 percent of the way there," the executive said. "He says, if we just do X or we spend X. He's a great executive that way."

As for *Lost*, it was such a high-degree-of-difficulty dive anyway, why not try to pull it off in the most unlikely pool in network television? McPherson proposed having *Lost* open Wednesday night at 8. Many on his staff were stunned. Who was going to tune in to a dense, challenging drama that early? Had McPherson decided in the end to just throw the show away? But that conclusion did not jibe with the all-out promotional effort he was putting behind the show.

Whatever McPherson's strategy, the Disney managers were still the ultimate masters of the ABC schedule. And they did not like the idea of *Lost* at 8 on Wednesday—or *Desperate Housewives* at 9 on Sunday. They had ideas about remaking Wednesday around reality shows, led by *Extreme Makeover: Home Edition,* which had started to do well on Sundays.

McPherson strongly opposed the all-reality idea for Wednesday. The home makeover show was central to his Sunday-night plans. It seemed like the perfect lead-in to *Desperate Housewives.*

The Disney side also presumed that *Desperate Housewives* was almost exclusively a female-appeal show, and thus would work ideally as a 10 P.M. anchor to Friday night, which was being rebuilt around a female-appeal comedy, *Hope & Faith,* starring Kelly Ripa.

McPherson was appalled. Friday at 10 was burying the crown jewel of that season's development. He wasn't the only one upset. When word of this suggested schedule got back to ABC's news division, they were apoplectic. A new entertainment show at 10 on Friday would displace the flagship newsmagazine *20/20*. And there didn't even seem to be a strategy to reschedule the program in another slot.

David Westin, the president of ABC News, felt sucker-punched. He had been sandbagged two years earlier when ABC's management wooed David Letterman for its 11:35 late-night slot without inform- ing Westin or anyone else in news, even though such a move would supplant *Nightline*. Now Westin could see it all happening again. Would his network dump its leading newsmagazine program for a new show about the soapy lives of suburban housewives?

When Westin got wind of the proposed new Friday schedule, he jumped on the phone to begin lobbying for *20/20*. Quickly, it became apparent to him that he was fighting against long odds. Michael Eisner and Bob Iger were both resisting McPherson's plan to slot *Desperate Housewives* on Sunday, instead insisting it go on Friday.

That was not McPherson's only problem. He had managed to fight off the reality gambit on Wednesday and now his bosses wanted the drama *Doing It*, now renamed *Life As We Know It*, the saga of teenage boys and their preoccupation with sex, to get the Wednesday-at-8 position.

Eventually, McPherson persuaded the Disney managers that *Doing It*, with its sex themes, simply could not play at 8. *Lost* could. That battle won, the bigger one still raged. McPherson wanted *Des- perate Housewives* on Sunday at 9; the Disney bosses wanted Friday at 10. The conversation got heated. McPherson did not mince words. He insisted on Sunday. Anne Sweeney backed him.

The standoff lingered through the last weekend before ABC's upfront, set for Tuesday. Westin continued to lobby as hard as he could for his newsmagazine. But he felt he was beating his head against the pavement. Westin still had not broken the news to David Sloan, the executive producer of *20/20*, that his program was threat- ened with extinction, hoping he would never have to know. As the upfront approached, Westin wondered how long he could hold out.

On Monday morning, *Desperate Housewives* still sat on Friday night at 10 on the schedule ABC would announce one day later. Westin didn't think he could wait any longer. About 11 A.M., he called in David Sloan. Sloan had no idea what was up. Westin told him he had some tough news. Unless something turned around in the next few hours, it looked like the entertainment division was going to abscond with the time period 20/20 had owned for two decades and hand it over to something called *Desperate Housewives*.

Before Sloan could react, Westin's phone rang. It was Anne Sweeney. "You're back on the schedule," she told him. "Fridays at ten." Westin, greatly relieved, thanked her and hung up. He turned to Sloan and told him the network had reconsidered; 20/20 was safe. "If I'd only waited fifteen more minutes, you never would have known," Westin said.

McPherson had won his showdown with the Disney management, but he had used some unique leverage. He knew that so much had been written and said about Disney's interference with the ABC operation, about Braun's ugly feud with Iger, and about the network's inability to land shows like *The Apprentice* because the entertainment chief could not commit to buying anything on his own, that this one time things might be different. Having anointed a new guy less than a month earlier, accompanied by a declaration that the new schedule would be all his, with all that stew boiling on the stove, the Disney hierarchy could not afford to take over the kitchen again, could they? What if McPherson, whom they knew to be both hardheaded and volatile, had simply told them to stuff it?

Unlike those who had preceded him in the job, Steve McPherson got what he wanted. He also made an impression. He had not led the ABC Entertainment division through a development season; he had commissioned none of the pilots. But one day before his first upfront presentation, he had put his personal mark on the new ABC schedule.

• • •

At CBS, Leslie Moonves was looking forward to his own presentation, primed to seize control of prime time once and for all. With both *Friends* and *Frasier* finally off the stage, NBC's crumbling Roman empire was wide open for the sacking. Moonves had strong doubts that NBC and Jeff Zucker could make up for the missing magic of those classic sitcoms with a diet of Donald Trump, *Joey*, and a cartoon about Siegfried and Roy and talking lions. Les went so far as to predict around the CBS offices that by January Zucker would be reduced to filling his schedule with five reality shows.

"The thing that Jeff does well is play for next week," Moonves said. "He's like the old Washington Redskins, the Over the Hill Gang. Play for next week, not next year."

Les was busy preparing his usual upfront film divertissement, this time featuring his character starting out in a saloon drowning his sorrows over the Janet Jackson fiasco and then jumping in a cab and running down Donald Trump (a dummy version thereof) in the street outside Carnegie Hall. Les was also stoked about the entertainment scheduled to cap off the presentation: a live concert by The Who, to celebrate the band's latest *CSI* theme song. Was anyone in that rocking Carnegie Hall audience going to call CBS the fuddy-duddy network now?

What Moonves did not know that week was that in the days leading up to the upfront, a new round of court intrigue was unfolding inside his parent company, Viacom. Most of the executives there had wondered for months, even years, how long the two men at the top, Sumner Redstone and Mel Karmazin, could continue to coexist. One of the other corporate officers said, "They never talked. Mel was down the hall from Sumner's office and they never made the walk to each other's offices. It was bizarre."

Moonves had grown close to Karmazin, as close as was possible, that is, with an executive who did not go in much for socializing. Others in the company assumed that Mel and Les were tight, were having dinners together all the time to talk about the company. But that was hardly the case. Moonves had only a couple of dinners with Karmazin; Tom Freston, Les's coequal running Viacom's cable operation, MTV Networks, had even less contract. He had lunch with Karmazin only once.

Karmazin baffled many of the other Viacom executives. "Mel would say, I don't want to watch any shows," one senior Viacom executive said. "I don't want to meet affiliates. I don't want to go out after six at night. That's it. I like coming at four-thirty in the morning."

Those were the hours of a radio morning-drive man, which, in many ways, Karmazin was. He had made his fortune in radio, running the Infinity group. Wall Street loved Karmazin for his lean, mean corporate style of management. But longtime Viacom veterans grumbled that Karmazin's radio group was dragging down the company's stock price. Moonves would hit great profit numbers with his broadcast group; Freston would do the same (or better) with the cable side. As one executive put it, "We would get tubed every year by Mel's operation, radio."

Worst of all, from Redstone's point of view, he felt as though Karmazin had taken his company away—or at least the day-to-day management of it. Karmazin was the active manager. Redstone, who still basically owned the company, was shoved to one side. He had no one really reporting to him.

Rumors swirled constantly that Redstone was trying to force Karmazin out. But the continuing cult-of-Mel on Wall Street seemed to keep Redstone from acting.

Until the spring of 2004. By then the company's stock performance was so disappointing that Karmazin's act no longer diverted The Street. Redstone decided it was time to act.

He had two logical, qualified inside choices to replace Karmazin: Freston or Moonves. Redstone could designate one of them as the successor. The other would then have to report to the winner—unless he decided he would rather move on.

Moonves had only worked at Viacom since its acquisition of CBS in 1999. Freston had worked for Redstone since he acquired Viacom, including Freston's bailiwick, MTV Networks, in 1987. More than that, Freston was seen inside the company as Redstone's guy, while Moonves was Karmazin's guy. A few executives knew that Redstone had personally told Freston on numerous occasions that he would run the company someday.

The next move should have been predictable, except for one thing. Freston had been vocal, both inside and outside the company, about his reluctance to move out of the MTV Networks job he loved and into what he saw as a tedious corporate supervisory position. In 2002, Freston had said, "I don't want Mel's job. You want that job? You want to spend all your time talking to investors, dealing with Sumner? How much fun is that?"

Only three days before the CBS upfront, Redstone called Freston to his suite in the Carlyle Hotel and gave him the news: He was going to move Karmazin out, get him to resign. That smelled like trouble to Freston. This was it: the call to step up and take the corporate job running Viacom. Freston, fifty-eight, was still enough of a sixties counterculture guy to conduct off-site MTV meetings in shorts, T-shirt, and Huarache sandals. He was still deeply reluctant about changing his lifestyle.

Redstone made the alternatives clear: Run Viacom for him, or stay in his old position—and work for Leslie Moonves. And by the way, Moonves happened to be on his way over to the Carlyle.

Freston left to sweat out his options. Soon Moonves arrived at the hotel and was ushered into Redstone's suite. Redstone broke the news that Karmazin was out and that he had called Tom Freston in earlier that day and offered him the job of president. Redstone was not finished. He told Moonves that Tom had not yet accepted the position—if he didn't, Sumner said he wanted to offer it to Les.

All of this sounded messy and troubling to Moonves, who asked Redstone if Karmazin had even been told yet that he was out. Redstone indicated he had been, but it sounded still somewhat uncertain to Les. When Moonves left the suite that day, nothing seemed to be settled—and Les was highly unsettled.

Freston, meanwhile, faced with the options of leaving the company, working for Les, or going corporate, realized he had little choice. The jig was up: no more MTV lifestyle. Besides, Redstone was sweetening the deal by throwing in the ultimate fantasy toy: the Paramount movie studio. The opportunity to play around in movies surely made the pill of corporate governance go down easier.

Freston, shrugging off his Hamlet-style reluctance, went back to Redstone and told him yes, he would succeed Karmazin as the president of Viacom. Where this would leave Moonves was not specifically addressed, though Freston had a strong suspicion that it would not go down well with his former traveling companion. He was right. When things got sorted out, and Les understood that Redstone had basically decided to bypass him by offering the top job to Freston, he was distinctly distressed.

After all he had done to build CBS into a serious challenger for network leadership, this was how he was being treated? After all the money he had made for Viacom, he was being passed over? And Freston, who, any fair observer would have to agree, did not have anything like the Hollywood background that Les had, was going to be handed the reins to Paramount Pictures? Between the two of them, which executive had experience running a studio operation? Moonves was certainly within his rights to question what was up with this move and what it would mean for him.

Among some of his closest friends, that's exactly what he did. "Les was absolutely livid," one of his Hollywood pals said. "He made a point of saying how unacceptable this was to him."

The question was what Moonves could do about it. The friend said that Les told him that his Viacom contract did have an out clause, but only if he was offered a CEO job. Was there such a job somewhere else that would interest him? There just might be.

That spring at Disney, Michael Eisner was facing a revolt among some of his board members, threatening his continued tenure. Eisner wanted to position Bob Iger as his successor, but the two of them seemed tainted by the company's recent performance—certainly, what had happened to ABC on their watch was no feather in their caps. If the board were to start looking around for someone who could fix the place, who could bring ABC back from the dead, surely Leslie Moonves would have to be on that list.

Les made clear to a small circle of his friends that he would listen to a feeler from Disney. But that was not a position he could actively pursue. In the short term, he was caught in this unacceptable situation.

No one inside the small Viacom circle aware of the management upheaval could guess what Moonves's unhappiness was going to mean. Would he quit? However unlikely that seemed, it was surely a concern. It certainly was to Tom Freston.

Freston had come to like Les through their trips to Havana and Rio. More important, Freston had come to have great respect for Moonves's abilities. He admired how involved Les stayed with every aspect of the television business, from picking shows to picking actors. To Freston, Les seemed "maniacal about his craft," and he viewed that as hugely valuable to Viacom.

The situation that Redstone had initiated by putting Moonves in second place behind Freston created not just the likelihood of a rift between the two men, but the real possibility that Viacom could lose Moonves and all those prodigious skills he brought to the table running CBS. Was there another executive anywhere in the country who could lead the broadcast side of Viacom as capably as Moonves had?

After taking just a short time to consider the impact of losing Les, Redstone got behind a potential solution. Why couldn't Tom simply share the job with Les? Surely, Moonves was far too important an executive to risk forcing out of the company this way.

A plan for coleadership of Viacom was proposed to Moonves and Freston on May 19, the very day of his upfront presentation in New York. Under the new plan, both men would be named copresidents of Viacom. Their duties would be more or less evenly divided, while they each would keep their separate areas of influence: Tom over cable, Les over broadcast. More significant, their contracts would be essentially identical in terms of compensation and all other particulars. It was a fair arrangement—in every way except one: Freston was going to keep the movie studio.

Moonves was still a bit bruised and confused by the rapidly changing developments of the week. It seemed that Freston had initially been offered the job, only to indicate his usual reluctance. Then the situation had swung around to where it looked like Les would be offered the job, only to have Freston step up and say, whatever his reservations, that he could not have Les get the job. And so Tom would take that initial offer after all.

The even-steven partition of authority had to appeal to Les more than being relegated to second place in a new Viacom configuration. But accepting the split depended on a deal that made it clear the division was truly equal. He had Ernie Del go to work to ensure that would be the case.

The day of the upfront itself, Les still felt the awkwardness of the situation every time he spied Mel Karmazin. Nothing apparently had been said to Mel about the plan, which would not be officially announced until all the paperwork was approved by all the principals. That might take weeks. At the party following the CBS upfront—as always, at Tavern on the Green—Redstone, oblivious to Karmazin's near proximity, indiscreetly lobbied for Les's agreement to the power-sharing deal with the one person he knew to be a logical intermediary, Julie Chen. Chen, the *CBS Morning News* anchor, had become the love of Les's life. Following Les's separation from his wife, the relationship had become public, though friends and business associates had known for some time that Les and Julie were a couple.

But a hard sell was not necessary. After almost losing out to Freston, Moonves had reason to be satisfied with the proposed deal for shared leadership. One of the few people aware of the machinations that had gone on inside Viacom that week saw Les that afternoon, just before he went on stage. His mood had completely changed, the executive said. "I saw great relief. Les was beaming."

·  ·  ·

For NBC, the opening of the new season was fraught with risk, one reason the network started it early, unveiling most of its new shows in the first week of September to take advantage of the huge audiences it would attract for the Athens Olympics. *Joey* opened well; it was no *Friends*, but it showed a lot of promise. Jeff Zucker professed to be elated. Critics were lukewarm, but not nasty, which was more than could be said for their comments about *Father of the Pride*. The critical reaction to the talking lions was mostly harsh, and the ratings, while relatively good, did not offer glimmerings of the

breakthrough on Tuesday night that NBC needed so badly. The rest
of NBC's early lineup generated barely more than a pulse with viewers in spite of the saturation promotion during the Olympics.

Still, the situation at NBC looked rosy compared with the early
news confronting Fox. That network's fall strategy—filling hours
with reality shows until the baseball playoffs began—stumbled from
the start. Fox got smacked for its lame, rip-off boxing series, *The
Next Great Champ*, which had been rushed onto the air to undermine NBC's big, expensive Mark Burnett entry, *The Contender*.
After all the nasty words between Fox and NBC, and even a lawsuit
defense that grandly wrapped *The Next Great Champ* in a First
Amendment flag, the public didn't give a damn. It was still a show
about boxing, and women steered clear. As happy as NBC was to see
Fox fall on its face, it had to worry that *The Contender*, with its far
more imposing price tag, was also going to face a tough pull with
women.

Fox's other high-profile reality series, *The Rebel Billionaire*, with
the British mogul Richard Branson trying to trump the Donald, was
yet another Xerox from Fox of somebody else's hit. It flopped like a
fish. About the only thing that clicked was another reality rework,
*Trading Spouses*, which looked so much like ABC's *Wife Swap* that
the latter's British producers eventually sued.

Steve McPherson, after seeing *Trading Spouses* get some strong
early numbers, could barely control his outrage. "The only thing I
underestimated was how unethical and desperate my competitors
are," he said. Fox executives, noting that McPherson could easily
have beaten their show to the air, dismissed him as a crybaby.

The network doing no hand-wringing at all was CBS. Leslie
Moonves had himself another incipient success, one that Fox's Preston Beckman liked to call a "colon-ized" hit, because it was a familiar title with a colon added—in this case, *CSI: NY*.

Moonves had scheduled the show on Wednesdays at 10, head to
head with the original *Law & Order*, which remained the quintes-
sential New York crime show. Before the season started, Les predicted that *Law & Order* would still prevail in the ratings. But when

the first showdown took place on September 22, *CSI: NY* defeated its established competitor.

That same night, another show had its premiere. Expectations for *Lost* were not nearly so high as those for *CSI: NY*. It was on at 8, for one thing, and for another it was on ABC, which had not launched a truly successful new drama since *NYPD Blue* almost a decade earlier. But a hint of buzz did surround the new series, largely because of ABC's exceptionally effective marketing campaign, which got a final blast in the *Monday Night Football* game that week.

Still, Steve McPherson could only hope in his wildest dreams that *Lost* might claw its way up to a 4 rating in the 18-to-49 audience. No matter what the show did, McPherson knew he would have to wait at least another week to see if the viewers came back. With a premise this kicky, audiences often took a taste and then moved on.

At the offices of *Lost*, J. J. Abrams, Damon Lindelof, Thom Sherman, and the rest of the show's staff were knotted up with trepidation about the show's prospects. Abrams, for all his accolades, had never had a true hit show. *Alias* was mainly a cult hit; *Felicity* had been a fad hit among young women and teens.

The day of the premiere, Sherman went around the office getting rating predictions. Most guessed that *Lost*—in the 18-to-49 demographic, which they all knew was the only thing that would matter to ABC—might hit a number in the "high 3's." Some thought it might go as high as 3.8, not a bad number at all for any 8 o'clock show.

Sherman thought everyone was lowballing. He stuck his neck out and predicted a 4.5 rating, a number that would indicate real hit potential—depending on whether it could sustain something close to that level over the next couple of weeks. Despite his professed confidence, Sherman slept uneasily that night.

Thom, who had been on the wild ride with *Lost* from the first day he heard Lloyd Braun's pitch at the ABC retreat, got a call the next morning a little after 7 A.M. from Jeff Bader, the network's chief scheduler. Bader said he had the ratings. Sherman's breath tightened in anticipation.

"Looks like about 18.5 million viewers," Bader told him, pausing for effect, "and a 6.8 in the demo."

"You've got to be kidding me" was all the stunned Sherman could think of to say.

Bader assured him it was true, and added a topper. With those 18.5 million viewers, the *Lost* premiere was the most-watched opening episode of a new series on ABC in *nine* years. Its 18-to-49 rating of 6.8 was the best of any new show on *any* network in four years. And to cap it off, the show's audience had grown at the half-hour mark, another sure sign of surging interest as new viewers tuned in throughout, while almost none left.

When Bader hung up, Sherman's head was spinning. He immediately dialed J. J. Abrams and told him the news. Abrams was almost speechless. "No way," he said. "It can't be."

Abrams had a long roster of people to call with the amazing news—all the staff members who had worked so hard on the pilot, and of course the cast. But he knew the person he had to talk to first.

Before Abrams could finish dialing Lloyd Braun's number, the former ABC boss reached him. Braun had already heard the ratings. He started by congratulating J. J. The writer, his voice charged with emotion, interrupted and said, "Lloyd, it actually did well." There was disbelief, or maybe shock, in his tone. Abrams told Braun how grateful he was to him for the opportunity to finally have a genuine, out-of-the-box, big hit. Getting teary, he told Braun: "It's a home run."

Braun, who sounded drained from the strain of the past several months, got emotional as well. He said all the thanks should go to Abrams for taking the kernel of Braun's idea and infusing it with the magic to make it a hit. They both agreed that the following week would be crucial. The show would have to hold up; the fans would have to come back for *Lost* to prove itself to those who still doubted that it could work on a weekly basis.

A week later, *Lost* retained virtually all of the audience from its premiere. Everywhere in the press it was celebrated as the first breakout hit of the year.

● ● ●

Four nights later, on Sunday, October 3, Marc Cherry attended a big premiere-night party for *Desperate Housewives,* thrown by his agents at Paradigm. Although the reviews had already been glowing, the kind Cherry could have only expected from close relatives, he felt overcome by nerves during the party. After ABC's pervasive promotion campaign, what if it was an instant flop? Would he and everyone at ABC have to go into hiding?

Cherry went home that night feeling physically nauseous from the fear that things had gone too well and some kind of bitter day of reckoning might be at hand.

Nerves had also afflicted Steve McPherson throughout that week. Even after the back-to-back set of spectacular rating numbers from *Lost,* McPherson felt crushing stress anticipating the first reaction from the country to *Desperate Housewives.* This show was much more his baby than *Lost.* McPherson had advocated the *Housewives* spec script, had made creative adjustments like replacing the narrator, and then had all but risked his future at the network in a give-no-ground battle with the Disney management to lock the show in on Sunday nights at 9, rather than Fridays at 10. What if the show didn't work there? That move was all on him.

For the first time in his life, McPherson felt the full responsibility of leading a network into prime-time competition. "You are publicly saying: I am the face and I'm saying this is what we're putting on," McPherson said, analyzing his role in the programming process. "This is when and where we're putting it."

The reviews for *Desperate Housewives* had been sparkling. The marketing effort, McPherson believed, had been outstanding; he could sense a national buzz growing around the show.

None of that helped calm his nerves. All the last week before the show premiered, McPherson repaired to his home gym, working out like a fiend, trying to muscle away the killing stress. By the time Monday morning rolled around, with the overnight ratings from Sunday due, McPherson checked his weight and found he had dropped fifteen pounds.

He was still so nervous he could not bring himself to check the ratings site on his computer that morning. Instead, he kept to his rugged regimen and hit the treadmill. That's where he was, running ferociously, head down, when his new wife, Jen (they had married in July), walked into the gym. She had a phone in her hand.

"You want to talk to Jeff Bader?" she said.

McPherson still could not bring himself to face the ratings music. "No," he said. "I'll get off in a minute."

"Well," Jen said. "You might want to know that you have the number-one television show."

"I'll get off," McPherson said.

At about the same time, the phone rang at Marc Cherry's condo. One of his production crew, a longtime friend, Joey Murphy, was on the line.

"We killed in the ratings," Murphy said. "We beat everything."

The numbers were, in every sense of the word, phenomenal. The pilot of *Desperate Housewives* had reached 21 million viewers, eclipsing the just-established record of *Lost* to become ABC's most-watched new series opener in a decade. *Housewives* also scored a 9 rating in the 18-to-49 audience, a number which was about three times ABC's overall prime-time ratings average for the previous season.

Cherry, overwhelmed, said, "Good, we'll be in the top ten, right?"

"Marc," said Murphy. "We're going to be the No. 1 show."

•    •    •

A few weeks later, J. J. Abrams had a poster-sized photograph made of the big airplane fuselage section that had been dumped on the *Lost* set in Hawaii. It was one of the most elaborate props in television series history. On one corner of the photo, Abrams inscribed a message of thanks to the executive who had made the acquisition of that real out-of-service plane possible, along with all the other extravagant touches Abrams and his crew had included in the pilot. Damon Lindelof and a third executive producer, Bryan Burk, added their signatures. Then they framed it, packaged it up, and sent it off to Lloyd Braun's house.

The *Lost* creators later learned that when the photo arrived it was another emotional moment at the Braun home. The autographed picture was going to be all Lloyd Braun had left to show for his quixotic campaign that, after much doubt, resistance, and not a little disrespect, eventually launched a monster hit.

Almost all, that is. A few weeks into the run of the series, Thom Sherman sent Braun an e-mail telling him all was going well with the show except for one thing.

"I don't know what's going on, Lloyd," Sherman wrote, burying his facetiousness. "But something is wrong with the voice at the start of the episodes, the one that says: 'Previously on *Lost* . . .' I think I heard TVs all over America switching off after they heard that voice."

When asked, the creators of *Lost* conceded that the voice saying "Previously on *Lost* . . ." every week sounded a bit like Lloyd Braun's. But it was only three words, and people might be imagining things. A lot of voices sounded alike. Besides, why would anyone want to risk the wrath of Bob Iger by having the guy he dumped from ABC still connected, in just the tiniest little way, a barely noticeable little voice-over, with one of the biggest shows on the network in years?

# CHAPTER FIFTEEN

# I SAW THE NEWS TODAY, OH BOY

O n Wednesday night, November 10, 2004, Leslie Moonves and several of his top executives sat in the ballroom of the Beverly Wilshire Hotel in Los Angeles. They were attending a dinner being held there that night, a fund-raiser for a Jewish charity.

Moonves and his guests had just settled down at the table after the cocktail hour. It was approaching 8 P.M., which of course meant that in the eastern and central time zones, prime time was just coming to a close.

Les and his colleagues had reason to be confident. Their Wednesday night was on the rise, mainly because of *CSI: NY*, which had enlisted Anthony Zuiker himself to serve as the showrunner. Still, Les's earlier prediction that *Law & Order* would be tough to knock off had proven true. *CSI: NY* had started strong, beating *Law & Order* the first weeks of the season, but NBC's old warhorse had come back more recently. Les wanted to make sure *CSI: NY* did not let up, and had suggested that Zuiker lighten the tone of the show a bit; the early episodes all had a dark, grim edge to them.

Just a couple of minutes until 8, Kelly Kahl felt the vibration from his BlackBerry and pulled it out to check the message. What he read startled him. A contact in New York was e-mailing him that the news department had preempted the final few minutes of that night's episode of *CSI: NY* during the East Coast feed because of a news flash. The subject of the flash: Palestinian leader Yassir Arafat had died.

"I can't believe this," Kelly said as he read the message. Moonves immediately wanted to know what he couldn't believe. When Kahl told Moonves that CBS News had taken *CSI: NY* off the air for a bulletin about Arafat, Les, by his own account, "went crazy."

He immediately demanded to know how such a thing could have happened. How could someone take over the network for this report without his knowing a thing about it?

As the full ramifications of what had occurred sank in, Moonves's fury rose. Every viewer in the country's two biggest time zones would have missed the ending to that night's *CSI* plot, meaning they would not know who the killer was. And for what? Arafat had been dying for weeks. Moonves and Andrew Heyward, the president of CBS News, had decided weeks earlier that Arafat's death did *not* merit interruption on the network. At most, they had agreed, CBS would run a twelve-second crawl at the bottom of the screen informing viewers that the Palestinian leader had died and they could get more information on their next newscast.

In this case, the damn local newscast was only five minutes away, Moonves realized. A memo had gone out describing all of this in detail. Who inside CBS News had dared to pull a stunt like this, in direct contradiction of his orders? Moonves was certainly going to find out.

Taking out his cell phone, Les pushed his way through the tables to a quiet place outside the ballroom and dialed New York. When the staff member manning the news desk answered, Moonves demanded to know who the hell was in charge there and had taken control of his network. The assistant told him right away. Karen Sacks, the senior producer of CBS's overnight news program, *Up to the Minute*, had been the official in charge, monitoring the news at that hour.

Moonves asked to be put through to Heyward. "How could this happen?" Moonves demanded with vehemence when Heyward got on the line. Did this woman really have the authority to do this?

Heyward explained that the news executive in charge did have the authority to take the air; that was the only prudent thing in case of a momentous event. But clearly there had been no call to do this, given the previous explicit instructions about Arafat.

Still steaming, Moonves said, "How many people have the ability to say take that off the air and put this on the air?" Heyward guessed it might be as many as twenty-five people.

Moonves was stunned. He thought only he and Heyward and maybe a couple of Les's other senior lieutenants had the power to interrupt the network's scheduled programming. Heyward promised to look into the situation and Moonves returned to his dinner.

To Les, this was simply too much. It was one more example of CBS News people being full of themselves, feeling like they were superior to the people in the entertainment division and everyone else in the company. And this incident was occurring only two months after the biggest scandal in the network's history: CBS News had been forced to withdraw its backing for a *60 Minutes II* report accusing President Bush of shirking his National Guard duty, because the documents it relied on as evidence had been shockingly, woefully insufficient in terms of authentication. After that disgrace, Les decided that the people in CBS News were not only not superior to everyone else at the network, they were responsible for tarnishing the good image of the rest of the executives and staff members of CBS. Now, just two months after this humiliating blunder, CBS News people were senselessly preempting the network's most important new show.

To Moonves, it only made it worse that he was learning about this outrageous act of stupidity while attending, of all things, a Jewish charity event. When he got back to the table, Moonves told the CBS group: "We were fucked by Arafat again."

The next day, Moonves ordered CBS to issue an extraordinary apology to its viewers for interrupting *CSI: NY*. The statement read: "An overly aggressive CBS News producer jumped the gun with a report that should have been offered to local stations for their late news. We sincerely regret the error."

Then Moonves announced that CBS would repeat the episode of the show on Friday night. After that, he fired Karen Sacks.

Inside CBS News, the latest trauma was just one more reason to be "sad and miserable," as one producer put it. Sacks had been respected and well liked. She told colleagues that she had simply had a mental lapse and somehow had lost track of time. Her friends sympathized with her, even as they acknowledged that she had stumbled into Leslie Moonves's crosshairs at the worst possible moment.

The calamities that had befallen CBS News, the network that, from the long-ago days of radio, had defined professionalism and prestige in broadcast journalism, had, by that point, become almost biblical in scale. It was like a rain of plagues. Even as Karen Sacks was emptying her desk, top executives and producers at CBS News were on tenterhooks awaiting the report of a special panel commissioned by Moonves to look into the document scandal that had rocked the network.

On September 8, *60 Minutes II* had made headlines with an explosive segment purporting to have proof of George W. Bush's long-bruited dereliction of duty while in the National Guard during the Vietnam War. Coming as it did just two months before the presidential election, the broadcast could not help but ignite partisan passions—and it did. Conservative bloggers attacked the report seemingly before it was even off the air, accusing CBS of basing it on bogus documents.

The fact that Dan Rather was the reporter only added high-test to the fire. Rather was such a bête noire to conservatives that groups had been organized for the specific purpose of attacking him for bias. Knowing that, CBS News staff members, including Rather and the report's producer, Mary Mapes, reacted with a circle-the-wagons kind of dismissal of the charges, decrying them as purely partisan and saying day after day that they stood by their report.

But evidence of the wafer-thin substance behind the documents kept mounting, much of it supplied by legitimate, nonpartisan investigators. Finally, after twelve days, CBS acknowledged that it could not authenticate the papers and, humbled before its enemies, apologized for the "mistake in judgment" that led the network to broadcast the report.

Like a bomb hitting an already teetering building, the discrediting of the report sent shock waves through CBS News. For years last among the network news divisions in every significant ratings comparison, CBS News had now made itself a laughingstock. As one shell-shocked producer put it, "We haven't had ratings for a while, but at least we had a reputation." One senior producer put it more bluntly: "CBS News is in the fucking toilet."

Most of those at CBS News not involved in the report had concluded long before the official apology that the documents, at a minimum, had been inadequately, even incompetently, vetted. That such a thing could have happened on a broadcast of such consequence, involving the President of United States, at a critical juncture in the election campaign, left the staff stunned and appalled. Many wondered how CBS could have taken so huge a risk on such a story without having it nailed down to the ground. Why even venture into these murky waters without incontrovertible proof? It was not as if most of the public didn't already know Bush had done *something* fluky and questionable while in the National Guard. The voters had seemed to acknowledge it and had moved on. Retracing that territory without new solid evidence seemed both reckless and self-destructive.

One CBS newsmagazine producer said, "My analogy is we fucked up the way Marcia Clark did at the O. J. Simpson trial. We didn't prove our case, and we left the guy free from further prosecution because of double jeopardy."

The list of people responsible for the disaster was long and profoundly significant, including Mapes—considered the best producer in the place, especially after she and Rather broke the accurate story of prisoner abuse in Abu Ghraib prison in Iraq. The scandal also involved many of the top executives at the news division, including the president, Heyward, and, of course, Rather himself.

Moonves, who obviously had done nothing to either produce the report or allow it on the air, was nonetheless shaken—"blindsided by what happened," as he put it.

He ordered up an investigation by the independent panel, headed by a former Associated Press executive, Louis Boccardi, and a former U.S. attorney general, Richard Thornburgh. Moonves said that he would stand by the results.

At a minimum, Moonves knew the panel's report was bound to be messy and inconvenient. If it involved Dan Rather, as it almost surely would, it would greatly complicate the still-incomplete plan to replace the anchorman on the evening newscast by the following May. Maybe Rather would have to take the fall immediately for his role in this debacle. Even if that could be avoided, could CBS still ease him off the broadcast in May or sooner without its looking like a delayed reproof? And if Andrew Heyward was implicated, that might even be worse, as it would necessitate an executive upheaval at news, something Moonves was not at all ready to initiate.

Since approaching Jeff Zucker four years earlier about the position of president of CBS News, Moonves had not looked anywhere else to find new leadership. During that time, he had actually grown closer personally to Heyward. Andrew, whipsaw smart, staggeringly voluble, and politically deft, had accomplished quite a feat running CBS News. Though the division finished third in every important ratings confrontation with its rivals—morning news, evening news, and live event coverage—Heyward was so adept at cost-cutting that he managed to keep the department profitable. He had also been dexterously diplomatic about one of the touchiest issues in the department: the personal relationship between his boss, Moonves, and staff member Julie Chen. Everyone knew about the romance. Julie was a host on the morning CBS News program *The Early Show,* which was based in New York. But once the relationship became public, Julie was with Les much of the time in L.A. As one senior CBS producer put it, "Andrew was quietly helpful to Les with the Julie issues. He got a special set built for her in the L.A. bureau so she could work on the morning show from there. It offended some people who could not get an extra five cents to cover the news."

But as this producer pointed out, the resentment at CBS News did not extend to Chen personally or her special status. One reason, the producer said, was Chen herself, who, beyond being a good professional colleague, was a sweet, lovely woman whom almost everybody liked. The other reason was that nobody questioned the basis of her relationship with Moonves. "People just thought they were two people genuinely in love," the producer said. "This was not some gold-digging psychopath. She was in love with the guy."

Chen was even on board with her fellow staff members regarding the fiasco about the documents. After the Bush story imploded, Chen was as deeply concerned as the rest of the staff. "How did they let CBS News fall apart this way?" she asked.

That was more a question for the man she loved, or at least for Andrew Heyward. CBS had seemingly grown content finishing last in news. When the division had been placed under his supervision three years earlier, Moonves did not feel comfortable navigating the world of CBS News. To him, the place still had a special aura, forged by legends like Walter Cronkite, Mike Wallace, and Rather. Movie stars and TV stars did not faze Les; the news stars left him slightly in awe.

But the main reason Moonves did little about the lowly state of CBS News was simply that news did not seem a priority. "There wasn't as much at stake financially," he concluded. "And the real mark of a successful network was entertainment, was prime time." At the end of each year, Les knew, people did not talk about which network was first in news. "The headline goes to who wins prime time, you know," he said.

For that and numerous other reasons, having to do with previous job cuts and the timing of news events, CBS had no plan of succession in place for its most important news position—even though its anchorman was seventy-two years old. NBC had announced that Brian Williams would take Tom Brokaw's place two years in advance. That was partly General Electric's obsessive-compulsive need always to have backup plans in place. But it also got Brokaw's audience familiar with his designated successor. NBC had orchestrated the same sort of transition on the *Today* show when it methodically introduced Matt Lauer.

Andrew Heyward was highly skeptical about naming Williams so far in advance. CBS could also have designated John Roberts, the White House correspondent, as the logical choice to follow Rather. Heyward believed NBC had made an early announcement about Williams not out of foresight but out of fear. He and Moonves had made a serious run at Williams themselves. If NBC had not made the commitment when it did, as his contract was ending, Les would have offered Williams the CBS anchor job.

Remarkably, despite Rather's age, there was no urgency at CBS at all to name someone else after Brian Williams fell through. Some talks about Rather stepping down had taken place as early as 1999, but after 9/11 all discussions stopped—it was though CBS recognized it had no one else on the staff, including Roberts, who could match Rather's stature in handling such a momentous event.

Finally, in June of 2004, Rather and his agent, Richard Liebner, met with Moonves and Heyward to thrash out a plan for Dan's retirement from the anchor chair. For several years, Rather had expected someone at CBS to hand him a gold watch and two weeks' notice; but he certainly wasn't going to abdicate voluntarily. During the talks that June, Dan proposed that he stay on until March of 2006, which would be his twenty-fifth anniversary as the CBS anchor.

Moonves and Heyward were not going to wait that long. Logically, an endpoint for Rather could have been targeted to the end of the 2004 presidential campaign. Dan could have anchored election night, then bid good-bye and gone off to work full-time on *60 Minutes,* a provision that had been in his contract for years. The only problem with this scenario was that NBC had already set it up for Tom Brokaw—he was retiring shortly after election night.

NBC had chosen Brokaw's last night of anchoring for December 1, giving him twenty-one years in the job. CBS could not reasonably grab time for Rather around the same date without being accused of stealing Brokaw's thunder. Finding a slightly later date might diminish Dan's farewell. At the June meeting, the specifics of a date for

Rather's departure were left open, with a vague sense that May 2005 sounded good, right at the end of the traditional television season.

Moonves was generous to Rather, telling him, "Dan, it should be when you feel it." But Les left the meeting feeling that May sounded about right.

That was where things stood when the Bush-report catastrophe landed on CBS News.

In the following weeks, all the main players in the story presented their versions of the events to Moonves's independent panel. Many were underwhelmed with how the investigation was being conducted. The interrogators, Boccardi, Thornburgh, and the lawyers hired to investigate, set up in a conference room on the nineteenth floor of the CBS "Black Rock" headquarters. The conversations were not even taped. Everything was done by handwritten notes. Rather especially bristled at what he perceived as a potentially stacked deck. After all, Thornburgh had been attorney general for the first President Bush, and Rather did not have a great history with that administration. He had been in the middle of one of the most famous live television contretemps in history with a sitting president: Rather intensely questioned President George H. W. Bush about his role in the Iran-Contra affair, only to have Bush come back and attack Rather for the famous incident where Dan had walked off the set and let the news go dark for several minutes.

That November, everybody inside CBS News was hearing rumors about who the commission was going to single out for blame. The atmosphere inside the news headquarters on West Fifty-seventh Street was poisonously tense. The *CSI: NY* incident did nothing to help. Moonves, though he professed to have no insight into what the commission might find, told colleagues that he expected people would be fired.

About a week after Karen Sacks paid the price for the Arafat incident, Rather learned that Les was scheduled to be in New York. He asked if they could meet in private. Rather and Richard Liebner journeyed over to Les's Viacom office on Forty-fourth Street, away from any prying eyes at CBS. Andrew Heyward did not attend.

Rather told Les he was concerned that his retirement from the evening news would get mixed up with whatever would happen as a result of the panel's report. Moonves said it was fair to say he was worried about the same thing. He did not want that event to be interpreted as dictating the terms of Dan's exit from the anchor chair.

Given Tom Brokaw's impending departure, Dan said he would prefer to make an announcement before December 1. Moonves agreed. "We don't want to step on Tom's toes." Then Dan said he wanted to talk to Moonves alone. Liebner left.

"I would really like the chance to do this on my own terms," Rather said. Moonves readily agreed and asked if he had a date in mind. Dan suggested March 9, which would be his twenty-fourth anniversary as anchor, as a possible target date. Moonves thought that sounded fine. Dan asked if he could be allowed just a little more time to think it all through. Les was fine with that, too.

On Friday, Rather quietly approached Gil Schwartz, the chief corporate PR executive for CBS, saying he was thinking of formally announcing his retirement. Gil suggested that whatever he decided to do, he should do it quickly because the next week was Thanksgiving, a week with a shortened news cycle. If it were put off until Wednesday, it would look like CBS was trying to bury the news.

On Monday, November 22, Rather spoke to his wife, daughter, and son. They all had the same message: Do it if you think the time is right. The next day, about noon, Rather put in one last call to Moonves.

"I've thought this through," Rather said. "I've made my last check-offs. My gut says this is right." His voice caught, and Moonves knew Rather was tearing up. "I'm comfortable with this. I appreciate your sensitivity, your understanding, your patience."

CBS News put together a release a few hours later. After twenty-four years, Dan Rather would leave the anchor chair on March 9. Just before the announcement went out, Moonves told his aides to make sure the panel investigating the Bush report knew about Rather's decision.

•   •   •

Tom Brokaw stepped down from *NBC Nightly News* a week later, to a chorus of praise for his distinguished career. Brokaw was going out on top: His newscast had dominated the ratings for years, and every time all three network news divisions covered a major event, like the just-concluded national election, NBC and Brokaw dominated them as well.

With the top-rated anchorman leaving, the television news business was rife with predictable speculation, centering on Brian Williams. The new NBC anchor was widely regarded as a smooth operator both reading the news and leading live, ad-libbed coverage. But few believed Williams was the equal of the three titans who had led the newscasts for two decades, at least in terms of his reporting background. Unlike Brokaw, Rather, and ABC's Peter Jennings, Williams did not have a résumé crowded with impressive fieldwork. The question mark always attached to Williams related to *gravitas.* Mainly, did Brian have any? And if he didn't, how long would it take before that caught up to him with the viewers?

Inside CBS, many of Rather's colleagues had long suspected that Dan had been hanging on as long as he could out of a conviction that Brokaw's exit would shake up the ratings and perhaps allow Rather to make a comeback of sorts before he, too, left the stage.

But the real sense of anticipation was located uptown, at the headquarters of ABC News. Peter Jennings had enjoyed a long stretch at the top of the ratings himself in the early 1990s (Rather had not been number one since the 1980s), and at sixty-five years old, Jennings was convinced he had another run in him. So was everyone else at ABC News. The arrival of Williams presented an opportunity. How was Brian going to measure up to the authoritative, stylish Jennings?

Everyone at ABC News was waiting for the first breaking news event, preferably something overseas, where PJ, as he was known inside ABC, could demonstrate his savvy, erudite approach and blow Brian Williams away.

Less than a month into Williams's tenure, the break came. On

December 26, 2004, one of the biggest earthquakes ever recorded erupted under the Pacific, engulfing huge swathes of Asian coast-lines in a massive tsunami. The destruction and loss of life were on a gigantic scale. The networks rushed to cover it. This was surely a story worthy of anchor-on-the-scene coverage. Williams and Rather packed their bags and took off.

At ABC, David Westin, the president of the news division, sent word to Jennings, who was on vacation in the Caribbean. Jennings called back. He sounded a bit hoarse, and indeed, the first thing he said was that he'd been having a respiratory problem. "My doctor doesn't want me to get on a flight all the way over there."

Like many others at ABC, Westin knew PJ's reputation for being a hypochondriac. But in this case there was no doubt he sounded pretty congested. Jennings was apologetic, wished he could go.

"Hey, if you're sick, you're sick," Westin said. "We'll send Diane." Westin could perhaps have asked his other anchor superstar, Ted Koppel, to fill in, but ABC was in the middle of a testy contract renegotiation with Koppel. Westin asked Diane Sawyer instead.

Sawyer rushed to Asia and reported on the devastation there. Few thought she provided quite the authoritative perspective that Jennings would have. Inside ABC it was looked on as a missed opportunity for PJ, but nothing more than that.

●   ●   ●

On January 11, 2005, CBS released the independent panel's volu-minous report. The conclusion: In its broadcast about President Bush's National Guard record, CBS News had suffered a total breakdown of its own standards. In apparent haste to break a scoop—fearing what seemed to be competition from the USA Today newspaper—CBS had failed to complete even the most rudimentary fact-checking. That resulted in reliance by 60 Minutes II on docu-ments whose authenticity had in no way been validated. The pro-ducer of the segment, Mary Mapes, either had been less than honest or else had deliberately misled her supervising executives about the provenance of the documents and her efforts to authenticate them. The executives in editorial control of the broadcast themselves had exercised shockingly little oversight.

As for Dan Rather, the panel found he was an overworked reporter who mostly went along for the ride on the story.

In its only sop to the network, the panel declared that it did not attribute CBS's actions to political bias but instead to its unchecked zeal to break a story. The panel also declared that it could not definitively say one way or the other whether the documents at the center of the controversy were authentic or not.

Moonves wasted no time. He ordered Mary Mapes fired outright, then asked for the resignations of three CBS News executives who had oversight responsibility for the report: Betsy West, the senior vice president; Josh Howard, the executive producer of *60 Minutes II*; and Mary Murphy, the senior producer on the broadcast.

Among those notably *not* asked to resign were Dan Rather and Andrew Heyward. The latter decision left heads shaking all over CBS News. Heyward was the guy running the department and he was left unscathed?

In a statement to the press, Moonves said, "The bottom line is that much of the September 8 broadcast was wrong, incomplete, or unfair. We deeply regret the disservice this flawed report did to the American public, which has a right to count on CBS News for fairness and accuracy in all it does."

Privately, Moonves admitted that while he had expected the panel to find serious flaws in the process of producing the Bush report, he was "shocked at the extent of the things that went unchecked."

Besides shame, the prevailing emotions inside the news division were bitterness and despair. Several of the people ousted, especially Josh Howard, were extremely popular, more so than Heyward. Many on the staff considered his escape either a cop-out or a payoff. Somehow Heyward had skirted the ultimate responsibility for the report, even though everyone else in proximate authority was kicked to the curb.

"Betsy West and Josh Howard were two of Andrew's best

friends," one senior CBS producer said. "How could he do this and save himself?"

How much authority Heyward had left was another question. "People think he's lost his Teflon," said another CBS News producer. "We're going to have a 100 percent impotent president. I personally think he should have been shown the door five minutes after this happened."

Heyward himself acknowledged that he had probably lost the backing of some on the staff. He had been ready to resign if Moonves had asked. But he didn't, and Heyward felt the report spelled out that he was not directly culpable for what occurred. Accepting the fact that some in his department would continue to blame him—wrongly, to his way of thinking—for what had happened to their colleagues, Heyward simply moved on. "I realized a long time ago this is not a popularity contest," Heyward said. "As long as I can look myself in the mirror and know I treat people fairly, which I do, once I've done that, I really can't worry about it anymore."

Morale in the department, already low, now penetrated the permafrost. "There's a pervasive paranoia in the building," a newsmagazine producer said. "People are asking, will we even have a news division in five years? TV news is a dying business; this didn't help us."

Moonves had no regrets about the severity of his actions. He felt to his core that the dismissals were totally justified—and necessary. "I don't know what would have happened if I hadn't ordered that," he said.

Some at the network assumed that Moonves had ordered Mapes to be fired, while the others were asked to resign, only because of legal concerns. They assumed that CBS had felt it could justify terminating only Mapes because her actions were provably egregious. With the others it seemed less clear-cut, and they presumed CBS was looking for safer legal grounds to stand on should any of those ousted choose to protest the resignation requests and sue. Josh Howard quickly gave every indication that this was his intention.

But one of Moonves's close aides said that none of that had anything to do with Les's motivation. Instead, it had do with a more classic—classical, really—brand of corporate leadership. The aide said this move was like something out of ancient Rome, where people who had fallen out of favor, but who were respected, were not executed; they were given the chance to fall on their own swords.

Moonves, this associate said, had always loved the *Godfather* films and the way the Corleone family handled their business. "Remember Frankie Pentangeli?" Moonves's aide said, referencing the character from *The Godfather, Part II* affectionately called "Frankie Five Angels." On the brink of testifying in a U.S. Senate hearing against Michael Corleone, Frankie had been convinced to choose another path. "When you respect somebody, you ask them to go into the bathtub and open their veins."

• • •

Exactly one week later, Moonves appeared at a news conference at the Universal Hilton Hotel in Los Angeles. Just married to Julie Chen over the holidays in Cabo San Lucas, Les was in a great mood. His network schedule was looking more and more like a winner across the board. But the reporters did not want to talk much about that. Instead Les was barraged with questions about the panel's report on the discredited *60 Minutes II* broadcast. A number of reporters wanted to know why he hadn't fired Andrew Heyward. One pointed out that when a naval ship runs aground, the captain loses his command.

"CBS News is not the Navy," Moonves shot back.

He was pressed about Rather's continuing reluctance to accept that the Bush story may have been wrong. Les defended Rather as a "top-notch reporter." The questions continued to focus heavily on the scandal. Moonves seemingly had no way to move past them, until one questioner asked whether CBS might use Rather's departure as an opportunity to move beyond the traditional single-anchor format.

"It's very possible it might not be the voice-of-God, single anchor that has been in existence for so many years," Moonves said. "It might be time to change it up and do something different."

This was a new theme for the press to chew on, and Les decided to run with it. He told the reporters he was looking for something "on the cutting edge," that he was considering "reinventing the wheel," that it was possible that the scandal might push the network to a more radical change. "As opposed to an evolution, maybe we're dealing with a revolution," Moonves said. He was even willing to encourage some wild speculation that CBS could work Jon Stewart of *The Daily Show* on the Comedy Central channel into the evening news in some way. "Jon Stewart is part of our company," Moonves said, referring to Viacom's ownership of Comedy Central. "We speak to him regularly about all sorts of different things."

The next day, the stories in the papers had shifted from the *60 Minutes II* scandal to Moonves's apparent commitment to shaking up the evening newscast in revolutionary ways, perhaps dropping the idea of an anchor altogether, maybe even hiring Jon Stewart to do the news. At CBS News headquarters, the executives who had been talking with Moonves about possible plans to follow the Rather era were stunned. Nothing so extreme had been discussed as a formal plan. Heyward and Jim Murphy, Rather's producer on the evening news, had kicked around the notion of moving off the traditional solo anchor, even using the phrase "voice-of-God anchor" between them.

Heyward then had mentioned the phrase in a conversation with Moonves just before Les left for L.A. Now it appeared the boss had borrowed it on the spot in the press conference, then just run with the whole idea of a revolution in the newscast when the press began lapping it up. Heyward had no problem with Les appropriating the phrase voice-of-God anchor, and he had to admire how skillfully Les had moved the press off the attacks on CBS News. But Les certainly went further than Heyward was prepared to go in promising a revolution. That seemed like an awfully big promise.

Moonves had even offered a timetable for this big shift, telling the reporters, "Come later this year sometime, there's going to be a very different show than the show that's on the air now."

•　　•　　•

In his later years at CBS, Dan Rather had become emotionally edgy, even fragile. On numerous occasions in public and occasionally on the air, Rather seemed on the edge of tears. Sometimes it was understandable, as when he visited David Letterman in the wake of 9/11 and was so overwrought that he had to be comforted by the comedian. Other times the emotion seemed out of scale, like the time when he was extolling the virtues of his then-producer, Tom Bettag, to a group of reporters and he became so choked with emotion he could barely speak.

On March 9, Rather's last night as the CBS anchor, viewers—and even his coworkers—had no idea what to expect. For his end-note soliloquy, Dan chose to resurrect his onetime sign-off of "Courage." In the past when Rather had used that variation on Murrow's "Good night and good luck" and Cronkite's "That's the way it is," viewers did not know what to make of it. It seemed yet another weird choice from the unpredictable Rather. But on his final night, Rather revived "Courage" as a kind of clarion call to continue to fight the good fight against enemies of the nation, against poverty, against prejudice. And he managed to get through the commentary without choking up.

The broadcast ended. As Rather stood up and an aide removed his earpiece, most of the staff of CBS News surrounded the desk and showered him with sustained applause. Embarrassed but appreciative, Rather waved and lifted his hands in little gestures of salute to his coworkers. Heyward stood at the desk with him and gave a brief speech as champagne and bourbon were poured. Heyward had not known what to expect, how Rather would be received by the staff in the wake of the disgrace of the Bush report, which had given such comfort to the critics of CBS News. In the days preceding Dan's final newscast, various old lions of CBS News had given interviews in the press, many of them harshly critical of Rather. Cronkite said he preferred to watch the competition and that Bob Schieffer would have made a better anchor than Rather. Mike Wallace said he found Rather "contrived." Rather loyalists had taken to calling these critics the "BOMs"—for Bitter Old Men.

Heyward had quietly put out word throughout the building that there would be a toast to Rather at the conclusion of the newscast that evening. Both Jim Murphy and Heyward were prepared to speak. But Heyward wanted to avoid the potential embarrassment of having no one else willing to jump in. So he set up what he called ringers. He arranged for two correspondents, Anthony Mason and Richard Schlesinger, both fans of Rather, to stand up and say a few words.

But Heyward underestimated the depth of respect and affection the rank and file still felt for Rather. The toast turned into a spontaneous testimonial. Staff member after staff member stood to recall a moment of professional guidance or personal kindness from the anchorman. Some talked about his doggedness, others his leadership, others his courtly manner. One younger correspondent, Jim Axelrod, recalled his father's funeral. He had been at CBS only a short time, and at the funeral he looked up and was stunned to see Rather standing in the back row of the synagogue. On the way out, Axelrod said, his ninety-three-year-old grandmother, having just buried her son, said to him, "Did you see Dan was here?"

The comments were warm and deeply personal. Dan managed to hold up emotionally, misting over just a few times. He even got through his own extemporaneous remarks, which, in typically grand Rather style, dealt with "the dream" of being a journalist, of "living a life of purpose." With only a hint of choke in his voice, Rather concluded, saying, "Don't let the dream die."

As much as the news division had been through with, and because of, Dan Rather, there was a sense in the studio that evening that CBS News was losing something it would never get back.

•  •  •

At ABC that same week in March, David Westin had a conversation with Ted Koppel, just before the only anchor *Nightline* had ever known was to leave for an extended vacation cruise with his family. Westin and Koppel had been talking about a new contract since November. Koppel, who was sixty-five, was not going to be staying

on at *Nightline*. ABC had long since decided that it needed to over-
haul the flagging program, bringing it back to a live news broadcast.
Koppel was well past the point where he wanted to work live starting at 11:35 each night. Westin was hoping to talk Koppel into taking over the Sunday-morning political discussion program *This
Week,* which, under host George Stephanopoulos, had collapsed in
the ratings.

The relationship between Koppel, possibly television's most
respected journalist, and his network had been frosty ever since
ABC's secret attempt in 2002 to hire David Letterman and toss
*Nightline* overboard. At the time an ABC executive, citing the millions of Americans getting news from cable channels and Internet
sites, said, "The relevancy of *Nightline* just isn't there anymore."

The wooing of Letterman—and the quote—enraged the staff of
*Nightline,* and especially Koppel, who had fought for years to establish the program as the only daily news broadcast on any network
after the evening newscasts. Once Letterman said no, ABC tried to
placate Koppel and his staff by guaranteeing them at least two more
years on the air.

But the two years had expired, and soon so would Koppel's contract. Westin wanted to convince Koppel to stay on, even though
some in upper management had long since decided he was an imped-
iment to improving the program. One senior executive's private opinion was that Koppel had been "mailing in" his effort for years.

Westin did not know if Koppel would go for the shift to a different program, but he was convinced that in the previous two months
they had made significant progress in the contract talks. Westin
believed he had a good chance of getting a yes out of Koppel when
the anchorman returned from his three-week vacation.

One night shortly after Koppel left, Westin and his wife, Sherrie,
hosted a dinner party for some friends and Peter Jennings attended.
Westin and Jennings were not especially close, but he found PJ in
excellent spirits that night. A number of the guests complimented
Jennings at dinner about how slim he was looking. He described the
diet regimen he had undertaken. It seemed obvious that Jennings,

who by then had been in the ABC anchor job for twenty-two years, was serious about getting himself into shape to challenge for news leadership again with Brokaw gone. Westin thought PJ actually looked a bit gaunt. As the night wrapped up, Westin fetched Jennings's lightweight black overcoat and helped him on with it, saying, "You know I've always coveted this coat."

Jennings, always an impeccable dresser, said he appreciated the compliment and added, "I'm going to get you one. There's a shop in Toronto where I have these made. You're a 44-long, right?"

Westin said he really didn't have to do that. But Jennings assured him that he was getting him a coat. Westin noticed that Jennings had been coughing a bit that night.

The next day, Westin and Sherrie left on their own vacation to Jamaica.

Two weeks later, on March 28, Westin returned to the office. He was due to fly to San Francisco with Jennings the following week to launch an ABC News Internet initiative called ABC News Now. Just as Westin was settling back into his office, Jennings appeared, carrying a package.

"Here's the good news," Jennings said. "I've got your overcoat," and he presented Westin with the specially ordered coat from Canada. "Now the bad news: I can't go out with you and do the press conference next week. My doctors want me to go in for a biopsy. They don't know what it is. I can't shake this cough. I've gotten hoarse again. They said it could be viral, or it could be a parasite, or it could be a lymphoma."

Westin told Jennings that his health obviously took precedence over a promotional trip to the West Coast. But he was not worried, because Jennings didn't sound worried.

The next day, Ted Koppel called. He was back from his cruise and he got right to the point. "I've thought about it long and hard," Koppel said. "And I'm going to leave."

Westin was shocked. "I thought we were about to conclude a deal," he said. "Ted, I don't even know how to respond to this. Can you give me any indication of why?"

Koppel said he really didn't want to because that would constitute a negotiation and he did not want to be talked into a deal. He said he had thought it through, had talked with his family, and it was simply time for him to go. Westin asked for a night to think all this over.

The next day, he called Koppel to say he agreed, reluctantly, with Ted's decision. They would work out the details of Koppel's exit from ABC the best way they could. He hung up. Aware that Jennings's CAT scan had been scheduled for that morning, Westin asked around about the anchorman. He had not come in. Westin started to fear something was terribly wrong.

The next day, Jennings called. "The doctors think it might be lung cancer," he said, clearly rocked by the news. Westin conferenced in PJ's friend, Dr. Tim Johnson, the ABC medical reporter (who also happened to be an ordained minister). Johnson told Jennings that he would consult with his doctors, help out any way he could. Westin told Jennings that whatever the news was they would all work through it together.

Later that day, ABC officially announced that Ted Koppel would leave the network in November. Given Koppel's stature, it was national news, particularly in the context of Ted being the third network news giant to announce his departure. That evening, Westin appeared as a guest on the *Charlie Rose* show on PBS to talk about Koppel's career. Westin gave Ted his due, but all he could think about was the much bigger problem ABC might be facing—an anchorman who was really sick.

Jennings came into the studio on Friday. He wanted to do the broadcast. Westin, almost the only one in the building who knew about the tests, thought Jennings looked like hell and sounded worse. Westin could not imagine how Jennings was going to get through a newscast. But he did not see how he could intervene.

From his office, Westin watched with building nervousness as Jennings began the newscast. In an almost surreal twist of fate, the bulk of the broadcast that night was about impending death—the Pope's. Jennings struggled throughout the first segment, stopping several times to catch his breath, to pull up his voice. He was so shaky that Westin, watching on his office monitor, began to panic. He asked himself: "I'm live on the East Coast. What do I do? How am I going to substitute an anchor in the middle of a broadcast? What if he can't do the second block?"

Phyllis McGrady, the top production executive for ABC News, burst into Westin's office, intensely worried. "What's wrong with Peter?" she asked. Westin, not able yet to say, told her, "He's not feeling very well. He's got this respiratory thing. Don't worry about it."

Jennings rallied in the second block. Westin breathed easier. But, badly shaken, he let his emotions slip when he turned to one of his aides, Sandy Sidey, and said, "I think we may have seen Peter do his last broadcast."

The following Monday, Westin was in San Francisco for the ABC News Now press conference. After the event, he, his wife Sherrie, and the chief ABC News press executive, Jeffrey Schneider, took a car back to the airport. Westin let both of them out, then called Jennings from the limo. Jennings gave him the news. "It's lung cancer. It doesn't look very good."

Westin saw Sherrie waiting outside the car and looking in at him. But he could not help himself; he was in tears. Jennings was breaking down as well, but he told Westin, "We're going to fight it." Westin promised to back him in every way possible. As he tried to encourage Jennings, saying that he was sure it would work out, Westin quietly berated himself for not putting it together sooner: the respiratory issues that kept Jennings from covering the tsunami; the coughing at the dinner party; even the weight loss. Beyond that, Westin knew Jennings's history as a smoker. He knew that when Jennings had traveled the world as ABC's chief international reporter he had been a heavy cigarette smoker. It was only after PJ had based himself in New York as the anchor and had two children that he had managed to quit—after a long struggle. He and his then producer, Paul Friedman, had gone as far as visiting a hypnotist in Boston who specialized in breaking the habit. But more recently, after 9/11, close friends knew that Jennings had become a smoker again, secretly grabbing a cigarette when he went out to walk his dog.

Unknown to most of his colleagues, Jennings had also had some heart problems. He was sometimes wearing a heart-monitoring device after several bouts of arrhythmia.

Westin had one more thing he had to tell Jennings. "Peter, we've got to announce this, because it's going to get out." He was afraid Jennings would fight that idea, arguing for privacy. But Jennings immediately agreed, saying, "I'll be in tomorrow morning, and I'll tell the staff and we'll send something out."

The next morning, Jennings composed an e-mail to go out to the staff. Westin had composed a draft of a message himself. The news broke around noon. Jennings went for a short walk in the park. Around 2, Westin went down to the anchorman's office and found Jennings. He looked awful, gray and exhausted. Westin sat down and asked how he was doing.

"I'm fine," Jennings said. "I really want to do the broadcast tonight."

Westin could not conceal his concern, though he said, "Peter, let's be clear. I want you to decide this. I'm not going to decide this."

Jennings read the concern and said, "You don't want me to do it because you think I'm going to embarrass you."

"Forget about that," Westin said. "You're not going to embarrass me. I'll do it any way you want. I'll have an anchor sitting right next to you who we'll just go to. If something goes wrong, we'll just switch the camera—so we will not go to black and it will be just fine. The thing is, you decide what should happen. But I'll give you my honest advice . . ." Westin paused. This was not easy. "People are going to be looking at you really closely tonight, and you don't want them thinking that you're sicker than you are. They may overreact if they think you're shaky on the air."

Jennings nodded, still apparently not convinced. "Well, I've written this thing I want to say." And he read Westin the statement he wanted to make as an end-note on the broadcast. In the message, he explained the news of the diagnosis, promised he would continue to do the broadcast when he could, even admitted that he had been "weak" and resumed smoking after 9/11. They agreed that he should tape the statement in advance and see how he well he could perform.

Jennings went into the studio, sat at his anchor desk, and got miked up. His statement was on a TelePrompTer. As he started to read it, Westin and other ABC News executives watched nervously in the control room. Westin had thought Peter sounded hoarse back in his office, but not actually as bad as he had been the previous Friday night when he almost could not get through the broadcast. As PJ started to read the statement, however, Westin cringed. He realized that when Jennings went on the air he projected his voice, more in the form of an oration than natural speech. Once on camera, he was pushing his voice, and it sounded really bad. Westin looked across the booth to his press chief, Jeffrey Schneider. The two men exchanged reactions of deep discomfort.

Jennings read the end-note three times. He could not get his voice to work. After the third take (ABC would later select the second take for use on the air that night), Jennings removed the mike from his tie, stood up, and turned to those in the control room. "Maybe I won't do the broadcast tonight," he said. "It wouldn't be fair to the viewers."

Westin walked up to meet him and said, "I think that's a really good call, Peter."

Jennings walked slowly out of the studio. The ABC News staff members looked on silently, as he disappeared into the elevator. It was heartbreaking. Jeffrey Schneider said, "That was like watching a heavyweight champion get knocked on his ass."

# CHAPTER SIXTEEN

# THE RESIDUE OF DESIGN

**M**idway into his first season running NBC Entertainment, Kevin Reilly was starting to feel uncomfortable. Like a man drifting far too close to a steam radiator, Reilly was feeling the heat.

The ratings were more disappointing than outright bad, but the trend line was frightening. NBC had dropped sharply in the November sweep. Ominously, CBS had started to win Thursday night consistently, and by sizable margins.

Moonves used the occasion to send a message to advertisers about the next upfront: "These ratings are absolutely going to translate into dollars, especially on Thursday night."

Reilly did not have to strain his eyes to pick out the chief clunker. At 8 P.M., the network's great hope for the season, *Joey,* the spin-off from *Friends* so lovingly crafted, so enthusiastically endorsed by both network and studio, was downshifting rapidly. Reilly could hear the gears grinding.

Another NBC executive summed it up: "There were six characters in *Friends.* We had one character in the spin-off and we sort of ended up with one-sixth the audience. I guess you could say Joey was delivering his share of the audience."

Jeff Zucker thought the *Joey* performance was "the biggest miss of the year," but in public he professed to be largely unconcerned.

After all, he pointed out, what GE really cared about was the profit figures, and unless there was some kind of historic collapse, NBC was highly likely to be just fine in that department. Even the Thursday-night losses did not overly disturb him. At the end of November, Zucker said, "Thursday remains by far our most profitable night. We'll generate more profits than last year. That's something the consumer press will never understand."

His calculation had everything to do with NBC exchanging the $10-million-a-week cost of *Friends* for the less than $2 million a week for *Joey*. But the ratings reduction vitiated the cost reduction. A few executives at competing networks had begun to track the attendant declines—far less severe at that point—in NBC's other crucial Thursday-night piece, *The Apprentice*. With *Joey* gone lame, Donald Trump was having to work that much harder to hold up his end at 9 P.M.

Although Zucker appeared unfazed on the surface, he recognized NBC's vulnerability. He could not help thinking how much worse off he and NBC might have been that fall: *Imagine how this year would be if we had bungled the Conan thing*.

Only a short time earlier, Zucker conceded, he had been in a "terrible predicament" over the Conan thing, which also involved the Jay thing, and was all about the *Tonight Show* thing. Zucker knew that the contracts for both his late-night stars, Conan O'Brien and Jay Leno, were coming to an end within eighteen months. While there was no reason at all to supplant Jay, who was handily winning the 11:35 time period over David Letterman on CBS, Zucker knew he had every reason to worry about what that would mean for Conan.

O'Brien, defying every early expectation, had grown into the leading comic/host of his own generation. At forty he was thirteen years younger than Leno. He had cemented his appeal with the young male viewers who always formed the core of the late-night audience. By 2004, having starred on NBC's 12:35 show, *Late Night*, as long as David Letterman had, Conan decided, as Letterman had before him, that it was time to move up to the big leagues, an 11:35 show. O'Brien was really a Letterman protégé, though he got along fine with Jay. He was enormously grateful to NBC for having made him a star and did not believe in making demands. He had representatives at the Endeavor Agency for that. And they continued to press Zucker: Conan could not stay permanently at 12:35.

O'Brien's representatives—"my Rottweilers," he called them— were growing so impatient with NBC that they seemed ready to chew through Conan's contract to free him. The day that happened, they were certain, ABC would be on their doorstep with an offer. *Nightline* was no longer sacrosanct—ABC had already tried to dump it for Letterman in 2002. Andrea Wong of ABC was calling Endeavor every two weeks to inquire about Conan's status. She knew that if ABC hesitated even one second, Fox would be clearing space at 11 P.M., intent on starting up a late-night franchise of its own.

Two years earlier, Fox's top executive, Peter Chernin, had come at Conan, checkbook in hand. The offer then was a cool $21 million a year. O'Brien was unsure about Fox's late-night prospects and still hoping the big enchilada, *The Tonight Show,* might be served up at some point. So he renewed his deal on *Late Night* for a relatively paltry $8 million a year.

What gave O'Brien a degree of comfort was his personal relationship with Bob Wright. Bob and Suzanne Wright had been guests at his wedding, not a common occurrence between star and corporate suit. But Wright, again defying his image as the squarest, most conservative man in any room, had been, from very early days, a Conan fan. While others at NBC had often denigrated O'Brien's talent, Wright thought Conan was NBC's "comedy future." O'Brien was profoundly grateful. "He did the right thing with me," Conan said. "I'm very happy to do anything Bob Wright asks me to do."

Within reason. O'Brien was not going to stay on at 12:35 indefinitely to make Wright happy. "I think I've proved I can do a show that I don't think has to exist at 12:30," Conan said.

That was in the spring, just a week after NBC announced it had extended Jay Leno's contract to host *The Tonight Show* until 2009. Even though it made complete sense for NBC as a business decision, because Jay showed no signs of flagging, the announcement left Conan's representatives stunned. When he got the news, Rick Rosen, Conan's principal agent, thought it was over for Conan at NBC.

Doors would open at ABC and Fox, maybe even CBS if Letterman showed signs of retiring; but this meant that Conan, like Letterman before him, was not going to reach his dream, *The Tonight Show*. Conan himself took the news calmly. That was his nature. For a star he was unusually levelheaded and non-neurotic. But Rosen vented about NBC's shortsightedness. Didn't they understand that this would mean that come 2005 there would be *three* comedy talk shows at 11:35 each night? And with the network losing ground in prime time, maybe Conan would give Jay and Dave a run for their money right away if NBC let him go.

Only Jeff Ross, Conan's executive producer, had any inkling that the game might not yet be over. "I don't know anything," he said. "I just have this feeling that something else might happen here."

Zucker himself had not shut the door. His public statements remained cryptic: "Conan is a huge star, and I believe he's going to have a long future with NBC with a lot of tremendous opportunities." Privately, to Ross and others, Zucker was all confidence, as always. "I'm going to work it out," he said shortly after extending Leno.

His plan would only succeed, however, if he could prevail on the man who now occupied Johnny Carson's chair to give it up voluntarily. Bob Wright analyzed it as a three-way negotiation—Jay, Conan, and the future of *Tonight*. He handed it to Zucker, with a message: "Living through the Letterman thing, losing one of those types of people is just terrible."

Zucker had not personally lived through the "Letterman thing," when NBC had lost a star to a network with no late-night franchise at all, and then watched CBS establish the only successful alternative to *Tonight* any network ever created. But Zucker believed that with the way television was changing, the prospects for launching a new star in late night were almost nil. If another network was going to start a competing show—he was certain ABC would eventually dump *Nightline* and try it—then the only one they could go to was

Conan. Even Jon Stewart, for all his brilliance hosting *The Daily Show,* seemed a bit narrow to Zucker to make the leap to network stardom. Conan, however, was established and ready to do battle with the big boys, Jay and Dave.

Whenever Zucker saw Rick Rosen, he would needle him mercilessly: "Have you called Bob Iger lately? Are you having dinner with Peter Chernin tonight?"

Finally, Zucker went to Burbank to visit with Leno. From his days running the Burbank operation, he knew Jay—as well as anyone could know one of the more impenetrable stars in television.

Zucker's approach to Leno had to be delicate. He couldn't suggest that Jay should ever stop working. Jay's reputation for having a work ethic was the stuff of legend: He made Viking oarsmen look indolent. His only interest outside his show was collecting cars and motorcycles, and no man ever dreaded retirement more than Jay Leno. Yet Jeff Zucker turned up on his doorstep intending to talk him into giving *The Tonight Show* up to Conan O'Brien.

The two comedians were not personally close, as Zucker was well aware. But he knew Jay did have one area of high sensitivity.

"Look, Jay, I'm thrilled that we have this agreement extending you five years, but I'm here to tell you I have a Conan issue," Zucker said. This was no news to Leno, who followed the machinations of late night more closely than any agent or executive. "I don't want to lose him," Zucker continued.

Leno had been there himself once, twelve years earlier, wanting this one show more than anything else on earth. He indicated that he respected Zucker's position. The name Letterman did not come up directly in the conversation, but Zucker let the connection float there, knowing that Jay had never forgotten and always regretted the way it had played out when he got *The Tonight Show* and Letterman was forced to flee to CBS. At that time, Jay suffered from the perception among some that he had schemed and undermined Letterman, whom Jay had once regarded as a friend. That ugly assertion had colored reaction to Jay—especially in the press—for a long time. And people who knew Jay acknowledged that he had never fully gotten over that. Now NBC was coming back to him with a replay. Same time, same station.

Zucker simply asked Jay to think over the dilemma. Over several weeks they had further conversations, always with the Letterman episode hanging in the air like a persistent fog. Bob Wright was certain this would be the crucial factor: that this time Jay would "get to be the good guy," that he would "end up being the hero." Wright believed that Leno could not countenance being seen as the guy who "pushed out Conan O'Brien." Wright predicted that Jay simply would not "want to be seen in that light."

When Zucker finally asked point-blank if Jay would agree to give up the show at the end of his five-year deal, Jay acquiesced, though he told Zucker he was unconvinced that Conan would be willing to wait that long. Zucker had some doubts about that, too, but when the reward is *The Tonight Show,* he had a hunch patience might be an easier virtue to acquire.

In late August, Marc Graboff met with Conan's representatives, who, besides Rick Rosen, included the head of Endeavor, Ari Emmanuel, and Conan's manager, Gavin Pallone. The group blanched a bit when they heard the terms: "Conan will be handed *The Tonight Show,* no later than June 2009. And yes, Jay is on board with this."

The negotiations over details like salary lasted another three weeks. O'Brien's representatives were not in the best bargaining position. "When it's the show that's been around fifty years, you know you're not going to be paid as much money," Rosen said. But Zucker was right. Conan was not going to pass up *The Tonight Show* for five years of trying to build an audience on ABC.

The deal was concluded on September 27. Jay would host for five more years, then Conan would take over. Jay made it official, announcing the news to his audience on that night's show.

Conan's agents were impressed with Leno and how classy he had been throughout. Jay called Conan and they had what Conan thought was a sincerely nice chat. Conan thanked Jay for his graciousness. A short while later, Conan also spoke with Letterman, who told Conan how happy he was for him. About a week and a half later, after some communication between intermediaries, Conan had another phone conversation with a late-night host.

"Hello, kiddo," the voice greeted him. Like others who had heard Johnny Carson in the years after his retirement, O'Brien thought Johnny's voice had softened a bit, perhaps from not performing anymore. But he sounded good, and it struck Conan that this was a moment he would remember the rest of his life: Johnny Carson was calling to congratulate him on winning the show.

O'Brien thanked Carson and tried to joke about the long wait until he got the job, saying, "If I live to see it." To which Johnny said, "Yes, it does seem like a long engagement before the marriage."

Mainly, Carson wanted to offer some insight into what Conan could expect. He said, "There are going to be nights when everything goes wrong. But at the end of each week it usually works out in your favor."

He had other bits of practical advice. Conan felt a little like Johnny was turning over his old Plymouth Valiant and telling him, "It sticks a little in third, and the brakes need realigning."

They spoke about a half hour. For Conan O'Brien, it was a bit like being blessed into the priesthood by the Pope himself.

A week or so after the deal was announced, Zucker heard from Leno, who said that when he went to do one of his regular weekend standup gigs, he was surprised at how many people came up to him and asked him why he was leaving *The Tonight Show*. Jay found himself having to explain that he would be staying around for five more years. Zucker thought that Jay was upset, and afraid that people might start thinking of him as a lame duck. Zucker felt that was absurd, there was no lame-duck aspect to this. He was sure that talk about the arrangement would be over quickly. He was proud of how adroitly he had managed the dangerous late-night situation, securing both his incumbent host *and* his successor. It was the NBC way, after all: smooth transitions; no broken china.

An NBC associate of Leno's from the comic's first years hosting the show had a different take. "They broke Jay's heart," the colleague said. "I know this guy like the back of my hand and I know they broke his heart. I know he feels betrayed." The associate pointed out that two weeks after the announcement, Jay started telling jokes about how lousy NBC was doing in the ratings. "He never did that in his first ten years in that job. They made him announce this on his own show. It was like they were saying: We're sticking it right up your ass. I'm sure he's already thinking about that magical moment when he moves over to ABC or somewhere and kicks the shit out of Conan."

But another NBC executive, who frequently saw Leno after his show, said Jay talked about the transition one night with unusual emotion. "I am not going to put Conan O'Brien through what I went through," Leno said.

• • •

As poorly as the fall of 2004 had gone for NBC, it was a prime-time nightmare for the Fox network in general and two executives in particular, Gail Berman and Mike Darnell. Berman was in charge of entertainment, and nothing on Fox was entertaining many viewers that autumn. Some of that was Darnell's doing. His heavy lineup of reality shows had crashed and burned. But Berman was ultimately responsible for the network's performance and she had little to console her.

There was one new drama, *House,* which critics liked, with a star, Hugh Laurie, who commanded the screen in a fascinating way. But the numbers were puny and, worse, the show's audience profile was old. The Fox executives were so unsure about the long-term viability of *House* that they sought to cut the order down from twenty-two episodes to sixteen. The studio producing it happened to be NBC Universal, and the request had to go to Jeff Zucker, now in charge of the studio. Zucker approved, because he wanted the studio to have a successful show. (He even interceded to get Laurie booked on *The Tonight Show.*) But the request from Fox did not fill him with confidence that *House* would stick around long.

Inside Fox, rumors floated about Berman's tenure. Few Fox

entertainment chiefs lasted long, because Rupert Murdoch had a firecracker-length fuse. The fall, aside from baseball, had been an unrelenting downer for Fox. Berman's future seemed to ride entirely on the strategy she had outlined in May. The network was holding back its biggest guns for winter.

The big guns in question were the action drama *24*, which Fox withheld so it could play all twenty-four episodes in sequence without repeats, and *American Idol*. As always, Fox executives made much of their vaunted patience with their treasured hit, how they steadfastly resisted the temptation to overuse the powerhouse talent show. They sniffed at NBC's folly in programming *The Apprentice* in two series during the season, noting that this was a sign of desperation and a sure way to diminish the phenomenon. With *Idol*, the self-sacrifice would pay off. Fans would only see one Idol crowned a year, and that would keep them coming back for more. They publicly congratulated themselves for their refusal to give in to the siren call of too many episodes of *American Idol* each season.

Of course, all of that was hogwash.

"We had enormous fights with them over the number of episodes," one representative of *American Idol* said. Fox kept pushing for more, and the production side kept resisting. Fox had no ownership stake in *Idol* and thus could not simply order up more rounds of the show. Fremantle and 19 Entertainment controlled the show, and they were the entities showing restraint.

"It was a big bone of contention between the show and the network," the representative of the show said. "If left to Fox, the show would be on seven days a week, fifty-two weeks a year."

Beyond the resistance from the show's production side, *American Idol* could not possibly have added a second series in the fall each year anyway—and not because of baseball. Simon Cowell, the acknowledged star, was simply not available to appear on *Idol* in the fall. He had signed no contract to do it, and he also had invented his own talent show in England called *The X-Factor*—an enormous hit, as it happened—and he starred in that one throughout the fall.

The question of how to do *any Idol* shows without Simon Cowell loomed over the series because Cowell's British partner, Simon Fuller, sued him in British court that October, saying Cowell had stolen the idea for *X-Factor* from *Idol*. Thinking Cowell might quit the show at the end of 2006 to bring *X-Factor* to the United States, Andrea Wong had skillfully put herself in position to pursue him for ABC. The situation left Fox facing its most daunting financial negotiation. Fox would have to pay Simon Cowell a fortune to keep him on *Idol*—and another fortune to buy *X-Factor* and keep it off a competing network.

For Mike Darnell, the day could not come fast enough when *Idol* would return and his morning calls to the ratings hot line would become joyful again. "After the fourth quarter, Mike desperately wanted to redeem himself," said one of his Fox coworkers. "And he saw the show that was going to redeem him."

It was called *Who's Your Daddy?* A contestant, a young woman who had grown up as an adopted child, would question a panel of eight older men and test them in various ways to help her discover which was her long-lost birth father. If she zeroed in on the right guy, she won $100,000; if one of the impostors fooled her, he took home the cash.

Darnell managed to produce seven episodes without many people at Fox knowing about it. Berman knew, of course, and expressed deep reservations about the concept. Mike said "upper management" had approved the show. When Beckman heard about it, he told Darnell the show sounded like an abomination and that they were crossing a line with this one.

Mike said this one was no worse than anything else they had put on. Determined and passionate as always, Darnell won approval to get the first episode of *Who's Your Daddy?* on the air. If it hit, the other six would surely find a spot quickly.

Darnell had pushed buttons before, but this one raised angry hackles even within Fox. One top Fox executive had an adopted daughter and told other staff members what a horrible idea this was.

Beckman thought that the young woman on the first episode was far too provocatively dressed and looked like she might be a porn actress. Darnell assured him that she was not. Beckman noted that her look made the first episode come across more like an episode of *The Bachelor* than a touching father-and-child reunion. "Guys are going to be staring at her breasts," Beckman said.

Darnell liked the show as it was. He felt a degree of confidence. After all, *Who's Your Daddy?* had elements that had spelled earlier success for Mike and Fox, including controversy and a sexy main character—and howling mad critics in the press. He knew "some people in the company were discomforted by it," but he argued, "It's a harmless television show."

Less than 6.5 million people tuned in; the show finished dead last. A day later, the Web site Gawker.com reported that the show's central figure *was* in fact an actress who had appeared in a soft-core porn film called *Seduction of Innocence*. An unrated version was available on DVD.

Two weeks later, all was forgotten, if not quite forgiven. *American Idol* returned and scored its biggest premiere ratings ever, pulling in 33.5 million viewers. Darnell, as always, supervised the Fox juggernaut. Even one of the Fox executives, appalled by the *Daddy* affair and hoping that this tawdry business might finally cause "upper management" to reconsider the free rein Darnell was always granted, cut Mike some slack, saying he deserved credit for being an early booster of *Idol*.

The Fox comeback hit full stride, with *24* roaring to new heights of success, and *House,* now located behind *Idol* on Tuesdays, suddenly taking off with big numbers. Fox called NBC Universal and upped its episode order back to twenty-two.

No one benefited from the warm bath of strong ratings more than Gail Berman. The day after the first *Idol* numbers arrived, one of her senior executives said, "Gail, today for the first time you can breathe."

With a Super Bowl ratings bonanza in February, Fox zoomed past NBC and ABC into second place behind CBS, closing every week behind more monster *Idol* numbers. All doubts about Berman evaporated. Her taste was vindicated. By March, Berman was such a hot

Hollywood executive, she was scarfed up by the new Paramount movie studio chief, Brad Grey. Peter Liguori, who had pushed the FX cable channel to significant success (abetted earlier by Kevin Reilly), took over for Berman.

Gail left Fox full of satisfaction. "I loved it, even in November, and it was pretty hard to love it in November."

She had some words of sympathy for Reilly, saying she felt bad that NBC's decline was happening on his watch. "But there's a lot of people who don't seem to mind it happening on someone else's watch," Berman said, clearly referring to Jeff Zucker.

"You know what," Berman said, not able to resist one last shot at the competitor who most irritated and provoked her. "You have to be able to point to something, sometime. This is what I stood for in this job, good or bad. This is what I stood for and it won an Emmy, or it changed television in some way. You gotta be able to say something about your tenure before you sit in front of people and say I'm the man, I'm the man."

• • •

At least in terms of NBC's prime-time performance, Jeff Zucker had less and less reason to think of himself as "the man"—not that he ever would have used such a crass term. But facts were facts: Fox had *Idol*; ABC had *Desperate Housewives* and *Lost*; and NBC had trouble.

So when Dick Ebersol, the president of NBC Sports, called Zucker on March 1, Jeff was only too eager to listen.

"How badly do you want football on Sunday nights?" Ebersol asked.

"Are you kidding?" Zucker said. "I really, really want it. And we need it."

Ebersol knew that, of course; he had a longer history at NBC than any other top manager, all the way back to his role in starting up *Saturday Night Live* in 1975. But before he began the challenging chore of lining up GE's support for the massive expenditure of acquiring NFL rights—$600 million a year, as Ebersol calculated it—he had to be sure of Zucker's willingness to make some sacrifices.

"Well, you're probably going to have to fork up something for this," Ebersol told Zucker. Zucker had no illusions about what it would take to get the NFL back on NBC, and he said to count on him. Besides, he trusted and admired Dick Ebersol.

The NBC sports boss knew his way around these negotiations. Ebersol had wrested the Olympics from ABC, once the network solely identified with the games. He had even managed to turn a profit despite the exorbitant cost—and cost was the reason NBC was no longer associated with NFL football, network television's most reliable ratings generator for over three decades.

NBC shrugged off the absence of football, saying it was a money pit—ABC was losing $150 million a year on *Monday Night Football*. And NBC was the house of hits: with *Seinfeld, Friends,* and *ER,* who needed football?

Now NBC did. Getting back in would take a fierce effort. Fox, CBS, and ABC all had the right to retain their packages as long as they ponied up what the NFL demanded. Ebersol anticipated that ABC would be vulnerable this time around because Disney, its parent, also owned ESPN, which had the cable package of games on Sunday nights, one that *made* money. Disney's priority clearly was not holding on to its ABC network package but ensuring that its cable deal was renewed.

NBC's own interest in Monday-night games was modest at best. NBC's Monday shows were not the problem; they were doing OK, especially after they added an emerging hit called *Medium*. More significantly, a game starting at 9 P.M. would run so long it would preempt Jay Leno, messing up NBC's lucrative late-night franchise every Monday for eighteen weeks.

But if the prime-time schedule could be moved to, say, Sunday night, in a switch with the cable package, NBC might get very interested. To Ebersol's surprise, the NFL seemed intrigued with the idea. When the league cut deals in November with CBS and Fox, well in advance of their expiration dates, the NFL included a new clause allowing the league to move some late-season games from Sunday afternoons onto the prime-time schedule. The NFL still wanted to make its one weekly prime-time network game a show-case for the league. Avoiding late-season games involving teams out of contention was increasingly imperative.

Ebersol was elated by the new development. He knew this so-called flexible schedule made much more sense if the prime-time game was on Sunday rather than Monday night. Teams made their travel arrangements far in advance. If Sunday games were moved to Mondays, rebooking hotels and charter planes for additional nights would be a logistical mess. But sliding a game from 4 P.M. to 8 P.M. on the same date would involve almost no heavy lifting.

Although Ebersol had begun his quiet maneuvering over the summer, the NFL negotiations had been disrupted by a shattering family tragedy. Over Thanksgiving, Ebersol was seriously injured in a private plane crash that killed his beloved young son Teddy. In addition to his grief, Dick endured months of rehabilitation from multiple fractures. Still, three months later, Ebersol broached the subject of rekindling an NBC-NFL relationship.

By the time he called Zucker on March 1, Ebersol could feel the ground moving toward NBC. He never really doubted Zucker's interest; Dick could read the ratings as well as anyone. If NBC could land a Sunday-night prime-time NFL package, it would elimi-nate the need for four hours of Sunday-night programming from September through January.

Having the NFL on Sundays would also free up *Law & Order: Criminal Intent* for use on another night. That spin-off had lost all its momentum when ABC inserted *Desperate Housewives* against it. Ebersol also believed football would provide a promotional launch-ing pad to display the network's other shows. Just that September, ABC had done a masterful job pumping up *Lost* during early-season *Monday Night Football* games.

Bob Wright, convinced that the pool of network television view-ers was drying inward from the edge, had urged Ebersol to go after the NFL. As Dick put it, "The base from which to market our wares is getting smaller and smaller every year. Football is the only thing, over the long haul, you can be sure is going to be somewhere remotely close in ratings to where it was when you started."

But Wright could not commit the necessary $600 million from the NBC budget. Only one guy could do that. On Sunday, March 6, Ebersol called the GE chairman, Jeffrey Immelt. As usual, Immelt was in his office working that Sunday afternoon. "What have you got?" he asked.

Ebersol said NBC was suddenly in a far better position to chase a deal with the NFL. "We really need this product for a variety of reasons," Ebersol said. "The single most important is, we don't have a mountaintop from which to make the clarion call about what's on our shelves. For the first time in history, if this comes to the street, it will come on Sunday night, which means on the most important night of the week we will have the only male product. It sets up our whole week. It fills four hours of prime time. For years we haven't been able to get arrested from 7 to 9 P.M. on Sundays, and now ABC has taken away 9 to 11."

Immelt said he understood, but Dick still had to offer something else. Ebersol knew that Immelt had long before suggested some kind of Olympics model to amortize some costs in the NFL. Ebersol said he had thought more about the Olympics idea and there was a chance that GE businesses like capital financing and health care could be worked into the mix. "I can put us in a position where we will get the ability to present first to the NFL on all kinds of different stuff—if we are willing to make a competitive deal."

Immelt liked the sound of that, but he quickly added, "Look, on the money thing, you have to find a way to pay for his—'cause we're not changing the rules."

Ebersol had been a part of the GE management culture long enough to know that meant any expenditure that would mean possible red figures was going to have to be accounted for somewhere else.

Bob Wright was thrilled about Immelt's general support and called a meeting to discuss how NBC would cover the NFL expense.

ABC was losing about $150 million a year on the NFL. NBC believed it could do better than that, mainly because on Sunday it would have four full hours of prime time to sell instead of the two ABC had on Monday.

Of course, with four hours of prime time blocked out, the entertainment division also might be able to get by with fewer programs in development. That's where Zucker came in. Was he willing to cut an amount from his budget that would help cover the risk of loss on the NFL? There was risk doing that as well. ABC had pared down its development-budget costs when it put *Who Wants to Be a Millionaire?* on four times a week—with ruinous results. But nobody at NBC thought the NFL was going to wear out its welcome and get canceled. Zucker agreed.

On March 11, Ebersol, barely out of a wheelchair and walking with a cane, was in his vacation home in Telluride when Immelt held a meeting in New York for top NBC and GE executives. He wanted to thrash out all the NFL issues, then take a vote on whether NBC would pursue a deal. Nobody thought any vote counted except Immelt's. But the CEO quizzed all the participants, including Ebersol, who was outside freezing on his deck because he was smoking a cigar. In deference to his wife, Susan Saint James, Dick never smoked in the house.

They discussed the obvious value in the deal. The six-year contract would include the right to broadcast two Super Bowls; every season NBC would get two playoff games; and that flexible schedule might mean several hugely important end-of-season games each year. Immelt took it all in and then turned to Zucker: "Jeff, you understand that this is coming out of your programming budget?" Immelt said. Zucker said yes, explaining that he would make it work by holding the line on development money. He added that, long term, it might also force tough decisions about how many times to renew aging shows because they got so much more expensive over time.

Satisfied, Immelt, referring to Ebersol by his formal first name, said, "Okay, Duncan, you've got your 600 million. Go run with the ball."

NBC expected to wait several months before they would have a chance to bid on the prime-time games, since ABC held exclusive negotiating rights until October 31. Ebersol was stunned when Roger Goodell, the NFL chief operating officer, called on April 15 and asked: "If I told you we'd be ready to negotiate really soon, how quickly could you be ready?"

Ebersol said he might need an hour. Goodell laughed and asked, "Why so long?"

"Because I'm still walking with a cane," Ebersol said.

Goodell explained that the NFL was about to close the ESPN deal with Disney and it looked like the deal would mean abandoning the option on retaining *Monday Night Football.*

When Ebersol arrived at the NFL headquarters on Park Avenue, they ushered him in through a back entrance and stashed him in a conference room while they finished negotiating with Disney. Dick understood that Bob Iger, now officially Michael Eisner's successor at Disney, was still in the building. About twenty minutes after Dick arrived, the NFL commissioner, Paul Tagliabue, ducked into the room. After a few moments of personal conversation about how Dick was holding up, Tagliabue said, "We have a signed piece of paper— they have walked away from the prime-time network package."

Ebersol said a quiet "Wow." Then he asked what the league had in mind. Tagliabue said that since all the officers were still in the city, they were ready to talk to NBC at once. "So when can we meet?"

Ebersol arranged it for the next afternoon, a Saturday, over at 30 Rock, the NBC building. A weekend was perfect, and not just because preserving privacy would be far less difficult; Ebersol knew he could skirt the building's ban on smoking much more easily on a Saturday. When the group sat around a conference table in Ebersol's big office, just about all of them smoked. After two hours, the group started to go over details of how the advertising sales might be structured. Steve Bornstein, a former ESPN and ABC executive who had become the NFL's top media official, caught Ebersol's eye and winked. Dick understood this meant the deal was done. He started to break into a wide smile. But as he looked past Bornstein, his eye caught a photo of his son Teddy taken the previous February. Ebersol had all he could do to keep from sobbing. Bornstein could see the tear crease Ebersol's cheek as he stood up and pretended he was leaving the room for an ashtray.

By the time Ebersol returned, everyone was standing, shaking hands. NBC would get Sunday-night football for six years at a cost of $600 million a year. The cable package on ESPN would shift to Mondays. *Monday Night Football* on ABC would have one more season and then disappear into television history. NBC and the NFL would make the announcement on Monday morning.

Ebersol left the building about 6 and, still charged up, decided to walk to his apartment. As he hobbled on his cane up Park Avenue, he passed a building at Sixty-first Street that he knew well. It had been for a time the home of the late Roone Arledge, the master impresario of television sports who had invented *Monday Night Football*—and who was, in every sense, Ebersol's professional father. Dick worked for Roone right out of college and had been his closest aide until he left for NBC. Ebersol looked up at what had been Arledge's apartment and thought of Roone's legacies: the Olympics, which Dick had brought to NBC; *Nightline,* now seriously threatened with the departure of Ted Koppel; and finally *Monday Night Football,* which as of that day was leaving Roone's network home, ABC.

Arledge had lamented ABC's loss of the Olympics, but he told Dick how proud he was of him for grabbing them. But the end of *Monday Night Football* on ABC would have surely broken Roone's heart, Ebersol knew. As happy as he was for bringing the NFL back to NBC, Dick could not help but be ineffably sad, thinking of the Arledge era passing into time.

Later that night, Ebersol decided he would show up at the set of *Saturday Night Live,* just to sit with his friend, the producer Lorne Michaels. Ebersol always got to Studio 8H only about thirty seconds before the telecast. Just as he took a seat next to Michaels, Zucker walked in from the other direction. Ebersol greeted him with a handshake and a huge smile. Lorne looked at the two men embracing and said, "If I didn't know any better, I'd say you two guys just made a football deal."

•   •   •

There were only a few tears at ABC about losing *Monday Night Football*. The league, after all, had forced ABC's hand by switching its prime-time package to Sunday night. And ABC already had some attractive options on Sunday nights. Both *Desperate Housewives* and the 8 P.M. reality show, *Extreme Makeover: Home Edition*, had better ratings than what *MNF* was scoring. If any network was in position to shrug off losing football on Sunday night, ABC was the one.

By the time the new NFL deal was concluded, ABC's position on Sunday night only seemed to be getting stronger. The last week in March, ABC introduced a new drama on Sunday at 10. It arrived without much advance publicity and seemed to be simply getting a tryout, filling in for another drama, *Boston Legal*, which was on hiatus until the May sweep.

It made sense to try a different show, because *Boston Legal* was losing a good percentage of the *Desperate Housewives* audience. The series that Steve McPherson selected to fill the slot was a medical drama with strong female appeal called *Grey's Anatomy*. The series had been on the shelf at ABC since the preceding spring.

*Grey's Anatomy* had strong supporters at ABC, mainly the same female executives who had pushed so long and hard for "girls' shows." Heather Kadin, the staunch champion of both *Lost* and *Desperate Housewives*, had been an advocate of a young writer named Shonda Rhimes. She had previously created a searing drama pilot for ABC about female war correspondents "out in the field having lots of sex," as Rhimes put it.

That script had caught the attention of Susan Lyne. But she had doubts about the sustainability of the premise. And Bob Iger told her he despised the show. ABC passed. But Kadin and Suzanne Patmore, then McPherson's top drama executive at the Touchstone studio, were so impressed with Rhimes's writing that they asked her to develop another show.

Rhimes came back with a script with a similar theme: young women on the firing line. But this time Rhimes put them in a recognizable television landscape: a hospital. The pilot was initially called *Surgeons,* though with its angst-ridden young people, Lyne took to calling it *My So-Called Surgical Residency*—after the famed but ill-fated former ABC drama about angst-ridden youth *My So-Called Life.*

The script was finished late and was up for consideration with several others for the last pilot order for the 2004–2005 season. This time Bob Iger did like the material. Steve McPherson at Touchstone was less of a fan. This was yet another serialized show, which Steve continued to have doubts about. For the last pilot pickup, he preferred a suburban police show. Kadin and Julie McNamara, the ABC drama team that had ardently backed *Housewives,* took matters into their own hands. They turned up in Lloyd Braun's office and made an impassioned case for *Surgeons.*

Braun liked the script, but he was inclined to reject the show because it violated his mantra that ABC's dramas had to be distinctively different. This was another medical show. But Kadin and McNamara argued that it was sexy and appealing to women and if *Desperate Housewives* ever did make it, this would be a perfect companion. The newly titled *Grey's Anatomy* won the order; it was the last show picked up by ABC that development season.

Casting was critical, as always. Lyne and some others had considered a young actress named Ellen Pompeo for a part on *Housewives,* but she lacked the force required. As Meredith Grey, the sexy, intelligent, but somewhat dysfunctional lead in *Anatomy,* she fit well. Sandra Oh, who had made such an impression in the film *Sideways,* took one of the other leads.

The biggest hurdle was the male lead, Meredith's love interest, so devastatingly handsome he was nicknamed "Dr. McDreamy." ABC could not find the right actor. The studio pushed Patrick Dempsey, but Lyne fought the suggestion tooth and nail. Dempsey had disappointed the network on several previous occasions and he was unusually expensive. Lyne reluctantly agreed to let him read.

With Pompeo, Dempsey seemed to fill out as a star. When Lyne saw the pilot, she said of Dempsey, "Put him in green scrubs and, my God, your heart stops."

Female hearts began stopping all over America on March 27, when the *Grey's Anatomy* pilot went on following a new episode of *Desperate Housewives.* From the first week, it held far more of the *Housewives* viewers than *Boston Legal* ever had.

The competition noticed. Nervous word began to spread, especially among executives at NBC: ABC just might have found *three* major drama hits in one season.

•    •    •

ABC's addition of *Grey's Anatomy* only made it all the more certain that NBC was facing the most ignominious fall in network history, an epic tumble from first place to last. And if that was not enough of a crisis on Jeff Zucker's plate, the show he was personally most connected to, *Today,* was edging ever closer to an experience it had not endured in a decade: finishing a week in second place.

The enormous weekly lead in viewers that *Today* had enjoyed over ABC's *Good Morning, America,* which reached as many as 2 million viewers during Zucker's run as executive producer, was shrinking perilously. One week in April, the two shows were separated by just 200,000 viewers. NBC publicly pointed to *GMA*'s near-shameless exploitation of *Desperate Housewives* as the main reason for its ratings surge. *GMA* was offering viewers "secret scenes"—really just outtakes—from television's hottest show every Monday morning. On Thursday, they were doing other tie-ins with *Lost.*

But it wasn't like *GMA* had invented some new scheme to lure viewers. Under Zucker, *Today* had just as aggressively exploited tie-ins with NBC series, like *Friends* and *Seinfeld.*

Besides, nobody at NBC was satisfied with excuse-making for the narrowing lead in the morning. No program was more important than *Today,* the most profitable in television, taking in more than $250 million a year. One of Zucker's close friends said, "I never saw Jeff so freaked before. They expected him to get in there and fix it."

"They" in this case was Jeff Immelt. Zucker had been the master producer of *Today*. Now the news division reported to him. Surely he could find a way to preserve NBC's morning superiority.

In fact, Zucker had been contemplating shaking the show up for some time. He didn't like the way it was being produced; it had become stale, empty of fresh ideas, the kind he had injected constantly in his years leading the show. By this time, *GMA* had appropriated most of those ideas, so the differences between the shows had become less and less defined. That meant viewers were simply choosing which group of hosts they liked best.

*Today* had always held the advantage there, because no morning host was ever more adored than Katie Couric. That spring, Couric remained hugely popular—but for the first time some research indicated that by some standards Couric was also becoming hugely *unpopular*. In an arcane likability measurement known as Q-ratings, Couric, who once seemed to have legitimate claim to the title of "America's Sweetheart," had suddenly started posting high negative scores to go along with still-high positive scores. Katie beat Diane Sawyer, the host of *GMA,* in popularity, but she now was also beating Sawyer—whose somewhat arch style contrasted sharply with the perky style attributed to Couric—in terms of negatives. Couric even had a higher negative score than Dan Rather.

Zucker had seen the numbers and had sat down with Katie in February, gently advising her to tone down some of the touches that viewers apparently objected to: her frosted hair, her glamorous clothes, her public superstar salary. At $15 million a year, a figure that some at NBC believed Katie had been overly willing to leak to the press, she was the highest-paid person in network news. Zucker trod carefully both because he still shared a deep personal bond with Couric—one friend described it as "a brother-sister kind of thing"—and because he knew Katie could be fragile. Some of her colleagues believed that Katie, who had relied heavily on Zucker's production skills at *Today,* felt somewhat abandoned when he went off to Hollywood.

One senior NBC executive said, "There hadn't been a strong producer of that show since Jeff left. In order to compensate for that,

Katie became larger than life. And that's tolerated by white men, but not by women or minorities. It just isn't. So that gradually blew up on her."

While Zucker wanted to shake up the production side, he had no interest in displacing a star as big as Couric. She was still the center of the *Today* show. Her contract ran another thirteen months. Zucker had made a quiet effort to extend her that winter and been put off. He knew why.

Leslie Moonves was already wooing Couric, dangling Rather's anchor job as well as an occasional spot on *60 Minutes*. Les could not formally chase Katie while she was under contract, but he could let her know he was interested—and he had. Les talked to Couric several times that winter and had other conversations with her agent, Alan Berger of CAA.

Moonves had no trouble remembering how he had begun the turnaround at CBS Entertainment: He hired Bill Cosby, the biggest star he could find. Grabbing Couric would be a similar coup, perhaps exactly the one to revive his moribund news division. For a star as big as Katie, Les could give up the talk of radically altering the evening news format. Katie could be the solo anchor at *CBS Evening News*. That would be revolutionary enough—nobody had tried a "voice of goddess."

That was part of the pitch. Katie could be the first woman ever to be a sole anchor—the face of a news division—at any network. Les could offer her something that NBC could not. NBC could have named Katie to the leading news role at NBC, but instead went with yet another man, Brian Williams. In private, Katie herself asked why only men had been placed in the sole anchor positions. (Both Barbara Walters and Connie Chung had brief runs as coanchors on newscasts, and met with rejection from both viewers and their male coanchors.)

The question Moonves posed to Katie was: What did she want to do with the rest of her career? When her NBC contract ended she would be forty-nine, the perfect age to launch a new chapter in her life. She had already been on *Today* for fifteen years, longer than any previous anchor. Did she want to continue in that role indefinitely? She had already reached the peak there. All that could really change in the future was losing finally to Diane Sawyer and ABC. What else could NBC offer? A spot next to Stone Phillips on *Dateline,* NBC's fading newsmagazine? Or a syndicated hour like the recently failed Jane Pauley show?

A deal for Couric would make a gigantic splash, drawing instant attention to CBS News. It would also be outrageously expensive. The figure $140 million for seven years floated through the rumor mill. Couric dismissed it as exaggerated. Still, if Katie could lead CBS out of third place in news it would be worth every penny to Moonves. And of course, removing her from *Today,* and potentially knocking that juggernaut off stride, would be an added benefit.

That said, Moonves calculated that the one thing he could not offer Couric was the bond she had with Zucker. He wondered if she would ever be able to walk down the hall to tell Jeff she was leaving.

Zucker himself reckoned that their personal closeness was perhaps his only counter to Moonves's blandishments. He could not, or would not, extend his budget to match a $20-million-a-year offer. Zucker had too many dominoes at NBC News that would fall as soon as a deal like that was public: more money for Williams, for Matt Lauer, for Tim Russert. If money was the factor, NBC was going to lose. Some inside NBC News interpreted the leaks of Couric's salary as an indication that money *was* a big factor to her, that she saw money as a measure of importance. "If I make more money than you, I'm more important than you," as one veteran NBC News executive put it.

Couric herself professed honest uncertainty. "I'm trying to figure out what I want to do," she said. Many of those close to her, including Zucker, believed her. So did Moonves, who thought the decision was probably "anguishing for her."

Couric at one point said she would decide by the fall of 2005, which led to speculation—not discouraged by CBS—that she had an early out clause in her contract. But Couric finally ended that rumor, declaring it was totally false. "I'm really fortunate and flattered that I have some opportunities," she said. "I'm trying to make a thoughtful decision while being in the middle of this media spotlight, which I am trying to ignore."

Zucker decided to blow up *Today*'s production side in April, firing Tom Touchet, the third executive producer to fill that role since Jeff himself left it in 2000. "The change is being made because of ratings. I'm being honest about that," Zucker said. "The gap has been closer in recent weeks, and that doesn't make me happy." The decision amounted to a vote of no confidence for Neal Shapiro, the president of NBC News, who hired Touchet. (He announced soon after that he was stepping down—opening the way for Zucker to put a personal stamp on NBC News.)

Relying on advice from his friend Dick Ebersol, Zucker reached into the sports division and plucked out Jim Bell to be the next EP at *Today*. He seemed to have the right pedigree for the job—not only did he have experience with producing live events but, with a beginning in sports and a degree from Harvard, his qualifications mirrored Zucker's own résumé. "He reminds me of me," Zucker confessed privately—in every way but physique, that is. (Bell had played defensive tackle at Harvard and still looked like he could.) Zucker paired Bell with an NBC News veteran, Phil Griffin, as the executive in charge of the broadcast.

The team arrived during what Bell called "dark days" for *Today*. With *Desperate Housewives* about to wrap its season with an enormous finale, *GMA* had its best chance to sneak past *Today* and actually win a week. If it did, it would deny *Today* a cherished celebration planned for the fall: 520 consecutive weeks—ten years' worth—in first place, a feat few shows in television history had ever recorded. That Monday, with more "secret scenes" from *Housewives,* the ABC program did beat *Today* by about 800,000 viewers. *Today* spent the rest of the week trying to catch up. By Friday no one was sure of the outcome. Matt Lauer went home, for the first time so worried that he waited for the call that would indicate how things looked. "There were a lot of egos and a lot of pride involved," Lauer said. "I don't know what it feels like to lose a week."

It could hardly have been closer: *Today* won by a scant 12,000 viewers. The *Desperate Housewives* season was over, but ABC had every reason to expect that *Today* would finally be toppled in September when *Housewives* and *Lost* returned. Watching from the sidelines, Moonves pondered whether a win by *GMA* might just be the last nudge Katie Couric needed to jump into his welcoming arms.

• • •

Moonves was eager to escape from a different relationship—his partnership with Tom Freston. After Viacom announced that he and Tom would run two separate divisions of Viacom, Les developed an idealized picture of this partnership, modeled after the best professional partnership he had ever witnessed: Bob Daly and Terry Semel at Warner Brothers. But in practice, the corporate relationship between CBS and MTV Networks, and the professional relationship between Les and Freston, was strained from the beginning.

Moonves had been open to the idea of a real sharing of leadership of the company, but he did not get the same feeling back from Freston. Two weeks in, Les decided it wasn't going to work. Neither man disliked the other, but they had almost nothing in common. "Different worlds," said Les. "Different universes." All the promised synergies of matching up CBS's broadcast assets with MTV's cable assets amounted to very little in practice.

Once in a while the two men would have breakfast if Les was in New York. But overall they spoke infrequently. Like Moonves, Freston could feel the culture clash. "The cable culture is younger, probably less reverent, more poorly dressed," he said. "The broadcast guys are older, with more of an overt sales perspective on things, more Hollywood." Freston sensed that to the CBS guys the MTV kids were "beatniks almost." Cable executives had long been accustomed to scoring points with advertisers by mocking the networks. Freston said, "Part of the initial mission of cable was we were the un-network."

Moonves could roll with that. The biggest source of friction was the Paramount studio. Les thought from the start that he would be involved with movies. He told Freston: "You know I really wanted the studio. So like, if you're ever going to make any big moves at the studio, you know, plug me in. I'd love to just know."

Moonves was clearly hoping Freston might take advantage of his vast Hollywood expertise. But Tom made his biggest move, selecting a new studio chief, without talking to Les. When he followed up on Les's request and let him know about the move, Freston had the impression that Les "fell off his fucking chair."

Freston had hired Brad Grey, the talent manager and producer, a principal in Brillstein-Grey Entertainment—and one of Les's closest Hollywood pals—to run Paramount. "What?" Les said when he caught his breath. "Brad Grey? Why would he take this job? Why would Brad leave this perfect life, making all that money, take a pay cut, and come over and do this?"

"Well, I convinced him," Freston said. "I think this is what he sees as the next station in his life."

Moonves later supported Freston all the way. He backed the choice of Grey enthusiastically in a board meeting, for which Tom was deeply grateful. But Freston still had the impression that Les was in a state of shock over the appointment. Some friends of Freston's speculated that Les might have preferred Tom to pick a loser, perhaps opening up the possibility that Les could get eventually get control of the studio. But Freston could only point to how supportive Les ultimately was of the appointment of Grey. Besides, the two copresidents of Viacom were commonly incentivized, which meant they should be rooting for each other, not hoping the other guy fell on his face. Still, when outsiders suggested to him that Les's competitiveness was not to be underestimated, Freston conceded that he had thought quite a bit about that.

The studio issue only reinforced the notion that Moonves, despite the equality of the contracts, remained at something of a disadvantage in this alleged partnership. Freston was and would always be closer to Sumner Redstone. One of Moonves's close L.A. friends related, "Les said out loud on the golf course one day that he knew he was in second place to Freston in that company."

Les had not heard a word from Disney about the job succeeding Michael Eisner, and told friends how surprised he was that they had not spoken to him. Strangely, his name never even surfaced when the press listed the final candidates Disney was supposedly looking at—even though by résumé and list of accomplishments Moonves was an obvious top-tier candidate. The position surely would have tempted Les, given the apparent second-place situation at Viacom. But Disney did not call.

Not Moonves, anyway. Disney did approach Tom Freston, who was in India when they phoned. The headhunter told him his name was on a "very very short list" of possible names to replace Eisner. Freston said he was flattered, but he had a contract. The headhunter said, "We're not afraid of Sumner Redstone." They invited him to meet the Disney chairman, former senator George Mitchell. Freston asked to think about it. But he didn't think long. Like most observers, he already sensed that Disney had decided on Bob Iger. If Freston met with Mitchell, Disney people would probably leak the news to prove they were sincere about searching for a CEO outside the company. Redstone would find out and all Freston's years of loyalty would be undone. Besides, would running Disney be that great a job, with its cruise ships full of people getting diarrhea and theme parks threatened with terror attacks? Freston called back and thanked the headhunter for the interest; but he said he would not want to waste Senator Mitchell's time.

Later, it became public that the eBay chairman, Meg Whitman, had interviewed for the job—the only outsider to do so. (Reports said that Peter Chernin from News Corp. had an exploratory meeting but declined an interview.) Freston sensed he was right about the search being a sham. Whitman only hurt herself within her own company, and Disney gave the job to Iger anyway.

Freston never talked to Les about the approach from Disney.

In March, with Viacom's stock still languishing, Redstone hatched what seemed like a reverse-your-field plan to unlock what he saw as the growth side of the company. He would ask his board to split Viacom into two separate entities: the cable unit and Paramount, with Freston as CEO; and the broadcast unit, including radio and billboard advertising, with Moonves as CEO. This was the direct opposite of Redstone's previous strategy of expanding to exploit synergy. Some on Wall Street questioned the move, others embraced it.

Moonves and Freston were in the latter category. Les especially liked the idea that he would be getting his own operation. No more second-place status. The fact that he would be in charge of the part of the company *not* expected to show financial growth was only a spur for Les to prove people wrong. Nobody had believed he could resurrect CBS and he had done just that. Now the CBS side of Viacom was supposed to be the lesser of the two halves. Les would see about that.

•   •   •

Moonves's competitive personality was certainly on display that spring when Mark Burnett finally unveiled his ultra-expensive boxing reality series *The Contender*. Burnett remained one of Les's most valued producers, and Les, in his kinder, gentler moments, saluted Burnett for generating the show that had transformed his network, *Survivor*. Moonves even bestowed a new Mercedes on Burnett for that. But business was business. When NBC scheduled *The Contender*, a show Les had bid on and lost, Moonves lined up an original episode of his powerhouse 10 P.M. drama, *CSI: Miami*, to try to knock the boxing show immediately to the canvas.

Burnett called Moonves to tell him the NBC executives thought he was being a bit vindictive. Moonves said to tell them to grow up. "This is a business and I've got a job to do," Les told Burnett, adding, "Don't you wish you were with me now?"

The numbers the next day reinforced Leslie's point: *CSI: Miami* had reached 21 million viewers, *The Contender* only 8 million. The show continued to demonstrate Burnett's skill at producing quality, nonfiction drama. And the numbers, especially for the Sunday-night slot NBC gave it, were never bad. They just were not up to Burnett's hit standards, nor worthy of what NBC was paying. The network passed on bringing *The Contender* back for another season. (Burnett subsequently sold it to ESPN.)

NBC still had a lot invested in Mark Burnett. After all, he had put them into business with one of America's most talked-about celebrities, Martha Stewart. Burnett, alone among television producers, had solicited Stewart at the lowest point of her career—just before she was sentenced to jail. Convinced Stewart would be seen as heroic when she emerged from prison, Burnett sold Stewart on two ideas: a total revamping of her syndicated daily show, and a reality show of her own, a new version of *The Apprentice*.

When Burnett told Zucker, Jeff agreed that signing Martha was a brilliant move; he, too, was convinced she would be a hot commodity when she was released. They made the deals with Stewart before she went off to Alderson prison in West Virginia in October. Burnett further ingratiated himself with his unwavering loyalty; he flew from L.A. to West Virginia every three weeks to visit her.

What was not quite spelled out in the *Apprentice* deal was whether Martha would be supplanting Donald Trump, filling it for him for one cycle, or supplementing him with a second separate show. Stewart had no doubt about what she thought the offer was: She would inherit the lead role in the original *Apprentice* as well as its Thursday-at-9 time period. Zucker expected that as well.

But they didn't reckon on Donald. As Trump wound up the third cycle of the program, he was not disposed to walk away from it. Some of Stewart's representatives believed Burnett was surprised by Trump's continuing interest in doing the show. They thought Burnett was expecting the mogul to walk away after three go-rounds. But the contract with Trump actually gave Donald a financial interest in the series; he was not just Burnett's star, he was his partner. And he wanted to continue his role on Thursday nights—he remained, after all, NBC's biggest series star.

While the show's ratings had slid a bit, they continued to be among the best NBC had. Burnett attributed the fall-off largely to NBC's collapse from 8 to 9 on Thursday, thanks to the now-woeful showing of *Joey*. But both Trump and Burnett conceded that they had miscalculated on the third edition of *The Apprentice*. Burnett thought a competitive setup between "street-smart" and "book-smart" contestants had backfired, and actually detracted from the series. Donald thought the problem was the cast, which he found utterly unlikable. Worse, he felt like the group had been selected without regard to his own preferences.

At a mass tryout in Trump Tower the previous fall, Trump had spotted several potential candidates, and he was shocked when the final cast was announced that none of those he liked had made the cut. "There was this girl I wanted," Trump said. "And a guy in dread-locks. I said I'd like to see if you could have them on the show. I wasn't being the typical Trump. I was being nice to a guy who worked for Mark Burnett. When I saw the eighteen they picked, I was saying: You didn't take one of my suggestions? Where was that beautiful girl I picked? They told me: Well, we didn't like them. I said: What the fuck? First of all, it's my show, and secondly they've got to work for me. What the hell are you doing telling me who should be on the show? I went through the roof. Then I became the real Trump."

With the shrunken lead-in, the lackluster cast, and Donald's evi-dent on-air distemper, some of the magic wore off *The Apprentice* in that third edition. But with Donald still expressing a strong intent to come back for more, Burnett decided to go for broke and pitch NBC on a double dose of *The Apprentice* for the fall of 2005, Donald *and* Martha. Why not, he figured: If *CSI* and *Law & Order* could do three shows a week, why couldn't *The Apprentice* do two?

Burnett was convinced that, post-prison, Martha would be "the biggest news in the fucking country." Of course, Trump had little reason to want his franchise diluted, and Stewart had no interest in doing a second-string show—one that Donald Trump would be get-ting a credit on. "That made her insane," one of her business associ-ates said.

Kevin Reilly was initially disposed not to play two weekly edi-tions of the show, leaning toward using Martha in the fall and rest-ing Donald. He wanted to "let the show breathe," which it surely would not with a double dose on the schedule. But Burnett, as Reilly described him, was "go, go, go." Reilly believed "contractual issues" with Trump were driving Mark's insistence that the double-header would work. Burnett argued that the Trump show was a rock-solid hit, and that Martha had such heat she would have an appeal all her own. Besides, he told NBC, "Why would you possibly change Thursday at 9? Do you guys really want to be responsible for really tanking your Thursday night? What if Martha didn't work?"

Not that Burnett had any real doubts on the latter point. He was always certain his shows would be hits. But it helped his argument for putting both shows on the air at the same time.

NBC finally agreed, but not for the reasons Burnett cited. Zucker had come around to thinking that *The Apprentice,* like *Who Wants to Be a Millionaire?, The Bachelor,* and several other unscripted megahits, might only have so many bullets in its gun. Doing a rapid 180 on his decision to reshape Thursday night just a year before, Zucker said NBC might as well maximize its gains while it could. If the *Apprentice* comet was going to flame out, Zucker wanted NBC to be ready to go back for comedy.

• • •

NBC held what is known as a "mini-upfront" in March, a kind of preview of its most promising projects for a gathering of advertising executives. Nobody could hide the ugly stain in the ratings results: The NBC schedule was in steep decline. *Joey* now looked like a bust. *Medium* had provided a little midseason boost, but nothing had come along that looked like *Desperate Housewives* or *Lost.* Reilly and some other NBC executives were excited about one new comedy they were introducing that spring: an American adaptation of the British sitcom *The Office,* especially because in Steve Carell they believed they had a hot comedy star. But Zucker was cool on the show, as he was on all single-camera comedies. At one point, he dismissed *The Office* as so narrow in appeal it was more appropriate for NBC's artsy cable channel Bravo.

Before the presentation, Randy Falco, the head of NBC's sales operations, observed that prime time was like football. "Control the middle of the field and you'll win." That meant focusing on Tuesday, Wednesday, and Thursday nights. Despite the travails of *Joey*, NBC was doing OK on Thursday. But Tuesday and Wednesday were fraying like old sweaters.

In front of the advertisers, an upbeat Reilly said that during development season he and his aides had thought a lot about "what we stand for and what we want to be in the future." He cited a line he had heard at an industry panel: "Television goes where NBC goes." He added, "I feel a mandate to deliver on that."

Then he introduced a batch of shows in development, including a comedy about a young man in a retirement community, a *French Connection*–era cop show, a sexy drama about an episcopal priest who had Jesus as an imaginary friend, and a rural comedy about a ne'er-do-well out to remake his life. The latter, *My Name Is Earl*, Reilly called "one of the smartest scripts we have." The advertisers seemed to have a good time.

About a month later, when the NBC brass flew in from New York and Reilly presented them the completed pilots, the reaction approached panic. One senior NBC executive said, "After seeing the pilots, I thought Kevin wouldn't last a week. There was talk of that."

Some of the New York executives were shocked, not because the shows were necessarily bad, but just at the fact that they had been made in the first place. "A young guy in an old folks' home?" one New York executive said. "What the fuck is this? There is no place anymore on a network schedule for a show like *Golden Girls*. I thought: *Who commissioned this idea? People in their eighties?*"

The network's highest-profile drama, *The E-Ring*, a Pentagon thriller from hitmaker Jerry Bruckheimer, met with shrugs: It was dull, disappointing. "*Zzzzzz*," said the New York executive. Nothing looked remotely like a breakout hit, or even much good, with the exception of *My Name Is Earl*, which got some laughs. But with its rural, downmarket characters, it hardly looked like the NBC brand.

Where were the shows with sexy young characters and story lines? Hadn't *Desperate Housewives* proved that was what the audience was looking for? The New York executives started calling Reilly "too narrow." One longtime comedy executive on the staff labeled him "fringe-y." Another executive chose "niche-y." One New York executive summed it up, saying, "Kevin, I think, is too nonpopulist for what's necessary to happen here now. His program sense is way too of *The Office* variety. He's a very nice man, but put him against Les and he's not going to make it."

As dangerous as the reaction to the development list was for Reilly, it was only slightly less risky for Jeff Zucker, who had selected Reilly for the top NBC Entertainment job. "Jeff is on the line for this," one senior NBC executive said. "He's on the point for it, because he can't say it was anybody else's decision; it was his."

Still, Reilly retained one very significant defender. Bob Wright called Reilly "the real deal." Part of that was his sense that Reilly, who had worked at NBC in the nineties, understood the place and got the fact that NBC needed distinctive new shows. Part of it was that Wright started to admire how Reilly held up when under the gun.

Just days before the upfront presentation at Radio City, Wright called Reilly in and sat him down in a conference room in front of a large group of NBC executives. Wright wanted to know every bit of Reilly's thinking on every show: Why do we need this? What do expect for this? About halfway through this grilling, Reilly got his back up. He stood up and told Wright and the others that he could go on and detail every element of the strategy, but the bottom line was that the shows that had been picked up for the schedule represented the best material they had, and this is what they had to do to start the climb back. Afterward, Wright and several others said they started to feel better about Reilly's moxie.

As for the schedule itself, NBC had deep cause for worry. *My Name Is Earl* tested sensationally—much to the surprise of some NBC executives in New York. They actually sent it back for four retests, not believing the first numbers. But there were no other worthy comedies to pair it with. Reilly pushed for creating an hour by matching it with *The Office*. But the early ratings on the British import were only convincing Zucker and some others that it was exactly as "niche-y" as they feared.

NBC considered bringing *The Office* back for the fall, but only on the cheap. They offered to renew it at a license fee of $660,000 an episode, about $300,000 less than any other comedy on television. The producers tried to calculate how they could pay their writers and actors. But they believed in the show so much they wanted to try. Then NBC offered an order of just eight new episodes and a slot in midseason. "NBC was saying: Okay, you want to play? You gotta go all the way with us," said Ben Silverman, the producer who purchased the rights from the British star Ricky Gervais.

Silverman flew to New York to meet with Zucker. He pitched his heart out in Jeff's office, citing how his show had held most of its lead-in, tiny as it was, from the fading comedy *Scrubs*. He pointed out that Steve Carell's upcoming film, *The 40-Year-Old Virgin*—from NBC Universal, no less—was already being touted as one of the potential comedy hits of the summer. "You could have a huge comedy star in one of your shows," Silverman pleaded. "You think he'll do TV again if this gets canceled?"

Finally, Zucker got angry. He accused Silverman of going around all over Hollywood telling people that Zucker wanted the show to fail. "You've been saying I didn't like the show and I let it die," Zucker said.

Silverman tried to explain that he had been saying Jeff didn't like any single-camera comedies. That did not placate Zucker. "Get the fuck out of my office," he said, and he essentially tossed Silverman out.

Silverman fled, but quickly sent off a fax to Zucker showing Ben's horoscope for the day, which said he would put his foot in his mouth.

*The Office* eventually got the spot on Tuesdays after *Earl*. NBC announced it was a thirteen-episode order, but actually it only ordered six episodes of *The Office* to be made, backed up by seven scripts. It was a show on the thinnest of ice.

The Sunday night before the upfront, Kevin Reilly and Steve McPherson, best friends and competitors, commiserated in

McPherson's suite in the Ritz-Carlton on Central Park South. Aptly, Reilly's suite was one floor below. The two men had the same jobs at two networks heading in opposite directions. Reilly would be up first the next afternoon and would face a skeptical crowd, while McPherson on Tuesday would be enjoying something close to a coronation. They both knew that this was just the way network television went: timing and luck. As they kicked around the vagaries of the business, their wives were in the next room, watching the latest episode of *Desperate Housewives* in their pajamas.

At the upfront, in the best self-deprecating tradition of those presentations, Reilly was featured in a video lamenting everything that had gone wrong that season with NBC. It was part of the general mea culpas being tossed around. Zucker led the way, telling the advertisers that NBC knew it had a rebuilding job on its hands.

But he continued to tout NBC's great appeal to upscale viewers, running through charts and graphs that put NBC's performance in the best possible light. Networks always did that; but in this case NBC was a network experiencing a historic crash: first to last in one season. And, as always seemed to happen with Zucker when he was doing the spinning, the wolves howled for blood.

One of the wolves was a former colleague of Reilly's, who unloaded on Zucker that upfront week. "I think people feel like he came in and rode the network down. And he did it with a disdain for everyone in the business. He didn't come out and say, 'I am coming in with a different perspective, here's what I don't know.' He came out and said, 'I know everything, fuck you.' He was very dismissive of everyone in town. He rode it down, and he keeps saying I was there for four years of bliss. I have issues with Zucker, because he's saddling Kevin with things he had nothing to do with. Kevin doesn't control marketing. Kevin doesn't get to control the schedule. So how the fuck do you do a ten-minute skit about him being responsible for all this bad shit? It's not right."

The comments were more of the same Hollywood harangue about Zucker, and they had no more impact on him. Zucker, as always, shrugged off the slams and went about his business.

NBC expected to take its lumps in the upfront sales, but it did not foresee a catastrophe. After all, it still had all those great upper-income demos to sell. Randy Falco, who ran the business side, predicted that NBC would still finish second in billing to CBS. NBC would drop about $500 million from the previous season's haul, he expected, with ABC gaining about a similar amount. "Ours is a business of momentum," Falco said. He called it "a pipeline business," not really different from films. "If you don't have shows in the pipeline that can take over for the *Friends* and *Seinfeld*s, it ultimately comes back to bite you in the ass."

But NBC had not yet been bitten. In fact, a year earlier, with *Friends* finally off the schedule, NBC had been able to sell on the come, adding revenue in a year when its competitors had expected NBC finally to start shedding some dollars. Instead, NBC had booked a record $2.85 billion in the upfront, well above CBS's $2.3 billion.

Falco was prepared to argue to the advertisers that NBC was still dominating certain audience groups. "That's why I think we'll end up probably not losing as much as a different network in our position would."

But Falco had not factored in how thoroughly unimpressed the advertisers were with NBC's new schedule, especially its unchanged Thursday night, led by the now-humbled *Joey*. Nor was he aware of the pool of resentment toward NBC that had been simmering inside a passel of the advertisers. When Keith Turner, the NBC head of sales, went into the marketplace asking for a 2 percent *increase* for NBC's new schedule, he might as well have hung a Kick Me sign around his neck.

Advertisers rebelled. They started talking about not buying NBC's schedule at all. The negotiations got ugly. As one senior NBC executive analyzed it, NBC was taking two years' worth of pummeling in one year. "They gave us a pass a year ago. We'd been number one for all but three or four years of the last twenty. With what happened the last ten weeks of the season, where we had another 10 percent fall-off, they just said: Uh-uh, no more. This was more than just saying your shows don't work. It was saying: We don't believe in you."

Another NBC executive wondered if the NBC sales department was being punished for years of "squeezing people" when it had all the shows everyone wanted to buy. "Our guys probably misread the market this year," the executive said. "And they're probably getting punished for years of hammering people." But the executive added, "There's probably no excitement about our schedule."

The extent of the punishment dealt out by the advertisers shocked NBC. When the final total was in, NBC had dropped almost $1 billion from the previous year's take. No network had ever taken a hit like that before.

Bob Wright came to blame ABC, at least in part. ABC had gone into the market first, because it was the network with the hottest shows. But Wright said ABC had sold far too low, getting only a 5 percent increase when it could have gotten 8 to 11 percent if it had played hardball. That move only set the sales level lower for NBC.

Wright did not overtly blame the NBC sales staff for its brazen demand to be paid more for finishing fourth instead of first. Nor did he slam Zucker for the fall-off in prime time's fortunes. But neither did he absolve him.

"Well, it's tough for him," Wright said. "But if you want to be in this kind of thing . . ." Wright gave Zucker credit for being broad-based, for covering a lot of ground and integrating the cable entertainment networks well into the company. But he said Zucker seemed more reserved. "He's feeling a lot of pressure," Wright said. "He's on the hot seat, no question."

Inside NBC, speculation rippled about the Wright-Zucker relationship. Once solid, it now seemed strained. One executive who knew both men well said, "I don't think he's giving Jeff any support at all. Emotional or otherwise. He's just like, leaving him out there."

That Zucker was out there was confirmed in hostile reviews in the press after the upfront. A venomous editorial in *Advertising Age* called Jeff "the network's biggest loser" and said he was running out of time to fix NBC. Some even nastier pieces predicted that Zucker would be out by December.

Those opinions were not likely to matter where Zucker's future really counted. That was in Fairfield, where Jeffrey Immelt took stock of the fortunes of the whole sprawling GE empire. "Keep in mind," said an executive with a strong relationship with Immelt, "GE's management style is to see not how great you do in handling success, but how you deal with it when there's water in the engine room. That's what's happening to Jeff right now. Anybody who thinks that Jeff Immelt is going to make a decision based on what he has seen in the last four months—well, that is never going to happen."

Zucker himself continued to be largely unrattled, whether from his boundless store of confidence or his abiding conviction that he had been through far worse than a bad television season. He put the turn in NBC's fortunes down to just that—ill fortune, or as the lead character in NBC's best hope for a comedy revival, Earl Hickey of *My Name Is Earl,* would have put it: "Karma." Earl's fate turned on the chance of a lottery ticket getting blown into his pants cuff.

"That ticket landed in NBC's pants cuff in 1994," Zucker said, referring to the year NBC found *Friends* and *ER* in the same season. "And, you know, it landed in ABC's pocket in 2004." Admittedly, he said, "You have to make your own luck. But it would be nice to have it land in our pocket again, too."

Zucker added, "I think the lottery ticket twirls in the wind."

He was right. As 2005 came to an end, with cable and the Internet inevitably siphoning off more advertising dollars, and more and more viewers finding ways to create their own program schedules on their own time, the four seven-night-a-week television networks faced a continuing hunt for new sources of revenue, while battling increased costs, and uncertain future reach. But, for a while at least, they still had the means to make magic, to generate a storytelling premise that could seize the attention of 20, even 30 million people a week. The next big hit remained out there, in the wind, twirling like that lottery ticket. All it took was a network smart enough, open enough, to reach out and grab it.

# A BRAND-NEW DAY

**M**arc Cherry enjoyed his ride on the hottest show on television as much as any program creator ever had. Midway through the first year of outrageous success on *Desperate Housewives,* Cherry went off to buy himself a house. By chance, the new next-door neighbor was the well-known L.A. disc jockey Rick Dees. As Cherry was looking over the house for the first time, Dees came out to empty his trash. He walked over and Cherry offered his hand. "Hi, I'm Marc Cherry," he said.

"You're Marc Cherry?" Dees said.

"That's how my life has changed," Cherry said. "Rick Dees knew who I was."

Of course, as one top program executive put it, "No show stays a buzz show like that for very long." In the case of *Desperate Housewives,* the inevitable backlash arrived extremely early, within three episodes of its second-season premiere. Critics tut-tutted about disappointing plots, suddenly pedestrian writing, unfortunate exaggerations in the characters. Backbiting among the cast was reported in some gossip columns: The rest of the women were jealous of the attention Teri Hatcher was getting. Agents kept close watch on who was getting paid what, and who was getting what perk. The women received fewer invitations to appear on *Oprah.*

Cherry himself was accused of empire building, going off too soon to lend a hand as co–executive producer on another project, *Kill/Switch*, a mystery-comedy. Cherry, chastened by the suddenly hostile comments, e-mailed the press, saying he was not giving *Desperate Housewives* short shrift. But he admitted that his creation had hit a few ruts early in its second season.

"Yes, we're trying some new stuff," Cherry said to Dave Bauder of the AP. "Some of it might work. Some of it might not. This, of course, is the nature of episodic television. They can't all be gems."

The audience didn't seem to mind—at least not yet. The early episodes of *Housewives* reached more than 27 million viewers each—well above the average of 23.7 million for all of the first season. It was almost always No. 1 or No. 2 among the most-watched shows on television.

*Desperate Housewives* certainly did not seem like a fluke. It was a huge hit in every English-speaking country in the world. "I have now lucked into this show that looks to be this worldwide phenomenon," Cherry said. "And what makes the story fascinating is that I was less than nothing in this town. My career was, for all intents and purposes, over. It's a fascinating story to tell, not a fascinating story to live. But it's one of those things where I go, I'm becoming like a legendary anecdote: Don't give up hope; remember Marc Cherry."

• • •

**S**teve McPherson had one of the most spectacular years any network programmer ever put together. Under his watch, ABC added three top-ten shows in one season, with *Desperate Housewives, Lost,* and *Grey's Anatomy.* Steve drew special praise for his marketing skill. The way he threw ABC's promotion effort behind *Lost,* a show he had opposed in its initial creative stages, was, even some detractors acknowledged, the sign of an exceptional executive.

One producer, who was much closer to the Braun/Lyne regime, said, "Whatever you say about these new people and their loyalties and how they revise the past, they are fucking good at marketing shows. That kind of broadcasting knack deserves success. Sure, they got lucky having the shows all produced and ready for them, but you make your own luck."

Still, during McPherson's second year in command, nothing ABC introduced worked very well. In the fall of 2005, the network had high hopes for another new drama, *Commander in Chief*, with Geena Davis as the first woman president. But the audience leaned toward older women, a trend that increased as the show proceeded. The original creator, Rod Lurie, was removed; Steven Bochco came in. But the ratings were all downhill. Another touted drama, *Invasion*, which got the coveted spot behind *Lost*, managed to drive away more than half of that show's viewers. And nothing McPherson tried in comedy promised to be a hit, though a summer reality hit, *Dancing with the Stars*, came back strong as a mid-season entry.

McPherson told several colleagues that he was beginning to feel the pressure. Some at ABC saw signs of slackening in corporate support, amazing considering how McPherson had been described as the most secure executive in television only months earlier. Steve's relationship with Anne Sweeney had soured, several of his friends said. Bob Iger himself made a somewhat surprising comment at one black-tie event. After he was saluted for turning around the network with *Desperate Housewives* and *Lost*, Bob got up and said to the crowd, "The first thing you should know is that the woman who actually put on *Desperate Housewives* is in the room tonight." He asked Susan Lyne to stand for applause, a gesture of such generosity that Lyne was touched.

In truth, the ABC schedule continued to be feast or famine, with some of TV's biggest hits surrounded by some of the biggest holes. And with *Monday Night Football* going away, McPherson faced the additional hurdle of having to fill two more hours of prime time in the fall. Still, he had led his network out of the ratings desert. For all the concerns, ABC—with the Super Bowl as its ace in the hole—was by most projections on track to win the 2005–2006 season in the 18-to-49 competition—an achievement Steve McPherson would be able to take justifiable pride in helping make happen.

• • •

**D**avid Westin had his own challenges at ABC News. Peter Jennings passed away in August, only four months after the announcement that he had lung cancer. ABC News had missed its best opportunity to surpass NBC in the evening news race. Westin now faced the task of replacing Jennings with a worthy challenger to Brian Williams at NBC. The decision was slow in coming, partly out of respect for Jennings, partly because ABC had a choice between two distinct directions: the steady-as-you-go course of experience, symbolized by Charles Gibson, the *GMA* host who had done well substituting for Jennings; or the full-blown shakeup, represented by the team of Elizabeth Vargas and Bob Woodruff, two correspondents from a younger generation: They were in their early forties; Gibson his early sixties.

Westin seemed to vacillate until the last minute, when he finally offered the position to Gibson with some heavy strings attached. Gibson would have to abdicate to the younger team after just two years, pushing him out before the next presidential election. Charlie read that as something less than half a loaf and declined the offer. That freed Westin to install Vargas and Woodruff, and to sell them as the future of network news, a future that would involve more news delivered on more electronic devices, from laptops to cell phones.

First the ABC team would have to succeed on television sets, however, and there they met with some initial resistance. In the first weeks of the Vargas-Woodruff partnership, ABC fell far behind Brian Williams.

• • •

**K**atie Couric had a vested interest in how the ABC situation unfolded, both in the morning *and* the evening. Still unsettled about whether to jump into the anchor chair at CBS, Couric had time to assess exactly how the ABC move would impact the competition. Several associates suggested that the choice of Vargas and Woodruff would only make it easier for Couric to jump. "That team she has to figure she can beat," said one NBC executive. If it looked as though Couric could get CBS into second place, it would be all the more incentive for her to take the shot. To lift CBS into second place would rank as a coup on par with David Letterman's initial takeover of late-night leadership, beating *The Tonight Show.*

For that and several other reasons, the handicappers at both CBS and NBC began to bet that Couric would accept Les Moonves's offer—once he was able to formally make one in May. Zucker seemed to be preparing himself—and the network—for the blow. One friend of Zucker's said, "Jeff has already gotten through the 'I'm pissed' stage and moved into the 'I'll deal with it' stage."

Zucker began talking about the options NBC had at *Today.* Campbell Brown had a lot of experience substituting, but Zucker also seemed high on a young anchor from MSNBC that *Today* had brought in on several occasions, Natalie Morales.

One reason the panic had subsided at NBC over the prospect of losing Couric was *Today*'s rapid comeback. Not only had *Good Morning, America* failed to mount the expected threat that fall when *Desperate Housewives* returned to the air, it seemed to have lost all the momentum of the previous spring. *Today* went back to beating *GMA* by 800,000 viewers or more each week.

In a way, that left Couric freer to embrace the CBS offer. One of Katie's friends, who was in on a number of discussions about her future, said, "If you had been listening to her, you would know that this was starting to sound like an ideal job for her."

More than anything it was the opportunity to make a real mark on television news that appealed to Couric. Her friend said, "The legacy stuff, she really cares about that. That matters to her at this stage of her career."

Couric sat down with the people closest to her and asked for advice. What she heard, the friend said, was that going to CBS was something she had to do. "The achievement of being the first woman solo anchor is a huge deal for her," the friend said.

The remaining unknown, several associates of Couric said, was whether Katie would have the stomach for the ferocious criticism that was sure to come, from the press, that would question whether the woman who once sang with Bette Midler in the mornings could command the respect necessary to be a true hard-news anchor, and from the right-wing forces that had hacked away at Dan Rather. Even the rumor of Katie taking the job was enough to unleash Rush Limbaugh, who pronounced her the only news talent CBS could find who was more liberal than Rather.

"She's gotta weigh all that," said one of her NBC colleagues, who nevertheless concluded that Couric was likely to leave NBC in May.

·   ·   ·

**A**ndrew Heyward departed his job as president of CBS News in October, after one of the longest runs ever in that position. That meant Couric would be wooed by someone new, Sean McManus, the highly regarded head of CBS Sports whom Moonves had selected to replace Heyward.

Of Heyward, Les said, "He was spent." Andrew had been trying to find some new formula for the newscast that would satisfy Les's demand for revolutionary change, but Moonves concluded, "His heart wasn't in it."

He chose McManus with some trepidation, knowing that the news division already shuddered at Moonves's apparent willingness to rip the place apart for the sake of change. He was quoted in a *New York Times* magazine piece saying favorable things about a cable show in England called *The Naked News* and even talking about wanting "to bomb the whole building" where CBS News was housed.

Choosing a man who had spent his whole career in the sports division seemed like an invitation for mass protest. "The expectations from people in news were so low, they thought I was going to bring in Sean Combs, not Sean McManus," Moonves said.

But McManus was well respected throughout the company, and the news staff was actually relieved. Roone Arledge, at ABC, had already proved that a sports leader could make a seamless transition to running news. Sean was also considered exceptional at handling talent. That looked like a prerequisite for landing a star as big as Katie Couric.

·   ·   ·

**S**imon Cowell was the most important star in the history of the Fox network. But he still remained willing to risk it all for the ultimate payday. For Alan Berger, who represented him, this made for overpowering leverage.

Before the start of what promised to be supremely difficult negotiations, Peter Liguori and other Fox executives made a show of discounting how essential Cowell was to *American Idol*. Liguori said, "We could do the show without him." But that position was belied by the lengths Fox went to to save Cowell's costar, Paula Abdul, after she was accused by a former *Idol* contestant of having a sexual relationship with him. Fox hunkered down, declined comment, and then commissioned its own "investigation," which helpfully absolved Abdul by saying the kid's claim could not be proved. If retaining Abdul was worth that much effort, how much further would Fox go to keep Cowell on the show?

That's what Berger was determined to find out. The safety valve for Cowell was his British hit, *The X-Factor*. If Fox wanted to play chicken, Cowell could go all the way. He would simply shift to that show and sell it to a different network—threatening to take a chunk of the *Idol* audience with him.

Berger, however, knew that the history of television was filled with stars who left their hits too soon to try other projects. "A bird in the hand," Berger said. He knew the Fox executives would come around. They did in September, putting on a full-court press to get Cowell signed. In a day of frantic negotiations between multiple parties, Fox executives ran from room to room in the Regency hotel in New York, lining up Cowell, Simon Fuller, Bob Sillerman—who had bought Fuller's company—Fremantle, and Sony-Bertelsmann Music, Cowell's record company. Even then, Cowell could only agree to a deal in principle because Fuller had not yet dropped his lawsuit against Cowell.

Simon was torn about making a deal at all, knowing it would mean that *X-Factor* likely would never play in the U.S. market. But the money was certainly going to be good.

Fuller kept nerves jangling at Fox by holding out until after the original trial date in England (it got deferred while a settlement was pursued). Even the usually blasé Cowell confessed that the situation became "rather stressful." Finally, the deal was consummated. Simon Cowell was on board for five more years of *American Idol.*

No financial figures were released, though a competing network executive said Fox had agreed to pay Cowell the phenomenal sum of $36 million a year. Alan Berger conceded that, for only ninety minutes of work a week, Simon Cowell was likely to be the highest-paid performer "per minute" in network television. (Berger acknowledged that maybe Oprah made more in syndication.)

The investment quickly proved justified as *American Idol* returned in January 2006, with bigger ratings than ever before. Simon Fuller said the show had "become definitive." It was surely the definitive blockbuster hit of American television in the early twenty-first century.

• • •

**M**ike Darnell, who still supervised *American Idol,* may have been the most amused observer of the lawsuit that Simon Fuller filed, claiming that Simon Cowell had ripped off the format for *Idol.* Mike continued to believe that any hit show was fair game for a "similar" show, as long as it had a twist of some kind. As soon as ABC struck gold with *Dancing with the Stars,* Mike swung into action, commissioning his own version, *Skating with Celebrities.*

The relentless cloning of reality ideas seemed to have taken some of the steam out of the genre. The dance show, and NBC's dieting contest, *The Biggest Loser,* were the only significant new entries in the reality field, while most of the standbys—*Survivor, The Apprentice, The Amazing Race*—saw some fall-offs in viewing. Nobody seemed to be coming up with hot new reality ideas, though Darnell made a deal with the director, Ron Howard, for an upcoming series that would put contestants through a realistic space simulation.

There was always *American Idol,* however. Darnell still could not sleep the night of the premiere, but he had every reason to rest easy as long as *Idol* was around.

Inside the Fox offices, Darnell was causing less consternation. Whether because the climate had changed for reality shows, or the management was holding him to a stricter standard, or because he was in charge of television's biggest phenomenon, a Fox executive said, "Mike has been forced to be more cooperative, and it's paying off for him."

•  •  •

Martha Stewart provided the latest evidence that reality programming was flagging. Whatever fascination the public had for Martha post-incarceration, it did not translate into ratings for *The Apprentice: Martha Stewart*. The show did not even open. In its first week on the air, Martha attracted only a little over 7 million viewers and scored a puny rating in the cherished 18-to-49 category.

Quickly, the whole second *Apprentice* idea looked like a major miscalculation. The hit version with **Donald Trump** was already sliding, diminished by the wretched lead-ins and probably too much exposure. Donald himself had the same thought: "I think there was confusion between Martha's *Apprentice* and mine," he told a radio station in November. "Mine continues to do well. The other has struggled very severely. I think it probably hurt mine, and I predicted it would."

Trump was right, even if not especially gallant. Two *Apprentices* were more than the public wanted to see. Martha came back with a shot of her own in *Fortune* magazine, describing an original plan that would have ousted Donald from his Thursday show, maybe even with her firing *him* on the opening episode of her *Apprentice*.

Mark Burnett and Jeff Zucker had talked about that one point. But neither thought that was a good idea in the end. NBC executives breathed a huge sigh of relief that they had stuck with Trump on Thursday because, even with lesser numbers, his show was still landing in hit territory. Martha had no appeal to men at all, and overall just never caught fire.

NBC announced, to no one's surprise, that there would be no further editions of *The Apprentice: Martha Stewart*. But Donald

Trump was going to get another shot. NBC ordered a new round of his *Apprentice,* to be set in L.A. this time—an unusual choice, given that Donald's connections were all in New York.

That L.A. show would be in addition to a finished version of *The Apprentice,* aimed for the second half of the 2005–2006 season. Trump and Burnett had expected to come back to their familiar Thursday-at-9 spot, but NBC had other plans.

.   .   .

**K**evin Reilly, buffeted by criticism for his supposedly niche-y tastes, added the biggest new hit comedy in eight years to NBC's schedule in the fall of 2005. *My Name Is Earl* was a smash from its first week on the air, even though it faced fierce competition—and special enmity from Fox, which could have had the series but turned it down. Before the season, Fox executives disparaged *Earl* as so antithetical to NBC's identity as the hip urban network that it had no shot.

The audience disagreed. *Earl* won its time period virtually every week in the fall, and was quickly the second-highest-rated comedy on television, after *Two and a Half Men* on CBS. Reilly also stuck by *The Office* as the companion comedy to *Earl,* even when it initially lost a big percentage of *Earl*'s audience, and even when outsiders continued to insist it would never claim a wide audience with its offputting characters and quirky pseudodocumentary style.

Inside NBC, executives finally embraced *The Office* when they saw how well it was doing with the network's traditional upper-income viewers and young men in general. That view was further validated when NBC made a deal with Apple's iTunes to make episodes of a number of shows available for downloading for $1.99 a pop. To the shock of some at NBC, the first week the NBC shows were available, four of the top five video downloads on iTunes were episodes of *The Office.*

Reilly was not among the surprised. He had been a stalwart champion of *The Office* from the start, even committing the near sacrilege of occasionally comparing the show to *Seinfeld.* Kevin actually meant that it was a highly original comedy that took many episodes before capturing the nation's fancy. Reilly did have one key ally in his campaign to save *The Office*. It was Jeffrey Immelt's favorite show. The GE boss loved to watch the episodes on the GE corporate plane. "He was crying with laughter," a GE executive said.

With Thursday night still sinking—keeping *Joey* at 8 had proved as wrongheaded as everyone had predicted—Reilly started thinking as early as October that NBC might play a bold card and move *Earl* and *The Office* to Thursday to try to re-create the NBC comedy lineup. The risks were huge: For all the erosion NBC had suffered, it was still finishing second on Thursday to CBS, because *The Apprentice* was hanging in with solid numbers.

Could Reilly's comedies come close to the ratings for *The Apprentice*? The last thing NBC wanted was to plummet from 9 to 10, undermining the still-potent *ER.*

Reilly decided he simply had to try. In January, he booted *Joey* off the air, moved *Will & Grace* to 8, and inserted a new comedy called *Four Kings* at 8:30. Obviously, Reilly did not make the moves alone. Jeff Zucker had to back the strategy, but he already wanted NBC to get back to comedy on Thursdays.

NBC defied expectations again. *My Name Is Earl* opened strong on Thursday. So did *The Office*. Suddenly, what Kevin Reilly had to say about television comedy made a lot of sense.

"NBC was sort of responsible for killing comedy, with horrible show after horrible show, all cut from the same cloth," Reilly said. "It wasn't just this network. Guys with no training, no life experiences, five minutes out of Harvard are getting $3 million a year and they don't have a thought in their heads. No singular vision. . . . There has just been too much entitlement and pure laziness in the comedy business. Frankly, the audience was watching a lot of crappy sitcoms. Now we're paying the price for it. I think what's happening is that they're just flushing it out and we'll see better voices rising to the top."

• • •

Jeff Zucker had been in the bull's-eye only a few months earlier for having selected Reilly as the creative leader to pull NBC Entertainment out of its tailspin. Having one success in the fall, *My Name Is Earl,* was not going to free either of them from critical scrutiny inside the company. But it did lighten the pressure.

For Zucker, the timing was crucial, because the steep downturn in NBC's prime-time results was greatly complicating his career plans. After tearing through every assignment at NBC like a man unmistakably headed for the top, the last year in entertainment had thrown up significant roadblocks. As much as Jeff Immelt favored him, Zucker could not count on taking the last step to a spot in line to succeed Bob Wright as CEO of NBC.

In October, Zucker told a friend, "They'll never give it to me with prime time in this shape."

That echoed the view of Zucker's persistent critics, who finally expected the man they regarded as the cocky spinmeister to get his comeuppance. When NBC hinted it was about to announce a major management realignment in mid-December, e-mails began flying among Zucker's detractors at the competing networks, predicting this might be the moment of his ultimate demise.

They could not have been more wrong. On December 15, NBC announced a restructuring all right, but the centerpiece was the elevation of Jeff Zucker to CEO of the NBC Universal Television Group. Just to make things clearer, NBC stated that Randy Falco, who previously reported to Bob Wright, would now report to Zucker, as would Dick Ebersol and just about everyone else at NBC. Wright remained the chairman and CEO of NBC Universal, but the question of succession had been settled. Jeff Zucker was next in line.

How such a development could have happened with NBC's prime time in such bad condition baffled some of Zucker's critics, but those who knew Jeffrey Immelt were surprised only by the timing: Apparently, there was a rush to get it done before the Christmas holidays. One executive who had relationships with both Zucker and Immelt pointed out that Zucker had solved the *Today* problems and had the cable operations performing well. "What matters to

Immelt is leadership," the executive said. "He sees things in Jeff. He knows he's a leader. He knows Jeff's people would die for him."

Immelt made another notable announcement the same day; he named Beth Comstock to lead NBC Universal's digital group. Less attention was paid to that move, but it was almost as significant—indeed, some at NBC immediately speculated that if Zucker stumbled again, Comstock might actually pass him in the race to succeed Wright.

Few in the television industry had anticipated Comstock's promotion because her background had been largely in public relations. She headed corporate PR for NBC under Wright, and then for GE, first under Jack Welch and then Immelt. The latter had come to be especially impressed with Comstock, and in 2003 he had elevated her to a new role at GE, chief marketing officer. Comstock had wowed Immelt in that position—she was behind a rebranding campaign that overhauled GE's ancient motto, "We bring good things to life," and created a new one, "Imagination at work." He gave Comstock a big GE award at a management conference in the fall of 2005, and a bigger compliment, calling Comstock "the most transformative leader we have had in twenty years."

What was less clear, at least to those trying to read the NBC tea leaves, was Bob Wright's role in the new appointments. They were all made under his name and several NBC executives claimed they were all Bob's idea. But one senior NBC executive said, "Bob didn't want this to happen." Wright had never been comfortable with the notion of naming a formal successor; he hated it when Andy Lack was set up in that position. Bob's mixed feelings seemed apparent when a reporter at the press conference announcing the change asked whether this formally set up Zucker to succeed him.

"Absolutely," Wright said with a kind of forced laugh. "All he has to do is survive 2006, 2007, and so forth."

On the other hand, Wright was quite comfortable with the addition of Comstock, whose marketing skill seemed especially well-tailored to NBC's plans to expand in the digital realm.

Zucker welcomed her as well. Then again, none of the backstage machinations seemed to trouble him in the least. Nor did the continuing put-downs from his detractors. One longtime competitor said on hearing of Zucker's promotion: "I just hope I'm treated that well when I fuck up."

But there was no question what the promotion meant. Zucker was headed for the top. "This is all about accountability for Jeff," said one longtime corporate executive. "You said you could run NBC. Let's see if you can."

Zucker himself observed that one result of the promotion was a continuation of the ongoing match between television's two top executive chess masters. "This puts me pretty even with Les," Zucker said.

·  ·  ·

**L**eslie Moonves confessed that 2005 had left him physically exhausted. The details of the split-up of Viacom, with all the haggling over who should own the name Paramount, the movie studio or the television studio, and who should own the famous Paramount lot, ate up even Moonves's usually deep stores of energy and attention.

But when the split was consummated in early January, Les was both elated and excited. He had his own empire, and he had big plans for it.

The usual group of doubters could not see how Les would be able to pull off his plan to make CBS as potent a growth company as the MTV group. One senior executive at a competing media company could not fathom how Les would wring value out of the deadwood among his assets.

"Moonves has radio and fucking billboards," the executive said dismissively. "They may be a great promotion machine, but he can't make a nickel out of them." But many other competing executives like Bob Wright expressed confidence in Moonves's abilities. "Time has proved he's the real deal," Wright said. On the more cautious side, another media executive said, "I think he's a very good competitor. I think he's done a hell of a job. And I think that over the next two years this will all look fine. Because he'll still be in that sort of growth CBS as been in—and in two or three years, he'll hit the same wall that NBC is hitting. And when he hits it, he'll have no place to go. He'll look like a ninny."

Les believed he had plenty of places to go. The developments late in 2005, with Disney making deals to sell episodes of *Desperate Housewives* on a video iPod, NBC making deals with iTunes for downloads, CBS making deals with Comcast for video on demand, played right into Les's hands.

"I don't think people are going to look at things the same way," Moonves said. "This is a pivotal year. The downloading and all, this is all heading toward that. The explosion has begun."

Moonves began to position CBS less as a network than a content company. "Content is essential," he argued, and CBS would continue to acquire and develop stores of desirable content. He demonstrated just how aggressive he was going to be less than a month into his tenure running the CBS Corporation as a stand-alone company. Moonves engineered another coup. He worked out a deal with Warner Brothers to fold both their mini-networks, UPN and the WB, and create a new fifth broadcast network, the CW. It was welcomed by the ad community and looked like a sure bet to begin making money—after the separate networks had spent years losing cash. The new network would be another outlet for creating potential hits, more content for that exploding world of technology Les was poised to exploit.

Content was also crucial to Les's larger plan, one so audacious it held the promise of shaking the television industry to its toes. Moonves intended to stage a showdown with the cable industry with a demand they pay a subscription fee for network programs. As revenue from advertising became threatened by the personalization of television programming, Moonves believed the time had come to force cable operators to pay networks for their shows, through a complex process called retransmission consent.

For years networks allowed cable systems to retransmit their shows for free, because that was the best way to maximize audiences. But the network financial model was obviously inferior to cable, which drew revenue both from advertising and from subscription fees. The networks had begun to extract value out of their retransmission rights in the 1990s by creating cable channels that operators put on their systems. But all along the cable operators had made it clear: If a network demanded cash for retransmission consent, it would mean war.

Moonves welcomed the war. He believed he had superior weapons. "If we stay as good as we are now," Moonves said, "and we have the NFL, and NCAA basketball, and we have David Letterman and *CSI* and *Survivor,* they're going to pay for it."

Cable operators could always refuse and take CBS off their systems, but Moonves did not believe many would dare if it meant depriving their customers of CBS's content. "As I say over and over again, you pay for the cable network which has *CSI* reruns, you're going to pay for the originals. It's only fair."

The increasing availability of satellite distribution only further emboldened Moonves; if he could make a deal with a satellite company, he would have even more leverage against the cable operators. They could deal with CBS or lose subscribers to satellite.

Winning this confrontation would certainly change every equation in network television's future. "That's my obligation," Moonves said. "To create multiple revenue streams, and this is the classic one. It would mean hundreds of millions of dollars of additional revenue."

Of course, losing it would be devastating, but Moonves did not figure on losing. He sensed the momentum in the business, even with all the technological advances, was moving toward the companies with the content people wanted to see. "I believe it's inevitable," he said. "It's a brand-new day. Who knows what the future is going to look like? That's why our content is so important."

Content, of course, was just another word for hits. The future Moonves envisioned could work only as long as CBS had the hit shows that people wanted to see. Nobody—or at best very few—was going to pay $1.99 to download episodes of *Threshold* or *Yes Dear* or to storm the offices of cable operators demanding their CBS-TV so they could see inferior shows.

"If anything, it's going to be more hit-driven than ever," Les conceded.

Again he had confidence that this development only played to his own strengths. Who else in the business had put a mark on so many hit shows? What other executive had read as many scripts, watched as many pilots, cast as many actors, sat in as many scheduling meetings?

But now that he had reached the pinnacle, running a bicoastal media conglomerate that included two broadcast networks, a pay cable channel (Showtime), a television production studio, radio stations, and outdoor advertising, how was Les Moonves going to continue playing the master showman?

First, by continuing to emphasize his home base. "The flagship is still the network," he said. "It still gets the most press, the most publicity."

But mainly he vowed to never stop reading the scripts, viewing the pilots, calling the shots on what programs America was going to see.

"I'm still thinking about the schedule all the time," Moonves said. "Am I always going to be in the scheduling meetings at the upfront? Damn straight. I'll be there. You know you can't keep me out of that scheduling room."

The scheduling room remained the vital center of network television, the beating heart of its aging, sometimes battered, but somehow still thriving life form. As long as what emerged from those scheduling rooms each year continued to divert, amuse, or thrill many millions of Americans, the program cycles would continue, the money would continue to flow, the beat would go on. The television business had become endlessly complicated, seriously challenged, and yet not much different than it had ever been. The networks, desperate to live on, had only one enduring assignment:

Let's put on a show.

# AFTERWORD

In October 2006, just about the time that the massively successful Internet search engine Google was offering $1.65 billion to buy a twenty-month-old website owned by two guys who started the business in an office above a pizzeria in San Matteo, California, CBS executives were trying to drum up interest in the revelation that they had secured new advertising commitments for one of their most prominent new programs of the fall season.

That deal, with some pharmaceutical companies and a retail outlet, was for a grand total of $1 million—not exactly up to the standards of YouTube, the video website that had become a media sensation and was being lusted after by every big company from Yahoo to Viacom to Microsoft, even though it had yet to turn even a modest profit. Still, CBS had every reason to expect some attention for its payday as well. The program in question was, after all, *The CBS Evening News with Katie Couric*, which, if not quite up to the standards of the media frenzy that accompanied YouTube's emergence as an Internet site offering videos of every description (and every level of legal or illegal provenance), certainly made a bigger splash than any other new TV program in the fall of 2006.

Couric's defection from NBC's *Today* show for the seat behind the anchor desk at CBS was *the* story of the network world in the fall of 2006, and certainly proved once again network television's unmatched ability to create head-turning, attention-commanding stars. Couric's arrival at CBS was nothing short of a national event, promoted—at a cost estimated at $15 million—like the entry of Cleopatra into Rome and covered in the press with only slightly less breathless devotion.

The result, an opening-night happening attended by more than 13 million viewers—about double what CBS had previously been attracting for its newscast—thoroughly validated Katie's status as a celebrity icon in American culture. CBS and its leader, Leslie Moonves, wanted a news star, and they got one.

A lavishly produced opening-night newscast went to great lengths to connect Katie, the first solo female network news anchor in history, with the long-ago greatness of CBS News. Opening with Walter Cronkite's familiar voice intoning her introduction, Couric's first newscast included pieces contrived to include glimpses of every famed leading figure from CBS News's past from the titan Ed Murrow to the first TV anchor, Douglas Edwards, to the lightning rod Dan Rather, to Cronkite himself. The message was clear: Katie belongs on this list.

And she just might. But that conclusion will have to come over time. The spectacular success of Katie Couric's first week as an evening news anchor was followed by a slow, and utterly predictable, descent back toward the status quo in the evenings: NBC first, ABC second, CBS third.

Still, in one area Katie triumphed without reservation: she proved that the network evening newscasts could still have impact, could still be talked about, could still count as valuable "content" in the network arsenal. More and more, as 2006 drew to its close, that was how the television networks, and the media companies that owned them, defined themselves—not as "programmers" but as "content providers." Virtually every bit of programming the networks came up with was designed to be made available only for initial use on a television set—after that, Katie and the rest of the content were unleashed on the digital world.

Nothing, not even the prodigious price tag placed on YouTube, proved the ascendancy of the computer-screen world over the TV-screen world more powerfully than the stunning dismissal in September of one of the television business's most prominent executives, Tom Freston, from his CEO chair at Viacom. Freston had served Viacom loyally for two decades, mostly as the leader of the fabulously profitable cable channel division MTV Networks. That proved to be insufficient for the Viacom chairman, Sumner Redstone, who pink-slipped the executive he had been closer to than any other in the company's history, openly blaming Freston for his failure to acquire another hot Internet outlet—the community-service site MySpace.

Rupert Murdoch and his News Corp. closed that deal for what in retrospect seemed like a paltry $580 million; Freston never had a chance to buy it. But not having the site, and suffering stock-price punishment because Viacom did not have it, were enough for Redstone. Freston walked out of Viacom's headquarters surrounded by two thousand saluting staff members. And then when YouTube became available, Viacom again fell short.

The very same day that Google turned the YouTube inventors into millionaires several hundred times over, CBS announced a deal with the website that would make video from the network's programs—including Katie's newscast, of course—available on YouTube, all for the price of a cut of whatever advertising revenue the website could sell adjacent to the CBS content.

As one CBS executive put it, "The hottest user-generated content site is another way to take our programming and achieve major expansion and set up another revenue stream." In other words, "We might be able to make a few extra bucks this way."

With the advertising model increasingly threatened as the financial underpinning of the network business, thanks to the increasing ease with which the audience could escape commercials, the media companies that owned the networks placed a premium on developing the correct digital strategy, one that forever sought to answer the big question: Where *else* can we sell this stuff?

It was no longer enough simply to have the best or most popular shows on during the prime-time hours every night; it was essential that consumers ("viewers" having fallen away as the chief target of the business) be given endless opportunities to locate the shows they wanted, and to watch them whenever they wanted.

In the first week of the new television season in September, a young female fan of the new ultimate must-see program, ABC's *Grey's Anatomy*, had no need to be home on Thursday night at nine, where ABC had boldly relocated the show as a direct challenge to the previous ratings champ, CBS's *CSI*. Instead, she could wait a day and catch it on ABC.com.

If she did, the presentation might have been considerably less glorious on her laptop than it would have been on the fifty-inch hi-definition plasma screen she had installed on a wall in her living room, but that was okay, too. The networks had concluded, reasonably, that a little extra effort to watch an episode of a favorite show could only be a good thing because that fan would be likely to decide (1) that the experience would be better on the big screen next time, inducing her to add to the show's first-play rating the following week, and (2) that it was a great thing for viewers to know they never had to miss a single episode of a show they loved anymore. As an executive from a competing network put it, "ABC won't lose that viewer ever again, not like we used to lose viewers occasionally because they couldn't be around for every episode."

Of course there was a number three: maybe it didn't matter at all anymore when the networks programmed their shows because viewers could simply watch them whenever they wanted. Whether there was enough advertising revenue to be accrued in these Internet replays or in the DVD sales of a hit series' entire seasonal run were questions still to be answered.

With 2007 looming, and questions about the sustainability of the traditional network schedule being fretted over inside offices in New York and LA, the networks continued to chase the technology beast running pell-mell and untamed ahead of them—even as they continued to spend ever more cash in their endless hunt for the hits that made for the best possible "content."

# INDEX

ABC, 3–4, 7, 10, 25, 147,
    197–201, 207–10, 225–52,
    351–53, 374–76
  advertising revenue, 40, 286,
    370
  Disney Company management
    and, 197–200, 226, 231,
    232, 234–35, 237, 240–41,
    251, 271–75, 283, 291, 294,
    295–96, 345
  Entertainment division, 84,
    107–201, 225–26, 271–75,
    285–96, 348
  football, 253, 345, 348, 349–50
  Friday-night programming
    (TGIF), 36, 225
  late-night programming, 295,
    326–29, 335, 336, 350
  management retreat, 208–10
  News, 294–96, 319–20,
    326–32, 376
  pass on *American Idol*, 9, 181,
    183, 226
  pass on *The Apprentice*, 9–10,
    199–201, 226, 296
  pass on *CSI*, 9, 115–16, 121,
    198, 226, 282–83, 289
  pass on *Friends*, 28–29
  pass on *Survivor*, 9, 67–68,
    79–81, 198, 226
  promotion of new shows,
    292–93, 304
  ratings, 84, 165, 197, 253, 275,
    285–86, 305, 307, 357–58,
    374, 375
  reality TV shows, 55, 76,
    80–81, 84, 92, 102, 106,
    107, 181, 225–26, 294, 375

  sports, 253, 304, 345, 348,
    349–50, 351
  2004 season, 10–11, 284–96
  upfronts, 9–13, 295
  *See also* Braun, Lloyd;
    *Desperate Housewives*; Disney
    Company; *Lost*; *Who Wants
    to Be a Millionaire?*; *specific
    shows*.
ABC *News Now*, 328, 330
Abdul, Paula, 25, 189, 190, 379
Abraham, Dustin, 118, 119
Abrams, J. J., 236–40, 251, 272,
    273, 283, 293, 304, 305,
    307–7
Abruzzese, Joe, 41, 75, 112
Addison, Anita, 68
advertising, 264
  ABC, 40, 286, 370
  *American Idol*, 182, 183–84
  CBS, 43–44, 112, 333, 369
  Cialis, 257
  Coca-Cola, 182, 183
  "make-good" ads, 286
  mini-upfront and, 83, 273, 364,
    364
  NBC, 22, 137, 212, 349, 365,
    369–70
  network total revenues, 4–5
  products embedded in
    productions, 73
  reality shows and, 226
  *Survivor* and, 75–76, 86
  Thursday-night lineup, 7,
    215–16, 333
*Advertising Age* magazine, 370
Agoglia, John, 262
Ahmanson Theater, 35

Albrecht, Chris, 35
Alexander, Jason, 42
Alfano, Joanne, 155
*Alias,* 225, 236, 237, 239, 241, 273, 304
*Alien Autopsy: Fact or Fiction?,* 96–97
Alliance Atlantis, 131–32
*Ally McBeal,* 148, 165, 175, 232, 244
*Amazing Race, The,* 380
*American Dreams,* 169
*American Idol,* 9, 20, 25–26, 175–76, 181–95, 225, 253, 254, 261, 268, 270, 341, 343, 378–81
Ancier, Garth, 52–64, 136, 150, 152, 279
Aniston, Jennifer, 31, 40, 138, 211, 217, 218, 220, 221
Apple iPod, 5, 387
Apple iTunes, 382, 387
*Apprentice, The,* 9–10, 17, 23, 199–201, 261, 262, 263, 264–67, 280, 296, 334, 362–64, 380, 381–82, 383
   *Martha Stewart,* 362–64, 381–82
Arafat, Yassir, 310, 311
*Are You Hot?,* 225, 226
Arledge, Roone, 145, 350, 378
*Arrested Development,* 25
*Average Joe,* 278
Axelrod, Jim, 326

*Bachelor, The,* 175, 225, 232, 233, 252, 268, 364
Bader, Jeff, 304–5, 307
Balcer, René, 122
Barrino, Fantasia, 25
Barry, Josh, 229
Bauder, Dave, 374
Bass, Michael, 141, 142, 147
Battaglio, Steve, 62
Baum, Stephen, 60
Beckman, Preston, 16, 53, 54, 54, 55, 61, 107, 108, 191–93, 261–62, 264, 303, 342
Bedrosian, Matt, 227
Bell, Jim, 357
Benson, Mike, 293
Berger, Alan, 19, 157, 194–95, 355, 379–80
Berman, Gail, 24, 103–5, 107, 108, 157, 176, 182–83, 185, 270, 340–44
Bettag, Tom, 325
*Bette,* 125, 132
*Beverly Hills Cop,* 114
*Big Brother,* 152
*Biggest Loser, The,* 380
*Big John, Little John,* 96
Bleeth, Yasmine, 59
*Blind Justice,* 289
Bloomberg, Stu, 84, 198
BMG, 179, 186
Boccardi, Louis, 314, 317
Bochco, Steven, 205, 289, 375
*Body and Soul,* 165
*Boomtown,* 278
*Boot Camp,* 107
Bornstein, Steve, 349–50
*Boston Legal,* 351, 353
Boyette, Bob, 36
Branson, Richard, 24, 303
Braun, Lloyd, 80, 197–201, 225–26, 229–30, 231, 234, 251, 265, 271–75, 285, 286, 289, 296, 352, 374
   *Lost* and, 207–10, 234, 236–41, 251, 281–84, 290, 291–92, 304–5, 307–8
Bravo, 364
*Breaking the Magician's Code,* 97–98
Brenneman, Amy, 42
Bright, Kevin, 28, 138, 216, 221
Brillstein-Grey Entertainment, 197, 239, 359
British television shows, 56, 80–81, 101, 151, 152,

176–87, 263, 303, 341–42,
364, 366–67, 378
Brokaw, Tom, 6, 145, 146, 315,
316, 318
Brown, Campbell, 377
Bruckheimer, Jerry, 17, 70, 114,
119, 120, 121, 122, 123,
365
BSkyB channel, 184
Buena Vista studio, 79
*Built to Last,* 264
Burk, Bryan, 207
Burke, Karey, 167–68, 169, 277,
279, 287
Burnett, Mark, 17, 77–78
    *The Apprentice,* 199–201, 265,
    362–63, 382, 383
    *The Contender,* 303, 361–62
    *Eco-Challenge,* 69, 72, 73, 78
    *Survivor,* 67–76, 81–82, 86–88,
    102, 361
Bush, George H. W., 317
Bush, George W., 311, 312–14,
317, 318, 320
Bushnell, Candace, 232
*Busted on the Job,* 97, 100, 101

Cable television, 5, 387–89
Cannon, Danny, 123
Canter, Kassie, 53, 62
Capra, Frank, 144
Capra, Tom, 144
Carell, Steve, 364, 367
Carson, Johnny, 336, 339
Carter, Graydon, 258, 260
Caruso, David, 42
*Castaway,* 207
Castro, Fidel, 259–60
CBS, 4, 5, 38–48, 279, 296–302,
303–4, 309–18, 358–61,
378, 386–90
    advertising revenue, 43–44,
    112, 369
    audience for, 7, 19, 39, 43–44,
    48, 71, 85, 297
    "The Bullpen," 68

Entertainment division, 30–31,
    39, 44, 126, 166, 355
News, 20, 149, 309–18,
    320–26, 355–56, 378
pass on *The Apprentice,* 200,
    201
pass on *ER,* 30–31
ratings, 19, 25, 27–28, 41,
    46–47, 48, 84, 132–33, 164,
    315, 376
reality division, 9, 17, 59, 65,
    68–76, 80, 81–89, 102, 103,
    106, 111–13, 133–34, 135,
    140, 175, 181, 254
scheduling, 111–13, 125–30
*60 Minutes II* document
    scandal, 311, 312–14, 317,
    318, 320–23, 324
Super Bowl "wardrobe malfunc-
    tion," 254–58, 297
Thursday-night lineup, 7, 19,
    33, 65, 111–13, 133–34,
    135, 136, 212, 254, 263,
    333, 383
upfront weeks, 18–23, 40–41,
    125–30, 297, 301–2, 333
*See also CSI;* Moonves, Leslie;
    *Survivor;* Viacom; *and specific*
    *shows.*
*CBS Early Show,* 22, 86
*CBS Evening News,* 355. *See also*
    Rather, Dan.
*CBS Morning News,* 302
Cecil, Bill, 73
*Celebrity Boxing,* 268–69
*Central Park West,* 41
*Chains of Love,* 60, 152
*Chair, The,* 106, 107
*Chamber, The,* 106–9
*Charlie Rose,* 329
*Cheers,* 215, 218, 219, 223
Chen, Julie, 22, 302, 314–15, 323
Chernin, Peter, 183, 184–85,
    335, 337, 360
Cherry, Marc, 2–3, 11–13,
    161–73, 373–74

ABC pickup of *Desperate Housewives* and showrunner job, 227–35, 241, 243, 252, 284–85, 294, 306
agent and embezzlement, 162, 165, 166, 170–71, 230
background, 162, 163–64, 287
casting and pilot, *Desperate Housewives,* 241–51
inspiration for *Desperate Housewives,* 161–63
Paradigm and, 171–73, 202, 204–6, 306
selling *Desperate Housewives,* 164–73, 201–7, 227–35, 291
Cherry, Martha, 161–63
*Chicago Hope,* 30–31, 33
*China Beach,* 30, 244
Christie, Julie, 106, 107
Chung, Connie, 355
Chvatal, Cindy, 117
Clooney, George, 32, 40, 116
*Cold Case,* 254
Columbia-TriStar television studio, 31
Comcast Corporation, 5, 234, 387
Comedy Central, 80, 324
*Commander in Chief,* 375
Comstock, Beth, 385–86
*Conrad Bloom,* 264
Constantinople, Alex, 147
*Contender, The,* 23–24, 303, 361–62
Conti, Chris, 168, 169
*Cop Rock,* 29
Corrao, Lauren, 78, 79
*Cosby,* 127, 215, 223
Cosby, Bill, 42–43, 355
Costas, Bob, 142, 143, 144
*Coupling,* 15, 254, 263, 279
Couric, Katie, 63, 143–44, 194, 354–58, 376–78
Cowell, Simon, 25, 176–80, 185–95, 341–42, 378–80
Cox, Courtney, 31, 138, 220

Crane, David, 28, 138, 216, 219–20
Creative Artists Agency (CAA), 19, 38, 157, 201, 206, 239, 355
*American Idol* and, 180–85, 194–95
Crichton, Michael, 30
*Crimson Tide,* 123
Croasdale, Bill, 19
Cronkite, Walter, 86, 315, 325
Cross, Marcia, 13, 246–47
*Crossing Jordan,* 158
Cruise, Tom, 148
*CSI,* 9, 22, 113–34, 135, 140, 175, 282, 297, 363, 388
financial partnership problems, 130–32
*Miami,* 361
*New York,* 303–4, 309–11, 317
pilot, 122–25, 126
scheduling, 125–30
*Cursed (The Weber Show),* 15, 136
Cut-downs, 127
CW network, 387

*Daddio,* 59
*Daily Show, The,* 324, 337
*Dallas,* 286
Daly, Bob, 37, 38, 41, 358
Daly, Tim, 42, 125
*Dancing with the Stars,* 375, 380
Danson, Ted, 42, 215
Danza, Tony, 128–30
Darnell, Carolyn, 95, 96, 107, 108
Darnell, Mike, 24–25, 265, 270–71, 340, 342–43, 380–81
*American Idol* and, 181, 182, 183, 187–88, 189, 191–93, 268, 270, 343, 380, 381
background, 95–96
persona and character, 99–100
reality TV shows at Fox, 91–109, 267–70, 340, 342–44, 380–81

*Who Wants to Marry a
   Multi-Millionaire?* and,
   92–93, 102, 268
*See also* Fox television; *specific
   shows.*
*Dateline,* 101, 356
David, Larry, 197
Davies, Michael, 78–81
Davis, Geena, 375
Dees, Rick, 373
DeGeneres, Ellen, 42
Delaney, Dana, 244
Del, Ernie, 36–37, 39, 46, 302
Dempsey, Patrick, 352–53
*Desperate Housewives,* 365–66,
   368, 387
   ABC/Touchstone and, 4, 5,
      11–13, 20, 170, 226–35,
      241–51, 273, 284–85,
      290–96, 306–7, 346, 351,
      352, 353, 357, 358, 373–74,
      375, 377
   casting, 241–51, 290–91,
      294
   efforts to sell, 164–73, 201–7
   inspiration for, 161–63
   Paradigm agency and, 171–73,
      202, 204–6, 226–29, 306
   pass by Krantz/Warner
      Brothers, 201–7
   pass by Lifetime, 170
   pass by NBC, 2–3, 167–69
   pilot, 241, 251–52, 285, 292,
      293
   premiere, 306–7
   time slot, 252, 293–96, 346
   *See also* Cherry, Marc.
*Diagnosis: Murder,* 48, 111, 134
DiCaprio, Leonardo, 119
Dick Clark Productions, 106
Diller, Barry, 96
Discovery Channel, 69, 78, 79,
   120
Disney, Roy, 234
Disney Company, 2, 9, 10, 37,
   133, 151, 165, 300, 360
   ABC decisions and, 197–200,
      226, 231, 232, 234–35, 237,
      240–41, 251, 271–75, 283,
      291, 294, 295–96, 345
   Buena Vista studio, 79
   deals with Apple iPod, 5, 387
   production studio, 28
   *See also* ABC; Eisner, Michael;
      Iger, Robert A.; Touchstone
      studio.
Dolgen, Jonathan, 46
Downey, Roma, 245
*Dr. Quinn, Medicine Woman,* 27
Dreamworks studio, 281
Driver, Minnie, 281
Dunkleman, Brian, 190

Ebersol, Dick, 53, 57, 142, 150,
   344–51, 357, 384
*Eco-Challenge,* 69, 72, 73, 78
*8 Simple Rules for Dating My
   Teenage Daughter,* 10, 225,
   286
Eilbacher, Lisa, 35
Eisner, Michael, 9, 10, 37, 80,
   198, 200, 235, 237, 251,
   271, 273, 295, 300, 349, 360
Elfman, Jenna, 42
*Emeril,* 155, 158
Emmanuel, Ari, 338
*Encore,* 264
Endeavor agency, 11, 206, 335,
   338
Endemol, 152
Ender, Chris, 45, 73, 81, 83, 85,
   127, 133
*ER,* 4, 15, 30–33, 38, 47, 48, 57,
   137, 140, 175, 213, 383
Erdman, Dennis, 201
*E-Ring, The,* 17, 365
ESPN, 78, 274, 345, 349, 350,
   362
Etz, Tony, 239
*Everybody Loves Raymond,* 44,
   126, 127, 128, 263
*Expedition: Robinson,* 79

*Extreme Makeover,* 225
  *Home Edition,* 294, 351
*Eyes Wide Shut,* 148

Falco, Randy, 53, 61, 155, 213,
  277, 364, 369, 384
Fallon, Jimmy, 139, 140
*Fame Academy,* 177
*Family Law,* 69
*Father of the Pride,* 15, 281, 297,
  302
*Fear Factor,* 151–52, 158, 212,
  278
Federal Communications
  Commission (FCC), 257
*Felicity,* 70, 237, 304
Feltheimer, Jon, 31, 46
Ferrell, Will, 139, 140
Fetters, Sid, 144
Fey, Tina, 14, 139, 140
Field, Syd, 119
*Fired Up,* 264
*Firefly,* 175
*Five Mrs. Buchanans, The,* 164,
  166
Flame TV, 201
Fleiss, Mike, 92, 93, 268
Flockhart, Calista, 148, 244
Fong, Wenda, 270
Ford, Harrison, 125
*40-Year-Old Virgin, The,* 367
*Four Kings,* 383
Fox television, 4, 16, 24, 28, 52,
  55, 78, 79, 157, 165, 170,
  232, 275, 303, 335, 340–44,
  378–81, 382
  cable channel FX, 25, 277, 344
  Entertainment division, 24, 25,
    95, 97–109
  pass on *The Apprentice,* 265,
    267–68
  pass on *Friends,* 29
  pass on *Survivor,* 80, 102
  ratings, 20, 24, 193–94,
    253–54, 343, 380
  reality shows, 6, 9, 20, 24,
    25–26, 56, 76, 82, 91–109,
    175–76, 181–95, 225, 253,
    254, 261, 267–71, 303,
    340–44, 378–81
  rivalry with NBC, 23–24
  scripted shows, 25, 41, 95, 244,
    340
  sports programming, 6, 20, 24,
    28, 254, 303, 343, 345
  upfront, 2005, 23–26
  *See also American Idol;* Darnell,
    Mike; *Joe Millionaire; Temp-
    tation Island.*
Franz, Dennis, 244
*Frasier,* 48, 136, 159, 218, 220,
  296
FremantleMedia, 179, 191, 341,
  379
Freston, Tom, 254–61, 297,
  298–301, 358–61
Friedman, Paul, 330
*Friends,* 4, 14, 15, 28–29, 38, 47,
  48, 54, 58–59, 65, 111, 136,
  137, 175, 254, 262, 263,
  280–81, 296, 333, 353, 369
  casting and pilot, 31, 32
  renewals, star salaries, and
    episode costs, 54, 58–59,
    159, 211–22, 334
  supersizing, 137–40
  *See also Joey.*
Frot-Coutaz, Cecile, 191
Fryer, Robert, 35
*Fugitive, The,* 125, 126, 132,
  133, 228
Fuller, Simon, 176, 179, 180,
  181, 191–92, 342, 379
*Full House,* 36
FX networks, 25, 277, 344

Gabler, Lee, 183
Gadinsky, Brian, 187, 190
Gallen, Sandy, 185
Garner, Jennifer, 237
Gartner, Michael, 145
Gaspin, Jeff, 181

Gawker.com, 343

General Electric, 1, 53, 212, 267, 315, 347, 348, 383, 385

*General Hospital,* 172

Gervais, Ricky, 367

Gibson, Charles, 376

*Girls Club,* 175

*Glutton Bowl, The,* 269

*Godfather, The,* 323

Gold, Stanley, 234

Goldberg, Shauna, 220

Goldberg, Whoopi, 215, 279

*Golden Girls, The,* 162, 164, 227, 228, 287

Goodell, Roger, 349

*Good Morning, America* (GMA), 147, 148–49, 353, 354, 357–58, 376, 377

*Good Morning, Miami,* 211–12, 214

Gore, Al, 150

Graboff, Marc, 73, 212–13, 214, 216, 220, 222, 281–84, 338

Grammer, Kelsey, 219

Grazer, Brian, 258, 259–60

*Greed,* 107

Grey, Brad, 258, 344, 359

*Grey's Anatomy,* 351–53, 374

Griffin, Phil, 357

Grushow, Sandy, 93, 94–95, 102–3, 175–76, 182, 183, 184, 185, 193, 194–95, 270

*Guiness Book of World Records* show, 100

Gumbel, Bryant, 143

Gunts, Bucky, 144

Gurvitz, Marc, 239–40

Haber, Bill, 38

Hanks, Tom, 207

Hansen, Libby, 233

Harbert, Ted, 15–16, 46, 139, 155, 239

Harding, Tonya, 268

Harmon, Mark, 35

Harrison, Gregory, 35

Hartley, Alix, 180, 181

*Hasty Heart, The,* 35

Hatch, Richard, 82, 83

Hatcher, Teri, 13, 40, 247–51, 273, 373

Havana Seven, 258–61

*Have Gun, Will Travel,* 116

*Hawaii,* 15

HBO, 35, 232

Helgenberger, Marg, 122–23

Heyward, Andrew, 149, 310–11, 314, 315, 316, 317, 321–22, 323, 324, 325–27, 378

High Horse Films, 117

Hill, David, 97, 99, 101, 102

*Hill Street Blues,* 205, 215

Hogan, P. J., 242–43

*Hollywood P.I.,* 128–30

*Homicide,* 31

*Hope & Faith,* 294

*Hopewell,* 122

*Hot Moms,* 247

*House,* 25, 340, 343

Howard, Josh, 321, 322

Howard, Ron, 258, 380

Huffman, Felicity, 245–46

Hunt, Bonnie, 290

ICM, 28, 216

Iger, Robert A., 9–11, 12, 151, 198, 199, 200, 234–35, 237, 240–41, 251, 271–75, 290, 291, 295, 296, 300, 307, 337, 349, 351, 352, 360, 375

*I Know What You Did Last Summer 2,* 123

Ilson, Sol, 36

*I'm a Celebrity, Get Me Out of Here,* 225–26

Imagine Entertainment, 201, 258

Immelt, Jeffrey, 267, 347, 348, 354, 371, 383, 384–85

Improv club, L.A., 34–35

Infinity group, 298

Inside.com, 62–63

*Inside Schwartz,* 15, 155, 158
*Invasion,* 375
ITV, 177, 179

Jackson, Janet, 255, 256–57,
 297
Jackson, Michael, 16, 187
Jackson, Randy, 25, 189, 190
*JAG,* 126
Janollari, David, 28
Jennings, Peter, 6, 319–20,
 327–32, 376
*Jenny,* 264
*Joan of Arc,* 131
*Joan of Arcadia,* 254
*Joe Millionaire,* 253, 268
 *II,* 254, 269–70
*Joey,* 14, 15, 23, 218–20, 281,
 297, 302, 333, 334, 362,
 364, 365, 369, 383
Johnson, Barry, 272
Johnson, Tim, 329
Jones, Paula, 268
Jones, Simon, 176–77
Josephson, Nancy, 28, 216, 217
*Judging Amy,* 69
*Just Shoot Me,* 58, 137, 139, 140,
 287

Kadin, Heather, 228, 229, 231,
 235, 239, 242, 250, 351, 352
Kahl, Kelly, 44, 45, 72–73, 76,
 84, 85, 111–13, 132–34,
 257, 309–10
Kaplan, Rob, 69–70
*Karen Sisco,* 232
Karmazin, Mel, 257, 297–302
Katzenberg, Jeffrey, 36–37, 281
Kauffman, Crane, and Bright,
 28–29, 138, 216
Kauffman, Marta, 28, 138, 216,
 219–20
Keegan, Peter, 39
Kelley, David E., 30–31, 87, 175
Kidman, Nicole, 148
Kid Rock, 255, 257

Kimmel, Jimmy, 11
Kingsley, Pat, 148
Kingston, Alex, 245
Klein, Debbie, 171–72
Kline, Kevin, 148
Knauss, Melania, 267
*Knots Landing,* 36
Kopelson, Arnold, 125
Koppel, Ted, 6, 320, 326–27,
 328, 329, 350
Krantz, Tony, 201–7
KTTV, 96
Kudrow, Lisa, 138
Kuhn, Robert, 170

*L. A. Law,* 31, 249
Lack, Andy, 53, 63, 146, 149,
 278, 385
Lagrasse, Emeril, 155
Larroquette, John, 279
*Las Vegas,* 279
*Late Night with Conan O'Brien,*
 5, 22, 334–35
Lauer, Matt, 316, 356, 357
Laurie, Hugh, 340
*Law & Order,* 15, 48, 57, 120,
 122, 205, 212, 303–4, 309,
 363
 *Criminal Intent,* 158, 212, 346
 *Special Victims Unit,* 57, 212
Lawrence, Sharon, 244–45, 247
*LAX,* 15
LeBlanc, Matt, 14, 54, 138,
 218–19
Lederman, Nina, 201
Lee, Sheryl, 290
Leno, Jay, 212, 334–40, 345
Letterman, David, 295, 325, 327,
 334–35, 336, 337, 338–39,
 377, 388
Levitan, Steve, 287
Levy, Frank, 35
Lewinsky, Monica, 269
Lieber, Jeffrey, 236
Liebner, Richard, 316, 317
Liefer, Stephanie, 231–32

*Life As We Know It (Doing It),* 289, 295

Lifetime network, 170

*Life with Bonnie,* 290

Liguori, Peter, 25–26, 344, 379

Limbaugh, Rush, 378

Lindelof, Damon, 239, 293, 304, 207

Littlefield, Warren, 30, 36, 47, 48, 49–52, 53, 54, 150, 262, 287

Littman, Jonathan, 113–16, 121, 133

*Lois & Clark,* 13, 39, 40, 248

Long, Howie, 249

Longoria, Eva, 13, 245

Lorimar Television, 36, 38

*Lost,* 4, 5, 207–10, 234, 236–41, 251, 272–73, 281–84, 289–92, 293, 295, 304–5, 307–8, 346, 351, 353, 358, 374, 375

Louis-Dreyfus, Julia, 245

*Love Boat, The,* 249

Lurie, Rod, 375

Lyne, Susan, 198, 210, 225–26, 229–31, 233, 234, 237, 240, 241, 251, 252, 271–75, 284–86, 289, 293, 351–53, 374, 375

Lythgoe, Nigel, 186, 190

*MacGyver,* 249

*Magnificent Seven, The,* 116

*Major Dad,* 27

*Making the Band,* 181

Mandel, Jon, 264

*Manhunter,* 116

*Man Show, The,* 80

*Man vs. Beast,* 269

Manze, Vince, 53, 54, 140

Mapes, Mary, 312, 313, 320–21, 322

*Married by America,* 269

Marriott, Evan, 268

Mason, Anthony, 326

Maynard, Ghen, 68–73, 76, 81–83, 91, 169, 181

McCluggage, Kerry, 46

McDougall, Charles, 243, 246

McGrady, Phyllis, 330

McGrath, Judy, 255

McManus, Sean, 378–79

McNamara, John, 228

McNamara, Julie, 228–29, 231, 232–33, 352

McPherson, Jen, 307

McPherson, Stephen, 10–11, 80, 120–21, 125, 130–31, 133, 232, 247, 274, 351, 352

   as ABC Entertainment chief, 285–96, 303, 367–68, 374–75

   *Desperate Housewives* and, 227, 229, 230, 235, 247–48, 285, 290, 292–96, 306–7

   *Lost* and, 241, 272–73, 289–90, 291–92, 293, 294, 304–5

   personality and temperament, 286–89

MediaCom, 264

*Medium,* 345, 364

Meisner, Sanford, 34, 35

*Melrose Place,* 41, 57, 123, 172, 246

*Men Behaving Badly,* 264

Mendelsohn, Carol, 123

Messing, Debra, 281

Metcalf, Mitch, 61

*Michael Richards,* 58, 60, 136

Michaels, Lorne, 139–40, 258, 350–51

Midler, Bette, 125, 377

*Midsummer's Night Dream, A,* 148

*Mike O'Malley Show, The,* 57

Miller, John, 53, 54, 140

Miller, Tom, 36

Mind Share, 167–68

MIPCOM, 184

*Miss Match,* 169

Mitchell, George, 360
*Monday Night Football (MNF),*
    253, 304, 345, 348, 349–50,
    351, 375
Moonves, Leslie, 18–23, 38–48,
    65, 135, 149, 153, 157, 164,
    170, 212, 247, 253–54, 263,
    265, 266–67, 279, 296–302,
    303–4, 378, 386–90
  background, 34–38
  CBS News and, 309–18,
    320–26
  "content" company concept,
    387–90
  Couric offer, 355–56, 358,
    377
  *CSI* and, 116–17, 121–32,
    134
  Freston and, 258–61, 358–61
  Havana Seven and, 258–61
  Julie Chen and, 20, 22, 302,
    314–15, 323
  personality and volatility, 28,
    45–46, 266
  Super Bowl "wardrobe malfunc-
    tion" and, 253–58, 261
  *Survivor* and, 72, 73–76,
    81–89, 111–13, 159
  upfronts, 18–23, 125–30, 297
  at Warner, 28–33, 36–38, 41,
    47, 138
Morales, Natalie, 377
*Mr. Personality,* 269
MSNBC, 377
MTV, 70, 78, 176, 254–57, 297,
    299, 358, 386
*Muddling Through,* 31
*Murder, She Wrote,* 39
Murdoch, Elizabeth, 184, 188
Murdoch, Rupert, 24, 25, 91, 99,
    184–85, 188, 341
Murphy, Jim, 324, 326
Murphy, Joey, 307
Murphy, Mary, 321
*Murphy Brown,* 249
*My Best Friend's Wedding,* 242

*My Name Is Earl,* 17, 365, 366,
    371, 382, 383, 384
*My Wife and Kids,* 225

*Naked News, The,* 378
Nash, Bruce, 102
*NBC Nightly News,* 145, 146, 319
NBC Productions, 131, 139
NBC Universal, 14–15, 19,
    49–65, 135–59, 211–23,
    277–81, 302–3, 333–40,
    353–58, 381–86
  acquisitions and mergers, 1–2,
    277, 278
  advertising revenues, 22, 137,
    212, 369–70
  coastal culture clash, 155–56
  corporate culture, 52, 53–54,
    287
  digital group, 385–86
  East Coast business division,
    155–56, 279
  late-night television, 5, 51, 53,
    140, 142, 212, 334–40, 345,
    376
  *Lost* opportunity, 281–84
  "Must See TV," 48, 262
  News, 64, 145, 149, 277,
    315–16, 318, 354, 355, 356,
    357, 376
  NFL deal, 344–51
  pass on *American Idol,* 181
  pass on *Desperate Housewives,*
    2–3, 167–69
  pass on *Survivor,* 80
  ratings, 14, 17, 19, 22, 23, 47,
    48, 61, 147, 158, 159, 212,
    253, 262, 266, 278, 279,
    280–81, 296–97, 333, 340,
    353, 357–58, 364
  reality shows, 9–10, 17, 23, 56,
    59–60, 199–201, 151–52,
    158, 181, 261, 262, 263,
    264–67, 278, 262, 296, 280,
    297, 334, 362–64, 380,
    381–82, 383

soap operas, prime time, 57, 58, 61
sports, 132, 142, 143, 344–51
"supersizing," 135–41, 153
Thursday-night lineup, 7, 19, 23, 32, 33, 48, 65, 111, 113, 133–34, 135–41, 155, 159, 211–22, 254, 261, 262–65, 266, 280–81, 302–3, 333, 334, 362, 365, 382–84
upfronts, 13–18, 52–53, 59, 364–66, 368–70
West Coast/Entertainment division, 3, 15, 16, 17, 30, 33, 49, 52–65, 135, 137–38, 139, 150, 151–59, 262, 277–79, 333–40
*See also Apprentice, The; ER; Friends;* General Electric; *Joey;* Reilly, Kevin; Zucker, Jeffrey.
NBC Universal Studios, 150, 340, 343, 367
Nealon, Kevin, 34
Neighborhood Playhouse, 34
Nelly, 255, 257
Nesvig, Jon, 100–101
Network television
  advertising revenues, total, 4–5
  benchmark, viewers 18 to 49, 6
  cable broadcasting of, 387–89
  cable competition and, 5
  digital and broadband competition, 5
  hit shows, need for, 5, 6
  news, 6
  satellite distribution and, 388
  scheduling room, 389
  series, producing at a deficit, 131
*New Detectives, The: Case Studies in Forensic Science,* 120
News Corporation, 2, 91, 183, 184, 195, 360
*Next Great Champ, The,* 303

NFL television rights, 344–51, 388
Nielsen Company, 19
*Nightline,* 295, 326–27, 335, 336, 350
*Nightly News with Tom Brokaw,* 145, 146
19 Entertainment, 179, 341
*Nip/Tuck,* 277
Noonan, Tom, 29
Norville, Deborah, 143
*NYPD Blue,* 244, 289, 304

O'Brien, Conan, 51, 53, 140, 142, 212, 334–40
*O.C., The,* 232
*Office, The,* 364, 366–67, 382–83
Oh, Sandra, 352
Ohlmeyer, Don, 33, 47, 48, 49, 51, 52, 53, 54, 55, 102, 262
Olsen, Mary-Kate and Ashley, 36
Olympics, 132, 142, 146, 183, 302, 345, 347, 350
Opinden, Laurie, 33
*Oprah,* 373
*Outrageous Behavior Caught on Tape,* 95, 97

Pallone, Gavin, 338
Paradigm agency, 171–73, 202, 204–6, 226–29, 306
Paramount, 24, 46, 300, 344, 358–59, 386
Paramount Television, 46, 131
Parker, Mary Louise, 244
Parsons, Charlie, 78, 79
*Pasadena,* 244
Patmore, Suzanne, 229, 351
Patterson, Ytossie, 104–6
Pattman, Andy, 171–73, 206, 227
Pauley, Jane, 143, 356
PAX-TV, 165
Pedowitz, Mark, 200, 274
Perlman, Rhea, 42
Perry, Matthew, 31, 138

*Peter Pan*, 242
Peterson, William, 116–18, 121, 122, 124
Phillips, Stone, 356
*Picket Fences*, 31
Pitt, Brad, 221
Poehler, Amy, 14
Poltrack, David, 128–29, 134
Pompeo, Ellen, 352, 353
*Pop Idol*, 176–77, 179–81, 183, 184, 187, 188, 191–92
*Pop Stars*, 177–78, 181
Powell, Amy, 54
Powell, Michael, 257
Pratt, Chuck, 172–73, 204, 205, 233
Probst, Jeff, 83
Prochilo, Doug, 68–69, 81

*Quincy*, 114, 122
Quinn, Colin, 52

*Ranger*, 48
Rather, Dan, 6, 20, 312–18, 320, 321, 323, 324, 325–26, 378
*Reality Check*, 29
Reality television, 56, 59–60, 67–89, 91–109, 151–52, 158, 165, 181–82, 212, 225–26, 262, 265–70, 341–44, 375, 380–81. *See also American Idol; Apprentice, The; Darnell, Mike; Survivor; specific networks and shows.*
*Real World, The*, 70–71
*Rebel Billionaire, The*, 24, 303
Redstone, Sumner, 257, 297–302, 359, 360
Reilly, Kevin, 15, 17, 277, 282, 284, 286, 333, 344, 363–64, 366, 367–68, 382–83
Rhimes, Shonda, 351–52
Richards, Michael, 57
Riggs, Conrad, 67–68, 69, 74, 79, 80, 87–88, 89, 199–200, 265

Ripa, Kelly, 294
Ritter, John, 10, 286
Rivera, Mariano, 20
Roberts, John, 316
Robinson, Anne, 152
Rockwell, Rick, 92–93
Roedy, Bill, 258
Romano, Ray, 44
Rosen, Rick, 11, 336, 337, 338
Rosenblum, Bruce, 205–6, 216, 217
Rosenthal, Phil, 44, 126–30
Ross, Jeff, 336
Ross, JoAnn, 73, 75
Roth, Peter, 97–99, 138, 205–6, 213, 214, 216, 217, 218–19, 221, 283–84
Russert, Tim, 356
Ryan, Jeri, 245
Ryan, Marty, 143

Sacks, Karen, 310, 317
Sagansky, Jeff, 30, 39
Saint James, Susan, 348
Sanchez, Rosalyn, 245
Sassa, Scott, 49–52, 55–64, 94, 99, 135, 138, 150, 152, 158, 271, 279
*Saturday Night Live (SNL)*, 14, 34, 52, 57, 92, 139–40, 212, 258, 344, 350
Sawyer, Diane, 320, 354, 356
Scalara, Ron, 84
Scanlon, Ed, 149, 150
Schieffer, Bob, 325
Schlesinger, Richard, 326
"Schmuck insurance," 31, 284
Schneider, Jeffrey, 330, 332
Schwartz, Gil, 318
Schwimmer, David, 31, 138, 220
Scott, Tony, 123
Scott, Willard, 143
*Scrubs*, 155, 158, 211, 214, 263, 367
Seacrest, Ryan, 190

*Seinfeld,* 15, 48, 49, 60, 197, 215, 216, 219, 223, 245, 249, 353, 382

Seinfeld, Jerry, 49–50

Selleck, Tom, 42

Semel, Terry, 38, 358

*Sex and the City,* 35, 162, 163, 201, 232, 243, 252

Shapiro, Mark, 274

Shapiro, Neal, 357

Shepherd, Harvey, 37, 38

Sheridan, Nicollette, 246

Sherman, Thom, 170, 210, 226–31, 234, 236, 238, 239, 251, 288–89, 293, 304, 305, 307

*Shield, The,* 277

*Shocking Behavior Caught on Tape,* 100

Showrunner (term), 30

Showtime channel, 389

Shriver, Maria, 143, 144

Sidey, Sandy, 330

*Significant Others,* 167–68

Sillerman, Bob, 379

Silveri, Scott, 220

Silverman, Ben, 367

Silverstone, Alicia, 169

Sitcoms, 162, 163, 164, 264, 265, 279, 297, 383. *See also specific shows.*

*60 Minutes,* 316, 355
  II, 311, 312–14, 317, 318, 320–23, 324

*Skating with Celebrities,* 380

Sloan, David, 295–96

Smoking Gun, The, 92–93

*Some of My Best Friends (Kiss Me, Guido),* 171

Sony-Bertlesmann Music, 379

*Sopranos, The,* 35, 197, 260

Sorkin, Aaron, 205, 266

Spelling, Aaron, 57, 236

*Spielberg, Steven,* 30

*Sports Night,* 245

*SpyTV,* 152

St. Elsewhere, 30

Star, Darren, 41, 201

*Stark Raving Mad,* 15

Stephanopoulos, George, 327

Stewart, Jon, 324, 337

Stewart, Martha, 17–18, 362, 381–82

Strong, Brenda, 294

Suarez, Flody, 287, 289

*Suddenly Susan,* 264

Super Bowl, 20, 25, 89, 112–13, 135, 343, 348, 375
  "wardrobe malfunction," 254–58, 297

*Survivor,* 67, 152, 159, 180, 226, 263, 380, 388
  ABC passes, 79–81
  CBS and, 9, 17, 59, 65, 68–76, 80, 81–89, 102, 103, 106, 111–13, 133–34, 135, 140, 175, 254
  The Survivor Company and revenue split, 75–76, 86–89

Sussman, Peter, 131–32

*Swan, The,* 24

Swedish television programming, 79

Sweeney, Anne, 273–74, 292–93, 295, 296, 375

Tagliabue, Paul, 256, 349

Tarses, Jamie, 80

Tartikoff, Brandon, 151

Tassler, Nina, 22, 44, 113–18, 121–22, 125, 131

Tellem, Nancy, 44, 83

*Temptation Island,* 103–6

Tenney, Jon, 249

*Texas,* 48

Thames Television, 177

*That Was Then,* 225

*Third Rock from the Sun,* 264

*Third Watch,* 55, 57

*This Week,* 327

Thomas, Tony, 286–87

Thornburgh, Richard, 314, 317

*Threshold,* 388

Timberlake, Justin, 255, 256–57
Time Warner, 2
Tisch, Larry, 38–39, 40
*Titans,* 57, 58, 60–61
TiVo, 2
*Today,* 15, 62, 65, 85–86, 135,
    143, 212, 214, 316, 353–58,
    376–77, 384. *See also*
    Couric, Katie; Zucker, Jeffrey.
Toffler, Van, 255, 256
*To Live and Die in L.A.,* 116
*Tonight Show, The,* 5, 334–40, 377
*Top Gun,* 114
Tortorici, Peter, 39, 40, 41, 43
*Touched By an Angel,* 48, 245
Touchet, Tom, 357
Touchstone studio, 80, 116,
    120–21, 130–31, 197, 232,
    272, 282–84, 286, 287, 289,
    351, 352
  *CSI* and, 115–16, 121, 198,
    226, 282–83, 289
  *Desperate Housewives* and, 206,
    227, 229, 230, 235, 242,
    243, 244, 247
  *Lost* and, 272–73, 282–84,
    289–90
  *See also* McPherson, Steve.
*Trading Spouses,* 303
*Trapper John, MD,* 35
Tripplehorn, Jeanne, 245
Trump, Donald, 199–200, 263,
    264, 265–67, 280, 297, 334,
    362–64, 381–82
Tucci, Stanley, 148
*Tucker,* 59, 60
Turner, Keith, 369
Turner, Ted, 50, 60, 61
*20/20,* 294–96
20th Century Fox television
    studio, 97
*24,* 25, 175, 201, 341, 343
*Twin Peaks,* 290
*Two and a Half Men,* 254, 263,
    382
"Two bites" (term), 283

Upfronts, 9–26, 40–41, 52–53,
    59, 125–30, 289, 295, 297,
    301–2, 365–66, 368–70
  mini-, 83, 273, 364, 364
UPN, 4, 176, 387
*Up to the Minute,* 310, 312
USA Network, 78, 388

*Vanity Fair* magazine, 258
Vargas, Elizabeth, 376
Vasgersian, Matt, 108
*Veronica's Closet,* 264
Viacom, 2, 21, 131, 255, 257,
    258, 297–302, 317, 324,
    358, 359, 360–61, 386
Vivendi Universal, 1

*Walker,* 48
Wallace, Mike, 315, 325
Wallou, Alex, 200
Walt Disney Company. *See* Dis-
    ney Company.
Walters, Barbara, 355
Warner Brothers, 27–33, 36–38,
    41, 54, 138, 283–84, 358,
    387
  *ER* and, 213
  *Friends* and, 213, 216, 217–18,
    220, 222
  pass on *Desperate Housewives,*
    201–7, 229
Warwick, Kevin, 186, 187, 191
Waterman, Pete, 180
Watson, Taheed, 104–6
WB network, 4, 52, 54, 64, 70,
    181, 387
*Weakest Link, The,* 151, 152
Weber, Steven, 136
Welch, Jack, 49, 53, 59, 145,
    151, 267, 278, 385
Wells, John, 30, 32, 55, 87
West, Betsy, 321
West, Chandra, 123, 126
Westin, David, 295–96, 320,
    326–32, 376
Westin, Sherrie, 327, 328

*West Wing, The,* 57, 158, 205, 266

*When Animals Attack,* 76, 95, 97, 98

*When Disasters Strike,* 97

*When Stunts Go Bad,* 97

Whitman, Meg, 360

Who, The, 297

*Whoopi,* 279

*Who's Your Daddy?,* 342–43

*Who Wants to Be a Millionaire?,* 55, 59, 76, 80–81, 84, 92, 102, 107, 180, 197, 198, 348, 364

*Who Wants to Marry a Multi-Millionaire?,* 56, 82, 92, 102, 268

Wiatt, Jim, 258

*Wife Swap,* 303

*Will & Grace,* 23, 51, 136, 137, 139, 140, 159, 211, 263, 265, 281, 383

William Morris Agency, 258

Williams, Brian, 315, 316, 319, 320, 355, 356, 376

Winfrey, Oprah, 380

*Wings,* 125

Witt Thomas Harris, 286–87

Wolf, Dick, 87, 205

Wong, Andrea, 80, 181, 183, 335, 342

Wood, Natalie, 35

Woodruff, Bob, 376

Wooten, Jamie, 164

*World's Deadliest Swarms,* 97

*World's Greatest Calamities,* 97

*World's Greatest Hoaxes,* 97

*World's Greatest Police Chases,* 76

*World's Scariest Police Chases,* 95

Wright, Bob, 1–3, 4, 18, 49–52, 53, 55–56, 57, 58, 59, 62, 64, 94, 151, 152, 155, 213, 215, 216, 222, 267, 277–78, 279, 335, 336, 338, 346–48, 366, 370, 384, 385–86

Wright Concept, The, 165, 171

Wright, Marcie, 162, 165, 166, 170–71, 230

Wright, Suzanne, 278, 335

*X-Factor, The,* 341–42, 379–80

*X-Files, The,* 165, 175

*Yes, Dear,* 388–89

*Yesterday, Today, and Tomorrow,* 144

Zucker, Caryn, 146, 147, 150, 151, 153

Zucker, Jeff, 13–17, 19, 21, 24, 146–48, 156–58, 282, 284, 314, 344
  background, 141–43, 194
  NBC Entertainment division chief, 62–65, 135–41, 151–59, 164–65, 168, 169, 181, 201, 211–22, 253, 261, 262–65, 266
  NBC president: entertainment, news, and cable group, 277–81, 296–97, 302–3, 333–38, 340, 344–51, 353–58, 362, 364, 366, 367, 368, 370–71, 382, 383
  NBC Universal CEO, 384–86
  *Nightly News with Tom Brokaw* and, 145, 146
  personality and temper, 149, 154
  "supersizing" idea, 135–41, 153
  *Today* show and, 63, 86, 139, 143–51, 154, 159, 353–58, 376, 384

Zuiker, Anthony, 114–21, 123, 309

Zuiker, Jennifer, 120

© FRED CONRAD

Bill Carter reports on the television industry for the *New York Times* and has written about television for almost thirty years. A graduate of the University of Notre Dame and a native of Brooklyn, New York, he currently resides in New Jersey with his wife and children.